The Free Church Through the Ages

The FREE CHURCH *Through* THE AGES

Gunnar Westin
Professor Emeritus, University of Uppsala

Translated from the Swedish by
Virgil A. Olson

BROADMAN PRESS
Nashville, Tennessee

Translated from the third edition of
Den kristna friförsamlingen genom tiderna
First edition, 1954; third edition, 1955
German translation, 1956

423–08037

Library of Congress card catalog number: 58–8926
Printed in the United States of America
4.F58K.S.P.

Contents

Contents

Foreword

IT IS A PLEASURE and an honor to be permitted to write a foreword to the English translation of THE FREE CHURCH THROUGH THE AGES. The author should need no introduction to Baptists. Long prominent in the Baptist World Alliance, he has been a familiar and revered figure in its gatherings. In his native Sweden, he is outstanding among church historians. His scholarship long since has won him a place on the theological faculty of the University of Uppsala, a quite unusual tribute to a Baptist in a country where the state church is Lutheran. An impressive shelf of books bears witness to the prodigious labors of his pen and is a tribute to both his ability and his industry. In addition to his duties in Uppsala, Professor Westin has found time to teach in the Baptist Theological Seminary in Stockholm and to assist in other ways in the life of his denomination in Sweden. In the first year of his emeritus status he employed his alleged retirement to lecture in this country, both in the Southern Baptist Theological Seminary and in other institutions of higher learning. His vigor seems unabated, and further volumes may be anticipated from his fertile brain and hand.

The book which is here given in its English form is the fruit of extensive research, part of it during a leave of absence from university duties. Obviously it arises from the sturdy convictions which have made the author a staunch protagonist of a free church in a land where religious liberty was won with difficulty: indeed, he has had an important part in later stages of that achievement.

As will be quickly seen by a glance at the table of contents, Professor Westin has given a comprehensive survey of the history of the free churches from the beginning to the present day. He rightly views the New Testament churches as "free." He rapidly sketches dissent from the Catholic Church of the Roman Empire and from the established churches of the Middle Ages, devoting the major portion of the book to the Reformation and post-Reformation periods. He has taken full account of the recent extensive research in the history of the Anabaptists and has given an inclusive picture of that often misunderstood and maligned movement. Yet he is not blind to the weakness of the Anabaptists. Although, as is to be expected, he covers the history of the Baptists, properly, in view of his choice of subject, Professor Westin by no means centers his attention on them. He endeavors to cover all the major and some of the minor free churches. For that reason he gives much attention to the British Isles, where free churches have been and are prominent, and especially to the United States, where they have enrolled the majority of the professing Christians. Americans will especially welcome the full treatment of the free churches on the Continent of Europe in the nineteenth and twentieth centuries. There Professor Westin is especially at home.

No one need fear embarking on a perusal of the volume because of the author's formidable scholarship. Professor Westin has sought, successfully, to tell his story in such fashion that those who have no specialized knowledge of the subject will find in his pages all that they require for an introduction. He writes readably and well. The hypothetical general reader can know that he is in the hands of a competent guide who commands the respect of the experts.

KENNETH SCOTT LATOURETTE

Sterling Professor of Missions
and Oriental History, Emeritus
Yale University

viii

Preface

THE PURPOSE OF THIS VOLUME is to give information concerning a current within Christianity which has received little consideration in the larger works of church history. The meaning of the central concept, the Christian free church, will soon become apparent in the reading of the book. Every reader of the Bible can testify that such a church can be found in primitive Christianity. It also is well known that such a movement exists today, even though there are many who have no adequate knowledge of its comprehensive nature, either in the past or the present.

Major emphasis has not been given to the indefinite number of unsettled free church movements which existed before the Reformation. Documentary material on these pre-Reformation movements is scarce, and they also exhibited a changeable character. Attention is thus concentrated on progressive movements during the time of the Reformation and their direct and indirect successors in the post-Reformation period. The Anabaptist movement in the sixteenth century and the enormous expansion of free churches during the nineteenth century naturally occupy a central place.

The pioneer struggle took place on the European Continent during the sixteenth century. In succeeding centuries the scene of activity shifted to the English-speaking world, and it was here that the fully developed free church blossomed. While the Continental movement was exclusive, disregarding culture and community affairs, the English-American free churches have been aggressively missionary and positive in their convictions regarding state and community welfare. The former group held to a principle of social isolationism; the later group fought against the social oppression created by community mores and state churches. The struggle in the seventeenth century for civil freedom, citizenship rights, and justice in the English-speaking world was the free church contribution towards democratic and autonomous church government. This campaign did much to determine modern historical development.

Reasons for, and development of, the free church movement and its main principles rather than doctrinal differences within the movement are discussed. No detailed discussion of the inner development of various denominations is presented, and biographical material is generally omitted. The span of both time and geography compels that concentration be restricted to the major theme. This volume is designed as a handbook in the area. The author knows that much more could have been written on the subject, but even one volume fills a need.

It is assumed that the reader already has some acquaintance with the general concepts of church history, which it is impossible, naturally, to cover in this treatise.

GUNNAR WESTIN

Preface to the Third Edition

When this book appeared in October, 1954, it was given a very good reception; manifestly it filled a real need. Already after a few months a third edition must be printed. There have been no major alterations, but a few typographical errors have been corrected and other small changes made in the interest of clarity. Some information about the Congregational denomination in Germany has been added. A few reviewers have pointed out that certain small revisions could be made, and one church leader has criticized the treatment of the early church. Although presentation of this subject obviously is fragmentary, it is doubtful that one can contradict it on the basis of contemporary documents. A brief appendix has been added.

G. W.

I

Early Development of
the Churches

THE PRIMITIVE CHRISTIAN CONGREGATION in Jerusalem—as
well as similar congregations in Antioch, Ephesus, Corinth, and
Rome—was a free church. This concept, the free church, will
be outlined in the course of this book. The term "free church"
has reference to distinct groups within history who through
the medium of preaching have accepted the gospel of Jesus
Christ by faith and have separated from the life of paganism
to bring forth fruits of righteousness. This formula is clearly
enunciated in the New Testament. "Faith comes by means of
preaching, and preaching by means of the power of the Word
of Christ" (translated from Swedish, Rom. 10:17). With these
words Paul attached the life of faith and the inception of the
church to a historic event, which can recur whenever people
meet. However, the primary basis of faith, that which accom-
plishes everything, is the grace of God. Preaching and faith are
functions in men's lives, as well as distinctives and principles
in the church. The "accepted word" was the foundation of the
church, and without this acceptance there would have been no
local assemblies. As every reader of the Scriptures knows, the
Acts of the Apostles and the Epistles in the New Testament
list a number of these churches located in various cities and
districts.

These congregations may be defined, therefore, as free
churches because they won adherents and members who, when
they freely accepted the word, turned away from the life of
sin and voluntarily were baptized. In Acts 2:42 the events that
followed are recorded: the new Christians "devoted themselves
to the apostles' teaching and fellowship, to the breaking of

bread and the prayers" (RSV). The serious exhortations in the Epistles reveal that the freedom to believe and to teach could be misused, and they also point out that definite demands were placed upon Christian conduct which differed from the pagan customs. It is not always easy for the historian to evaluate correctly motives and dynamics, but he must take account of a person's statements and testimonies. Consequently, the historian must give full attention to the testimony of the primitive Christian assembly concerning the ministry of the Holy Spirit, which was the first seal of Christ's own work, as it was understood by those who were the bearers of the good news in the earliest periods. New Testament writers have described how the assembly as a historic experience became God's *ekklēsia* throughout the realm of mankind. A large number of individuals compose this congregation. It is with the comprehension of the empirical church, rather than a dogmatic concept, that church historians are primarily occupied.

Again it can be established that the primitive Christian assembly was a free church in that it had no relationship, subordinate or co-ordinate, with any constituted authority or the state. For these churches there was a clear line of demarcation between the church and the "world." The dominion of the Roman emperor and the kingdom of Jesus Christ were two entirely separate domains. The early Christians could never conceive of any union between governments of this world and God's *ekklēsia*. From a religious point of view, these churches scattered throughout the Roman Empire were fixed points in making known the good news concerning Jesus, crucified and risen. The Christians considered themselves as strangers and pilgrims on the earth. They had their citizenship (*politeuma*) in heaven. It was self-evident to Paul that the churches of that day should remain free in their relationship to the Roman Government. Any complete alignment with an anti-Christian state, or even a semi-Christian state, has ever remained a serious peril for the church. This concept, even in later years, has always been clear to discerning observers. Throughout the centuries many Christians have not only been aware of this peril but they have sought to act consistently according to this in-

2

sight. This important factor in early history will be developed in this volume, showing examples even down to the present day.

Within the local congregations there were found divergent offices, such as those of the elders (*presbuteroi*) and bishops (*episkopoi*), and also deacons to take care of practical matters. There were several elders and bishops in each congregation, constituting the directive group. Sometimes the Scriptures speak of pastors and teachers, but no clear line of demarcation can be drawn between these and the former offices. Certainly it is impossible to find any church hierarchy such as that which became prominent later in the papacy and the episcopacy. Even in this way the Christian congregations were free churches, yet there existed a strong bond of spiritual fellowship among them. As local minority groups in Jerusalem, Antioch, Ephesus, and Corinth, the Christians did not stand isolated. All sensed a deep union in Jesus Christ. This sense of belonging together caused the church to be described in spiritual language as the body of Christ, indicating its universal character. God's *ekklēsia*, which in Paul's letters is given strong emphasis, has a fellowship characteristic reaching beyond the boundaries of nations and races.

This polity was prominent among the local Christian assemblies long into the second century. Bishops and elders (*episkopoi* and *presbyteroi*, cf. Phil. 1:1 and Acts 20:28) made up the leadership, and there was no clear mark of distinction between them. The suggestion is not valid that the elders and the bishops in the local congregations obtained a sacramental position similar to priests and mystagogues within Judaism and the heathen religions. It is natural that elders and bishops exercised leadership in matters of doctrine and also in the baptismal ceremony and the observance of the Lord's Supper. This was, however, a matter of organization within the local churches. These leaders did not have the designation which was common to the priesthood, nor at this period is it possible to find the use of the altar or any direct influence of Temple worship. Altars came into use during the early part of the third century, when church buildings began to be erected. A reveal-

3

ing testimony concerning church order is found in one of the apologies written at Rome during the early portion of the third century. Pagan antagonists had inquired why the Christians did not have altars and temples, and the Christian apologist replied that even though they had neither temple nor altar, there was no secret about whom they worshiped. The writer continued, "Is it not better to build a temple for Him in our souls, to hallow a place for Him in our hearts?"

When the missionary advance following the apostolic period, A.D. 90 to 180, is traced, it is evident that the original characteristics of the early churches were still maintained. New churches were established and the older congregations increased their membership, but the free church concept was still maintained. The method was still preaching, teaching, conversion, faith, and baptism. All of the sources from this period agree that there existed no other way of uniting with a Christian assembly. During the entire second century, and even into the third, the Christian churches were independent minority groups within predominantly Jewish or pagan communities. These churches can be defined as free in that membership was voluntary and separation from the state was clearly marked.

During this period, and until the latter part of the second century, it is not possible to discover any centralized church authority, for the local churches were independent, yet with a real sense of relationship to one another. As in the days of Paul, letters were directed to the local assemblies, not to any bishop or superintendent. That this policy was maintained is evidenced in the First Epistle of Clement of Rome (A.D. 95 or 96) and in Polycarp's letter to the Philippians a few decades later. The Ignatian epistles to the churches in Asia Minor written in the opening decades of the second century reveal the same condition. Throughout the Roman Empire it is possible to discover these minority groups, independent churches which majored in the proclamation of the gospel and the observance of the ordinances. In one of the apologetical writings from the close of the second century, the Christian churches are compared to islands which are protective havens for ships. In a world that is ravaged by the storms of sin, God has given these meeting places to which those who desire to be saved may flee. It is in this that the exclusive character of the churches and the separation from the world is strongly emphasized. There was no thought of churches embracing an entire populace but of minority groups composed of individual Christians. The testimony from this period indicates that the churches exercised great care concerning the ordinance of baptism and the instruction of catechumens. Several of the church scribes during this period of the second century reveal that great demands were laid upon the members of the Christian congregations.

By the middle of the second century the itinerant prophets, evangelists, and teachers exerted considerable influence in the Christian missionary expansion. These leaders were not servants of any one particular church, but they visited the local congregations and were often received with respect and given a hearing when it was evident that they had been supplied with special spiritual gifts of grace. It was also agreed that the prophets would be permitted to pray and offer thanksgiving as much as they desired at the observance of the Lord's Supper. As yet there was no rigid obligatory ritual to be observed at the communion service. Writings from this same period indicate that these itinerants, at least in some places, were held in higher esteem than the local church leaders, such as the elders, bishops, and deacons. The tendency, therefore, during the second century was that the latter group mentioned began to guard more carefully their positions in the congregations, and after the middle of this century there began to appear evidences of a monarchial episcopate, the leadership of one man in the congregation. One man became the leader of the assembly because he elevated himself over the others and because at this time he had won a recognition which entitled him to his unique position. The process of centralizing the local congregations began to take place when these leaders (bishops) began to come together for synod meetings. These meetings had their beginning during the latter portion of the second century.

It was during this period that the bishop at Rome began to

issue statements implying that he was the head of the churches. With the development of this centralized authority there was pressure on the congregations and the various church groups to accept a standard of orthodoxy in matters of doctrine as well as polity. The so-called ancient Catholic Church arose from this situation, and it was supplemented by the Judaistic ideas of officials and offerings, the Roman juridical concepts, and the practical needs for church authority. It was primarily the monarchial bishop's claim to his personal authoritative teaching, especially that of the bishop at Rome, which more than anything else gave evidence of the new church order. A hierarchical and sacramental pattern was now created with specific appeal to the Judaistic types in the Old Testament. Such sacrificial priests with their holy places and altars were, of course, not found in primitive Christianity. For this reason it took some time before the new ecclesiasticism, with its authoritative bishops and magical sacraments, could win complete recognition. At the same time that this change in ecclesiology was taking place, the writings of the New Testament were being formulated into a canon, and the so-called apostolic statements of faith were being drawn up. These latter statements originally arose from the simple confessions of faith required of baptismal candidates.

Even at the end of the first century, as the sources reveal, the gatherings of Christians were simple edificatory meetings. The well-known account from this period is the letter which the governor of Bithynia sent Emperor Trajan. After careful investigation, the governor had this to say: "They maintained that their fault or error amounted to nothing more than this: they were in the habit of meeting on a certain day before sunrise and reciting an antiphonal hymn to Christ as God." The Christians then bound themselves with an oath to maintain certain moral standards. Besides this, they declared it was their custom to meet together and "partake of a meal." This letter also gives evidence that the Christians came together on the Lord's Day—Sunday.

In his famous *Apology*, Justin Martyr from Rome, about A.D. 150, gave the following account: "On the day called Sunday,

6

all who live in cities or in the country gather together in one place, and the memoirs of the apostles or the writings of the prophets are read for so long as time permits. Then, when the reader has ceased, the overseer [*proestos*] instructs us by word of mouth, exhorting us to put these good things into practice. Then we all rise together and pray." Then followed communion. Justin also indicates that the Christians came together on Sunday for worship, because this was the day that Jesus Christ rose from the dead. Other meetings were conducted to help look after the needs of the members, as well as to proclaim the gospel. Advice was given to the church that a careful record of membership be maintained, "name for name." This was necessary in order to maintain a rigorous church discipline.

In the meantime, the church made great numerical gains by reaching the masses but neglected in many instances to enforce church discipline. The spiritual customs became less demanding, and the ancient Catholic Church gradually began to lower its requirements. This condition, together with increasing sacerdotalism, led to a division which began in the middle of the second century and came to be known as the first separatist congregation. The strict procedure of excluding members no longer was maintained. There is evidence enough that the Roman episcopate dominated the church by about A.D. 200, a situation far removed from the association of the original local assemblies. The free church concept had been overruled by a pretentious authoritative church order. The hierarchical program, the magical-mystical sacramental concepts, and the declaration of a rigid, dogmatic orthodoxy were marks of the growing ancient Catholic Church.

During the latter portion of the second century there remained groups of believers which in simplicity maintained the principles that had come down from the period of apostolic primitive Christianity. The larger church termed these groups as heretics. The justification of making this evaluation of the free churches will not here be discussed. The Roman Catholic theory that its type of church institution, hierarchy, and sacramental liturgy can be traced to the constituent and primary elements of primitive Christianity has had many defenders

7

throughout the centuries. The Church as a mysterious organism, with its miraculous institutions of grace maintained by sacrament and cult ceremonies, has won adherents even from the ranks of Protestantism.

For others, history is clear that these institutionalized churches were strangers to the New Testament pattern. Whether the primitive churches' simple concepts ought to be directional guides for Christianity in future periods is a question for later discussion. It is possible to accept the New Testament message and example either as an authoritative rule or as a historical picture of basic concepts, yet undeveloped, which naturally are subject to change. The Protestant groups and the state churches generally have made commitments to the latter type of interpretation. Churches and fellowships which follow the free church heritage have regarded the New Testament as being authoritative in matters of organization as well as belief.

II

Free Church Movements
as Heresies

Marcionism and Montanism

The process of development which transformed the original Christian congregations to a sacramental, authoritarian Church took place during the latter portion of the second century, as has already been stated in the previous chapter. This change did not take place without protest. The Christians were only a few decades removed from the apostolic period; therefore, they were keenly aware of the procedures among the primitive churches, the simple forms of government, the unified observance of baptism, the celebration of the Lord's Supper in its original design, as well as the moral rigorism which was a part of the Pauline spirit. If the tendency to develop a monarchical episcopate, which became marked during the latter portion of the second century, could not be stopped, the centralized Church, on the other hand, could not possibly hinder the development of opposition movements. It is during this same period that the first mention of infant baptism is made in historical sources.

Characteristics of the free churches were maintained, but it became increasingly clear that the institutionalized Church was becoming more and more infiltrated with Judaism. A revival of Pauline teachings, which caused a schism to occur in the Church at Rome, laid the foundation for a new Christian movement—*Marcionism*. Marcion was a prosperous owner of ships from Asia Minor (south coast of the Black Sea), who early in this period opposed the trend the orthodox Church was taking. He came to Rome, and there he attracted a large following. When he separated from the Church, probably about A.D. 140, a large number of people followed him to establish a

9

separate church. This movement spread rapidly, so much so that Justin Martyr was able to write a few years later that it had "spread among all nations of mankind." It is evident that this reaction met a real need, for large numbers regarded it as a necessary return from Judaism to a purified form of Pauline Christianity. It is possible, Harnack suggests, that the Marcionites also called themselves "Paulicians," since the Paulicians who appear in the Middle Ages "were easily transformed Marcionites."

The most significant of Marcion's teachings was repudiation of the close tie the Church had with the Old Testament, especially its sacerdotal system. The imitation of Judaistic practices in the Church was regarded by many as a departure from both the example and teaching of Jesus as well as from the Pauline concept of the gospel as free to all. Marcion and his followers rejected the allegorical method of interpretation, which made it possible to apply the Old Testament practices to the congregation's way of life. He did not approve the Judaistic teachings of righteousness, and in this he was in accord with the words of Jesus. The Sermon on the Mount was evaluated highly. The gospel was to him something entirely distinct from the legalistic requirements of the Old Testament. It is apparent that Paul was the great authority for Marcion. Another factor to consider is that Paul had been put aside by the second century theologians in preference to the teaching of the Logos on the one hand and the idealistic teachings of Judaism on the other.

Marcion's sharp opposition to the Old Testament and Judaism misled him to take a moderate dualistic outlook regarding the Creator and the Saviour—maintaining the existence of two Gods. Many have interpreted this position as being a form of gnosticism. In this old controversy it is now possible to gain a measure of clarification, for investigation supports the conclusion of Hans Lietzmann, who maintains that the source and motive of Marcion's thesis in this question does not arise from the gnostic framework of thought. Neither in its origin nor in its outgrowth is Marcion's teaching dualistic. In his sharp rejection of the assimilation of Judaism in the

Church, he desired to purify the Church's message and, further-more, to accept the Pauline writings as the only authority for Christians. It was only a "purified" version of Luke's Gospel that Marcion approved as satisfactory. He also expunged those portions in the Pauline epistles which he believed to be Ju-daistic interpolations.

Interest for present purposes is not so much in Marcion's speculations concerning one interpretation or another. The main question is whether or not he was a supporter of the free church concept when he left the official Church to set up his own organization. Rigorous moralism and an ascetic view of the Christian life contributed greatly to holding this new fellowship together. The Marcionites rejected the multifar-ious complexities in the life of man. Fasts, temperance in eat-ing and drinking, and sexual austerity identified them. Their congregations were firmly united in living a quiet and with-drawn life. This made a strong impression on the great Church, especially when many of the Marcionites were led to martyr-dom.

The Marcionite movement was promptly noticed by the heathen writers of literature. Philosopher Celsus, who was a strong critic of the Christians, dealt with this movement in one of his polemical treatises, ca. A.D. 180, as a separate branch of Christendom. Tertullian from Carthage declared, about A.D. 200, as had Justin in Rome forty years previous, that the Marcionites had spread over "the whole world." From the numerous opposition writings during the second century it is possible to determine that this movement had spread through western Asia Minor, Corinth, Crete, the large cities such as Antioch, Alexandria, and Edessa, and even as far as Carthage and Lyon. Rome was the headquarters and main point of de-parture. The Marcionite movement was consequently a major competitor to the primitive Catholic Church and was regarded as a peril. This was particularly true in the East. In the region of Syria, even during the fourth century, the Church fathers issued emphatic warnings about this sect. In Armenia during the fifth century Marcionism was pointed out as dangerous. In the meantime, the movement began to lose some of its force in the West. Because of the severe imperial edicts against heresies, Marcionism was outlawed even in the East, but it continued to remain alive in small villages and concealed places for a hundred years. In the process of time it was absorbed into Manicheanism, a new movement. In the early Middle Ages the Marcionite type of separatism was represented by the Paulician movement.

Another free church movement which arose during the same period and extended its influence far and wide, though heterogeneous in character, was *Montanism*. Basically it was a movement which sought to maintain the office of the original church prophet. It also became a well-defined opposition movement against ecclesiasticism in the official and institutionalized Church, which developed during the latter portion of the second century. This movement had its origin in the spiritual experiences of Montanus, who resided in the heart of Asia Minor.

It seems that a form of early-church pietism had been preserved in the secluded valleys of inner Asia Minor. When Montanus, according to his interpretation, was suddenly laid hold of by God's Spirit, probably in the early portion of the seventh decade of the second century, there was a sympathetic response on the part of many who desired a similar experience and consequently united with Montanus. It was the imaginative interpretations of the book of Revelation which stimulated the group. Soon a tension arose between those prophets and evangelists who had no local responsibilities and the officials who were directly responsible for the local churches. This tension increased quite naturally after the middle of the second century, when the primitive Catholic Church organization became more exclusive. Warnings against false prophets had appeared early, and in many instances the evidence reveals that the admonitions were justified. When the Montanistic movement, whose members called themselves "the new order of prophets," broke forth from its birthplace in Phrygia, these apprehensive warnings were revived. Montanus had experienced ecstasies and probably spoke in tongues. In the great Church this was considered a strange phenomenon, and consequently definite measures were taken to oppose this new movement. The essential features of this revival movement were not, however, the ecstasy and the *glossolalia* but the emphasis on declaring the message of salvation and holiness in the light of signs of the imminent end of the world. This major emphasis on holy living was a real contrast to the slackness and worldly conformity which, to a great extent, characterized the Church during this period. The most serious charge made by the early episcopal-type Church was that Montanus and his two leading prophetesses, Prisca and Maximilla, claimed to have received a direct revelation from God through the Holy Spirit. This concept was diametrically opposed to the conviction of an official apostolic succession, which only could come through the sanction of the Church.

The Montanistic congregations generally did not lay as much emphasis on ecstasy, prophecy, or on speaking in tongues as other groups in later church history. The basic emphasis centered on the three popular "Spirit-filled" prophets and their ministry. Others naturally followed in the line of these prophets, and they attempted to give a good account of themselves. The high-sounding claims of possessing special revelational insight, the one-sided emphasis on apocalyptic types, the practice of rigorous asceticism, as well as unbridled ecstasy, became weapons for attack in the hands of their opponents. Antagonism became sharp, and the justification of such a revival movement was drowned out in the waves of excessiveness. Consequently, the Montanists were rejected as a fanatical sect by their opponents, and on the basis of this opposition evaluation, the critique of this movement throughout history has been conclusively negative.

The success of the movement was great in the beginning. The center of this activity, including leadership personnel, was Pepuza, a city in Phrygia. A central treasury was established, and offerings made it possible for the church to maintain itinerant preachers. When the bishops and other leaders in the great Church came together in their synods, they decided to excommunicate the followers of Montanus. This action created a movement with autonomous characteristics, an independent fellowship. Peculiarly enough, there now gradually developed within the movement a more tightly knit organization, which included the creation of various types of officers. Montanism advanced rapidly in nearly all directions; even in Rome it made an early appearance. Eusebius has recorded that the early Montanist disciples in Rome laid claim to the fact that they were in the unbroken succession of prophets from the apostolic period. This prophets' movement soon plagued the Church in Alexandria and Egypt, a fact evidenced by Clement of Alexandria's anti-Montanistic outbursts in his work *Stromata*. In western North Africa no less a personality than Tertullian was won over to this new faith. Tertullian wrote a masterful reply to the critics of Montanism in his work *On Ecstacy*. He argued for the importance of understanding that beholding the glory of God, being overshadowed by God's power, quite naturally causes a person to lose control of his mind and common sense. Another important emphasis the Montanists stressed was that laymen are priests and ought earnestly to assume their priestly prerogative, even in the administration of baptism and the Lord's Supper. Like other groups, the Montanists regarded Paul as the great authority.

It is significant to note that in Gaul, where Montanism won adherents quite early, Bishop Irenaeus of Lyon exercised milder forms of opposition, while in Asia Minor the synods brought strong measures to bear. This fact is evidenced from the communications that were sent to the churches in that area. Irenaeus' close association with the churches of Asia Minor indicates his position of intervention, but toleration for the Montanists did not result. Instead the schism became more acute, even in the western countries. After the Decian persecution, the Montanists shared the Novatians' insistence on enforcing rigorous church discipline, especially for those who fell away from the Christian faith during the time of persecution. Montanists were now opposed even more vigorously. Soon the great Church denied the validity of baptism administered by the Montanists.

About the year 370, Epiphaneus, a writer of church history, declared that he knew of flourishing Montanist congregations in Asia Minor. Later yet, Hieronymus testified concerning the existence of Montanism even in its old environs. Since a historian in the fifth century maintained that the movement was found in Asia Minor and could not be uprooted, it is natural to conclude that Montanism was a powerful movement. As it was with the Marcionites, so it was for the Montanists: the imperial pronouncements against heresies during the Roman state-church period made it mandatory to destroy all dissenting movements. One of the emperors, Honorius, A.D. 407, decreed the death penalty for all Montantists. This peril caused the group not only to become more solidified but more closely united with other heretical movements. Glimpses of this movement were found in the Orient during the eighth century.

The established Church's dread of heretics and mysticism could not completely subdue Montanism's insistence on the primitive pattern that it was possible to personally experience God's power through the work of the Holy Spirit. Those in the great Church considered this phenomenon of personal inspiration as the work of demons, since this was before some in monastic orders began to advocate similar experiences. The monastic revival was a movement within the Church after the pattern of schismatic movements. Although there was no direct relationship between mystical monasticism and the free church movement, it may be stated with a degree of certainty that the cloisters and monasteries were filled with people who desired fellowship based on personal holiness.

The great significance of Montanism for the future was the strong emphasis on salvation, the teaching of holiness, and a severe, critical attitude toward worldliness and carelessness within the Church. The contribution of Tertullian, the Montanist, in explaining this point of view was of real significance. Throughout history the strict moral lessons and ascetic practices were destined to fill an important function in the life of the church.

Novatians and Donatists

The significant separations which occurred during the third and fourth centuries had special causative reasons. Even during

earlier periods of history, the question had arisen of how rigorous church discipline could be maintained when the church
embraced all classes of people. Later, when periods of religious
freedom made it easy to fall into moral laxity, the problem of
discipline again appeared. The question became particularly
acute in view of the schismatic and separatist movements
known as the Novatians and the Donatists.

The first to appear were the *Novatians*. The question of
forgiveness or penance for mortal sins committed after baptism had earlier been a topic of much discussion. Now again,
during the Decian persecution in the middle of the third century, the same controversy blossomed. Involved were those that
had fallen away from Christianity. During the persecution,
scores of Christians undoubtedly wilted in their faith while
others forsook Christianity completely. Now the question was
posed: What should be done with these *lapsi* (backsliders)?
How should they be received by the congregations? Around
these issues the controversy raged. Both in Rome and in North
Africa the churches had initiated mild requirements for the
restitution of those accused of immoral conduct, making it
comparatively easy to be tolerant toward those who had been
deserters from the faith. Against this procedure there arose
considerable misgiving and finally, definite opposition.

At the same time, around A.D. 250, there was an election to
fill the office of bishop at Rome. Novatian, a presbyter, stood
for the position that the Church should enforce strict discipline,
and he opposed the idea that deserters of the faith should be
received back into the Church. Novatian won many adherents
who elected him bishop in opposition to one previously elected.
As bishop he continued to work for his own objectives. The
orthodox bishop's synod in Rome dismissed Novatian and excommunicated him. The rigorism of the ancient Church was
still desired by many, and therefore Novatian became the
leader of opponents in their struggle against the great Church.
It was at this time that the term *katharoi* (the pure) came
into use. This is the term the Novatians applied to themselves.

The movement became widespread, even in Africa and Asia
Minor. In Africa especially it appeared that the Montanists

16

forsook their cause in great numbers to join forces with this new opposition movement. In many sections Novatianism was the predominant form of Christianity. Even in Carthage the Montanists supported Novatian's claim to the episcopate. Novatian churches grew up in both the East and the West, and through a well-knit organization under the leadership of the bishops, this movement came to be a separatist church group parallel with the orthodox Church. Emperor Constantine and his successors occasionally showed great consideration to the Novatian bishops. During the fifth century this church had as strong a position in Constantinople as it did in Rome. The adherents of Novatianism migrated as far as Gaul and Spain in the West and to Syria in the East. By this time, however, the movement had lost many of its original characteristics. There is information to the effect that Novatians were found in the Orient as late as in the seventh century.

When the orthodox Church, in the first half of the fourth century, came under the protective custody of Emperor Constantine, and in a real sense became a state church, the debate over keeping the Church pure from those who had committed mortal sins was again revived. Even at this time the question was related to those who had recently backslidden in the time of persecution. Immediately after the Emperor's edict, A.D. 313, which gave toleration to Christianity, this problem became seriously acute. Out of this controversy there emerged the movement known as *Donatism*. As previously mentioned, so now again an election of a bishop proved to be the spark that set off the conflagration, but this time it was among the churches in North Africa.

Belief among various church groups that the bishop recently elected in Carthage had been consecrated by one who had failed to maintain a steadfast faith during the Diocletian persecution resulted in refusal to recognize the new bishop. Dissenters elected a bishop of their choice to take his place. A deep cleavage in the North African churches resulted. At first appearance the parties seemed to be uniformly strong. In fact, in some places the schismatic group was the stronger. From then on the movement was known as Donatism after Donatus

17

the Great, who for a generation was the powerful leader of this new fellowship (until A.D. 350). This schism in Africa became a delicate matter for Emperor Constantine, who at this time assumed the position of protector of Christianity.

Attempts to win over the Donatists were fruitless. The question now arose as to what disposition should be made of church property which had been closed or confiscated during the persecution. When the property was to be returned to the Christian churches, there were both orthodox churches and the strict Donatist churches which laid claim to the buildings. Because he sought to unify and strengthen the empire, the Emperor was faced with a difficult problem. His desire for unity made him sympathetic with the normal, Catholic-type churches—in North Africa, as elsewhere; but it could well be that churches of Donatistic persuasion would not recognize directives coming from the Emperor and his officers. Thus a new problem arose concerning the relationship between state and church.

At two significant synods, one in Rome, A.D. 313, and the other in Arles in Southern France, A.D. 314, this question of unity was seriously considered. At both of the synods the Emperor had taken the initiative to win over the schismatic group, but agreement between the rival groups could not be reached. At the synod of Arles especially a large representation from various western sections formed the strong, authoritative majority in the synod. The Donatists had little chance. They were censured, and their claims were rejected. The state, which possessed the power and the authority, was now ready to suppress Donatism. The Emperor had considered this from the beginning. He therefore issued an edict legalizing the confiscation of Donatist churches and property and forbidding Donatist rebaptism. When there was an outbreak of agitation of a social nature, he used military force against Donatists, many of whom became martyrs. When the Emperor became more aware of how widespread Donatism really was and with what high-pitched enthusiasm it held forth in various places, he gave up the idea of trying to bring about conformity by force.

The Emperor's perplexity over this problem was due to the

fact that it took him by surprise just as he had emerged as the protector of Christianity. There must have been indecision and uneasiness on all sides when the Donatists, after their reverses in the synods, appealed to the court of the Emperor. Vacillating in his position toward the Donatists, the Emperor dispatched a notice, A.D. 321, to the governmental leaders in North Africa that the judgments and proceedings against the Donatists should be nullified and that they should be "turned over to the judgment of God." This was a clear acknowledgment of the failure of the first attempt to settle a question by means of a church-political alliance. Constantine's attitude about this problem remained the same, however, as is indicated by the fact that he granted money both to orthodox priests and Roman congregations to build new church buildings in instances where the Donatists had kept possession of the older church buildings. Also, during this period the Emperor was concerned about Arianism, a schism more serious and widespread.

How was it possible for Donatism, with its moral rigorism and its disregard for Rome and the synods, to become so quickly a power in the North African churches in competition with the orthodox Church? About A.D. 330, some 270 Donatist bishops (leaders of local churches) gathered for a synod in Carthage, and according to Harnack's findings, it is difficult to believe that the orthodox Church had many more bishops in this church province. This church division, which conformed to the usual pattern of such events, also took place in the area where Tertullian and Cyprian had made such remarkable contributions to the church. Understanding of Donatists' great progress partly lies, undoubtedly, in the Montanistic free church tradition, to which even Tertullian had committed himself. In contrast to this free idea, bishops under the influence of Cyprian stressed the solidarity of the church. These two converse influences must have created a rift, preparing for the Donatist protest to find ready acceptance.

There is still another important circumstance that bears observation. Carthage and Rome had long been hostile toward one another, and so this new outward expression appeared as a

19

survival of the anti-Roman tradition. The left radical wing of Donatism expressed itself in enthusiastic nationalism which, coupled with the anti-Roman spirit among the natives, added up to a Donatistic folk movement. The right wing party took things quietly, organizing groups which included outstanding men of culture. In both instances these parties became a "break-from-Rome" movement, which continued with undiminished energy during the entire fourth century. The history of the Donatists differs from other opposition movements in that it primarily remained geographically bounded within its original territory. Information has been found concerning the existence of a Donatist church in Rome and one in Spain.

When in 316 Donatus the Great became the foremost bishop within Donatism, the movement obtained a strong leader. Through his gifts of teaching and eloquence, Donatus made a deep impression. During the time when more lenient emperors reigned, Donatism found free opportunities of expression. When one of Constantine's sons, during the decade of 340, began to exert powerful pressure against Donatism, he was met with real steadfastness. The Emperor sought to win leading personalities over to the cause of the orthodox Church by offering them gifts of money. Donatus could not be enticed; he refused to receive money from the Emperor. He considered this a bribe and condemned the procedure with the rejection: "What does the emperor have to do with the church?" With these words, Donatus gave the free church movement for all time a slogan, a slogan that has often been repeated. The persecution during the time around 340 could not make the Donatists give up their convictions. Donatism was now clearly a free church movement from this point of view: it stood adamantly opposed to any intermingling of state power with the organization of the church.

Donatus the Great died in exile about 350, but a new leader of significance stepped forth to assume the new responsibilities within the movement. This was the Spanish Parmenianus, similar to Donatus in piety and leadership. The Emperor now had new concerns, for the great Church's inner strife was revolving around Arianism and the christological controversy.

However, during the short reign of the pagan Julian, which began about 360, all of the "heretics" found easier breathing. Even for the Donatists this was a great time. Donatists emphasized their digressions from the orthodox Church by thoroughly cleaning the church buildings which had been returned before using them. They reordained preachers that came over to their mission, and they rebaptized individuals who came from the great Church, which now had become state supported. Donatist expatriates returned, and because of the reclamation of the church buildings, the movement was able to make new advances. When many came to join the Donatist cause, it became necessary to examine everyone scrupulously. During the last decades of the fourth century Donatism was a strong free church movement in North Africa.

During the time of Parmenianus' leadership there were two distinct directions which became evident in the movement, a radical and a conservative. After the death of Parmenianus (392), there was a period of serious conflict between these two sides. Without a strong and able leader who could act with authority, Donatism was weakened because of inner conflict. At the same time, the orthodox Roman Church had a great theologian and leader in Augustine, who came to the forefront in North Africa. After his early years spent in Carthage and also a residence in Italy, Augustine returned to Africa as bishop of Hippo Regius, not far from Carthage, where he became the dominant person in the Church of that area. This area was populated with many Donatists, and for two decades Augustine sought to win these heretics back to the faith which they had renounced.

At first, Augustine sought to convince the Donatists with theological arguments. The Donatists' strong position in North Africa, however, could not be eradicated by arguments, not even by those of Augustine. Consequently, the famous theologian changed his method and instructed that the Donatists must be resisted and overcome by means of force. Augustine set up a theoretical apology for the punishment of Christian heretics, which during the Middle Ages became the merciless way of the Church to overcome its opponents. This role of

21

Augustine is seldom mentioned, so as not to detract from the reputation of the great church father.

Compulsory laws were again revived, Donatist property was confiscated, and churches were closed; then Augustine was satisfied. He had taught, according to Luke 14:23, that the Church should "compel them to come in." It was held as proper to force incorrigibles into the Church: *cogite intrare!* When it proved impossible to bend these nonconformists and when they in turn made violent accusations against the Church, it was decided to try to settle the question at a conference in Carthage, 411. The records state that there were no less than 279 Donatist bishops and 286 Catholic bishops who took part in this important meeting of discussion. The Donatists had two outstanding leaders in the forefront, and on the other side Augustine stood out as the foremost leader. The discussion centered on the problem of the wheat and the tares. The Donatists pointed out that in Jesus' own explanation, recorded in Matthew 13:38, it is the world and not the church which is the field. No tares should be tolerated in the church. The Donatists also accused the Church for its ruthless persecution of individuals who held contrary views. The victory naturally went to the great Church, and in particular to Augustine.

There immediately followed a severe persecution, and new compulsory laws from the Emperor were issued during the next few years. Donatist meetings were forbidden with the threat of the death penalty, churches were closed and confiscated, the members of the churches were deprived of their civil rights, and many received sentences of high fines. The Catholic Church's first great and inhuman persecution against other Christians was against the Donatist free church. This method could not continue for many years, for even here it became evident that brutal persecution was not effective to crush a spiritual movement. Donatism lived on for at least two hundred years.

The split in the North African territories could not be healed. The State Church went its way; and the Donatist free church, with its emphasis on church discipline and regenerate church membership, continued in its path, even though now

22

its influence was reduced. The end for both parties came two centuries later with the Mohammedan invasion and its great display of power. During the first centuries of the Middle Ages there were many that still held radical opinions about Christian freedom. Even though feeble, the many opposition movements reveal that the free church line was far from extinction.

Paulicians and the Cathari

It is difficult to ascertain the correctness of Harnack's cautious statement of opinion that it is possible that the Marcionites called themselves Paulicians. If this is correct, then the eighth-century Paulician movement could be regarded as a continuation of earlier movements, such as Marcionism or even Montanism. The truth is, however, as Harnack explains, that there is no documentary evidence for this theory. However this may be, the fact remains that the *Paulicians* arose in Asia Minor as a strong movement in the eighth century and that the movement had a distinct dualistic character. Generally speaking, the dualistic sects in the countries of the East have had wide ramifications appearing under many different names.

Paulicians were found in Syria and Armenia even in the seventh century, but where they came from and how they obtained their name is unknown. They had no direct historical relationship with the Manicheans, for they not only stood in opposition to them but condemned them. To be sure, there was an intermingling of all of these groups. During the ninth century some anti-Manichean writings appeared which could possibly have reference to the Paulicians. There is also evidence that the Paulicians came to certain places in the Balkans after they had stayed at Byzantium. During the eighth and ninth centuries, the Roman emperors in the East made the Paulicians the object of persecution, finally driving them out, for this group had become a powerful factor even in the city of Constantinople. There were several waves of persecution, and fleeing refugees went to the Balkan territories where nonconformists and opposition groups were received. From this area the ideas and the organization of the Paulicians spread.

23

Missionaries were sent out, and progress was especially significant in the southeastern portions of Europe.

The characteristic of Paulicians was stress on a holy life. They believed in separation from the nominal Christian populace, who were satisfied with the ceremonies of the Church as well as other religious forms. They had their own preachers and opposed the special consecration of ministers and the system of church hierarchy. It has been stated that they even minimized the sacraments. From one point of view this is correct, for they laid all their emphasis on the inner life and not on material things. They clarified this by saying that they worshiped God alone, not material things. They opposed the use of the symbol of the cross, church buildings, clerical vestments, and the celebration of the Mass. They called themselves simple Christians.

There was a similar group, a branch of Paulicianism, which was called the Bogomiles. This appeared in Bulgaria during the tenth century. Records indicate that the name was derived from a priest named Bogomil. One branch of the movement has also been known by the name of Phundagiagitae. No noteworthy difference is found between the Paulicians and the Bogomiles. The Bogomiles appeared in the same territory to which the Paulician immigrants from Asia had come, and so the historic connection between the two movements is fairly clear.

This leads to a crucial question, the origin of the extensive European movement known in history as the *Cathari*. As has been already stated, this term had been used by the Novatians during the third century when they applied the meaning by endeavoring to keep the church pure through strict discipline. When the Cathari appeared at the beginning of the eleventh century in the western territories of Europe, they revealed that their way of thinking and customs were in principal agreement with the opinion and orders of the Paulicians and the Bogomiles. It is natural then to affirm that there is a direct historical connection, even though it is impossible to point out all of the links in the chain. This portion of history is obscured by the same problem as the study of movements already mentioned. Research evidences are likewise similar for the opposition movements which follow. The historical material documenting these groups was often destroyed because these groups were heretics. In most cases research on the free church movement in the late Middle Ages must be based on the reports of the antagonists or the one-sided material obtained from the law courts.

During the eleventh century the Cathari spread rapidly and pressed on even to the western parts of Europe. The outreach, however, was not only in a westerly direction, for large areas of Germany were touched by their missionaries. In France they were called *Bulgari,* which also means they were classified as identical with the Bogomiles which lived in Bulgaria. Other proofs of this affinity can be pointed out. Foremost is the similarity in doctrinal questions and customs. Likewise, they were similar in their opposition against the dogmas and cult ceremonies of the great Church. During the twelfth century the Cathari reached out and won wide support, first because of their severe persecution in Bulgaria and the territories of Byzantium and again because of the closer union between the lands in the Balkans and the lands in the West during the Crusades. From this point of view the meaning of the Crusades cannot be overemphasized, even though it is impossible to discuss the details here.

The unifying element among all of the heretical groups that were opposed to the Church during this period was the emphasis on the difference between the material and the spiritual world, a concept which had roots in the Gnostic dualism of earlier centuries. In some respects this emphasis was a legacy from Paulicianism. This idea had also been prominent among the Marcionites and the Montanists. Pervading was a major insistence on the demand for holiness, separation from all worldliness, and the reception of the gifts of the Spirit. A consecrated Christian ought to renounce worldly property and home life and instead devote himself to Christian missionary activity and a life of piety. These requirements could not be applicable for all the members of the congregation, however, but only for those in the highest places, those that were called "the perfect" (*perfecti*). The remaining members in the fellowship could live a normal life on earth, but they were to seek their spiritual care from the itinerant teachers and spiritual guides. Naturally, there were requirements for these common "believers" (*credentes*) as well. They were to take note of the regulations and follow a life of asceticism and godliness which was separated from that of the worldly populace.

The Cathari preachers and apostles, "the perfect," carried considerable influence. Preaching and prayer were the foremost elements in their worship. They emphasized the spiritual; consequently, they had little use for the ordinary sacraments, including the Lord's Supper. The only sacrament was a kind of spiritual baptism called *consolamentum*. This baptism elevated recipients to a high plane so that they claimed to be above the regulations and edicts of the Church. It was natural that they would soon be exposed to the most severe persecution. It became one of the most cruel undertakings of the Middle Ages. It is understandable that the churchmen and their defenders saw in the Cathari dangerous enemies to the Christian faith, for the dualistic nature of their fundamental doctrine broke down the Christian concept of God and also attacked the doctrine of Christology which had been accepted by the Church.

Because of the widespread acceptance of these heretical ideas among the masses, the Church became terrified and sought to resist with forceful measures. To be sure, the court reports were magnified in order to justify their measures; however, it is certain that the Cathari was a substantial power. It is highly improbable, as one source claims, that two-thirds of Europe was overrun by these sectaries. The bloody annihilation in the Albigensian Wars, 1209 to 1229, gave witness to the fact that many political and personal elements were united in this conflict. This war of twenty years and the persecution which followed had a measure of success, for after a few decades the Cathari played no significant role. The complete organization of the Inquisition, which was established by papal decree, 1232, gave the Church a weapon by which it could systematically eradicate heretics.

Waldensians

Another movement, the *Waldensians,* attracted large numbers of followers during the period just studied. From many points of view this group went in the same direction as the Cathari, but it was not dualistic. "The poor men from Lyon" was one of the most remarkable opposition movements against the Medieval Church which arose before the Reformation.

A full account of Peter Waldo (or Valdéz) is not necessary. The story is well known—how Waldo, a prosperous merchant in Lyon, suddenly turned his back on his business and the things of the world to attire himself with poor clothing, live the life of an ascetic, and go out to preach in city and countryside. It does not appear that he had any relationships with the Cathari groups which were also prevalent in France, his homeland, nor is it possible to hold that he received any promptings or opinions from them. This movement seems to have arisen within the borders of the Church, and if any predecessors and teachers are to be named, then mention should be made of the wandering preachers in France who in earlier times had moved in opposition against the Church and had appeared as the missionaries to the people.

It is clear, however, that the Waldensians had definite similarities with the Cathari. This was evidenced especially in many points regarding the question of opposition against the Church's teachings and customs, such as the offering of the Mass, purgatory, the hierarchy, the property holdings of the Church, priesthood, pilgrimages, saint worship, and other elements of a lesser nature. Both groups strongly doubted the validity of sacraments administered by unworthy priests, and in this they were united with movements already treated. It was not this negative aspect which was the most important, although these points were prominent in the eyes of the defenders of the Church.

When Peter Waldo appeared about 1170 as a wandering preacher, there was a significant group of followers who associated with him. Characteristic of these adherents was that they were very faithful to the two basic principles of Waldo:

27

The Bible is the only conclusive authority in faith and action for the Christian, and the Bible in the vernacular coupled with the interpretation of Bible doctrines is the greatest need. From this point of view the Waldensians became a fellowship of Bible preaching. There were two classes of followers: "Christ's paupers" (*Pauperes Christi*), made up of people who left civil life, and the "friends" (*Amici*), people in conventional occupations. In this respect the Waldensians can be compared to the Cathari division of the "perfect" and the "believers."

Preaching by laymen (even by women), which now had its inception, became an impetus and emphasis which resulted in a free church movement of several centuries' duration, and it was independent of the Roman Church. Waldo was opposed by both the pope and the councils; his Bible translation did not win approval; and his preaching missions were condemned as being heretical. After his first appearance things began to happen quickly. The preaching fellowship soon developed into a free church fellowship. The followers of Waldo organized societies (*societatēs*) in various districts, and sometimes they were given the name "congregations" (*congregationēs*). Conversion was followed by a time of testing. After certain ceremonies, converts were admitted to the primary classes, "brothers" and "sisters." During the time of persecution it was more difficult for members to hold together and, in any case, to make an outward advance. The movement had to go more or less underground. Worship services were maintained in conventicles, and the Waldenses assembled in these little *scholae* for edification and for watchcare over the members. Similar "schools" later appeared among the Anabaptists during the period of the Reformation.

Waldo soon assumed the title of bishop and declared himself to have spiritual authority to ordain presbyters and deacons and to administer the sacraments according to the Word of God. Already before 1210 the movement had developed to the point that it was no longer a movement of simple fellowship made up of poor preachers, who, two-by-two, wandered about in the manner of Jesus' disciples, but an independent group of believers with a determined opposition against the

28

Medieval Roman Church. This development occasioned many difficulties, especially in the conduct of the Waldenses in other countries. Outside of Southern France a similar movement had grown up in Northern Italy, and this group expressed its independence by opposing the Waldensian branch in France and, in particular, Waldo's demands. This brought about a serious schism. It soon became evident that the Italian branch of the movement was stronger and could more easily outlive the fierce persecutions which were setting in. The Waldensian movement spread also to the territories of Germany, and it seemed to have had a widespread acceptance among the people, especially after the persecution which was primarily directed against the Waldenses in the central and southern parts of Germany during the early portion of the thirteenth century. Even in other territories of France and in Northern Spain the Waldensian movement progressed rapidly and also met with the opposition of the Church. Of all the groups the Medieval Roman Church attempted to condemn, this free church organization was the strongest and best organized. Therefore, the campaign was intense.

Early the Waldensians established two important fundamentals, which in later periods were taken up by others and have been preserved by many groups even until the present day. They taught that the Christian should refrain from the use of the sword to kill one another and that he should not swear an oath in any form. The Sermon on the Mount was the basis of this strict rule of living. The Waldenses preached penitence and conversion, and from the time of conversion and joining the free church congregation, the responsibility remained to live a Christian life according to the demands of the Sermon on the Mount and other portions of Scripture. The preachers richly supplied their messages with Bible quotations which became identified with the biblical character of the movement. The demand to translate the Bible into the various languages of the people became more intensified.

It has already been mentioned that there were similar traits in the reformation movements of the Cathari and the Waldenses. It is clear that Waldo did not sense any direct re-

lationship and dependence between the groups. This phenomenon has already been encountered: similarities do not
necessarily imply relationship. As has already been intimated,
the Waldensian movement was historically closely related to
the Church, and its biblicism gave it a distinction. During the
great persecution and at the courts the two movements often
were considered identical.

The attempt to stop Waldo and his preachers by prohibition
and banishment failed; it took some time before the Church
found a way to conduct opposition proceedings. At the beginning the Church seemed to consider the matter carefully, for
it resolved to win back many by organizing an anti-Waldensian
movement called "poor Catholics." During this same period
the mendicants appeared. However, it was not long before
fires of persecution had been kindled, and from 1211 to 1214
the Waldenses were burned in France and in Germany. Even
in northern Italy there were martyrs, even though these northern Italian Waldenses withdrew into the Alp Mountains in
the north to protect themselves from this extermination.

It is impossible here to describe the fate of the Waldenses.
In several countries the movement was nearly wiped out, yet
remnants were found, for example, in the territories of Germany even until the end of the fifteenth century. The Waldenses of northern Italy united with the Bohemian Brethren
in the early portion of the sixteenth century. Later they were
influenced by the Calvinistic Reformation, and after this time
they gradually lost their specific Waldensian character, becoming more and more a part of the Reformed church. Up unto
the present day there exists a Waldensian church in Italy ex-
hibiting some of the old characteristics, a Protestant free
church organization from the twelfth century. This is altogether a unique free church movement, and it illustrates the
strength and spiritual power of this form of organization.

Lollards and Hussites

About two centuries after the Waldensian movement had
spread over the European continent, a similar movement arose
in England. This was *Lollardism*. We know very little about

the circumstances of this movement before the remarkable accomplishments of John Wycliffe from about 1370. It is very uncertain whether any of the people in the Waldensian movement ever migrated to England, even though England had an active communication with the Continent. Certainly the people in England must have known about the Waldenses. Under any circumstance, however, during the middle of the fourteenth century, coming out of the streams of Augustinianism and biblicism, there appeared certain groups in England which were characterized by lay preachers and the free church ideal, similar to the ideas of the Waldensian movement.

John Wycliffe, during his studies at Oxford, came under the sway of an influential Augustinian theologian, Thomas of Bradwardine, who taught justification by faith and warned against depending upon works. Wycliffe caught up this line of reasoning and soon became an ardent student of the Bible, which is evidenced in some of his philosophic writings of about 1360. As a professor in Oxford and in good favor with the administrative powers, it was not very long before Wycliffe was drawn into the church political struggle, especially the national resentment against the pope's levying revenues in England. In this instance the teachings and the theories of Marsilius of Padua regarding natural rights played an important role. From 1370 on, Wycliffe in famous treatises set forth the relationships with the pope and hierarchy. With a zeal he proclaimed the Christian's ideal of poverty and stated that both spiritual and worldly authority and the right of possession depended on vassalage to God, the supreme Lord. If one stood in grace and followed rules of righteousness, one justly held earthly status, but if this were not the case, one forfeited both authority and personal possessions. This thesis worked against both the pope and royalty.

Later Wycliffe began to probe into questions regarding the authority of God's Word and the nature of the church. In both instances he went against recognized opinions. In his important apology for the Bible, the *Truth of the Scripture (De veritate sacrae Scripturae)*, the reformer clearly vindicated the Bible alone in all matters of faith, and on this point he lost the support of the learned scholars. These scholars knew full well that the Waldenses and other reform groups had earlier championed this thesis concerning the Scriptures and that the Church had condemned them for this conviction. The keen thrusts and the sharp expressions which Wycliffe employed in his writings reveal that his antagonists had become serious in their opposition to him. While others set aside the Scriptures, Wycliffe declared that the salvation of the believer and the foundation for all church dogma was found therein. He perceived that the Bible alone was the guiding principle for judging what was false doctrine. It was therefore imperative to determine the correct understanding of Scripture. The Lord had by grace revealed the correct understanding of Scripture, and Wycliffe now perceived that this was the living Word. Only if a particular dogma was in agreement with the Bible was it worth maintaining. Contempt for the truths in the Bible was the cause of all of the evil in the church; the primary task of the preacher was to study and declare the Word of God. It followed, therefore, that every believer was a priest and by faith he might receive power to give spiritual food and nourishment to the children in the church.

This teaching concerning the priesthood of all believers and the responsibility of every Christian to spread the knowledge of God's Word became the basic principles of the expanding Lollard movement. According to Wycliffe, the heretic was not the one who ministered the Word but the one who because of sin was separated from God. The bishops and priests who followed worldly pursuits and in word and deed denied the Scriptures were the real heretics. On the contrary, believing laymen who held to the Scriptures were the church's true defenders and followers. This became the theoretical basis for future preaching by laymen.

Along with this bold writing, Wycliffe produced another book which was of no less significance. It was his treatise *On the Church* (*De Ecclesia*), which later came to have tremendous significance in Bohemia. It is here that Wycliffe's Augustinian theology is most clearly presented: The basic question regarding the church is that the fellowship is made up of the predestined ones, and these make up the body of Christ. Consequently, no one can be the head of the church save Christ, and even the pope cannot be absolutely certain that he belongs to the predestined. The believing laymen have Christ as their priest, shepherd, bishop, and pope. According to Romans 8:30, it is the grace of God alone that brings justification and glorification, and this grace no one can merit. In this treatise Wycliffe also wrote about the various officers of the original congregation, repudiating any authoritarian position in the church for a pope or hierarchy. Papal indulgences are useless, for God does not forgive sins on the basis of money. God does not sell righteousness, but he is the only one who can grant forgiveness and absolution of sins, and this only to those who show a right spirit of repentance. According to this thesis, the entire sacrament of penance is worthless.

The last two works discussed were the foundation of the movement which Wycliffe originated. Wycliffe, from 1378 until his death in 1384, carried on a struggle against the Catholic Church's regulations with extreme rigor. When his tract on the Lord's Supper appeared, it was clear that he was also heretical on the sacramental questions. Because of this, many forsook him, especially the mendicant monks. Proceedings against him were now instituted. He was driven from Oxford and retired to a rural pastorate where he and his associates translated the Bible and from which he sent out the poor traveling preachers. Because of his connections with the court, Wycliffe was spared the death of a heretic at the stake. The movement continued on after Wycliffe's passing by keeping active the conventicles and through missionary activity of the itinerant preachers. The translation of the Bible by Wycliffe and his followers is one of the great epochs in the history of the English church. One of the reasons for translating the Bible was to enable the leaders of the country to read the Scriptures and then restore the church to its original functions established by Christ. This is a basic principle, the privilege and the right to reform.

The numerical strength of the movement cannot be measured, but the influence was not insignificant, as can be attested by many circumstances. The followers of this Bible-preaching movement were called Lollards, which some have suggested comes from the Latin word *lollium,* meaning "tares." In the Papal Bull issued against Wycliffe this term is used, meaning the enemy who sows tares among the wheat. Other explanations for this name are found, but in this connection they lack any significant meaning.

No able leader was ready to take over after Wycliffe was off the scene. Persecution increased, and therefore the movement was forced, for the main part, to live underground. In the year 1401 an edict was announced that all incorrigible heretics should be burned. Archbishops did not stop at anything, and they saw to it that the movement was resisted with both literary weapons and the threat of the stake. In 1409 an act was publicized which forbade all preaching that did not have the permission of the bishops and all translation of any text into the English language, or even the reading of a text, without the approval of the English church council. All of the writings of Wycliffe were to be destroyed. At the Council of Constance, 1415, Wycliffe was condemned as a heretic, and this increased the frenzy of the persecution in England. A few years later the bones of Wycliffe were exhumed and burned at the stake.

Lollardism won adherents, including some outstanding personalities who were quickly eliminated. Transcribing of the Bible translations was necessarily done in secret. It was dangerous work, in view of the zealous attempt to root out the translations. There were many copies, however, which outlived the devastation. Even the work maintained in the conventicles by the "poor preachers" might have had more significance than it is possible to clearly document. There were certain weaknesses which naturally attached themselves to the movement. Especially it appears that the understanding of doctrinal concepts did not carry a corresponding sense of evangelism. At least this was true of Wycliffe himself. But during times of martyrdom, peoples' spiritual crises and newly won convictions seemed characterized by great earnestness and unshakable steadfastness even unto death.

The Lollards were peaceful, Bible-reading, conventicle be-

lievers and in this respect can be contrasted with that movement in Bohemia in the fifteenth century, the Hussite movement, which resorted to weapons to promote its cause. That
the movement continued until the time of the Reformation is
seen by the fact that now and then its adherents were martyred
and some of them were led to join secret groups. The opinions
and ideas of Wycliffe had become so entrenched in the life of
the English church that it was impossible to root them out.
The marks of this movement show up clearly in traditions such
as independent Bible reading, aversion to the official church-
ism, and the fellowship in conventicles, convictions magnified
in Puritanism and the free churches ever since the period of
1560. In English separatism, "the dissenting mind" has an old
history.

Another group which developed on the Continent and became a powerful movement in Bohemia in the early part of
the fifteenth century was the *Hussite* movement. John Huss,
professor at the University of Prague and pastor of the Bethlehem church, early became fascinated with the ideas of Wycliffe. As an author, Huss did not possess much originality,
but he reproduced the ideas of Wycliffe and became their
strong exponent in the heart of Europe. These were altogether
different from the heterogeneous ideas and statements that
formerly had been broadcasted on the Continent by the Cathari
and the Waldenses. Here were two theological professors that
supported the criticism of the Church and propounded a positive Bible interpretation.

The movement in Bohemia, like that in England, was intermingled with nationalism. In both instances there was registered opposition against that strange prince who resided in
Rome and laid claim that he was not only the vicar of Christ
upon earth but also the ruling prince in the world. In Bohemia
there was also an aversion to the Germans, many of whom had
extended their influence by obtaining important positions
within the hierarchy. Czech nationalism was further stimulated
because the Germans controlled one of the favorable spots in
the country, the University of Prague. Tension arose from this
resentment, and finally the Germans left the University to the

Czechs and went to Leipzig to establish their own university in 1409. When the ideas of Wycliffe about philosophy, theology, and practical church work became united with a strong Czech anti-German nationalism, it was natural that a powerful "break-from-Rome" movement should develop.

About 1380, when a Bohemian princess became the queen of England, the Czech nobility and student groups became closely related to the University of Oxford. This was during the time when Wycliffe's ideas were being debated by the students. Shortly after, the writings of Wycliffe were disseminated even in Bohemia. It was in this manner that John Huss became acquainted with Wycliffe, and after this he became the foremost proponent of the principles of the English reformer. Huss had an important position in the University, and as a preacher he exhibited unusual ability in winning adherents. It was in his preaching that Huss first exhibited the Wycliffe practice of criticizing the Church, thereby establishing himself as a reformer. To say that Huss was original is not possible, but he added new coals to the fire and gave the ideas a new force when he applied the Wycliffe message to the prevailing conditions in Bohemia.

The result, of course, could have been anticipated. The pope and the Church authorities interfered, schism was unavoidable, and Huss had to choose between silence or the dangerous course of rallying the people of Bohemia to his cause. The primary ideas were those made popular by Wycliffe: The Bible is the only authority for the Christian in matters of faith and conduct; the church is a fellowship of the predestined; and the church knows only one head, namely, Jesus Christ. At the same time, the hierarchy and other church groups were exposed to violent criticism on the grounds of degeneracy and immorality. For a time it appeared that Huss, through his Czech writings and his enthusiastic preaching, would be able to pull the entire nation with him, but even within the church in Bohemia he discovered strong powers which opposed him. When in 1414 he was called to appear before the church-reform council at Constance, Huss went with confidence that his cause was right and that it was secure. But the resulting decision was that the reformer should be imprisoned. After a prolonged period he was burned at the stake in July, 1415.

This attack on Huss became a challenge to Bohemian nationalism as well as to the free church movement. The details of following events do not belong to this presentation. The Bohemians divided into conservative and radical parties, and both of these parties did not hesitate to stand up against the papal crusade army with the sword. Nor did they do less when they opposed each other. The conclusion of this unusual reform was that a minority group inaugurated a peaceful free church movement. This occurred in 1467, when the so-called United Brethren (*Unitas Fratrum*) was formed. This group selected its own pastors and used the title "bishop" for the outstanding leader of the fellowship. In consecration it borrowed help from the Waldenses.

Back of the formation of the United Brethren stood a religious personality of great spiritual power and originality. He seems to have become a convert of Wycliffism without any direct intermediation by Huss. This man was Peter Chelzicky, of whom little is known. He was not a priest but a layman. Even if Chelzicky had been with the Hussite movement from the beginning, he had come to his own convictions regarding the primitive life of the free church by a personal study of Wycliffe's writings together with the Bible. In several writings he set forth his ideas for the Czech people and at the same time energetically taught the principles of Wycliffe so that the ideal of poverty and the right of laymen to work in the church was zealously motivated. Chelzicky took a definite stand against both the conservative and radical parties and their use of the sword. The Christian congregation, as in the early church, should remain completely free in its relationship with the state. The Christian's relationship to the worldly powers and the life of the state should be negative. A believer needs to refrain from all business affairs and offices. Cultivating the land and labor with the hands are the most suitable ways of life. Chelzicky became the father of the Bohemian Brethren, even though he died in 1460, a few years before the *Unitas Fratrum* was established. Under a great leader, Lucas of Prague, the movement progressed steadily so that at the time of Luther it was of such significance that the German reformer sought to make contact with it. Luther was acquainted with the devotional books of the Brethren. Lucas of Prague as bishop gave the movement a stable character so that it could live through the most difficult persecutions.

During the national and church struggle for freedom, there developed an apocalyptic emphasis. Ever since Joachim of Floris in the twelfth century had set forth his teachings about the new dispensation of the Holy Spirit, the expectancy of the new kingdom of God had been widespread. This was also true in Bohemia. From the interpretation of Wycliffe's teachings pertaining to possessions there arose certain ideas concerning social rights and the sharing of personal property within the Christian brotherhood. In this regard the Sermon on the Mount played an important part. As in the Lollard movement, individual Bible reading and fellowship in conventicles ultimately resulted in free churches. In Bohemian regions the Cathari and Waldenses had migrated earlier, so this part of the world was not a stranger to free groups. These churches of the Brethren rebaptized people who came from the Roman Catholic Church, not because they were opposed to the principle of infant baptism but because they did not approve of the backslidden Church and the priests' administration of the sacraments. Among the United Brethren both infant and adult baptism were practiced. Later, however, when the mode of adult baptism became a criminal offense in the violent campaign against the Anabaptists, the United Brethren, in a synod in 1534, decided to discontinue entirely the practice of adult baptism. In questions pertaining to the sword, oaths, and magistracy, the Brethren took the same position which was held later by the Anabaptists. Heavy demands were required of Christians, and church discipline was rigorous.

III

The Reformation Period, 1525–1600

Problems and Developments in Research

As has been stated previously, the account of the development and tendencies within the free church movement during the late Middle Ages has been far from exhaustive. Simultaneous with the movements considered were other groups which did not separate from the Church but remained active within the ecclesiastical framework. Some of these parties were absorbed within the Catholic orders, brotherhoods, and guilds, while others lived piously within the Church as local groups of mystics with no thought of servering relations with the pope or the Catholic Church.

In the latter part of the Middle Ages, however, inner unrest took hold in many parts of Europe. Against the pope, church institutions, hierarchial pronouncements, routine observances of the sacraments, and the world of passive, nominal Christian laymen there were set up definite demands of living a personal life of faith, voluntary adherence, trust in the words of Scripture, and the layman's activities in the religious life. Against the Church—which laid claims in its priestly, sacramental functions to be the dispenser of grace and miracles—stood groups of believers, societies, and churches which stood for holiness. It was this traditional form of Paulinism which lived on and spurned the influence of Judaism in the development of the Church and religious cults. In some instances this opposition stream turned into a radical enemy of the world and was quite often associated with the forerunner of apocalyptic ideas, Joachim of Floris.

Opposed to Thomas Aquinas' concept that the church should become more adapted to the culture of the world were free

39

congregations that stressed personal holiness, abstaining from all compromise, isolating from activities in society, and maintaining an ethic which was based upon the Sermon on the Mount. The great German church historian, Ernst Troeltsch, in his well-known volume *The Social Teachings of the Christian Churches,* pointed out that this type of piety, to which he gave the name "sectarian," developed throughout the history of the church as one of the two major sociological types in Christendom. The other type Troeltsch termed that of the "institutional" or "established" church. Between these two types there had been an unbalanced struggle from the second century until the Reformation. Later this "sectarian" type became a problem within Protestantism. Troeltsch did not use the term "sect" in the sense of a value judgment, as it is so often used. He simply sought to designate a special sociological type which, through perpetual reference to primitive Christianity and the Bible, sought to apply and carry out the important principles of the gospel. He correctly recognized that the term "sect" has ordinarily had an opprobrious connotation, given it by established churches which claim to be the only true and right representatives of Christianity in history.

The priestly hierarchy claimed to have the apostolic tradition, sacramental grace, and the jurisdiction of the Church. The free churches, on the other hand, stressed voluntary fellowship patterned after the practice of the early church, the demand for holy living, and the absolute authority of the Bible. The sects maintained that these ideas and principles of primitive Christianity were not simply starting points for the historical development of Christ's church but that they were ideals and patterns for all generations. This sociological type, therefore, is legitimate and can be justifiably placed in contradistinction to the institutionalized church. For this view Troeltsch has won a large following, particularly among the secular historians and the sociologists.

According to Troeltsch, the development of the free churches (sects) was favored by the fact that during the latter Middle Ages a social revolution took place when the new and rapidly growing city culture became important. Earlier the development of a feudal culture had been a vital factor of significance in the influence of the institutionalized Church. The independent position of the laity in the cities, according to Troeltsch, was a powerful competitor to the rigid framework represented by the Church and the priest. Consequently, the laity aided the unrest and opposition which the leaders of the free church maintained. There is significance in this: one has only to be reminded of the special role performed by the Waldensian weavers and cloth manufacturers. Here there were similar circumstances, but one must be careful about drawing conclusions. It seems most reasonable that these trades enhanced the spread of the movement and its communication of the message, and even this has meaning for a movement.

Earlier, while considering Wycliffe, mention was made that the new ideas concerning natural laws were receiving considerable attention. Some basic concepts of democracy for both the state and the church were developed from this humanism, especially by Marsilius of Padua. These democratic ideas were to bear fruit in several ways. It is not now possible to document this thought fully, but with all of the developments of the latter Middle Ages kept in mind, it may be assumed that the free churches' doctrine of the absolute divine order of natural rights had been influenced by the teachings propagated by Marsilius and others.

Here a third tendency should also be mentioned, the way of radical individualism. In the Middle Ages and later, some stood in opposition to the Church and demanded faith in the Bible, New Testament conversion, and a consecrated life, without being united in the shaping and constructing of free groups and free congregations. Individual mystics or Christians "of their own design" appeared early who recognized no binding association, whether it be with the institutionalized Church or the sects. These were the unorganized spiritual men who were well represented in the Reformation era. These men and women went to the extreme left in their radicalism, and they were often absorbed in apocalyptical speculations. They could with the same zeal oppose either the old Church or the new association, a free church with its sacraments and church

41

discipline. This is a point to be remembered in considering some of the involved problems during the period of the Reformation.

In historical writings produced in the periods under study, all of the so-called sects were summarily considered as satanic heresies, a verdict which the courts of inquisition had established. It was natural under these conditions, then, that the chroniclers should dismiss these groups without attempting to gain a documentary understanding or an objective judgment. The general rejection by the courts left no room for further investigation within the authoritarian society of the time. A similar situation arose when the chroniclers attempted to describe the Anabaptist movement during the time of the Reformation.

This prejudging and condemnation of the free church movement has been carried on even in later times, a truth illustrated by subsequent Protestant historical accounts of the Anabaptists in the time of the Reformation. This attitude of malignant prejudice began to take shape even before the local phenomena of degeneracy which developed among the Anabaptists of Münster in 1534–1535.

For Luther, the Anabaptists and their churches were insane *Schwärmer* (swarmers) which ought to be kept under control by the government. He never ceased to identify them with the fanatics of the Peasants' Revolt and the Zwickau prophets' leader Thomas Müntzer, although Müntzer never was an Anabaptist. As a threat to the state, Luther believed, these heretics ought to be exterminated. In the same manner, Zwingli complained that these people were disturbers of the peace and fanatics which the authorities must resist with force. As will be shown, these were not empty words, for they were translated into practical, bloody persecution. Only in recent years has a serious research attempt been made among historians to reconstruct a true picture of the Anabaptist movement.

Several noteworthy church historians of the present generation have broken with the old prejudices and have given a factual, scientific investigation of Anabaptism which cannot be discussed here in detail. Even at the end of the nineteenth century attempts were made to reconstruct the story with more clarity. Some of these research scholars were Ludwig Keller, Josef von Beck, Johann Loserth, Karl Müller, and Walther Köhler. Through the work of these men and others it became increasingly clear that the Anabaptist movement was a third branch of the Reformation, alongside the Lutheran and Reformed movements. This new understanding meant that now the movement could expect a careful investigation. Such, in fact, has constantly grown from the time of World War I. This factual interest has been clearly expressed in the newly revised and enlarged critical commentary of Zwingli's *Sämtliche Werke* [*Complete Works*].

Historical study of the free church movement was quickened in 1925 by the Mennonite fourth centenary observance of the beginning of the Anabaptist movement, 1525. During the last twenty-five years a thorough work of investigation has been in progress. In 1925 the large *Gedenkschrift zum 400jährigen Jubiläum der Mennoniten* [*Memorial Volume for the Four-Hundredth-Anniversary Jubilee of the Mennonites*], including contributions by Johann Loserth and Walther Köhler, made such an impression that it initiated a new period of historical understanding. An important forward step came when the German Society for Reformation History, whose membership includes some of the leading church historians of Germany, sponsored the publication of a series of sources which had to do with Anabaptism. The first large volume appeared in 1930, and now there are several more. Loserth published a volume in 1929 which has had great significance in seeking to determine how to judge the various tendencies in the Anabaptist movement. This has stimulated others so that new significant volumes dealing with the same subject have appeared both in Switzerland and in Hesse. At the same time, the work on source materials has been substantially increased.

Those that have financially underwritten the publication of this source material in recent years have been the American Mennonites (descendants of the old Anabaptists). This group has furthered the cause of investigation from other points of view as well. Earlier the Mennonites from Holland had made good contributions, but most of their work was confined to the history of their own country; consequently, Mennonite history received a rather narrow interpretation. In 1913 the German Mennonites published the first part of a comprehensive yet incomplete *Mennonitisches Lexikon* and later initiated the *Mennonitische Geschichtsblätter* [*Mennonite History Papers*]. It was Christian Neff and Christian Hege who pioneered in the project. The American Mennonites, however, have done more than the others, for they have popularized and given this research financial assistance and have added scholarly contributions of good quality. During World War I and the distress in Europe the program of research was weakened and all but ceased, but then work was again commenced in earnest when the American Mennonites were able to guarantee the financial support of publishing the new volumes.

It is a strange fact that the American Mennonites, who in their principles have maintained a distance from the world and its culture in general, should in this matter reveal both a sacrificial willingness and a conscious responsibility to make their own investigations. Such men as C. Henry Smith, John Horsch, Harold S. Bender, and John C. Wenger are diligent and well informed, well able to develop this project. During the last thirty years the American Mennonites have published the *Mennonite Quarterly Review,* a stimulating research quarterly. Even in the great universities of America this matter has received considerable attention. Roland A. Bainton of Yale has made a significant contribution in this regard.

In all of this spirited investigation, the thesis established by Karl Müller and Ernst Troeltsch has been confirmed: The Anabaptists were a separate branch of the Reformation movement. Therefore, the earlier and common concepts about Anabaptism can be dismissed. The movement did not grow out of the agitation of Thomas Müntzer and the Peasants' Revolt, nor was it, as many have maintained, a revival of heretical groups from the Middle Ages that believed in the necessity of good deeds for salvation and sanctification. Such interpretation has had a large place in Lutheran circles. Zwingli was certain

44

in his evaluation that the Anabaptist movement was a relapse into the type of piety exhibited in the Middle Ages. With this type of judgment many have ignored the central religious position of the Anabaptists regarding repentance, conversion, and a life of holiness by means of faith and free grace.

Through the publication of many significant original Anabaptist documents, scholars today have a long list of source material never before available. The first volume of the new series in 1930, German Society for Reformation History's *Quellen zur Geschichte der Täufer* [*Sources for the History of the Baptizers*], correctly pointed out that earlier historians had a poor understanding of Anabaptist viewpoints, development, and church life because the historical material they had was so fragmentary. In view of this, commonly accepted conclusions concerning the significance and the thought patterns of the Anabaptists have been unreliable and superficial. Historians have come to see that a real historical evaluation of this Reformation free church movement was only in the primary stages of development. United with the American Mennonites, these European scholars have made great preparations to publish original sources, and publication undoubtedly will continue.

This is the first time that the scholars have had full material assembled, so they now can reach conclusions about what the Anabaptists taught and practiced in their congregations. Because of the ample publication of these resources it will be possible to set forth more clearly the distinction between the biblical-, congregational-type Anabaptist and the radical, individualistic, or chiliastic groups in the Reformation. There has long prevailed a bewildered intermingling in the designation of these groups. It is recognizable that it is not easy to draw the lines clearly, but with the aid of a liberal supply of new material uncovered in recent years it should be possible to make certain definite distinctions.

This brief treatment of the free church movement in the Reformation will be concerned essentially with the Anabaptists. The word Anabaptist, or rebaptizer, was not used by members of the group. It was a nickname which they did not care to recognize. According to their belief, they did not baptize again; they recognized only one baptism, the baptism of believers. Thus the term "Anabaptist" is here employed from a historical point of view.

The material in this study is arranged chronologically and geographically to follow development of the movement: beginning in the Swiss Reformation at Zürich, spreading in Switzerland and into southern Germany, branching eastward into Tyrol and Moravia and westward into Strassburg, the Rhine Valley, and the Netherlands. In many of these areas of Anabaptist expansion there arose problems which deserve special attention. In this book it is only possible to give this subject a general description, which is hardly adequate for a movement with such wide ramifications.

Origin and Development of the Swiss Free Church Movement

When Huldreich Zwingli came to Zürich in 1519 as the chief priest of the *Grossmünster* [Great Church], he began a twelve-year ministry which had widespread consequences. Already Zwingli had won the reputation in humanistic circles for his scholarship and his critical insight. His intellectual disposition brought him in close contact with Erasmus and his struggles against the superstitions among the monks and the priests. At the universities in Vienna and Basel, Zwingli had good opportunity to become acquainted with the critical arguments against the Church, new arguments based upon the study of the Bible which challenged the faith and life of the established Church.

Zwingli did not want to be called a Lutheran, and he desired that the reformation at Zürich should claim to be independent in its program from the Lutheran reformation. His eagerness in this matter increased when Luther, after the Diet of Worms, was publicly denounced in an imperial edict and was also banned by the Church. Zwingli declared that, while serving as a priest at Einsiedeln, he had started to study and expound the Scriptures on the basis of Erasmus' Greek New Testament, published in 1516. He stated that he had committed the Pauline epistles to memory, and he had even studied the old church fathers. When in 1519 Zwingli moved from Einsiedeln and began his ministry in the leading city of the Swiss Confederation, Zürich, he was already a long way on the road to the Reformation. Early he had become acquainted with the writings of Luther, many of which were printed at Basel, the center of humanism. After the Leipzig disputation in the summer of 1519, interest began to increase in the German monk who so fearlessly disputed the papal authority in the Church. Zwingli never was willing to acknowledge any dependence upon Luther. Later when these two Reformers met in theological debate, Zwingli was all the more convinced that he should maintain his independence.

The reformation proceedings in the city and canton of Zürich went slowly, even though Zwingli proclaimed the gospel and made the Bible the most important book of the Church. He said that he would go back to the basic source and preach Jesus Christ as Saviour. Incisively he attempted to correct all of the incongruities of the Church: indulgences, inferior cults, and heathen remnants of various kinds. In spite of this, and in spite of his preaching of "God's pure word," it was more than three years before there was a break with Rome. The situation was this: Zwingli had now become a political figure and was closely aligned with the city council in Zürich. As a well-known patriot and one who was active in political affairs, he would have to move cautiously in a reformation of the Church. His humanistic ideologies made him unwilling to start any strife or schism, a characteristic of his patron instructor Erasmus.

In the meantime, in the summer of 1519, Zwingli became very ill. This experience deepened his personal experience, as was clearly evidenced in his later preaching. After this experience of nearness to death, his preaching was marked by an emphasis on free salvation through grace. At this time he also refused to believe that unbaptized children were condemned to go to hell. He later clarified himself by stating that belief in cleansing from original sin through baptism is sheer superstition. The question of the relationship between personal salvation and baptism early came into the foreground in the Swiss Reformation. Even in 1521 discussion regarding baptism was current in the circles around Zwingli. The Anabaptists later emerged from this environment. It was quite natural that the teaching concerning the Lord's Supper would soon become a burning issue, for every reform of the worship service stumbled over the Mass, the venerable central ceremony in the Church. A reform in this sphere of worship would have to be accomplished by legal procedures. Zwingli co-operated with the council, which was the political authority in the city and the canton. Therefore, he was able to have the council call a meeting in January, 1523, which has been termed the first disputation in Zürich. The Reformation was thus in a real sense under the leadership of political powers, and the groundwork was laid for the evangelical state church pattern which became characteristic of the German section of Switzerland.

In the articles which were considered in this disputation and the exhaustive exposition of them by Zwingli, there is an entire series of questions which became burning issues between the conservative and radical Zwinglians. The Scriptures were affirmed to be the only authority in matters of faith and practice, and their interpretation was not to be dependent upon church authority. Every Christian who should come to the Scriptures with a humble spirit would receive the truth under the guidance of the Holy Spirit. Jesus Christ alone was recognized as the way to salvation, the Head of the church, which is his body. All who believe in him as their personal Saviour were seen to be organically united with him and were truly God's children. In the same article Zwingli denied that the Bible gives evidence of any special ordination of preachers in the sense taught by the Catholic Church. The New Testament knows only of preachers of God's word, and they were the ones which were now needed. In the last of these articles and in their interpretation, Zwingli indicated that it was easier to believe that the unbaptized children of Christian parents were not condemned to hell than that they were thus punished.

It should be pointed out that as early as January, 1523, Zwingli touched on such issues dealing with scriptural authority, the true believers, the genuine church, the correct office of the preacher, and baptism. Obviously these questions would continue to awaken increased discussion in Zwinglian circles, and soon it was possible to see how unrest was developing in Zürich. Close to the city there were two places where radical pastors ministered, Simon Stumpf and Wilhelm Reublin, the latter becoming married in 1523. Reublin aimed through his preaching to build a congregation of true believers. Both of the ministers mentioned also preached against the Church tithe and other gifts to the Church. This radical group was strengthened by the interest of two important men, inhabitants in Zürich. They were Konrad Grebel and Felix Manz. A layman and a colporteur, Andreas Kastelberg and the minister from Zollikon, Johannes Brötli, also joined this group. One of the most zealous was Ludwig Hetzer, a learned humanist from the area of St. Gall.

The rising wave of radicalism in the spring of 1523 disturbed Zwingli and the council. That year in June, Zwingli preached a sermon which was intended to be an answer to the claims of the radicals. The message was also given because the claim was being made in the Catholic cantons that in Zwingli's precinct there was a complete disorder in the church. In this respect Zwingli's work was being misrepresented. The Bishop of Constance, under whose jurisdiction the church at Zürich remained, sought to exercise his authority, but in vain. Therefore, Zwingli had to clear himself, and the result was this sermon. It was in this sermon that the eloquent and successful reformer accounted for the different groups among the church people in the city.

The first mentioned were the evangelicals, the believers who were Zwingli's followers and who knew that the nature of man is such that it is impossible to build a pure church in this world. It is necessary to accept the law and order of men in everyday practice, for only gradually can a godly righteousness change conditions in society. The other group were the radicals who agreed on a godly righteousness, which they insisted should be applied as a demand of the divine law and immediately practiced in the social life of the community. Zwingli accused these radicals of not taking into account human inability or the merits of Christ. The last-mentioned fact is repeated again and again: the Anabaptist demand of a sanctified life was interpreted as a relapse to the doctrine of good works and holiness based on deeds. Two other groups were also mentioned, the indifferent and the old Catholic believers, but these play no significant role in the present study.

Zwingli now stood in a situation similar to that of Luther during the Peasants' Revolt. It seemed advisable to preach the law and order of man, for the concepts concerning godly righteousness and grace had gone so far that many of the people seemed to have lost all of their sense of obligation to the Church and the priests. But Zwingli's attempt to hinder this trend in Zürich was unsuccessful. The truth of the matter was this: no church reform had actually been brought into the city. Mass was still celebrated, and the council had not worked out any procedure for accomplishing reform. Probably during the summer of 1523, the radicals appeared before Zwingli and sought to encourage him to go from word to action. Then the question arose concerning the building of a schismatic church (*eine Sonderkirche*), to which only genuine Christian people could belong. Believers should be required only to live according to the gospel, not to pay the tithe or church taxes. Here the question crops up concerning the free church in the Reformation.

Zwingli gave an account about this at the court proceedings against the Anabaptists in the spring of 1525. He could also give the information that Konrad Grebel at this time had sought to persuade him to join the radical reformation but that he had refused. Even Felix Manz and others had pressed him to take action in the cause of the Reformation, but still he hesitated. They had, however, said Zwingli, begun to conduct meetings about a block away from the Great Church (*Grossmünster*) to organize an independent congregation. In the fellowship of these conventicles and meetings were laymen who read and interpreted the Scriptures and openly criticized both the leaders of the city and of the church. This came to the attention of the council, which naturally disapproved. Zwingli's close association with the council and his calculated cautiousness when reforms were carried out caused him to feel responsible for what might happen. When some attempted violently to overthrow the images, unrest grew; and when resistance followed against the employment of the tithe and the church gifts, this unrest increased against the authorities. The council gave orders that some of the radicals should be put in prison.

This action by the council did not solve the problem. The council had to publicize a meeting, the second Zürich disputation, to set forth the views pertaining to the use of images and the Mass. This meeting took place in October, 1523, and it was better attended than the first disputation. It is estimated that approximately nine hundred people took part in this conclave. Zwingli began by presenting a clear case against the Roman Church, and in this instance all were with him, even the radicals. Among the radicals there appeared, for the first time in public, Balthasar Hübmaier, the most learned and prominent preacher in this period of the free church movement. He had become a doctor of theology the same year as Luther, 1512, and had taught in the universities at Freiburg and Ingolstadt. He had been a close disciple and friend of Johann Eck, Luther's major opponent. For a number of years Hübmaier had gained a respected reputation as an outstanding preacher and priest of the cathedral at Regensburg. That was before 1521 when he came as priest to serve the little village Waldshut on the Rhine, bordering Switzerland, only a few miles from Zürich.

Even in the early stage of the disputation Hübmaier entered the discussion. He maintained the conviction that help ought to be given to those individuals who had been led astray into the pit of error which the devil was forming within the Church. Examples of such delusions were the use of the Mass and images. He praised the council, which had convened this disputation for the purpose of settling the strife and disunity which had arisen. The best solution would be to proclaim the pure Word of God, for Scripture alone was the final arbiter in these matters, and nothing else could take its place. In this respect even Christ and Paul had used the Scriptures against Satan and evil adversaries to win their cases. The same thing would take place if one set God's pure Word against the Mass and icons in the church; that which is built on the Word is

51

eternal; it is impossible to destroy God's truth. *"Die Wahrheit ist untötlich"* ["Truth is indestructible"], is the motto which Hübmaier inscribed on nearly all of his writings.

In this disputation and in later discussions pertaining to the Mass, Hübmaier revealed that he was a capable student of the Bible, but at this time he was not extreme in his opposition against the established Church. Konrad Grebel, however, revealed that he had long been eager for immediate and radical action. Especially concerning the Mass, Grebel showed his impatience. There had been much talk about this question; Grebel insisted that this was the time for action. The present meeting should act as a church council to tell the priests how they should handle this matter. Zwingli made one of his characteristic replies: The council would undoubtedly find the correct solution pertaining to the reformation of the Mass. Then Stumpf, one of the radical priests already mentioned, objected that Zwingli had no authority to give this matter over into the hands of the council, for the Holy Spirit had already made a disposition of this case. Therefore, Stumpf indicated he would oppose any decision of the council which went contrary to God's decrees. He undoubtedly meant the Bible.

On the third day of the disputation, Grebel, who was a layman and a humanist well at home in the Greek New Testament, returned to the question of the Mass. Possibly he was not a good speaker, or debater, for he requested that those who were present and better able to present this matter should step forward. This drew out Hübmaier, and he again acted as spokesman. He announced that he did not even want to use the term "Mass" but rather to speak of Christ's testament, a remembrance of his excruciating death. Here Hübmaier and Zwingli had the same point of view: emphasis was given to the Lord's Supper as a symbolic, fellowship meal, a seal of sins forgiven, a help and strength for faith, and a remembrance of Christ's death. No one, Hübmaier argued, could hold to the established Mass if he preached the Word of God. Worship ought also to be conducted in the language of the people, and both elements naturally ought to be used at the communion. Hübmaier added that if anyone could show him from the

Scriptures where he had gone astray in this presentation he would be willing to learn, and as a disciple of Christ he desired in all things to obey God's Word.

It can be stated that during these days of October the anticipated Reformation in Zürich was decided, as well as in several other cantons in Switzerland. The radical contingent wanted a council decision from this meeting which would direct the reformers to act according to the decisions of this disputation. Hetzer, as secretary of the disputation, had the minutes printed and published in the form in which matters had been discussed; and Grebel had already given his own opinions on the controversial questions. Zwingli and his followers wanted to maintain their separation from Rome, but they wanted to leave the execution of this partial reform in the hands of the council. It was resolved that they should have reform. On this all were agreed; but there was no formal decision which clarified how far reform should go. Not much could come out of such a decision. The council appointed a commission and gave it orders to publish a pamphlet which would clarify the issues for the people. Zwingli soon had such a tract prepared, and in it he took the position of the middle road in the Reformation. The council declared that until further notice the old order should remain and that anyone who attempted on his own to change matters would stand in jeopardy of being punished. Zwingli and his associates thereupon traveled hither and yon to enlighten the priests and the people regarding this matter.

Because of this attitude of moderation, the established church order of worship stayed approximately the same for another year and a half. However, by the close of the year 1523 the radical groups had become impatient, and a separation from Zwingli seemed unavoidable. These radicals zealously studied the Bible, and it was at this time that a biblical stream became an irresistible movement. "What say the Scriptures?" This was the primary question. The distribution of the Bible had also increased greatly, largely because of the printing house in Basel, only a few miles northwest of Zürich. In September, 1522, the first edition of Luther's translation of the New Testament appeared, and already in December of the same year an edition had been printed in Basel. During the years 1522–25 no less than twelve editions of this translation appeared, indicating the zeal of the people to study and learn directly from the Scriptures. This interest in the Bible can be seen later when the Anabaptists were examined by the authorities. Even unlearned peasants in the country and laborers in the cities were found to be familiar with the message of the Bible. Zwingli on one occasion stated that people no longer needed to turn to the priests for an understanding of the truth, for in the rural areas this desire for Bible study had inaugurated "schools" which had become very independent.

Among the scholars this enormous Bible interest and study have led to a variety of questions. How much the medieval opposition movements influenced these Bible study groups is not easy to determine. It is possible that in many places the influence of earlier groups did play a role. One thing is clear: a strong new current came into being, a Bible-study movement resulted in a free church development. The disputations in Zürich during 1523 had stimulated wide interest concerning Bible matters dealing with the Christian church, the company of believers, sacraments, and the position of laymen. At the same time, the radicals, many of them laymen, continued to preach faith and a Christian way of life which was far removed from the way of the world. This led to conversions which were revealed later at the examinations of the believers. Soon the question of baptism became a burning issue.

Baptism, even at the close of 1523, had not played any significant role in the discussions. Zwingli had, of course, made a few references to the fate of the unbaptized children, and this reply became necessary only because of attack. With the zealous Bible study which was going on and which led, to a great degree, to a separated church (*Sonderkirche*), there would come sooner or later the question concerning the place of baptism in the first Christian church as presented in the Acts of the Apostles and the Epistles. The radicals continued their "schools" (conventicles) and Bible studies, and it is understandable that the question concerning the meaning of infant baptism must have been discussed, for in the spring of 1524 some began to balk at bringing their children to the priest to be baptized. This situation occurred in a few places outside of Zürich, and the two learned gentlemen, Konrad Grebel and Felix Manz, were among the leaders of this movement. Consequently, the council issued an order that all children should be baptized, as was customary in the "unreformed" Catholic Church. In this matter there would be no reform.

The first document which clarifies the attitude pertaining to baptism among the radical groups during this period is a letter which Grebel, Manz, and other associates wrote in the early part of September, 1524, to the German agitator, Thomas Müntzer. The Swiss radicals had come upon a publication of Müntzer, and they were happy to find one who was of the same mind as they were, even in the criticism of the evangelical reformers. In the matter of baptism, they wrote that they had never found any mention of infant baptism in the Bible, and therefore they considered this act meaningless and even contrary to Scripture. They stated that they knew that Müntzer understood this, and therefore they pleaded with him not to go contrary to the eternal Word and continue to baptize infants; for according to the Scriptures only believers were to be baptized. They also earnestly warned Müntzer in his use of violence, and this warning was needful, for the addressee was one of the most vehement agitators in the Peasants' Revolt. Here the ideas of pacifism began to be expressed, a concept which was to become a distinctive of the biblical Anabaptist movement.

The revival in Zürich could not be restrained by the council's actions against the Anabaptists, but there was not a large number of adherents. Many of the radicals had not advanced so far in the matter of baptism. In the letter of September, 1524, to Müntzer, the writers stated that there were hardly twenty who accepted the Bible in this question; most were still held in conformity to human authority. Zwingli had repeatedly spoken to the radicals in an attempt to calm them down, but in vain. At the close of 1524, Zwingli revealed that he had lost his patience, for in a publication aimed at the radicals who advocated insurrection he suggested severe penalties for those who opposed infant baptism. He charged these radicals with bitterness and quarrelsomeness and showing a carnal attitude. He admonished his followers unflinchingly to look the devil in the face, who was trying through these doctrines to reinstate justification by deeds of law.

This action of Zwingli did not frighten the antipedobaptists to silence or retraction. They took instead what they regarded as the only consistent position—baptism of believers. The movement now spread in many directions in Switzerland—St. Gall, Graubünden, and parts of northern Switzerland—as well as in southern Germany. Waldshut especially came to the forefront, for it was here that Hübmaier presented his evangelical messages. It was quite generally known that the situation in Waldshut had taken the form of a radical biblical movement. In Zürich or in the near vicinity the radicals first went from words to action. When the council's proceedings against the antipedobaptists went unheeded, another disputation was convened. Immediately following, in January, 1525, a new order demanded that all those who had failed to baptize their newborn infants must now have them baptized within one week or suffer the risk of banishment. The council and Zwingli worked together.

The council went even further and gave the order that all strangers among the radicals, those who were not residents of the city or canton of Zürich, were to be banished. This order was carried out. Such persons as Grebel and Manz who were residents in Zürich were made to comply and remain quiet. All private "schools" (conventicles) where these questions were discussed were to be closed. This was a type of conventicle act, and its aims were to bring about peace and unity in the church. Instead there was now an open and irreconcilable break between the Zwinglian reformers and the Anabaptists. One of the most zealous of the radicals, a former monk by the name of George Blaurock, became the obvious leader. Grebel first baptized Blaurock, and then Blaurock followed by baptizing fifteen others. Now the die was cast. From this time on until the present day the question of believers' baptism in place of infant baptism has not ceased to cause uneasiness among Christians in the so-called "Christian" countries of the West. It is obvious that this pulling out from the state church was a consequence of the free church principle. It is interesting to note how zeal for Bible study gradually led the forces of opposition further and further. In the summer of 1523 the issue was a separatist church, and its advocates sought to have Zwingli join them. A year later there was the debate over the question of antipedobaptism, which resulted in a sharp conflict. At the beginning of 1525 the practice of the new baptism was initiated.

The first baptism, held in Zürich, was preceded by a revival. The radicals now faced the question of breaking with the Catholic Church in its interpretation of the sacraments. The issue was not only the reformation of the Mass, which had already been debated; the Church's practice of baptism was now under attack. This did not stop with opposition to infant baptism. In January, 1525, the Anabaptists had their specific beginning when they baptized believers coming from the Roman Church who had been baptized as infants. The motive was not, as earlier, that they had been baptized in a reprobate church but rather that the New Testament says nothing about infant baptism. The new baptism was not considered by the Anabaptists as a rebaptism, for they never accepted baptism of infants as baptism at all.

Modern research founded on authentic source material has clarified this point: in the group of Zwingli adherents, Anabaptism was established in January, 1525. It is manifestly clear that the earlier agitators who came with Müntzer and Storch into the Lutheran territories of Germany were not the original Anabaptists. Further, it is an indisputable fact that it is not the sects in the Middle Ages that explain the origin of the Anabaptist. No leading Anabaptists have given any intimation that they recognized themselves to be dependent upon any of the earlier movements. It is natural, however, that these opposition movements prepared the ground and had some significance on the Anabaptist development. The earlier

57

"schools" and Bible study conventicles were a favorable milieu for the development of this new persuasion concerning the questions of baptism and the church. The rapid spread of the Anabaptists can be explained partially because of these circumstances.

From Zwingli's writings concerning the beginning of the Anabaptist movement in the Zürich area, it can be concluded that these radicals zealously proclaimed their new faith. In one place Zwingli pointed out that the radicals campaigned in every corner; in the streets, in the stores, in every place they attempted to start a discussion. On the other hand, it must be stated that Zwingli, by his sharp criticism, did not abate their desire for contest. Now that the Anabaptists were a recognized group, Zwingli organized his arguments regarding baptism and had them printed in a book, published in May, 1525. During this entire year Zwingli was engaged in a dispute with the Anabaptists. Zwingli met opposition. The first one to rebut the arguments of the Zürich reformer on the question of baptism was Balthasar Hübmaier of Waldshut. He was a well-qualified opponent, and Zwingli was well aware of the seriousness of the situation. Hübmaier had, in February, already issued a challenge over the manner of baptism. In April the former priest from Waldshut was baptized by Reublin, who had been driven out of Zürich and had come to Waldshut. In July his reply to Zwingli on the question of baptism was ready.

Within Switzerland the Anabaptist movement spread rapidly, somewhat dependent upon the refugee Anabaptists from Zürich who traveled extensively with their new message and their new practice of baptism. In Zürich actions against them continued. They were imprisoned, examined, and received punishment in form of fines and banishment. In March, 1525, the council announced the edict that anyone who would be baptized again would be banished. Zwingli was now alarmed. In his sermons and in his writings, he campaigned for an established national church and a reformation that would be moderate. He wrote that this battle was the most difficult in which he had been engaged, more so even than his opposition to the Catholic Church, and this had cost him much labor. He considered this situation so serious that he would have to take on the additional labors, because it was now no longer a question of baptism but of insurrection, separatism, and serious errors. It is not surprising, therefore, that the Anabaptists on their side were not too charitable in their judgments of Zwingli.

New centers of Anabaptism had developed in St. Gall, where Hübmaier had visited and had won many followers through his powerful preaching; in Bern, where another leading Anabaptist had won adherents; in Basel, where the influence of Hübmaier and other radicals was strong, as well as in Schaffhausen and Appenzell in northern Switzerland. The spread of this movement cannot here be described in detail, for it would take altogether too much space. We can only be satisfied to draw a few strokes which show the trend of the Swiss Anabaptist movement during the fifteenth century. The reason for detailed consideration of events in Zürich is that developments here became the pattern for the free churches which were later established. In a number of places this pattern was followed in both the rise of Anabaptists and the resistance against them. In the latter case the example of Zürich had fateful consequences. The council's new edict in March, 1526, was a terrifying act. Grebel, Manz, and Blaurock were condemned to severe imprisonment on bread and water; no one could visit them, not even in case of illness; they were to rot and die in their cells. If anyone recanted and then again fell into this delusion, he would be drowned without compassion.

A mandate appeared later that everyone must be faithful and attend his parish church. Anabaptists were allowed no room or board. Severe punishment threatened all those who did not respect this decree. In this barbarous fashion the men of the Zürich reformation attempted to exterminate an evangelical movement of which they did not approve. But the Anabaptist movement grew. One bailiff stated that of the more than a hundred Anabaptists in his district, only thirteen had retracted. In northern Switzerland the powerful influence of Hübmaier caused the authorities considerable concern, for the movement grew in defiance against all measures. "Hübmaier wins unusual support," wrote a bailiff, and he added, "he appears as a prophet." Groups gathered together out in the woods or in the homes. In January of 1527, when Felix Manz was drowned in the Limmat, a river that flows through Zürich, the council followed its words with actions. Blaurock had to run the gantlet and was chased out, for he was a stranger; if he returned, he would also be drowned. Grebel had died of the plague in the summer of 1526.

While Zürich set the pace of persecution, in other areas of Switzerland there was both the spread of the new movement as well as persecution of it. In St. Gall, Grebel remained for a few weeks in the spring of 1525, and it was here that the movement found two prominent leaders, namely Lorenz Hochrütiner and Wolfgang Ulimann, whose father was a leading citizen in the city. Ulimann was baptized by immersion by Grebel. Aspersion otherwise had been the prevailing mode. It did not take long before there were approximately eight hundred baptized believers in St. Gall. Here, too, the council went against the group by following the example of Zürich. The work of Hübmaier in St. Gall has been mentioned before. It is an interesting fact that the conventicles in St. Gall were called "readings," and those that led these groups "readers." These terms are recorded in an official document of this period. The Reformation leader who recorded these chronicles (*Sabbata*), which contain so much information about the conflict in this period, was Johannes Kessler. His record is a remarkable deposit of source material pertaining to the early history of the Anabaptists. Kessler took a definite stand with Zwingli and his middle-road position.

It seemed the council in St. Gall and the moderate reformation won an early victory over the radicals. Zwingli's book on baptism in the spring of 1525 was a real help in that it was read publicly to the people. The Anabaptists protested loudly. After a formal disputation, the council made a clear decision: the private assembling of people was forbidden. The Anabaptists were not allowed to administer the sacraments, on pain of banishment for them and their families; rebaptism was punishable by fines. At the same time, the council and the moderates had to implement reforms in the still unreformed Church.

Through the severe police measures it seems that movement was forced to break up, and in a short time their strong influence in St. Gall was lost; this extended to the surrounding areas of the city. Some ecstatic and eccentric exaggerations were made to discredit the movement. The movement did not completely die out, for as late as 1553 its marks could be seen in a disputation which was held. Even as late as 1639 the city archives made mention of an Anabaptist schoolteacher, as well as other Anabaptists who were found in the rural areas. At this time, of course, their religious way of life had no real influence in the canton. St. Gall had used the methods that Zürich had employed to keep the movement under control—fines, imprisonment, banishment, confiscation of personal property, and death.

In the canton Appenzell, close by Zürich, the movement spread in the same manner as in other areas, and in a few months thousands had joined, according to the statement of the chronicler. Here again the name of Hübmaier is foremost in the work. Great open-air meetings were conducted, and according to the records, multitudes were baptized in the streams and rivers. The movement here was characterized by strong ecstasy, if the animated description of the one who writes the chronicle can be considered trustworthy. The earnest preacher Blaurock visited Appenzell shortly before his martyrdom in 1529. At the beginning, the council moved carefully, for the movement had a strong hold on the people, and it developed that many persecuted and exiled Anabaptists came in from surrounding territories. From Appenzell there soon went a large number of emigrants to Moravia where the Eastern branch of the Anabaptist movement developed.

In the central canton Bern, which also became one of the reformation areas of Switzerland, the conflict was even more remarkable. Here the reformation movement under the leadership of Berchtold Haller became a great concern to the state, so that it was difficult for the Anabaptist free church ideas to win converts. The council at Bern had considered the question of Baptism as early as 1525, for Anabaptists were found there early that year. From Waldshut one of Hübmaier's associates,

Jakob Gross, came in 1526, and his ministry in these areas brought unrest. A son of Hochrütiner from St. Gall also visited there, and influence from Basel had considerable effect. Haller and the council followed Zwingli's and Zürich's deportment with great interest, but the leaders of Bern were wary about employing the death penalty. They chose rather expatriation. In the summer of 1527, Zürich, Bern, and St. Gall drew up an agreement detailing the handling of the sectaries, and this severe mandate was in force for a number of years until in 1531, when each canton established its own regulations. Before 1528 Bern had made no definite commitment to the way of the Reformation; therefore, it is understandable that the pressure of the radicals at this time could be a delicate question for the moderate reformers in relation to the Catholic reactionary party. Therefore, the Anabaptists were imprisoned in order to isolate them from the reform movement.

The first known investigation of Anabaptists in Bern was in the spring of 1529. Emperor Charles V issued a mandate on January 4, 1528, which was confirmed at the imperial Diet of Speier in the spring of 1529. The basic intent of these decrees was that all Anabaptists should be punished with the death penalty. Bern quickly followed others in this persecution, in a few cases even drowning some, otherwise inflicting imprisonment or banishment. Zürich, Bern, Basel, and St. Gall in January, 1530, united in an agreement to carry on common suppressing measures against the Anabaptists, since the movement had grown and had become a threat to the cause of the evangelicals.

Even in Bern this despised and persecuted movement had a long history, which will be described in the pages that will follow. Here we have satisfied ourselves with a few lines from the original historical documents so that later we can tie this up with succeeding developments. It is a fact that in the canton of Bern the free church movement became a tenacious, continuing phenomenon; yet, on the other hand, with equal tenacity the Reformation church in the canton with the council opposed the radicals with brutal persecution for a long time.

Reference has already been made that the canton and the city of Basel played an important role in the separation between the institutional, established church and the free churches, or "sects," to use Troeltsch's expression. As has been stated before, Basel was a center for humanism and for the printing of books during this period. This city had been an old gathering place for the Waldenses as well as for those who sympathized with the older church opposition movement, the "Brethren." One chronicler relates about the "Bohemian sect" which was in the city. But Ludwig Keller's theory that the "old evangelical congregations" were a basis for the Anabaptist movement cannot be substantiated. Testimonies concerning the ideas of the Anabaptists appear as early as 1524. Oecolampadius, the reformer in Basel, received a letter from a friend in France who desired information concerning the situation in the city, for he had heard that there were some who could be found in the city who postponed baptism until an individual was mature. Basel was the gathering place for all types of religious enthusiasts, even Italian humanists and rationalists, as well as German mystics, such as Denck, Hetzer, and others. Even Hübmaier had been there and had learned to know Erasmus. Hübmaier's influence was felt, according to the testimony of Oecolampadius.

It is evident that alien, migrant preachers brought the new ideas to Basel. Within the peasant population the movement took hold when the outsiders came. In August, 1525, a group of Anabaptists were discovered, a group of strangers that had emigrated into the territory, and they were the first ones to gather a free church. They assembled daily in the home of a craftsman, according to information, to read, preach, and talk about baptism. It did not take long before this little circle practiced baptism. Two important men came to Basel, Lorenz Hochrütiner from St. Gall and Ulrich Hugwald, the humanist who was associated with the university and for some time was head of the new movement. It is said that many adherents came from among the personnel of the printing establishments, which is understandable on the basis of the profuse distribution of Bibles, of which Basel was the center. For a period Hugwald gave up his connections with the chair of learning to go out and "earn his bread by the sweat of the brow." Later he gave up his association with the movement and returned to the university to continue for many years as a professor.

The mode of procedure which the opponents of Anabaptism followed in other cantons was well known. Already in August, 1525, Oecolampadius had a disputation with the ardent Anabaptists, but the official procedures were slow in being carried out. Oecolampadius wrote an account of this disputation, and this caused Hübmaier, from Nikolsburg in Moravia, to publish a reply in 1527. The reformer from Basel immediately answered this with a testy publication. In the summer of 1526 the first mandate appeared: those that were baptized were to be banished from the city and its surroundings. This was followed by a prohibition against conducting conventicle meetings close to the city. By this time, the movement had grown. Felix Manz even spent some time visiting in the city. During the years 1527–28 many great speakers visited Basel, and Oecolampadius complained about the activity of the Anabaptists. Many leaders in the movement in southern Germany made their way to Basel, and it should be pointed out that already by this time the Hollanders had visited the city. From the investigations of these years, the results show that those who were interrogated had been baptized in other places, some in Zürich, some in Waldshut, some in Augsburg, etc. Wolfgang Ulimann, from St. Gall, also came to Basel, a friend and fellow worker with Hochrütiner. Ulimann, because of prominent family connections, had been liberated from prison on several occasions. When Ulimann came as a traveling preacher to Basel in 1528, he was promptly driven out. Later he ministered to emigrants on their way to Moravia, but together with a company of adherents he became a victim of cruel executioners in southern Germany. In the winter of 1529, Blaurock was also imprisoned in Basel.

In June, 1527, Oecolampadius had another disputation with the Anabaptists, which was followed by a number of mandates from the government. It was now unlawful for the Anabaptists to hold meetings in the woods or the homes, to give shelter to any preachers, and to baptize. In March of the following year, new regulations were imposed which brought threats of banishment, fines for participating in conventicles, and new measures against the harboring of preachers. It was at this time that many of the Anabaptists left Basel to go to Bern, where one of their number, Hans Hausmann, was later drowned. Because of the persecution in Basel the movement spread out into the rural areas, and this became a characteristic mark of the Anabaptist movement in the canton of Basel. This austere policy continued in the reformation of Basel, where in February, 1529, the new state church was established. In Basel, as in other places, the council justified suppressive measures with the accusation that the Anabaptists were defiant of the law and disturbers of the peace; for the sake of God's word, no one was persecuted, they protested.

All Anabaptists in Basel, including anyone that visited their meetings or befriended them, were to be put in prison on bread and water and occasionally undergo torture in order that they eventually might swear off their waywardness. For the obstinate ones this meant life imprisonment. After this, if any of the followers should recant after having sworn off their heterodoxy, they should be executed by the sword. Now there followed imprisonment of many, both in the city and in the country. The foremost teacher of the Anabaptists at this time was Konrad Winkler, who suffered a martyr's death in Zürich, where he was drowned in the Limmat. The first Anabaptist execution in Basel was in January, 1530, and at the close of this same year a new mandate was issued: those that repented would be pardoned, those that resisted would be banished, and if they should return they should be drowned.

The movement was defeated by the enforcement of these draconic enactments. Martyrs grew in number; the flourishing time of the movement was past. The free church congregation in Basel had already dispersed by the spring of 1528; however, the underground movement continued. With new oppressing measures of 1529–30, there was little prospect for the free church to exist even as a catacomb church. At this same time, Oecolampadius indicated in a letter that he was satisfied that no place of refuge could be found for the Anabaptists within the canton of Basel. At the close of the decade in 1530 very few Anabaptists could be found in the vicinity of Basel, and this condition naturally continued. Through means of the court jurisdictions the movement disappeared gradually until it was extinct at the end of the century.

The Anabaptist movement soon appeared in the canton of Schaffhausen, largely because of its close proximity to Waldshut, from which it received strong influence from the German branch of the movement. Some have laid emphasis on the fact that Thomas Müntzer visited in the neighborhood of Schaffhausen a few weeks in the fall of 1524, but the most salient influence on the movement seems to have been that of Hübmaier from Waldshut. It was in Shaffhausen that Hübmaier found refuge; and it was here, during a very critical period, that he wrote some of his best-known manuscripts. The cause of the Reformation proceeded slowly in Schaffhausen as in Bern and Basel. It was at the close of 1529 that the Reformation was officially accepted in the canton. Sebastian Hofmeister, the reformation leader in Schaffhausen, like other Swiss reformers, then had revealed a certain ambiguity over the question of baptism. Hübmaier has mentioned this in one of his writings.

Although in Schaffhausen the Waldshut refugee, Hübmaier, was given hospitality, for leaders there refused to conduct their affairs as did the Catholic authorities in the vicinity, nevertheless tolerance could not long be expected for a movement that everywhere was exposed to bloody persecution. In November, 1527, the first death penalty for an Anabaptist was pronounced, and in the beginning of 1530 many Anabaptists were committed to prison. The high point of the movement seems to have been during the years 1525–27, and another revival occurred in the middle of the 1530's. The minutes of the council for 1535 indicate that no less than forty-one cases of Anabaptists had been acted on. It is possible that this increase of indictments might have been caused by the fanaticism of the Münster calamity.

The reformation movement, which became established early in Waldshut, was of much the same character as that which has been described concerning the Swiss Reformation. Geographically this little town was separated from Switzerland by only the river Rhine, but it belonged to Austria under a strong Catholic territorial administration. When Hübmaier came to Waldshut in 1521, a new church epoch was introduced. It soon became apparent that Hübmaier was reading both Luther and Zwingli and that he had come to a radical biblical position. Mention has been made already of Hübmaier's association with the Zwinglian groups in Zürich, and it was pointed out as well how he became a leading personality in the Swiss Anabaptist movement. No one could measure up to Hübmaier, either as an influential preacher or as a learned scholar. It is natural, therefore, that in the summer of 1525 Hübmaier became the one to refute Zwingli's book on baptism.

Hübmaier's powerful position in Waldshut made the Catholic authorities of the Austrian territories feel uneasy, and consequently Hübmaier, because of the threat of armed attack in the fall of 1524, willingly left the city and asked for his discharge. He took his refuge in the near-by Swiss territory of Schaffhausen, where he in one of his most renowned books, *About the Heretics and Those Who Burn Them,* struck a blow for the cause of tolerance and freedom. Hübmaier was considered by many as being indispensable to Waldshut, and therefore he soon returned to the city and won, as it seems, the population to the cause of the new church. The threats of the Catholic leaders still remained. When baptisms began to occur and Hübmaier himself was baptized on Easter, 1525, the tensions increased. It was Reublin, who has been mentioned before and who had been expelled from Zürich, who baptized Hübmaier. Hübmaier then later baptized approximately three hundred of the members from his congregation. More followed later. Hübmaier resigned as priest but then became the pastor of the free church which displaced the established Church.

The altogether unusual took place in Waldshut, for the cause of the Reformation developed in an evangelical free church with the baptism of believers as the accepted practice. It was natural that there would be those in the city who would oppose such a radical development. When Hübmaier, in July, 1525, opposed Zwingli in his writing on baptism and explained

67

that infant baptism was unknown during the time of the New Testament, this caused a great sensation. Zwingli answered in November of that same year, and Hübmaier wrote a reply to this in a new baptism tract a few weeks later, but because of the threatenings from the Catholic lords he was not immediately able to have it printed. The tract was published the following year in Nikolsburg, where Hübmaier had taken refuge.

Hübmaier, because of his learning and his many associations, occupied a unique position among the early leaders of the Anabaptist movement. His exchange of letters with Oecolampadius in Basel indicates his influence in that city, where both his acquaintanceship with Erasmus and his company with other humanists built up his reputation. His visits in Zürich, St. Gall, and other portions of Switzerland had given him a reputation as a preacher, theologian, and debater. In Catholic circles he was known as Johann Eck's student and collaborator at Ingolstadt University, where for a time he had been vice-rector. His abilities as a preacher in Regensburg were well known, establishing his reputation in the Church. When Hübmaier went over to the radical branch of the Reformation, it must have caused a great sensation. The Catholics had their eyes opened early to see what was taking place in Waldshut, as well as in the intimate connections with the Swiss Reformation. The city was considered important to the Hapsburgs, for it was a principal stronghold on the Rhine on the way between Constance and Basel. Therefore, the threats of the Austrian military powers were serious, and it was a question whether or not Zürich should send help to defend the city. But the radical development which the Reformation took dampened these ideas of help from Zürich.

The question of Hübmaier's part in the unrest which spread in the countryside of southern Germany is much debated. It seems clear that Hübmaier's social concern made him want to aid those people who were oppressed and poor, but it is also clearly evident that he wanted Waldshut and its inhabitants to be good subjects of Austria, if only freedom were given to the cause of the Reformation. The opposition measures by the Catholics were soon in full operation, for in the beginning of

December, 1525, Waldshut was conquered, and all of the reformation movements were forcibly destroyed. Hübmaier escaped with difficulty, and he made his way to Zürich. There he
was put in prison and had the sentence of death over him. He
was tortured so that he was broken in body, so much so that he
finally wrote a retraction of his faith, but it was just as much a
reply to charges. He was fortunate to be able to get out of the
city. He then made his way to southern Germany, where sometime during the summer of 1526 he stopped over to visit the
rapidly growing free church in Augsburg. Later he went to
Moravia through the cities which were well known to him,
Ingolstadt and Regensburg.

During this time when the free church and Anabaptist movements were spreading over large areas of northern Switzerland
and southern Germany, Zwingli continued his battle against
the radical reformation, while at the same time he attempted to
accelerate his own reformation of church life. It is significant to
realize that the radical men's measures accelerated the moderate reformation, such as their complaint over the low morals of
the clergy and over the general indifference in the lives of
Christians, which also pointed attention to incongruities with
which Zwingli and his associates had to take issue. Because of
the radicalism of the Anabaptists, however, the whole cause of
Reformation met with special discredit with the strong Catholic
population in Switzerland and elsewhere. It must be remembered that most of the cantons held to the Catholic Church,
detesting even the moderate reformation in Zürich and other
cities.

Zwingli's greatest concern during the later years of the 1520's
seemed to be the rapidly growing Anabaptist movement. Several references have been made to his writings on baptism during 1525. He emphasized that the circumcision of the Old
Testament was a prototype of infant baptism. In the summer
of the same year, in a writing concerning the office of the
preacher, Zwingli was severe in his attack on the right of laymen to preach, and he urgently warned his followers against
their teachings. Even in this writing, like his book which was
a reply to Hübmaier's book on baptism, he zealously cam-

paigned against the new teaching on baptism. A person does not have to be frightened by the doctors whom the Anabaptists highly acclaim and quote. This undoubtedly had primary reference to Hübmaier. When the Anabaptist movement progressed and enlarged during 1526–1527 and was soon regarded as a dangerous threat to the country, Zwingli gave himself to writing a detailed book against the Anabaptists. Published in 1527, it was the last great attempt of Zwingli to defeat his opponents by theological arguments. In this refutation of "the tricks" of the antipedobaptists Zwingli emphasized especially that election takes precedence over both circumcision and baptism.

In February, 1527, the Anabaptists had congregated in Schleitheim in Schaffhausen, and there they drew up a confession of faith which became very significant. It was given a wide circulation in the Anabaptist groups. Zwingli obtained one of the handwritten specimens in the fall of 1527, and he took up each article to refute it, point by point, in his new book already referred to. These seven Schleitheim Articles, so-called, are of great interest, for they are the earliest known doctrinal statements among the Anabaptists. Hübmaier had written before concerning the doctrine of baptism, but here is a brief confession which gives remarkable testimony of the direction of faith and practice during this period. Hübmaier was at this time in Moravia, and the older leaders, like Grebel and Manz, were already dead. It seems that the leader of this first Anabaptist synod was Michael Sattler, a former monk from southern Germany, who was mentioned in the records of Zürich's council as early as the fall of 1525. He had visited Strassburg and was known to the reformer Capito, as his letters reveal. Sattler, like Hübmaier, was a strong biblicist. He objected to the radicals' concept of the "inner word" and the mystics' loose individualism. He desired order in the free churches, and this is indicated in the seven Schleitheim Articles. At this time, Sattler was ministering in Württemberg, but this work was soon stopped. Later, in the spring of 1527, he was apprehended by a Catholic executioner and tortured to death. This martyrology, together with a letter from Sattler, appeared as an appendage of the printed editions of the Schleitheim Articles.

The individuals that took part in this Anabaptist synod are unknown. Probably some of the previously mentioned men like Reublin, Blaurock, and Brötli were present. The preface of the Articles indicates that there was disagreement within the movement which led to the conference and the Articles. It was the sagacious and temperate men of the Anabaptist movement who drafted the plan, for they desired to avoid the errors of those of a mystical trend. The "false brethren" for which this was intended are not easy to identify, but divergence from the particular points which the Articles certify as being correct evidently was involved. Consequently, these seven Articles are not a complete statement of faith, but these are written out of a polemic situation to avoid a break in the fellowship because of misunderstanding on certain important questions. The major contents of the seven Articles can be summarized as follows:

The first point pertains to baptism. The Anabaptists were united in holding that baptism is for all those who have been converted and whose lives have been changed, and who believe in faith "that their sins are taken away through Jesus Christ," and are willing to be buried with Christ in order that they may rise with him. Therefore, infant baptism, which is from the pope, is ruled out, it is further stated. For their new assurance, they refer to the Scriptures and the examples of the apostles.

The second article makes clear that excommunication—dismissal—shall be used in three stages against those members in the congregation who have fallen into sin. The reference is to Matthew 18. The third article deals with the Lord's Supper, or as it is called, the breaking of bread, which is observed as a memorial service. Those that partake of the bread and drink of the wine should previously be united with the congregation, Christ's body, of which Christ is the head. This takes place through baptism. The Lord's Supper is only for those who have one God, one faith, one baptism, and one Spirit.

The fourth article has to do with separation from the world and the external church system. The genuine believers should

71

be a congregation separate from all evil which the devil has planted in the world, and even from "all popish and anti-popish deeds and services" as well as from the snare of unbelief and such things on which the world holds a high premium. The genuine believer should get out of Babylon and the worldly Egypt; whatever is not in accord with God and Christ the believer should detest and avoid. Neither must the Christian use the sword—"the devilish weapon of violence." Christ has said that a person should not oppose the wicked.

In the fifth article the inner nature of the church is considered. It states that the congregation should be united around *one* shepherd, according to the Pauline arrangement, who should perform all of the spiritual duties. The shepherd should be supported by the congregation which appointed him, for those that serve in the ministry of the gospel should live by the ministry of the gospel. The pastor is responsible to the congregation which has the power to dismiss him if he falls into sin.

The attitude toward authorities and the state is considered in the sixth article. There it is stated that "the sword" is God's order for those living in the world outside of Christ, that the authorities will punish and even execute those that do evil but protect those that do good. Those that live within Christ's ideal come under the discipline of the church, and none of its members can hold office in the government. They have only God's Word with which to punish; they are armed with truth, righteousness, peace, faith, and salvation.

Finally, the Anabaptists made clear that they were also united in their opposition to taking oaths, for according to the command of Christ, the godly are forbidden to swear an oath. This is illustrated. This last and seventh article concludes as follows: "Christ is outright yes and no, and all who seek him in sincerity, will understand his word."

The Schleitheim Articles were held in high esteem among the old Anabaptists, which is evidenced by the many copies and printed editions. Even in Holland the Anabaptist movement excited interest so that the Articles were translated into Dutch and printed in 1560 and 1565. Therefore, in the western

European branch of Anabaptists these Articles were considered the essential concepts of the Anabaptists, whether they were called Swiss Brethren, Hutterites, or Mennonites. These Articles created uneasiness in the camp of the opponents, which is evidenced not only by Zwingli's large volume presenting a detailed refutation against the Anabaptists but also by Calvin, who wrote a refutation. Calvin had been requested to do this after one of his followers had sent him a copy of the Articles. Calvin's treatise was in Latin, and the remarkable fact is that already by 1544 it had been translated and published in the English language.

It should be pointed out that these Articles make no mention of community of goods (Christian communism), which historians generally give as a characteristic of the Anabaptists. The other factor, for which one can search in vain in these detailed Articles, is an explanation of the apocalypse and chiliasm. The pertinent points in their proclamation have to do with instruction concerning baptism and the congregation, church discipline, Lord's Supper, separation from the world to live a life of Christian ethics, Christian pacifism, the free church leadership by means of a pastor, refraining from service or office in the state and municipality, and refusing to swear an oath. One may consider separation from the existing cultural pattern, pulling away from the state and its environment, as fanatical narrow-mindedness, but otherwise these Articles give no impression of any association with the so-called *Schwärmer*.

About the year 1530, in all of the Swiss cantons where Anabaptists were to be found, a united campaign using the most severe methods sought to exterminate these heretics and their doctrines. All during the remaining portion of the sixteenth century it became evident that this inquisition had failed. Of course, the formal movement was defeated and it had to live underground, but it was never completely uprooted. In some areas the Anabaptists were completely liquidated, but to a great extent the movement showed remarkable powers of self-preservation. During the periods of the 1530's, disputations or religious convocations were used to try and convert the Anabaptists, but these methods met with feeble results. Such a convocation was conducted at Zofingen in the summer of 1532, and it has been reported that it continued for nine days. Another great disputation was conducted in Bern, 1538, and this continued for six days, but with no results. The more the reformation churches in the cantons gained a secure establishment in their new circumstances and their lines of separation were clearly drawn against the Catholic Church, which continued as the power in the majority of the cantons, the more intense became their demands for uniformity.

Zürich, even in this respect, was the one to show the way. A tightly knit church organization developed. A baptismal register was initiated, as well as a requirement to register all church marriages. By means of such measures the churches were able to maintain control over the baptized and their families. The council passed a law in 1530 that made it compulsory for all residents to attend church, followed by the so-called moral mandate. One of the points in this act was directed against the Anabaptists, for it complained that they wanted to destroy all authority and regulations. The officials and the priests were commanded to keep a record of all separatists. Now church uniformity was to become a reality. The Anabaptists' articles on their opposition to carrying arms and to swearing an oath were taken to be a form of anarchy. The Anabaptists did not want to have anything to do with the offices in the state or municipality. Their ethical ideals were taken from the New Testament, and their personal convictions of faith had to be a vital experience. A voluntary congregation of believers was for them a sufficient fellowship; this led to a passive attitude toward the community and made them oppose the payment of the tithe to the church. Within Switzerland, in the meantime, it was impossible for them to establish a well-organized church life, due to the severe persecution. In Zürich at the beginning of the 1530's, there were three convictions condemning the guilty to death by drowning. After Zwingli was slain in 1531 in a battle with Catholic forces, persecution was by no means relinquished. His successor, Heinrich Bullinger, was just as implacably opposed to the free churches, and his judgments of the Anabaptists in his chronicles have been the basis of a one-sided judgment of this movement for several centuries. In other cantons there seems to have been a vacillation between harsh and mild treatment, but in the principal rule there was strong uniformity: all inhabitants were to belong to the Reformed state church.

The pressure on the Anabaptists was increased after the catastrophe of the foolhardy experiment of political fanaticism at Münster when the Anabaptists came to grief. A pronouncement in Zürich, 1535, indicates this. It was obvious that Bullinger was behind this enactment. If the Anabaptists did not obey the law, they would be treated like other malefactors according to the "divine, civil, and imperial laws." The reference was primarily to the death penalty for Anabaptists in the edict of the emperor, 1528. When the great exodus began to take place, the property of these refugees was confiscated. During the period of the 1560's when the migration to Moravia increased, new measures were undertaken, partly of an economic nature and partly as coercive personal repressions. To the former category belongs the practice of barring the Anabaptists from the unions and craft guilds.

Even in Bern difficulties increased after the fruitless disputation of 1538. Orders were given that the Anabaptist teachers and the church leaders should be interrogated by means of torture and then executed. Men and women who belonged to the Anabaptists were to be banished, the more obstinate ones executed. The question of the Anabaptists came up also in the Confederation Diet during the sixteenth century, when both the Catholic and the Reform cantons united in the extermination. The most severe punishment was to be death by drowning.

During the latter portion of the sixteenth century it was not uncommon to encounter Anabaptist migrants from Moravia and the Netherlands who came to Switzerland to win followers and to urge migration. Several of these strangers were imprisoned and prosecuted, but their ministry bore fruit in a great exodus. The civil leaders of the cantons thought it best to suppress these migrants with prohibitions. In some instances, such as in the period of the 1580's, the authorities confiscated all the property of those that had any ideas of running off to Moravia or Holland. The traveling preachers, however, could not be restrained, and the growth of the Anabaptists even during the 1580's was strong. In June, 1585, the Bern government directed a paper to the council at Zürich, which recommended a discussion to consider the Anabaptists, as the movement grew and stronger measures would be demanded. It was pointed out that all attempts to educate these erring ones by means of persuasion were without result, and even the penalty of death and burning at the stake had not been effective. After all of these brutal attempts to exterminate, this complaint does seem strange.

During the same year, 1585, there was a meeting of the synod of the Reformed church. The concentration, as at earlier periods, was now to be on preventive measures, such as the reforming of the conditions of the preachers, increased and better preaching, raising the standards in the education of children, and exercising a stronger program of church discipline. The battle against the Anabaptists must continue, it was stated, as long as they refused to live as members of society, refused to take oaths and to go to war, weakened the population by migration, broke up households, and deprived the country of able-bodied defenders. A mandate followed in the same year which took up all of the former types of punishment, even torture and the death penalty. The last was reserved for the leaders and all those who instigated emigration.

In a petition written by the Anabaptists, 1589, presented to the council at Zürich, the major emphasis was that a Christian life should bear fruit which is representative of a true and living faith. In this instance, they continued, one must follow the New Testament, because this has priority over the Old Testament. In the latter, ethics is built on retribution; in the former, love is the law. There should be no inconsistency between the Word and the life of a Christian. It is this latter attitude which reveals the Christian, for he is created unto good works and is to be God's instrument. The Anabaptists repudiated the accusations that they wanted to win salvation by means of works so as to make the merit of Christ of no account.

The question of baptism was also treated in this detailed exposition, which is characterized by a calm and factual presentation.

One point of great significance was the rapid dissemination of Anabaptist literature, and at this point the officials of the cantons had to yield, for they were unable to stop this underground traffic. The remarkable hymnbook *Ausbund* spread the Anabaptist ideas in hymn form through Switzerland and southern Germany. The foundation of this book was the songs of some of the oldest Anabaptist martyrs, such as Manz, Blaurock, and Hut. The first copies of this book were transcribed by hand, but in 1570 or 1571 it was printed. At an examination of the Anabaptists in Zürich, 1590, several books were mentioned which were read in the Anabaptist groups. The Anabaptists now had also started to write chronicles which later became very important. At the close of the sixteenth century, the Anabaptists were still in operation, and they were to hold forth yet a good deal longer in various territories of their native land.

The Southern German Anabaptist Movement

The Anabaptist movement which has been written up thus far has often gone under the name of Swiss Brethren. At first, this movement was essentially identified with Switzerland, but persecution and edicts of banishment in the various cantons forced the movement to spread not only within Switzerland but in the near-by countries. The Anabaptists fanned out in many directions—in the East to Tyrol, in the North to the territories of southern Germany, in the Northeast to Moravia, and in the Northwest to Alsace and down the Rhine Valley until contact was made with the people from Holland. Because of the close proximity with Waldshut and the strong influence of Hübmaier, the movement of the Swiss Brethren early became a factor with which to contend in the area of southern Germany.

The German Reformation at this time had not made much of an impression in southern Germany. A Catholic reaction had also set in in the northern Rhine region, for in 1524 all of the newly converted priests were forced to desert their parishes in Baden and Württemberg. Only in Waldshut was it possible for the reformers to continue a little longer. Irrespective of the radical conversion of the reformation movement in Waldshut, due to the influence of Hübmaier the city certainly expected to share with other places the consequences of the Catholic counteraction. The social unrest in these regions made for reaction, and Hübmaier, like other Anabaptists who had an interest in reform, came out strongly against serfdom and oppression. The Church was a financial power of significant proportions; the tenants and the renters were the oppressed. There are various interpretations concerning the co-operation Hübmaier is supposed to have given in drawing up the so-called "Twelve Articles" which became the platform of the peasant uprising. All of Hübmaier's ministry was opposed to the established Church and the feudal system. Earlier this peasant unrest had broken out in other portions of Germany, and even during the late Middle Ages these uprisings were not uncommon.

The attitude toward the Anabaptists in Germany was the same as in Switzerland. Luther and his associates, even before the rise of the evangelical Anabaptists, had vigorously opposed the radicals, *Schwärmer,* in the Lutheran districts. The radicals were driven out of Wittenberg by 1522. Both Luther's professorial colleague Carlstadt and the spiritualistic Müntzer, together with Storch, were definitely opposed. Later it became a general practice in Lutheran areas to lump together all radicals under one title, *Schwärmer,* wild enthusiasts and fanciful dreamers. Consequently, the entire Anabaptist movement has been tagged with this title, even to the present day, and little attempt has been made to make any clarification between the various streams within the so-called radical movement. The bitter antagonism of Luther, Melanchthon, Justus Menius, Urbanus Rhegius, and Johann Bader during the period of the 1520's and 1530's indicates that the movement was widespread, and it was decried as being extremely dangerous.

In this connection the previously mentioned edict of the emperor, January 4, 1528, should be considered. This edict was given the greatest importance during the German-Roman imperial reign. While Lutheranism was by degrees winning some acknowledgment and freedom through the Diets of Speier in the 1520's, the Diet of Augsburg in 1530, and the Diet of Nürnberg in 1532, these same edicts had a crippling effect on the Anabaptist movement. It was decreed that the baptism of believers (rebaptism) should be punishable by death, without the benefit of trial before any spiritual authorities. It was only necessary to confirm that this serious crime had been committed, and death by burning or by the sword would follow. Even those who were not themselves rebaptized but who refused to allow their children to be baptized were to be treated in the same manner. These mandates by the Catholic emperor were reaffirmed at the second Diet of Speier in 1529, and consequently all of the territorial states in the German Empire, both Catholic and evangelical, issued similar edicts in their local domains, estates, or municipalities.

Against this background, consideration should also be given to the primary Lutheran confession of faith—the Augsburg Confession—which condemned the Anabaptists in several articles. When this Confession was presented to the Diet in Augsburg in 1530, it followed the same line of antipathy toward the Anabaptists which had already been spelled out in the political edicts. Moreover, the Lutheran territories were becoming much like the Catholic and Reformed countries: the organization of a national church demanded strict uniformity. There was no religious freedom; all were forced to follow the rigid religious regulations. As for the Anabaptists, this meant a martyr's death, or in some cases, banishment.

One of the first localities in southern Germany to become an Anabaptist center was the free imperial city of Augsburg. Hübmaier was born in this vicinity, in the village of Friedberg, right outside of Augsburg. (This is the reason why Hübmaier carried the name "Friedberger" or "Pacimontanus.") It was natural, therefore, after the difficult experiences in Zürich during the winter of 1526, that Hübmaier would retreat to this territory. Before his arrival, however, other radicals had been active in this area. It is difficult to determine

79

what part Hübmaier may have had with the earlier development of the movement in Augsburg. His theological writings undoubtedly were known, especially his two books on baptism. He possibly had friends and acquaintances there from the days of his youth.

In the summer of 1524, Ludwig Hetzer, who belonged to the radicals in Switzerland, visited Augsburg. He did not stay long, for he soon returned to the Anabaptists in Zürich. Hetzer, like so many foreigners, was banished from Zürich where there was an attempt in January, 1525, to round up all of the Anabaptists. Again Hetzer fled to Augsburg, remaining as a guest of a printer. It was this printer who later printed the translation of the prophetical books of the Old Testament on which Hetzer and Denck had collaborated. In Augsburg, Hetzer gathered around himself a group of men and women who were dissatisfied with the reform of the Lutheran preachers; this situation precipitated the action that led to Hetzer's banishment from the city during the latter part of September, 1525. Hetzer probably had never been baptized as an adult, but he belonged to those learned mystics who were then active. After this Hetzer was in Basel, Strassburg, Worms, and other places, as well as in Zürich for a period.

It is believed that Hans Denck came to Augsburg in the fall of 1525. Denck had received the position of principal in the St. Sebaldus school in Nürnberg in 1523, and he was an outstanding man in the city. There were a number of Lutheran radicals here who disapproved of the local Lutheran reformer, Andreas Osiander. They had undoubtedly been influenced by Müntzer's spiritualism and Carlstadt's radicalism. Denck was one of these opponents. He was accordingly banished from the city in January, 1525, on the grounds that he cherished certain "erroneous teachings," although he was not at this time an Anabaptist. Denck made his way to Switzerland, where he stayed in St. Gall from Easter of 1525 until the fall of the same year. It was natural for him to fall in line with the great movement which was active at St. Gall. After this he came to Augsburg to earn his living as a private tutor. It was at this time that he became prominent among the followers of Hetzer.

Denck, like Hetzer, was a zealous Bible student and translator. Denck undoubtedly was influenced to take the step of baptism by Hübmaier, who during the spring and summer of 1526 lived in the vicinity of Augsburg. It is very likely that Hübmaier administered the act of baptism himself. It is probably correct that this was the first baptism within the fellowship of the early Anabaptist movement in Augsburg. In the beginning, Denck was a zealous preacher of baptism. This is one reason why the movement spread so rapidly in Augsburg and in near-by regions to the north. The movement was also accelerated because of the many new persons who came into the city. Soon Augsburg was a new center for the Anabaptists. Only Strassburg at this time could challenge Augsburg to the right of being the headquarters for the movement in the German districts.

One of the new men to come to Augsburg was Hans Hut. He was a bookbinder and colporteur from Thuringia who also felt at home in Luther's city of Wittenberg. During his travels, Hut came in contact with the critical ideas concerning infant baptism. When he heard of these arguments against pedobaptism, he went to the great reformers in Wittenberg for clarification, but he did not receive any convincing answer. This was in 1524. Later Hut objected and did not permit a newborn child to be baptized, for he was certain that infant baptism was neither necessary nor required, especially when no one could prove the contrary to him from the Scriptures. The consequences were that Hut, together with his family, had to leave home. Finally he came to Nürnberg, becoming acquainted with the radical groups, especially with Denck, in whose home he was received. After a time of considerable traveling, Hut came to Augsburg where Denck was then residing. Denck had also been baptized by this time. In the latter part of May, 1526, Hut was baptized by Denck. The Anabaptist movement in southern Germany now obtained in Hut one of its most prominent and industrious preachers. Hut traveled extensively in Bavaria, Swabia, Franconia, and Austria, and as a zealous lay preacher he was very successful. Hut meant much to the movement in Augsburg as well as to these other areas. When Hut returned to Augsburg in the early part of 1527, he helped organize the congregation and arranged for the election of a chairman. One of the characteristics of Hut's confession of faith was his belief in the imminent return of Jesus Christ. He also dabbled in eschatological concepts, which were not noticeable during the earlier days of the Anabaptist movement. These ideas got Hut into variance with Hübmaier in Moravia, but more of this shall be mentioned later.

Several leading personalities in Augsburg joined with the Anabaptists, such as Eitelhans Langenmantel, a well-known citizen among the class of patricians, who was baptized by Hut in February, 1527. Other important men, whom Hut baptized the same month, were a priest, Jacob Dachser, who earlier had been a teacher in Ingolstadt, and Sigmund Salminger, a Franciscan monk from München [Munich]. Both of these men were pillars in the Augsburg congregation. The church elected both of them as chairmen and further elected a man to be responsible for the care of the poor. New adherents came from many different classes of people, and even from the immigration into the city the church received additions. In August of the same year, 1527, the important Anabaptist synod was held. It was a unique meeting, with the leader probably being Denck. It is thought that a number of inner difficulties of the movement were considered. However, not much is known about the "Martyr's Synod," as it is called. Hut, who had by this time visited Moravia, took part in this synod, and shortly thereafter he was imprisoned. Others whom the synod sent out to be evangelists quickly met with martyrdom. Urbanus Rhegius a few weeks after the synod published a document against the "new order of baptism." There was also in this writing a reference to monastic piety.

The city council in Augsburg now decided to set up strong restrictive procedures. Already, in the same month in which the Anabaptist synod was held, a number of members were thrown into prison while others had to endure torture. Among those who were imprisoned were Salminger, the chairman of the church, Dachser, and Langenmantel. When the soldiers broke in on one of the meetings, they were able to arrest such preachers as Hut and the Waldshut noteworthy, Jakob Gross. By means of threats and persuasion, the authorities attempted to get the members to deny their faith. In the meantime, the Lutheran clergymen, by means of instruction, were to induce the heretical preachers to retraction. A disputation was held but without results. A threatening mandate came out in October, 1527, with the order that baptism was not to be withheld from children, and that all should be satisfied with the church worship and avoid "crooked preachers." Even giving them food or housing was forbidden.

There were a number of members who found it expedient to turn from "the error" of their way, but others remained true, which meant that they were banished. Among those who were banished was Langenmantel. In the spring of 1528, Langenmantel was executed with the sword. He had produced a number of theological writings as well as composed some hymns. Hut, Gross, Salminger, and Dachser remained in prison. Hut especially suffered much torture. On one occasion as he lay exhausted on his bed of straw, it is reported that he knocked over a light so that a fire started. He received such severe burns that he died a week later. In spite of his death, he was condemned; his body was burned in December, 1527.

Various types of punishment were executed with dispatch, and the pressure on the congregation was exceedingly great. In the place of the imprisoned chairmen new leaders arose. The martyrdom of the faithful had created sensational news, and it had attracted many to the congregation. Immediately after Hut was burned, large numbers were received into the church, including many immigrants from various places. During the winter of 1527–1528 many of those who had been sent out by the synod returned to Augsburg. Great baptismal services were conducted. The Lord's Supper was observed secretly in the homes, and new evangelists were sent out.

In April, 1528, the deathblow came. The police surprised a meeting at which there were about a hundred delegates, bound them two by two in fetters, women and men. The new chairman was condemned to death and executed, the foreigners were driven out of the city, and hard punishment was inflicted upon the others. The refugees scattered in many directions, some toward the west to Strassburg, others toward the east to Moravia. Several of the banished leaders made their way in another direction. Some were executed, one in Bamberg, one in Passau, and one in Stuttgart. After this, the Anabaptist church in Augsburg could not continue to exist. No more could Anabaptists from other places come into the city, for a careful watch was set up at the gates of the city. Informers blossomed, and no one dared to harbor an Anabaptist. It was impossible for the Anabaptists to assemble in the city, but in the wooded districts close by it was still possible to meet. The imprisoned leaders, Gross, Salminger, and Dachser, broke down under the severe punishment. In the middle of 1531 all three of these men had signed retractions. In 1535 the Anabaptist church in Augsburg was no longer in existence.

The work was not entirely closed in Augsburg, for occasionally an Anabaptist visited there. This was the case of the renowned Pilgram Marbeck from Tyrol, engineer, preacher, and author of theological literature. He had occasion to visit in Augsburg in 1528, and it is even possible that he was at the Martyr's Synod in 1527. However, he was busy in Strassburg and other places until the early part of the 1540's when he returned to Augsburg as a trusted professional man to work in the employ of the city until his death in 1556. The great influence of Marbeck as an intercessor for the Anabaptists seems to have been before this final period, but he continued to be a leader in the movement.

A little Anabaptist congregation was established in München [Munich], capital of Bavaria, by 1527. The communicants met in a secret place in a suburb of the city. As soon as this was discovered, a terrible persecution broke out; some were cruelly tortured, others were burned at the stake or executed by the sword, some were drowned, and others were fortunate enough to escape. Concerning one of the martyrs burned at the stake, George Wagner, who displayed great faithfulness, there was written a brochure which was circulated as a candid testimony of the Anabaptist deportment in time of death. After the emperor's death penalty edict against the Anabaptists at the beginning of 1528, the brutal policy of the Catholic dukes in Bavaria became even harder and executions increased. How many scores of martyrs there were is not determinable, but the number of Anabaptists in München was never great. The last martyr to be executed was as late as 1586.

In many parts of Bavaria where Catholics continued to rule, it is to be expected that persecution did not minimize. The dukes gave out the order that all Anabaptists should be executed. Those Anabaptists who retracted should be killed with the sword; those that continued in their faith were to be burned at the stake. Even death by drowning was applied to the Anabaptists. It is estimated that during the next decade over two hundred were executed in Bavaria. Among these were many travelers who passed through the country on their way from Moravia or Switzerland. The bishops in Regensburg and Passau carefully scrutinized their districts, and as soon as some Anabaptist was reported to the authorities, the discovered heretic was cut down. Despite all of this, Anabaptists were still to be found in the dukedom at the close of the century. Even in the period of the 1580's a strict mandate was dispatched, especially with reference to the immigrant Anabaptists from Moravia. In spite of this, it is reported that in one year about six hundred were converted and migrated to Moravia where the Eastern branch of the movement lived on. More edicts were pronounced, and the brutal uprooting of this cause continued. The consequence of all this persecution was that the movement was finally uprooted. At the turn of the century, 1599–1600, it appears that the free church movement had completely disappeared in this Catholic dukedom. After two hundred years, the Anabaptists were back again, but this time they were invited to come from the Palatinate territory to dwell in Bavaria as colonists to develop animal husbandry and to cultivate the soil.

In the meantime, an extraordinary monument to the Anabaptist movement in Bavaria is found. Among the imprisoned Anabaptists in Passau several hymns which became the basis of the remarkable hymnbook *Ausbund* were composed sometime during the 1530's. Originally this was made up of fifty-one songs, and later the number was increased considerably. It is easy to sense the basic, characteristic lessons running through the songs in this hymnal—songs of faith, hope, and trust in times of tribulation. In the beginning these songs were distributed as hand copies, and after about thirty years the first copies were printed. These songs have been reprinted in many editions both in Europe and America, and they have been the subject of considerable research because they represent a special type of piety which up until the present has been little known.

Anabaptists were found in a number of other cities in southern Germany, such as Ulm, Memmingen, Passau, and Regensburg. Persecution against the Anabaptists was similar in these places as in the others mentioned. The underground movement was not able to continue very long. In Franconia, which is also north of Augsburg, the free imperial city Nürnberg early became the center for both the Renaissance and the Reformation. Andreas Osiander was the leading reformer and Lutheran pastor here. During the year 1524, a number of radicals became dissatisfied with the halfway conditions which they believed to be developing in the Lutheran reformation. One of these radicals was Hans Denck, the schoolteacher to whom reference has already been made, who became "a thorn in the flesh" of the church leaders at Nürnberg. Within a year, January, 1525, Denck was deported from the city.

In the following year, the authorities of the city warned all of the residents to beware of all those who discounted infant baptism, the sacrament of communion, and who looked for Christ to return to set up an earthly kingdom. In March of 1527 the council of Nürnberg sent a letter to Strassburg stating that the Anabaptists were dangerous and that no rebaptizers would be allowed in the city as long as this sect was inclined toward revolution and wanted to destroy all authority. Further, the council decided that no Anabaptist literature should be sold, distributed, or printed in the city. At the same time, a similar communication was sent to Regensburg, where Anabaptists were to be found. It was here that Hübmaier had old associates.

At this same time, in the spring of 1527, the council at Nürnberg had a priest executed who had been won over to the cause of the Anabaptists by Hans Hut. The council also gave permission to circulate an attack against the Anabaptists, drawn up by the Lutheran pastors of the city. These wrote that the "evil, satanic poison" of the Anabaptists should be resisted with all force, both by punishment from the state and the unremitting instruction in the Word of God. As is so often the characteristic of these polemical writings, the Anabaptists' opinions are exaggerated and usually illustrated by reference to the extreme mystical, chiliastic groups. Infant baptism was defended by referring to the Old Testament, and the Anabaptists' "false, mendacious, soul-murdering ideas" were refuted with the usual arguments. When most of the other cities accepted the edict of the emperor, 1528, that all of the Anabaptists should be put to death even without trial, the council at Nürnberg refused to accept such a sweeping policy of extermination. Consequently, the persecution followed the ordinary pattern.

The refugee Anabaptists were driven out of the city. Even in the surrounding neighborhood of the city a number of men and women were imprisoned at the beginning of 1529. In June, 1531, the theologians and the jurists united in a dictum that the Anabaptist movement must be resisted, not only with the Word of God but with the instruments of worldly weapons; they now recommended both burning at the stake and the sword. The Lutheran reformation in Wittenberg had by this time come to the position that the death penalty should be used against the rebaptizers. Consequently, these measures were carried out in Nürnberg. However, it is known that even in March, 1541, there was still a group of Anabaptists who existed in the city. All of the radicals were to be imprisoned on orders from the council. Some of these radicals retracted, while others were driven out of the city and its surroundings. In this way the movement was defeated in this Lutheran territory.

From Franconia the movement continued in its northerly direction to Thuringia, where it branched out both to the west and to the north. Anabaptism had now come into the central territory of Lutheranism. This occurred during the years 1526–1527 and naturally caused Luther and his co-workers to oppose the Anabaptists more sharply. The agitation of Müntzer and the Peasants' Revolt had taken place in this central area of Germany. When the new congregational ideas, including baptism, became known, the movement received a local coloring, especially because of the previous revolutionary circumstances. This movement had a strong apocalyptic emphasis. It won adherents from the groups which had been misled by the "Zwickau prophets." The principles of the peaceful, biblical, and anti-worldly Anabaptists which now appeared appealed to many in these areas of Germany. The civil and religious authorities were not careful in making distinctions, for they classified together in one group the peaceful, biblical movement with the chiliastic Müntzer movement and its consequential phenomena. On the basis of this indiscrimination, persecution against these biblical Anabaptists was carried on without any compassion. Luther vehemently wrote against the movement; he could see nothing but anarchy and blasphemy in this work. Accordingly, there could only be one kind of punishment—death! Justus Menius, the Lutheran reformer in Thuringia, in 1530 wrote his refutation against the Anabaptist teachings. At the same time, the Wittenberg theologians made a pronouncement that the death penalty was appropriate for Anabaptists. Death came by burning, the sword, or drowning. The landgrave, Philip of Hesse, who was Luther's friend, was an exception among the evangelical princes, for he did not employ the death penalty against the Anabaptists. Instead, conviction could bring life imprisonment. Among imprisoned Anabaptists were some from Saxony and others from Hesse. These Anabaptist "criminals" were given penalties according to their citizenship; those from Saxony were executed, those from Hesse were imprisoned. In either case, those that repented were set free. Around Gotha, Eisenach, Schmalkalden, Frankenhausen, and Mühlhausen, as well as farther east in Halle and Orlamünde, Anabaptists and free churches were found.

The bloody persecution did its work; it destroyed multitudes who could not be forced to surrender their convictions. By the middle of the sixteenth century the movement was declining;

gradually these Bible-loving people were uprooted, many of them fleeing as refugees. Moravia became a haven for the refugees; however, misunderstandings and oppositions here divided them from the Hutterites. The movement continued longest in the north around Mühlhausen; even in the 1570's, records indicate a little assembly whose leaders were executed. The entire movement in Thuringia seemed to be highly colored with the opprobrious radical imprint; however, it is now clear that it was an outgrowth of the southern German free church movement. It is evident that it was the radicals within the Lutheran movement, before the Anabaptists appeared, who had exerted a great influence on the lives of the people. To mention names of individuals in the Thuringian movement is not of particular interest here, for there were no important personalities among them. The backgrounds of the many martyrs are varied. What is of interest, however, is that the Anabaptists carried on operations in Luther's own area, in the territory of Saxony and around Weimar, Erfurt, Leipzig, and Wittenberg, and they were even imprisoned in such a historic place as Wartburg. It is understandable that with such formidable opposition as this the Anabaptists could never build a strong and growing congregation in Thuringia and the territory of Saxony.

The beliefs which the Anabaptists in this central German free church movement taught and preached can be gathered from the minutes of a trial. The accused was a traveling preacher, Ambrosius Spittelmaier, who even as a university student in his home town, Linz (which is within the territory of Austria, a few miles south of Passau), had been baptized. It was the zealous Hans Hut that won the young man to this hated and persecuted Anabaptist movement. Spittelmaier became an assiduous Bible reader and interpreter. In 1527 he left Linz and traveled to Passau and Regensburg, where he found spiritual kinsmen. Later he went to the very center of the southern German movement, Augsburg. From here Spittelmaier made his way to Nürnberg to meet a family by the name of Nadler, who had been recommended by Hut. Nadler held a leading position in the Anabaptist congregation in the city. Hans Nadler, who originally was from Erlangen, was a passionate preacher who traveled extensively.

By this time, as we have seen, brutal persecution had started against the Anabaptists in Nürnberg. Spittelmaier was soon thrown into prison, but Nadler was fortunate enough to escape. A series of examinations followed, some of them implemented with torture, which was common. The records from these trials present much information concerning the Anabaptist teaching and preaching during this period. Spittelmaier undoubtedly had been indoctrinated by early theological teachers, especially Hübmaier, who was in Moravia, not far from Linz, at the time when Spittelmaier had become an Anabaptist. In Augsburg, he might have met Denck and others. Hut was settled in his convictions at this time, and it was through him that Spittelmaier had been won to the new movement.

The first point which Spittelmaier presented at his trial was the absolute authority of Holy Scriptures. This is the rule for faith and life. He stated that he had proclaimed God's Word in every place in which he had been received. Christ was for him God's eternal Son, yet identical with man in flesh and blood, who through his suffering and death secured God's grace for men and prepared a heavenly kingdom, of which Adam had robbed mankind. It is necessary to receive this gospel with a living faith and in truth become Christ's followers in order to obtain salvation. The true faith is not simply an outward acknowledgment but an experience in the heart, and it is revealed in a Christian conduct which, above everything else, demonstrates love to fellow men. Spittelmaier especially emphasized the conviction concerning the fellowship among true believers; they are members of Christ's body and as such should serve one another.

This Anabaptist went on to say that in the congregation true believers are equal; no man is above the next one. Only one office is recognized, namely the minister of the Word, and he holds no higher rank than others, only greater responsibility. At the fellowship meetings held in different places there is only the reading and interpretation of God's Word. When Spittelmaier was asked about the community of goods, he replied that he knew of no organized Christian communism, but only the expression of love to the brethren which Christ had commanded. A Christian may own property, but he must always keep in mind that it belongs to all the brethren. From this point of view, a Christian does not own property for himself alone, but he puts it at the disposal of his needy brethren. This is exactly the same interpretation of community of goods which was suggested in the testimonies of the Swiss Brethren. One may conclude that this attitude of the community of goods was the general rule among the Anabaptists, except among the Hutterite congregations in Moravia and other places, which will be considered later.

Spittelmaier did not believe in infant baptism, since neither God nor his Son had instituted it, but it had come into the church after the apostolic period. God seals a covenant with those who are accepted as his children, and those who are to be baptized must come to a knowledge of this covenant before baptism. Therefore, the order is first preaching. He who has come to a saving faith is baptized, but this should remain a free choice for each individual. Regarding the Lord's Supper, he said that Christ's body and blood were not the bread and wine which the priests employ during the Mass. The one that states that Christ's own body and blood are there in actuality deceives the people with a "lot of humbug." The communion which Christ held with the disciples and that which the priests now conduct are as different as black and white. Jesus' words must be understood as being figurative, just as are the words, "We are members of Christ's body." Mariolatry, saint worship, and similar relics Spittelmaier dismissed with strong expressions. According to this Anabaptist preacher, the break with the Catholic Church was in every respect decisive.

The Anabaptist prisoner expressed himself well, using a careful selection of terms when he spoke about Christ's second coming. He maintained especially that no one knew the day and the hour of the return of Christ. He believed, like so many in the history of the church, that the end was near, as all signs indicated. Therefore, one and all should take heed to himself, keeping his accounts straight and in order that he may appear before Christ on that great day. When Christ shall appear, he will be the King of a new kingdom, and all believers will take their places with him there.

Finally, Spittelmaier gave a detailed account of the Anabaptists' relationship to authority. He repudiated the standing accusations against the Anabaptists, that they were guilty of disturbance and the overthrow of government and all authority. The magistracy is ordained of God, but this office should not be used to supervise those who are God's children. In this portion, Spittelmaier was very critical of all types of authority. As other Anabaptists had answered, so he said that a true Christian does not need supervision by either sword or force; for the Christian of his own free will and through the leading of God's Spirit will exercise justice and righteousness. Only those who are nominal Christians need a magistrate who can keep them in line—otherwise one person would poke out the eyes of another. For the Anabaptist there can be no question of any holding of office in worldly government. The Anabaptists have never carried on any conflict with the magistrate, nor have they designed any plots against the legal authorities. Their mission is, in a peaceful way, to make God's Word known so that all may come to the knowledge of the truth. The Christian shall give that which is due to the magistrate, but no magistrate shall rule over the conscience. The Anabaptists cannot be driven from God's Word by any princely ordinance.

Such opinions, as mentioned above, caused the courts to impose the death penalty. In February, 1528, Spittelmaier was executed by the sword at the castle in the vicinity of Nürnberg where he had been held prisoner.

The Eastern Branch of the Anabaptist Movement

It early became apparent that the message of those in the Swiss Reformation who demanded a free church composed of believers (*eine Sonderkirche*) won approval in the east and northeast, especially in Tyrol and Moravia. The Anabaptist movement expanded in nearly every direction, and as has been shown, it was treated with about the same brutality in each locality.

For a number of decades Moravia, however, was an illustrious exception. Moravia became the "land of Canaan" where thousands of refugees found security, many of them Anabaptists who emigrated from different parts of Europe. This land of opportunity presented itself at the same time that the Anabaptists were expanding into southern Germany. The Swiss Brethren were the ones who opened up the lines of communication. The Danube flows only a few miles north of Waldshut, Zürich, Schaffhausen, and St. Gall. As the river continues its eastward direction, it passes by in a wide curve to the northeast such cities as Ulm, Ingolstadt, Regensburg, Passau, and Linz. In all of these cities, the Anabaptists early gained a foothold. A few miles farther, the Danube River's edge borders the city of Vienna, and directly to the north of this city lies the great territory which was the asylum for so many refugee Anabaptists during the sixteenth century. The shortest route from Switzerland to the "promised land" was overland through Tyrol. It will be seen that not even this haven was in the long run a safe retreat.

The first important name in Moravia's free church movement in the time of the Reformation is Balthasar Hübmaier. He has been introduced already in the study of the Swiss and southern German movement as a man of erudition, eloquence, and ability to pioneer new ways of thought. Hübmaier came to Moravia in the summer of 1526, after experiencing many hardships. His radical reformation of church life in Waldshut had caused a catastrophe for the city, because the Austrian soldiers finally made a cruel assault on the city. In Waldshut Hübmaier had cleared away all popery; he had become married, had been baptized, and also had baptized several hundreds of the inhabitants in the city. His flight through Zürich and Augsburg has already been related. Later Hübmaier continued through the cities on the Danube, Ingolstadt and Regensburg, where he was well known both as a professor and a cathedral preacher. Hübmaier soon came to Moravia, and for about a year he not only was a responsible leader of the rapidly growing free church but also the illustrious teacher of theology. It was in this new country that Hübmaier composed most of his twenty-five writings. Printed copies of these tracts have been preserved to this present day. From this point of view, Hübmaier was the foremost theologian and apologist for the Anabaptists.

When Hübmaier made his way to Moravia, he must have been aware of the fact that this territory had been a cradle for free groups in previous centuries. Earlier the Bohemian Brethren had practiced rebaptism in this country, and at this time there was a degree of religious freedom being observed. The landed nobility in Moravia showed that they were susceptible to the new ideas of Lutheranism. This fact was especially true of two nobles, Leonard von Lichtenstein and his brother, who in their territory around the little city of Nikolsburg gave considerable liberty for evangelical teaching. Even other nobles, because of their rivalry against the hierarchy, had begun to listen to the new tones being sounded forth from Wittenberg and other centers of reform movements. An Evangelical Lutheran congregation existed in Nikolsburg before Hübmaier came there in July, 1526. Many of the leading Anabaptists came to Nikolsburg, and it was here that Hübmaier gained a strong position of leadership under the protection of von Lichtenstein, who was baptized and joined the Anabaptist group. A well-known printer from Zürich also came to Nikolsburg, and consequently Hübmaier was able to have all of his current writings printed, the number of which was about eighteen.

Nikolsburg now became an active center for the Anabaptist movement. Hübmaier baptized a great number of people. The entire evangelical group merged into the free church movement, of which Hübmaier was the recognized leader. From outside of the city great numbers of persecuted Anabaptists came to seek asylum. The unusual preaching ability of Hübmaier, together with his astute ability as a writer and theologian, as well as his firm leadership, promised to build a reform work of great importance. Neither the Catholics nor the Lutherans were able to stem the tide in Nikolsburg at this time. It is estimated that approximately twelve thousand people joined the fellowship of the Anabaptists of Nikolsburg. Probably many of these were temporary visitors, for it can be shown from the records of the court trials, which were held later in Tyrol and southern Germany, that the majority of those on trial had been baptized in Nikolsburg or otherwise had visited there. Johann Kessler, the chronicler from St. Gall, said he could verify that about six thousand people had been baptized by Hübmaier during his great activity. Of the personalities who are well known, there came to the city such men as Hans Hut, Hans Nadler, and Leonard Schiemer. Schiemer became one of the most successful evangelists. Later, after he was put in prison in Tyrol and placed on trial, Schiemer testified that he had baptized many inhabitants in several districts within Austria and Bavaria. Schiemer has been called the first Anabaptist "bishop" in Austria. He suffered a martyr's death at Rattenberg, Tyrol, in January, 1528, a few months before Hübmaier.

Among such a multitude of Anabaptists in Moravia it became evident that there would be differences of interpretation on several points. Several of the newer leaders, especially, began to oppose some of the points in Hübmaier's theology. One of these was Schiemer, and another, even more important, was Hans Hut. While Hübmaier continued to minister in a manner considerate of the community and the authorities, Hut lived in a chiliastic dream, declaring that a new kingdom was soon to be inaugurated, that Christ's return would occur on Pentecost, 1528. The implication of this message was that the false preachers and the powerful authorities would have to give an account of themselves. The sanctified, after a time of scattering, would be gathered together to be with the Lord in his new kingdom. Against these radical ideas Hübmaier asserted his authority and his theological scholarship. Hübmaier in his writings had taken a positive position regarding the magistracy and the sword, that is, the power and authority of the state. On the other hand, the majority of the Anabaptists took a negative attitude toward the magistrate, and they were totally opposed to the use of force and the sword.

The war against the Turks, which was an acute problem in the eastern part of Europe, demanded watchfulness, sacrifice, and man power. When the radical Anabaptists now declared that they would neither participate in any form of war nor pay taxes to the support of war, they were regarded by the ruling powers as traitors. This problem has persisted until the present day. There was a middle way open with Hübmaier and his principles toward the community and the state, but for the strict Anabaptists there was only one way—refusal to have anything to do with the state. Hans Hut became the great leader of this phalanx of the Anabaptist movement in Nikolsburg, and he continued as such for a number of weeks, from the close of 1526 until the beginning of 1527. A number of other individuals joined Hut in his convictions, especially his prophetic eschatological schemes, which attracted great interest. Among the followers of Hut was a man named Jacob Wiedemann. As has been often pointed out already, Hut was much appreciated in his evangelistic endeavors, for he won great numbers of people in different places to the opinions and convictions of the Anabaptists' position. Hut had much success in Vienna and several places in Hungary. His teachings about the return of Christ were also eagerly received by many who lived under the threat of martyrdom. A strange twist of circumstances came about; Hübmaier now stood in the same position in the great Nikolsburg congregation as Luther did in the Wittenberg unrest, 1521–1522, and Zwingli in his opposition against the radicals in Zürich, 1524–1525.

Two disputations were arranged between Hübmaier and his opponents. At the later disputation, Hübmaier presented fifty-two articles based upon the writings of Hut, which were a strong refutation of Hut's ideas. *Rechenschaft [Account]*, Hübmaier's final writing, January, 1528, touched upon the questions and the discussion at the disputation. Much of the discussion centered on the second coming of Christ. Hübmaier accused Hut of deceiving the people by setting a date for Christ's return. Furthermore, the discussion also dealt with the sword and the relationship of the Christian to the civil authorities, together with a number of dogmatic questions on which there were divergent points of view. These disputations were not able to bring about any reconciliation between the two parties. After Hübmaier had been arrested, imprisoned, and martyred in March, 1528, the moderate Hübmaier element within the movement began to lose its power and influence. Persecution soon came to these territories, and it became apparent that the radical phalanx was going to continue to survive under a strong leader.

The two von Lichtenstein brothers could no longer maintain their line of tolerance against the king and the emperor. The directives against the Anabaptists came with implacable severity. Hübmaier's protectors were now constrained to obey their governmental superiors, and consequently Hübmaier, the foremost of all Anabaptists, was imprisoned in Vienna. Ferdinand I and his men had received alarming reports about the growth of the Anabaptist movement in Austria, and furthermore it was announced that Hübmaier, during his reformatory work in the Waldshut years, had been a radical opponent to the Austrian government. This man whom publicity had pictured to be so evil and dangerous was now within reach of the authorities in Austria, so now transportation to Vienna was quickly arranged. In Vienna, Hübmaier was constrained to appear at several trials. Finally he wrote his famous reply, the twenty-seven articles of his *Rechenschaft*. In defiance to torture and the threat of death, Hübmaier refused to be a turncoat. Judgment fell. On March 10, 1528, Hübmaier was burned at the stake. Three days later his wife was drowned in the river Danube.

This execution caused a great sensation, not only in the Anabaptist circles but far beyond, for Hübmaier was well known as a university man and a great preacher of the gospel. One of his former Catholic friends, the erudite John Faber, one of the Reformation's foremost opponents, felt constrained to leave an explanation concerning the proceedings against Hübmaier. Faber had been present at Vienna, and he had personally attempted to win Hübmaier back to the old Church. Faber also wrote another tract directed against Hübmaier's pamphlets, in which he considered Hübmaier to be the foremost theological interpreter among the Anabaptists. Hübmaier also seems to have maintained a certain respect and consideration for his old friend, for he apparently was prepared to make a number of admissions during the negotiations.

Among the Catholic opponents, Hübmaier was considered

to be the leading theologian. Both as a preacher and writer, Hübmaier was without question the foremost of the early Anabaptist leaders. The discernment of Faber often has been mentioned, but there is other information that supports his contention.[1] Hübmaier won this reputation as an able author because of his pioneering and early insight into the question of baptism. Most of his twenty-five writings were naturally small (the book on baptism refuting Zwingli was one of his largest, 70 pages), but they were a distinct contribution in the theological debate by a man whose education and position of importance had earlier afforded him a place of high honor in the Church. That Hübmaier could not be ignored is also shown by the polemical writings which were directed against him by Zwingli, Eck, and Faber.

In this presentation it is not possible to make a close examination of Hübmaier's theology. This must be done elsewhere, perhaps in connection with the preparation of the scholarly edition of Hübmaier's works, which is now under consideration. Only a brief summary of the main points of Hübmaier's teachings will be considered in this survey. The main features of his ideas are as follows: the position of prominence was given to the Scriptures, the highest authority in matters of faith; there was an insistent demand on a Christlike life (faith *and* works); great thought was given to the doctrines of the church (congregations) and the sacraments. In conclusion it should be mentioned that he considered and discussed some of the divisive questions among the Anabaptists, such as the attitude toward the magistrates and the sword, in other words, law and its enforcement.

Hübmaier's understanding of the Bible as the only conclusive authority for faith and life was presented as early as the second disputation in Zürich, 1523, which has been mentioned before. From this time on, Hübmaier pressed the claims of this conviction in preaching and writing in order to convince

---

[1] At the Council of Trent, 1545–64, the commission on censureship enumerated the foremost men and leaders among the heretics, including such names as Luther, Zwingli, Calvin, Balthasar Pacimontanus [Hübmaier], Schwenckfeld, "and a number of others who are similar."

others of its logic and its primacy. The church fathers, councils, and the interpretations and instruction of men are meaningless beside the Scriptures, for by the Scriptures all must be judged. Further, all of the institutions in the practical life of the church, the use of cult forms and traditions which are not in conformity with the Scriptures, are also forbidden. The Holy Spirit's enlightenment and guidance make the Scriptures clear to the believer. Expressions such as the "inner word," or "inner light," as used by the mystics, were not employed by Hübmaier. In some instances he could demand a slavish interpretation of the Scriptures, but he learned that the Word is the best interpreter for the Word; that is, that obscure passages should be interpreted by the aid of those portions in the Word that are clearly understandable. In a few instances, like Luther, Hübmaier employed the concept of God's secret will, which is undiscernible in the Scriptures, in contrast to the clear will of God revealed in the Scriptures.

In the doctrine of salvation, Hübmaier was at one with the various reformers in the main essentials. Justification is God's work. Man obtains salvation through acknowledgment of his sins, being born again through faith, and the practical results of his faith are shown in his confessions and in his struggle against the old "Adam." Justification is by faith alone, not through the merits of man, but only because God declares one to be righteous. Faith is also a work of God, for he has given us his Holy Word through which our faith is quickened. Only God is active in the work of justification; man is passive, and he only receives. The question of God's secret will and predestination played little part for Hübmaier, especially after he came to see that all that an individual needs is in the revealed will of God. Hübmaier's theology provided a wide latitude in the operation of man's free will. In this regard he was closer to the humanists and Zwingli than to Luther, a devotee of the Augustinian point of view. Hübmaier was acquainted with Luther's *On the Bondage of the Will* (1525). Hübmaier wrote two articles pertaining to the freedom of the will.

The one who has been born again and who is truly a believing person performs good deeds; the good tree bears good fruit. The Christian life is a testimony of the true faith; otherwise there is no faith. Absolute obedience to the Word of God, faithfulness in life by serving in love, sacrifice unto death— all of these are, according to Hübmaier and other Anabaptist scribes, the expression of a living faith. One can and must appeal to the converted will of a newborn person and impress the importance of a true Christian life. It was the want of this in the Reformation circles that made the Anabaptists impatient and critical. Hübmaier never published any expressions concerning his ideas of the law and the gospel; it was the practical interests which dominated his writings.

The greatest sensation which Hübmaier created was his concept of the congregation (church) and the sacraments, especially baptism. He took the same position in his doctrine of the church as the Zürich Anabaptists. The church is a congregation of true believers (*Sonderkirche*) which are separated from the parochial congregations of the national Church, upon which both Zwingli and Luther established their Reformation churches. Hübmaier never wrote any detailed thesis concerning the church, and only passing references are made to this subject in his other writings. The universal, spiritually composed church is Christ's body, and this church is made up of all believers. Individual local churches in various places are to be composed of believers, just as local churches in various districts are spoken of in the Scriptures. A person joins one of these local congregations by being baptized, which should be preceded by faith and a public testimony of faith in Christ. These individual churches are also a part of the universal church—all believers together in one church, Christ's body. Within these local congregations there should be a careful preservation of the members and the exercise of church discipline. This became a distinguishing characteristic of the Anabaptist congregations.

Much could be written about Hübmaier's teachings concerning baptism and the Lord's Supper, but only a few lines will suffice for this presentation. It should be underscored emphatically that when Hübmaier denounced the sacrament of infant baptism and published his arguments for the baptism of believers in the summer of 1525, in an attack on Zwingli, he blazed a new trail. Acceptance of his arguments would have led to the overthrow of the national and territorial church organization, which Luther and the Reformed theologians carried over from the Catholic Church. Because of these circumstances, Hübmaier and his Anabaptist associates were looked upon as radicals who were overthrowing the established order, opponents of princes, governments, and rulers. At times the baptismal question is sidetracked as a secondary matter in the study of Anabaptist history. Great stress is given to the social peculiarities or the Anabaptist understanding of the church. Such emphasis disregards the fact that the most potent attack against the prevailing Church establishment and the Christian social order made by the Anabaptists was their dismissal of the old traditions concerning baptism. Earlier rebaptizers—who had appeared, for example, among the Waldenses, Hussites, and Bohemian Brethren—had not generally implied that they rejected infant baptism; they had not wanted baptism to be performed by an apostate church.

Hübmaier taught that two sacraments ought to be perpetuated. These are the only sacraments that Christ had established; therefore, these ought to be observed as a confession and obligation. He did not mention the remaining five sacraments of the Catholic Church which he had rejected, but he presupposed early that these had already been abolished in the groups to which he turned. According to Hübmaier, baptism is a witness and an acknowledgment of an inner transformation within man. The subject had been born again, and baptism was the expression of his justification. It has a future directive, for it is an obligation and a promise. God performs no direct work of grace in the water, yet baptism is not a meaningless ceremony. It has been commanded in the Scriptures, and it becomes an entrance into the fellowship of the congregation. Baptism was an important matter with Hübmaier, and this is evidenced by his six writings dedicated to this subject. He brought up all of the arguments to which later writers have returned. In the theological discussions with Zwingli, baptism played a leading part, and the position of Hübmaier was essentially this: There is no place in the Scriptures that indicates that infant baptism was commanded or that it was practiced during the apostolic period. All the witnesses from primitive times indicate that faith preceded baptism. For the Catholics who placed tradition beside the Bible, this insistent reference to the Bible was not so difficult; but for Zwingli and Luther, who always appealed to the Bible in their opposition against the Roman Church, this insistence of Hübmaier was irritating, which is evident in Zwingli's rebuttal.

In the question concerning the Lord's Supper, Hübmaier found it easier, for both Zwingli and Luther had removed the superstitions around the offering of the Mass and had opened the eyes of the people concerning the meaning of communion, with everyone partaking both elements. It is altogether clear, however, that Hübmaier's teaching about the Lord's Supper was dependent upon his teaching concerning baptism and the church. Only in such a church, as Hübmaier could define it from the Scriptures, could the Lord's Supper be legitimately observed. He never outlined a detailed exposition of this sacrament, but it is easy to discover his main ideas. The Lord's Supper is first of all, according to the Scriptures, a feast of remembrance centered on Christ, and it is also a meal of fellowship which binds the participants in love to one another. This latter point became a central feature in Hübmaier's teaching on the subject.

As has already been explained, Hübmaier did not agree with other Anabaptists in their opposition to authority and the sword. This position became of great importance for later Anabaptist evaluation of Hübmaier. There were those who did not want to acknowledge any association with him, for in this crucial question he had not agreed with those who were to determine future development within the radical movement. Anabaptists developed in two directions: toward pacifism or toward a chiliasm which urged concepts of violence and power. The latter came to a sorry conclusion, for it developed in the isolated degeneracy of the Netherland–west German movement, the Münster kingdom and its catastrophe of 1535.

Against such radical dreamers Hübmaier had stood unrelentingly opposed.

But the same time, Hübmaier could not follow the direction of those who taught that it was not right for one to assume positions of responsibility in public offices or to appeal to any court under the jurisdiction of a worldly magistrate. In Waldshut, Hübmaier had been forced to realize that a legal defense of a city could take place, even though superior powers there were great. He had learned in Moravia from the von Lichtenstein nobles that a Christian magistrate could also serve the gospel.

Hübmaier's teachings about the magistracy and government was influenced by such experiences. Obedience to the magistrates, who are God's messengers, must be given by all citizens. Because of sin, law and order must be maintained. Therefore, the judicial power must function, and it must be supported in its authority to punish. Otherwise the entire judicial system would be meaningless. Even capital punishment must be allowed for grave penalties. The magistrate must also take a position in regard to war and peace, and it is possible for a true Christian citizen to maintain employment in government positions. Hübmaier considered war as a punishment for sin, and if this were the case, then the Christian would be free to participate in war. The Christian ought, however, to be reluctant to hold offices in the civil government and to seek the office of the magistrate or a commission in the judicial system. The magistrate should be critically examined, and if he orders something which is contrary to God's Word, then a Christian can no longer support such a magistrate. He must oppose such a leader, yes, even try to have him unseated.

Hübmaier was estranged from his brethren because of other questions as well. He sanctioned the taking of oaths; he opposed the theory of the community of goods, and he never practiced it. The moderate middle way which Hübmaier followed had little success during the sixteenth century. In the next century the Baptist movement appropriated this idea, and to a large extent these convictions are still maintained among Baptists.

The death of Hübmaier in flames was a devastating blow to the large multitude of people who looked to him as their leader, especially in that it signaled the beginning of persecution in various parts of Austria. Several leading Anabaptist preachers and evangelists had ministered in this country, as has already been stated. These preachers worked down the valleys towards Tyrol and the Brenner Pass, as well as in the central areas of the country. In Linz, Steyer, Vienna, Salzburg, and a number of other places there were congregations where some men already mentioned, as well as others, proclaimed the gospel. Both from Moravia and Tyrol came streams of people who merged in Austria, but cruel persecution beat the movement down. As usual, many of the persecuted fled to other countries. Moravia received a good share, still being a place of refuge.

Tyrol early came into close contact with the Swiss movement, for many of the early Anabaptist leaders had close associations there. As a neighboring country to Switzerland, Tyrol had to take in a number of those who had been driven out of their home territories. To give a detailed account of the spread of the movement in Tyrol is not necessary here. Already by 1526 the movement had spread through the Inn Valley and other places. A congregation was even found in Innsbruck, and one account states that in 1529 there were Anabaptist groups in over a hundred places in the various valleys in Tyrol. The movement was so full of life that the Catholic authorities tried with all their power to root out the heretics. In November, 1527, there was an edict published against the Anabaptists. Mention has already been made concerning Leonard Schiemer who was martyred in Tyrol in January, 1528. This was the initiation of a series of executions by means of burning or the sword. In the early part of 1529, a more stringent edict was issued which demanded that even those Anabaptists who recanted should be executed and the homes in which the Anabaptists met should be burned.

George Blaurock, one of the prominent earlier Anabaptists at Zürich, also came to Tyrol. After Blaurock had been deported from Zürich, he met with great success in various places in Switzerland, and in the spring of 1529 he was active in Tyrol. Here he was the same zealous revival preacher that he had been in Zürich. Now he visited many places in Tyrol, preaching, baptizing, and strengthening the congregations and the little groups. He even assumed the leadership of a congregation, whose chairman had been imprisoned at Innsbruck, tortured, and burned at the stake. It was not long before the same consequences fell upon Blaurock. It is natural that Blaurock was cautious, holding his meetings in secret and concealing himself as much as possible. But the movement was altogether too large to remain secret. The "Anabaptist hunters" who were sent out were many and inconsiderate, and the authorities in Innsbruck were pressing the local police to do everything they possibly could to arrest Blaurock. In the middle of August, 1529, this goal was achieved. After the usual horrible torture, Blaurock, with another comrade, was burned alive at the stake on September 6, 1529. This took place at the city of Klausen, where Blaurock had one of his headquarters.

The bloody persecution continued, and after a few months, in the beginning of 1530, the authorities in Innsbruck could report to the Austrian government that more than seven hundred Anabaptists had either been executed or driven out of Tyrol. Notwithstanding this, one of the local authorities reported in 1538 that in one of the valleys the Anabaptists were increasing and were well received by the population. In many instances these people revealed a courageous faith by zealously witnessing, which must arouse wonder. The pressure became increasingly strong, and a total extermination of the movement seemed inevitable. It was at this time that many decided to turn to their friends in the faith in Moravia and form a closer fellowship with them. In this connection Jakob Hutter, one of the leading Anabaptist men in Tyrol, came to Moravia and assumed a leading position.

Before this association between Moravia and Tyrol is discussed, a few words ought to be said about the development in Moravia. As has been mentioned, Hübmaier had a number of opponents in his great congregation at Nikolsburg. One of these men was Hans Hut, who did not stay there long. Another was Jacob Wiedemann. The main question revolved around the attitude toward the magistrate and the sword. The two parties were designated as *Schwertler* (men with the sword) and *Stäbler* (men with the staff). Even after the death of Hübmaier the opposition continued, for his followers did not want to give in to the radical demands. The opposition group increased through immigration from Switzerland and other places, and the newcomers did not want to give in. They held their own fellowship meetings and were active in other ways. The Anabaptists' protector, Leonard von Lichtenstein, sought to reconcile the differences so that this group could join with the larger congregation, but he failed. This small group was then told to leave the city, and under the leadership of Wiedemann a contingent of these people, between two and three hundred, went to Austerlitz, not far from Nikolsburg. They were invited here by one of the nobles of Kaunitz. This was the group of Anabaptists which began to practice Christian communism in its original form, which later became so characteristic of the eastern branch of the Anabaptist movement.

Jakob Hutter came to the congregation in Austerlitz in 1529. He had become an Anabaptist in his home province in Tyrol. There he traveled as an evangelist and even became the leader of one of the congregations. When the grim persecution became even more severe, he decided to flee to Moravia. In this way Hutter came to the place of freedom, first as a negotiator and later, from 1533, as a leader of a radical group that had broken off from the Austerlitz congregation in 1531. In a small settlement, Auspitz, this group had found a new refuge. It seemed that there were difficulties in the fellowship over the community of goods which led to this division. It was at this time that Hutter was instrumental in establishing the small villages or community houses (*Bruderhöfe*), which became characteristic of this branch of Anabaptism. Hutter was a strong leader in this Auspitz congregation, and soon he had gathered around himself, by means of the growing influx from Tyrol, a well-organized fellowship with a series of Brethren villages in Moravia. From Tyrol alone came hundreds of Anabaptists, and it was at this time that the movement received the designation "Hutterian Brethren"—Hutterites. This was the branch of the eastern movement that was able to outlive the difficult trials.

Hutter did not remain long at the head of this pacifist and Christian communistic movement. King Ferdinand I and the government in Vienna could not be reconciled to the fact that the nobles in Moravia gave asylum to the Anabaptists, so in 1535 the Diet was constrained to enforce obedience to the edicts of the emperor and the king. Hutter, fearing for his life, returned to his home province in Tyrol. Here he was soon put in prison, cruelly tortured, and on February 25, 1536, he was burned at the stake. His wife was executed a short time later. The story of Hutter's martyrdom became a matter of soul-stirring accounts among his adherents. Hutter did not write much, neither was he much of a theologian nor a teacher.

In spite of everything, the Hutterian Brethren remained in Moravia, and during the sixteenth century no less than eighty vicinities contained these communal households—Houses of the Brethren. Because of the great reputation of the Hutterites in agriculture and handicraft, they were in demand by the nobility and country barons. These Brethren therefore took advantage of the many possibilities during the entire period of the Reformation to live and work in the close confines of the capital of the Catholic Hapsburgs. The details of their experiences have been recorded in their history and constitute unique chronicles. This history has been preserved to the present.[1] It gives an account of the "difficult scourges" and persecutions during the years 1536–1554. After the Peace of Augsburg in 1555 there was an easing of tension, even for the Anabaptists. The period 1555–1565 is recorded by the chronicler as "the good days" for the congregations, and the time from 1565–1592 was designated as the church's "golden era" (die goldene Zeit). It is estimated that at this time there were fifty brotherhoods with a membership of twelve to fifteen hundred. Some of these were found in Hungary, where a number of immigrants had come in later periods.

[1] Josef Beck, Die Geschichtsbücher der Wiedertäufer in Oesterreich-Ungarn— von 1526 bis 1785. [The Historybooks of the Anabaptists in Austria-Hungary— from 1526 until 1785], Vienna, 1883.

During the latter portion of the sixteenth century there were a number of capable leaders and preachers within the movement. Only one of these persons will be mentioned here, for he drew up an *Account of the Faith* for the Hutterites, which has been considered the confession of faith among these Brethren. His name was Peter Riedemann. Early he began his work in the movement. He was from Silesia, but as early as 1529 he was among the Anabaptists in Austria. He was taken prisoner, and after three years in prison, "through the providence of God," as recorded in the chronicle, he was restored to freedom. He then made his way to Moravia and joined the congregation in Auspitz, which soon sent him out as an evangelist. Coming to Franconia, he was apprehended and placed in prison at Nürnburg, and after a number of years he was released in the summer of 1537. He then went to Austria and Moravia. An invitation soon came from Anabaptists in western Germany saying that they needed assistance. Riedemann, in 1539, journeyed to Württemberg and Hesse, as he says, to "garner much fruit for the Lord." Once again, a year later, Riedemann returned to Hesse, but this time he was imprisoned, to be released again in 1542. Returning to Moravia, he labored as a preacher in the churches where he was greatly respected by the members. He lived until 1556, and he was one of the few notable leaders who died a natural death. As a servant of the Word of God and a leader in the churches, Riedemann was held in great respect and veneration in the Anabaptist chronicle. Of the twenty-seven years that Riedemann ministered in the movement, no less than nine of these years were spent in various prisons.

Peter Riedemann was the foremost theologian and ablest hymn writer among the Hutterites. Above everything else, his *Account of the Faith* is considered to be his most important work. After Hübmaier there was no one in the eastern branch of the Anabaptist movement who could measure up to Riedemann. Not too much is known concerning his education, but since he willingly and ably used his pen, it is presumed that he had good training. It is apparent that Riedemann spent his long years of imprisonment in working on his theological subjects. In 1543 he submitted his dogmatic tome, *Rechenschaft unserer Religion (Account of Our Religion)*. It was printed for the first time in 1565, and it has gone through several editions, even so recently as in the present century when the Hutterites in America arranged for a new edition. The influence of this volume has been great in this segment of the Anabaptist movement.

Peter Riedemann, like his Anabaptist predecessors in theology, stressed the importance of anchoring everything in the words of the Bible, for he maintained that this was the only conclusive authority. With Hübmaier he agreed that the Holy Spirit worked in and through the Word to make it living and clear. Only by means of such an inner contact with the Spirit would a person be able to come to the correct interpretation of Scripture; otherwise there is only pure, literal interpretation. He taught that the propitiation and redemption of Christ was fully accomplished for man's justification. Christ is not only justification for believers but he also works righteousness and godliness in them. "When many accuse us that we attempt to achieve justification through our own works, we reply no." This was Riedemann's explanation. By means of repentance and faith one must come into possession of salvation and sanctification acquired through Jesus Christ. Believers, therefore, are grafted into the true vine and consequently have the power to bear the fruits of a Christian life. As other Anabaptists, so Riedemann with no uncertain sound declared that a Christian must be a disciple of Christ and live a life of holiness, in which faith is demonstrated by good works. This is like both Lutheran and New Testament thought and expression.

On the question of baptism, Riedemann agreed with the other Anabaptists. He easily cited all of the references in the New Testament where baptism of believers occurs. Any effect of the sacraments, as such, outside of a personal faith and prayer was unknown to him. This is true of the Lord's Supper, which by itself is impotent as a means of grace or forgiveness of sins. It is a symbolic meal of communion for fellowship and for remembrance, a reminder of the truth. Church discipline must be maintained, and this can even lead to exclusion from

109

the congregation. Riedemann developed a great interest in the lessons concerning excommunication, and he attempted to enlarge this concept exhaustively from the Scriptures. This question was closely related to the views concerning the church or congregation, which were common among Anabaptists.

According to Riedemann, the congregation should select preachers or elders by voting or casting lots, for not all were to be trusted with the ministry of the Word and the administration of baptism. This required a special personality. In this he was in agreement with the earlier-mentioned Schleitheim Articles. Likewise, in respect to a person's responsibility to the magistrate, Riedemann maintained that a Christian must obey as long as there is nothing that is contrary to God's word. When conflicts arise, the Christian "must obey God more than man." The conscience is free, and the Christian is responsible only to God; therefore, the magistrate has no dominion over faith, nor can it molest the conscience of mankind. A Christian cannot use the sword, nor be a person of civil authority, nor use force. It is at this point that the Hutterites' negative opinions come to the fore, especially pertaining to the magistrate and the community. This was one of the points of difference between the Hutterites and the followers of Hübmaier.

Another point of difference was Riedemann's teachings concerning the community of goods. If all of the sanctified enjoy all spiritual things in common, then they ought to show the same communal spirit in material things. The sharing of life and love among the true Christians demands this community of goods, for among such Christians there must be nothing that stands between them. The account in the book of Acts about the community of goods in the early church was quoted. With the biblical point of view that the Hutterites possessed, it is natural that this example in the Bible would strengthen their faith and make legitimate a Christian community of goods.

Riedemann was an enthusiastic promoter of good hymns. He quoted from many places in the Scriptures to prove his point and also showed the practical points of view. He was an able hymn composer, and even today there are still forty-five of his hymns in the Hutterite hymnbook. As has been mentioned previously, the Hutterite hymnbook *Ausbund* early became a meaningful book in the history of the movement.

The Western Branch of the Anabaptist Movement

The Swiss Anabaptist movement, which went out from Basel northward along the Rhine Valley, progressed rapidly as a strong off-shoot of the original movement. The Reformation had earlier taken hold in this area, especially in Strassburg, the capital city of Alsace. Two of the influential men in the reformation in southern Germany, Martin Bucer and Wolfgang Capito, had already come to Strassburg in 1523. Both of these men were strongly influenced by Luther, but they also had active associations with the Swiss to which the correspondence of Zwingli and Oecolampadius bear witness. Both Bucer and Capito were radical in their criticism of the Catholic Church's teaching of the sacraments. In this respect, they were closer to Zwingli than to Luther. Both men also appeared to have made certain inferences from the sacramental view of infant baptism. At the beginning of their reform they were inclined to break completely from the Catholic Church in this doctrine of baptism. Capito, especially, seems to have held an opinion which drew him into a closer relationship with the Anabaptists. Even in the question of church discipline, these men came close to the Anabaptists in many points. They finally decided, however, that there was a practical advantage in retaining infant baptism.

Evidence indicates that the question of baptism was already acute in Strassburg when the radical groups from Zürich began to appear in 1524. Zwingli received a letter from Strassburg requesting aid in opposing Carlstadt and his followers, who proclaimed ideas about the Apocalypse and antipedobaptism. In the middle of December, 1524, Zwingli replied by stating his position in Zürich. He wrote about the opponents of infant baptism and how he had shown out of the Scriptures that baptism was not only the initial matter for those already believers but also for future believers, such as infants. Zwingli, even in Strassburg, was considered the foremost defender of the traditional mode of baptism. In this letter, Zwingli gave

111

reasons for this position, and they are the usual ones: circumcision, Jesus' blessing the children, and household baptism in the Acts of the Apostles. This correspondence at the close of 1524 indicates that there was a real difference of opinion over the interpretation of baptism in Strassburg.

Since the authorities in Strassburg during these early days maintained a political attitude of tolerance, many persecuted persons from other districts came there for asylum. The influence of the humanistic groups in Basel was also very significant. In the summer of 1525, Hübmaier came to Strassburg to see if he could have his book on baptism, which was against Zwingli, printed. This visit is believed to have been decisive for the radical Anabaptist movement in the city. Soon after, an Anabaptist congregation emerged, and it grew rapidly. Capito had earlier mentioned in a letter to Zwingli the seriousness of the baptismal question in Strassburg. In a letter to Luther's fellow worker in Wittenberg, John Bugenhagen, Capito wrote in the fall of 1525 about the visitor from Waldshut who had insisted on the necessity of rebaptism, as if "salvation was dependent on water." Even Jakob Gross from Waldshut visited in Strassburg for a period, and he was examined by Bucer. In the spring of 1526, another active Swiss refugee Anabaptist came to Strassburg. He was Wilhelm Reublin, and it was natural that the debate over the mode of baptism should blossom up again. The Anabaptist congregation was now growing in numbers. A few months later Ludwig Hetzer, Hans Denck, and Michael Sattler came to the city, and therefore the unrest increased.

With such an accumulation of outstanding men, the new Anabaptist movement was bound to make an effective impression on the city. The question now arose for the reformers as to whether these men could be tolerated. In the beginning of the Anabaptist work in Strassburg both Bucer and Capito opposed the idea of force, but it was becoming increasingly difficult to maintain a tolerant attitude when this movement was growing so rapidly. Capito was very obliging. He had, for instance, taken Hetzer into his home as a guest. Even Sattler was received as a friend and enjoyed a friendly relationship with the reformers in the city. He remained here only a few months, however, for it was not long after that he was martyred, as has already been mentioned. Sattler was so moderate in his opinions and in his missionary activity that neither Bucer nor Capito evidently came to grips with him. On the contrary, opposition against Hetzer and Denck was much more severe, which is evident in a writing which Bucer published against the Anabaptists in the summer of 1527. Earlier a public disputation had been held between Bucer and Denck, after which Denck was banished from the city. As has been stated before Denck was a mystic. After this action taken against Denck, a stricter church policy was initiated by the council.

Bucer, who was the leading reformer in the city, stated his principles clearly: an attempt should be made to convict and convince the Anabaptists, to win them back to the Reformed church. If this was not adequate, then the council must take these persons in hand. Subsequently, imprisonment and banishment were not only initiated but they were continued as methods of punishing heretics. The death penalty was never used in Strassburg as a method to quench the spread of the Anabaptist fire. In the summer of 1527 the council issued a strict mandate concerning the Anabaptists in which all of the inhabitants were warned to beware of these erring people, to have no intercourse with their teachers, to invite no heretics into the homes, to give them no food, drink, nor protection. Many Anabaptists were imprisoned, tried, and banished. A year later, an Anabaptist meeting was raided; the members were put in prison and placed on trial. The same thing happened a few months later when Reublin, who has been previously mentioned, and Pilgram Marbeck from Tyrol, an outstanding engineer, arrived in the city. A long trial followed, and in some instances torture was inflicted. Bucer was seeking to win his goal—a unified Reformed church, but in this he failed. In a letter to Zwingli in the summer of 1529, Bucer complained that the inconsiderateness of the Anabaptists had forced the council to oppose these heretics with greater severity. Bucer wrote with a cold indifference about the hard punishments the Anabaptists were receiving. It is evident that

Bucer lost his patience and tolerance when the free church movement upset his reformation plans. In contrast, Capito was able to maintain his benevolent attitude for a few years, but after 1533 he too arrived at the opinion that the Anabaptist movement was dangerous and must be warded off.

When Pilgram Marbeck came to Strassburg, Bucer's unrest increased. Marbeck was an esteemed man in the practical work of society, and he was a clear and convincing defender of the Anabaptist position. Marbeck had joined the new movement earlier, perhaps in his home town in Tyrol. His name has already been mentioned in connection with the Anabaptist work in Augsburg. Marbeck has related how he was reared in the Catholic Church, later turning to the "Wittenberg gospel." New insight later made him leave Lutheranism. According to his testimony, he then decided to follow God's guidance, be obedient, and be baptized. In the meantime, he had obtained a good position in the Tyrol community, where he was a member of the council in his home town of Rattenberg. He worked as a mining engineer and also as a mining judge. Perhaps he attended the Anabaptist synod in Augsburg in 1527, which has already been mentioned. How long he had been an Anabaptist at this time is not certain. Under any circumstance, when Marbeck was converted to the Anabaptist movement, which in Tyrol was being severely persecuted, he had to forsake all of his opportunities, responsibilities, and bright future possibilities to make his way to a strange country. His property was confiscated. When he came to Strassburg in the fall of 1528, the strife over the question of baptism was already in full swing.

At the beginning, Marbeck was also esteemed in the city of Strassburg, partly because of his craftsmanship and partly because of his outstanding character. He built some unusual aqueducts and water channels, at least for that time, in the adjacent valleys. He also took part in the conventicles and the Bible fellowship, and his zeal for the Anabaptist ideas and their application to the church soon became apparent to all. He soon was the real leader of the Anabaptists. Bucer and his associates could not tolerate this, for as has just been mentioned, more severe policies had been inaugurated by the authorities

114

since the summer of 1527. Even though the Reformed preachers, with Bucer at the head, were against Marbeck, he still had
many supporters among the city leaders. Bucer's letters to
Zwingli, Oecolampadius, and Blaurer (Württemberg's reformer) indicate that he was impatient over Marbeck's activity as he had been toward the previously mentioned Anabaptists. Bucer condemned the layman theologian from Tyrol as
"a stiff-necked heretic." It was not only baptism which caused
the reformers and the council in Strassburg to continue proceedings, but Marbeck, like some of his brethren in the faith,
also declared that a Christian could not use the sword or swear
an oath.

It was apparent that a man like Marbeck could not long be
allowed to engage in religious activities. Marbeck's special
training also made him an able scribe. When he distributed
two of his writings about Anabaptist doctrines, the measure of
antagonism was filled full. The censors acted; Pilgram Marbeck was apprehended and put in prison. Capito visited him
in prison, but no accord was reached. At the close of 1531, Marbeck requested of the council that he be allowed to present his
views in a public disputation with the reformers. He was
granted only a colloquy before the council and a few others. At
this time Marbeck defended his thesis with enthusiasm. He re-
proached Bucer and his men that they did not stand free in
their preaching but took protection under the princes and
states; therefore, it was no wonder that there was no fruit from
the word. The council then declared that Marbeck must leave
the city as long as he rejected infant baptism and wanted a
gathered church (Sonderkirche). In a farewell message to the
council, Marbeck gave an account of his views, more completely
defining them; for in matters of faith only God can judge a
man. In January, 1532, Marbeck left Strassburg, for the political suppression in the city was becoming unbearable. The jour-
neys and ministry of Marbeck for the next few years are only
vaguely known, but it is certain that he spent some time in
Tyrol and in some of the cities of southern Germany where he
had good connections with important families and where his
craftsmanship was in great demand. He finally came to Augs-

burg, as has been mentioned, and lived there until his death in 1556. Marbeck's reputation as a theological writer by this time was widely recognized.

During the Strassburg period, Marbeck came into contact with the well-known mystic, Caspar Schwenkfeld, who already in his home territory of Silesia was considered one of the Anabaptists, although he actually never was. Schwenkfeld had expressed himself understandingly about the Anabaptists, but nevertheless he basically took the same doctrinal position that Denck came to: baptism, the Lord's Supper, and an organized church are of no real importance for those who are genuinely spiritual people. Schwenkfeld did not recognize water baptism, only the baptism of the Spirit. He and Marbeck consequently got into a theological tussle, which cannot be discussed here in full detail.

The background of this difference stemmed from the opposition between such mystics as Schwenkfeld, Sebastian Franck, and Melchior Hoffmann on the one side and the Anabaptists, who organized biblical congregations on the other. It is difficult to draw a clear-cut line of demarcation between these two groups. However, in the writings which Marbeck and Schwenkfeld directed at one another, it is possible to outline the main points of difference so that an evaluation can be made. Sometimes the group typified by Schwenkfeld has been called "the nonorganizational mystics" to contrast it with the other group, the biblical branch.

In 1542 Marbeck published a two-hundred-page book, *Vermahnung* [*Admonition*], which has sometimes been called *Das Taufbüchlein* [*The Little Baptism Book*]. Schwenkfeld replied to this work by writing *Judicium* [*Judgment*], attacking Marbeck's book and the Anabaptist movement. Marbeck countered with another large volume, *Verantwortung* [*Vindication*], in which the Anabaptist teachings were treated. Johann Loserth has said that this book as a piece of controversial writing is one of the most unique in all of the polemical literature during the Reformation era. Its first part deals with baptism, and the latter part states the theological position regarding such doctrines as original sin, adoption, God's Word, the

116

church, the Lord's Supper, and the faith of the fathers. This book was written between 1542 and 1547, and in later periods it has been given great consideration. Only three manuscripts are still available. Loserth had the book reprinted in 1929. This book was highly respected among the southern German Anabaptists for a long time, but later it disappeared when the Anabaptists had to withdraw from that area of Germany. It is true that references were made to it a few times by the Anabaptists in Moravia, but Marbeck was never an important name among them, as their chronicles indicate.

As has been often stated before, spiritual life was active in Strassburg, an important center of culture and communications, during the latter portion of the 1520's and the early portion of the 1530's. Unrest increased considerably when Melchior Hoffmann arrived in the city in the summer of 1529 and started proclaiming his chiliastic and apocalyptic ideas. Formerly, when Hoffmann had been active in Lutheranism, upon the recommendation of Luther he had ministered in the provinces along the Baltic Sea, and at one time even visited Stockholm, Sweden. Hoffmann was not at this time an Anabaptist, but he was a Lutheran with a bent toward mysticism. It was not until 1530 that he was baptized, and then he began to make inroads among the Anabaptists in northwest Germany and Holland with his chiliastic interpretations, of which more shall be said later. This is something of the background of the fanatical movement which ultimately degenerated into the radical catastrophe at Münster, representing a different type of movement from that principally discussed thus far.

When Hoffmann made his two visits to Strassburg in 1529, he was not at the head of his unique branch of the Anabaptist movement. His interpretations outlined visions and revelations, his apocalyptic program won adherents and caused great concern for Bucer and his co-workers. When Hoffmann returned to Strassburg in 1533 with the idea that the new kingdom of God was going to be established there, he was put in jail and remained there ten years—until his death. The Anabaptist movement increased in the city, and it seemed impossible even with imprisonment and banishment to eradicate the movement. As the death penalty was not employed against the Anabaptists, because there was a milder handling of these cases and because of the effective persuasion by the reformers, several Anabaptists were won back to the Reformed church. The reputation was abroad that Strassburg therefore was more successful in keeping the Anabaptist movement under control than other areas. In the early part of 1533, the council at Bern wrote to Strassburg to inquire concerning the means that were exercised to suppress the Anabaptists, for in Bern all restrictive measures had little effect. Strassburg answered that no special plan had been used, only that the Anabaptists had been permitted to remain in peace as long as they promised to be obedient in the external regulations and did not occupy themselves with baptism. The recalcitrant were, however, exiled.

The free church in Strassburg therefore was able to live on. At the Strassburg church synod in 1539, one of the central problems under consideration was how to combat the Anabaptist movement. The Genevan reformer, John Calvin, there pressed the campaign against the dreaded Anabaptists. Bucer also continued his struggle against the heretics, which is evident in his commentary on the Gospels. The Anabaptist congregation lived on, and in the year 1556 the church had about one hundred members. After this, the membership decreased until the emigration from Switzerland during the seventeenth century gave a boost to the entire Anabaptist movement in Alsace. It was not only in Strassburg that the Anabaptists fortified themselves but in other parts of the province as well. Through the persecutions the movement spread into the province, but there the Catholic Church was still in power and exerted heavier pressure on the Anabaptist heretics. Severe persecution took place. The edict of the emperor in 1528 and the order from the Diet of 1529 concerning the death penalty for Anabaptists was reissued by the authorities in 1561. In spite of this, at the close of the sixteenth century there were still some congregations remaining in the province.

The electorate Palatinate, which lies north of Strassburg in the Rhine Valley, also soon became aware of Anabaptism. In and around the cities of Landau, Heidelberg, and Worms the

Anabaptist movement was already in progress, as it was in other southern German cities. Anabaptists from Thuringia even migrated down to the Palatinate, and ministers came from the Anabaptist headquarters in the east, Nürnberg. Denck was active in Worms sometime after his expulsion from Strassburg, and it was here that he and Hetzer worked on their translation of the Old Testament prophetic writings.

In the beginning of 1528, Johannes Cochläus, from Frankfort on the Main, the prominent, forceful Catholic foe of Luther and all reformers, wrote to Erasmus and begged him to take action against the Anabaptists, because in the princely electorate the opinions of the council were divided so much that the judgment against the imprisoned Anabaptists dragged on. That represented a danger for the country because the Anabaptists were spreading out. Already eighteen thousand had come into Germany, reported Cochläus. Erasmus was not much impressed by Cochläus' plea for a polemical writing against the Anabaptists, for the great humanist never wrote the requested tract.

The Anabaptists could expect no greater mercy in this Catholic region than in other places, even if the death penalty were not immediately employed and even if the prince showed himself tolerant toward the cause of the Reformation. An edict was issued which referred to the emperor's edict of 1528, but the immediate actions were confined to imprisonment and persuasion, greater fines, and in some instances, banishment. In some places the prisons were filled with Anabaptists. Soon, however, the coercive philosophy of other places was adopted. Anabaptists had forfeited the right to live, and executions took place. Men were executed with the sword, women were drowned. Even those who repented were punished, and many were banished. Many of these refugees finally came to the free cities of Moravia. In the Moravian chronicle it is estimated that about 350 persons were executed in the Palatinate during this period. This number has been challenged by historians, for it was thought to be too high. From the examination of the records one can see that these Anabaptists were the same peaceful type as have been studied before. They seemed to have been acquainted with the seven articles of the Schleitheim Confession. Like believers in other places, they also contributed a number of hymns to the highly esteemed Anabaptist hymnbook *Ausbund*.

The deathblow against the Anabaptists in the Palatinate around 1530 seemed to check the movement for some time. After 1544, when the Lutheran church first became established, there appeared a succession of evangelical princes; and then the Anabaptists, who were early opponents of Catholicism, were granted a degree of liberty to carry on their work. It was during this period that the Hutterites in Moravia continually sent preachers to the Palatinate, and it was at this time that the emigration to Moravia increased. The situation was that the Lutheran electoral princes attempted to win back the Anabaptists to their church, and this should come about through teaching and discourses. But even strict regulations were laid upon the Anabaptists, and if this did not bring them around, then greater pressure would be exerted. In order to win the Anabaptists by peaceful methods, a religious colloquy was arranged in the vicinity of Worms in 1557. About forty Anabaptists took part, of whom nineteen were leaders of their respective congregations. The topics of discussion were baptism, magistracy, holding of civil offices, church discipline, taking oaths, and withdrawing from the national church. As usual, the opponents of the Anabaptists were declared victorious, and therefore they commanded that all Anabaptist leaders and strangers should immediately leave the territory of the Palatinate. In the meantime, the subjects of the electoral prince were warned to keep away from any Anabaptist discussion groups.

Some of the Lutheran theologians from near-by areas who took part in the discussion gathered at the close of the meetings at Worms and decided among themselves to recommend to their rulers that hard measures be exacted against the Anabaptists. They recommended the death penalty for those who refused to join the national evangelical church. This recommendation was published in 1557. Among the signers were Philipp Melanchthon, Johannes Brenz, Johannes Pistorious, and Jakob

Andreä. Andreä was active in the Württemberg reformation and the University of Tübingen. For decades he carried on an active campaign against the Anabaptists without specifically getting at their essential ideas. This was the situation, more or less, of all of the leading Lutheran theologians. Against this condemnation, the Anabaptists in Moravia published a larger defense document. This action confirmed the union between the Anabaptists in the Palatinate and the free church movement in Moravia.

To be sure, a sharply worded mandate from the prince followed the pronouncement from Worms, but the prince did not seem to think that the mandate should be taken seriously. After a number of years, the otherwise vigorously hunted Anabaptists were still to be seen in the land, as long as they remained quiet. The Anabaptists showed themselves in the Palatinate, as in other places, to be skilled craftsmen and enterprising people. The political tolerance continued under Prince Frederick III (1559–76), who led the country into the Calvinistic Camp. Calvin, his patron teacher, accordingly wanted him to subdue all of the Anabaptists, first by attempting to win them over to the Calvinistic point of view. When this did not work out, the prince had to resort to force. In this effort he was also encouraged by the imperial ambassador. The old history was repeated: imprisonment, banishment, confiscation of property. When the Anabaptists complained that they had no sufficient opportunity to present their case, the prince called a new religious convocation in Frankenthal in 1571. These meetings continued for three weeks, and fifteen Anabaptists attended from the Palatinate, the imperial cities of southern Germany, and Moravia. It is believed that even some delegates from Holland were in attendance.

This discussion in Frankenthal is probably the most remarkable occurrence in the German Anabaptist movement during the latter portion of the sixteenth century. One of the foremost Anabaptist men from Alsace, Diebold Winter, was one of the active debaters for his cause. The Anabaptists from the Palatinate were very hesitant about participating for fear of reprisals. Winter had also taken part in their earlier convocation of

121

1557, and he now declared his dissatisfaction with the minutes of that gathering which had been written. In the thirteen questions that were presented to the Anabaptists at the Frankenthal convocation, it was impossible to arrive at any unity. Instead, the party of power again claimed that it had won the theological debate. The great report of over seven hundred pages was immediately published and is a good resource for obtaining an understanding of the Anabaptists' opinions. A reprint edition was immediately published in Holland, and this indicates at this time the close connection between the Anabaptists of the Rhine Valley and Holland.

The electoral prince became ill-humored when he saw that his attempt at unity did not materialize, and it was apparent that there was no other recourse than the usual methods: banishment and confiscation of property for those who did not recant. Those that capitulated and went over to the Palatinate national church regained their property. Thus the policy of suppression was carried out. Yet at the close of the century there still were complaints about the presence of the Anabaptists. New edicts were announced, which emphasized such punishments as confiscation and banishment. The Moravian Anabaptists received the persecuted refugees and took them into their settlements, and in this way the Hutterite movement was strengthened considerably. Only a weak assemblage remained in the Palatinate by the time the Thirty Years' War scourged the nation.

In Hesse and Hesse-Nassau the Anabaptists made their entrance at the end of the 1520's. It was here that the energetic Melchior Rinck was a minister of the new ideas, and he won a good number of adherents. In the treatment of the Anabaptist movement in Thuringia some brief mention was made of the tolerant attitude in religious matters for which the landgrave, Philip of Hesse, was known. He maintained that only spiritual methods should be employed to convert the heretics to the right position, and he persistently refused to do as other Lutheran rulers in executing Anabaptists. However, other severe measures seemed necessary to him. Melchior Rinck had been a priest in Hersfeld, close to the Anabaptist settlements in the western part of the electorate of Saxony. In 1528 Rinck was converted to this new movement, and he developed a center for the Hessian Anabaptists around Hersfeld. Philip attempted by various means to win Rinck to the Lutheran church, but not even the Marburg professors could persuade him. He was therefore put in prison, to be banished in the spring of 1531. When Rinck later returned, he was soon apprehended and returned to jail, together with a number of delegates who had just attended a conventicle which he had held. It was in this connection that heavier forms of punishment were proclaimed against the Anabaptists in Hesse. Rinck was condemned to life imprisonment.

The landgrave Philip made one final serious attempt at reconciliation when he, in the fall of 1538, convened a religious conference between the Lutheran theologians and the imprisoned Anabaptists. The leading men among these Anabaptists were Georg Schnabel and Peter Tasch. Tasch had close association with England. Even Bucer in Strassburg had been invited, and he took part in his conciliating and clever manner. Something unusual took place here: the leading Anabaptists made an agreement to return to the Reformation church on the grounds that certain reforms would take place in the church. Among these reforms was the demand to instruct the children in the evangelical teachings, which led ultimately to the establishment of confirmation in the Lutheran church. The achievement of the churchmen implied also that the leading Anabaptists should work for a return of all their followers to the church. This plan succeeded in several instances, especially because Tasch was able and willing in this respect. It was Bucer who suggested this plan to the landgrave, and he followed the results with keen interest.

Through his wise and tolerant church policy, Philip of Hesse had actually obtained some results which were unique, but it did not result in a return to the church by the entire Anabaptist movement. A large number held fast to their convictions, and the landgrave wrote in a letter, in 1544, that he was of the opinion that the Anabaptists who would not return to the church, as Schnabel, Tasch, and others had done, should be exiled from the country. Many of the Anabaptists who were turned out of Hesse went to Moravia, and here is another meaningful connection with this protective asylum. In all of his efforts to build a unified Lutheran church in his territory, Philip never set aside his principles of refusing to employ the death penalty. Therefore, he could write in his will—he died the early part of 1567—that he had never condemned anyone to death on the grounds of holding to a faith which he did not recognize to be true. In his long period of rule he had, like many, the opportunity to take note of the failures in moral life among the people, even where the Reformation had succeeded, and he had appreciated those who worked toward a better manner of living.

Because of the stringent measures against the Anabaptists, the movement was curtailed in its expansion and opportunities. Only minor remnants remained until the time of the Thirty Years' War; then these too disappeared. The Hessian movement had played no little part in establishing and fortifying the Anabaptist activities in the electorate of Saxony, Moravia, and Holland.

Holland stands close to the center of Anabaptist activities in the western branch of the movement. In northwest Germany and Holland the movement had its own special characteristics and a long and remarkable history.

In Holland and the near-by territories the Anabaptist movement made a great impact from 1530 on. It was here that the movement obtained its special characteristic, and it was here that it later received a new name after the foremost leader, Menno Simons. The designation Mennonites came later to be transferred to Anabaptists in other countries. The movement in Holland distinguished itself in several respects from those movements considered thus far. For one thing, it exceeded all of the other Anabaptist movements in the number of adherents. In some portions of the country, no less than a fourth of the population were Mennonites. Because of this, the movement made a positive contribution to the culture of the nation, even though this was not marked at the beginning. Finally, it should be pointed out that the movement in Holland enjoyed some freedom due to the religious freedom of the country, especially after 1570. The early history of the movement in Holland was similar to that in other areas of Europe, including the difficult times of martyrdom. In the early period the movement was marked in its character by a strong eschatological influence, and it is no coincidence that from this apocalyptic segment there went the fanatical phalanx that established the new kingdom at Münster. This degeneration of the Anabaptist movement can be largely credited to the earlier apocalyptic prophecies and visions of Melchior Hoffmann, who was quite influential in this part of Europe.

It is believed that the earliest associations that the people in the Netherlands had with the Anabaptists was via Basel and the Dutch colony existing there. Erasmus Rotterdamus, living in Basel, had exercised an attraction over his fellow countrymen, and Basel was much like Strassburg, a gathering place as well as a thoroughfare for various representatives of cults and reform movements. The Anabaptist movement's advance northward in the Rhine Valley soon led to the Netherlands. One of the larger adjacent stations en route was Cologne. The associations between Holland and the movements in the Palatinate and Hesse have already been mentioned. During the late Middle Ages, Cologne was an important stronghold for free movements, including the Waldenses. The place was prepared. The official records of 1531 mention the presence of Anabaptists, and two years later an active ministry was in progress in Cologne. One of the Lutheran "spiritualists," the brother-in-law of Carlstadt, Gerhard Westerburg, came to Cologne. He had connections with the Anabaptists of Münster. The movement in the Catholic city Cologne was forcefully beaten down, but a segment of the peaceful Anabaptists seemed to have early assembled into a congregation, which was in the city when Menno Simons visited there during a two-year period, 1544–1546. In the decade of 1550 there was a large congregation in Cologne, but persecution became very severe. In 1558 the leader and the most important man in the congregation was imprisoned and executed. It was this same year that Menno Simons again came to Cologne, this time to reach an agreement over an important question with the brethren in southern Germany. This, however, did not work out. During the next decade several people were martyred, but the congregation lived on until it was completely devastated by the Catholic inquisition at the close of the century, 1599–1600. The Anabaptists in Holland, Switzerland, and southern Germany maintained a close association with the congregation in Cologne. In 1591 a large conference was held in this city among the Anabaptists from Holland and Germany.

Specifically, the work of the Anabaptists began in Holland in 1530 when a congregation was organized in Amsterdam under the leadership of Jan Volkerts Trijpmaker. He was one of the disciples of Melchior Hoffmann, and he was also affected by Hoffmann's eschatological speculations. Hoffmann was one of the Lutheran preachers who espoused the new ideas concerning the end of the world and the imminent return of Christ. Before Hoffmann started baptizing, he ministered in Holstein, which was subordinate to Denmark, and in Kiel, and East Friesland. He was zealous to dispute and expound the allegorical-mystical interpretation of the Scriptures, which won wide acceptance. He had no theological training; he was a furrier. Earlier when Hoffmann had visited Strassburg, which has already been mentioned, he was undoubtedly influenced by Anabaptist opinions there. Conversely, he must have won followers to his views from various groups of Anabaptists, especially concerning his visionary revelations and the imminent approach of the last days. In 1530 he accepted the new baptism, but for the greatest period of his ministry he was a Lutheran free preacher of the radical type.

In the summer of 1530 Hoffmann was in East Friesland and led a great revival. It was at this time that Luther began publicly to warn concerning him. In the city of Emden, Hoffmann won a large following. It was to this city that many Anabaptists fled from several sections. Hoffmann, it is learned, baptized three hundred persons at Emden, but he was soon constrained to leave the city. He then appointed the recently mentioned Trijpmaker as the preacher in Emden, but he, too, soon had to flee. Hoffmann broke even more with Luther and the Lutherans when he wrote his new opinions concerning the question of baptism. After some time, Hoffmann made his way to Holland and worked there about a year. This was the time of building the foundation of the Anabaptist work in Holland. Hoffmann even visited the congregation in Amsterdam, but he had to save himself and flee. Again he came to these territories, and at this time he came into contact with Jan Matthys, the one who would be the revolutionary in the Münster kingdom disturbance. These two came into conflict over the question of baptism, for when the rebaptized martyrs became numerous, Hoffmann thought it would be best to refrain from baptism. Later he even retracted his ideas about baptism and once again espoused the views of infant baptism. Besides this, Hoffmann seemed to have opposed the tendency to use violence, which Matthys and others had advocated and which had its tragic fulfilment in the Münster kingdom episode in 1535. Hoffmann now definitely stayed away from the use of weapons and encouraged obedience to authorities. Hoffmann disappeared from these territories after his trip to Strassburg in 1533. The primary significance of Hoffmann is that he for a short time was a connecting link between the southern and the northern Anabaptists.

The Anabaptist movement in Holland thus had a poor beginning, for the radical view of the imminent approach of the millennium had won too many adherents. Two men from Holland, Jan Matthys and Jan Beukelssen of Leiden, sought to set up the kingdom in Münster with the sword and violence, thereby departing far from the right way. There they attempted to have a compulsory church life, which was altogether foreign to the free church movement which has been traced thus far. When this fanatical enterprise in Münster was crushed with blood and totally uprooted, it caused much confusion in many places. Even in the Netherlands, in the spring of 1535, there were a few attempts to bring about a revolution with force, and the cause of the peaceful Anabaptists was rendered more difficult. During the same time, the movement had great difficulties because of a radical businessman, David Joris, who earlier had been a zealous exponent of reformation in his native city Delft. During the middle of the decade of 1530, Joris was baptized. He traveled much—he was also in Strassburg—and after the Münster catastrophe he felt that he was called to be a prophet. He was of a loose "spiritualistic" type, and he established a new party. The deathblow finally fell in 1538 when some of his family were executed, but he, together with some of his own, escaped. He remained in seclusion but spoke and wrote in behalf of his convictions. Finally, he escaped in 1544, traveling to the south, and emerged in Basel as a wealthy businessman with the assumed name of Johan of Brügge. There he was able to conceal his former activities and gain a position of social standing. But the "Jorisites" continued for a long time in Holland, Friesland, and Holstein.

After 1535 it was expected that hard persecution would come from Catholic rulers. It was the strict Catholic emperor, Charles V, who was the ruler of the land and who had from the beginning opposed every expression of the Reformation in the Netherlands, even during the Lutheran period. After the Münster catastrophe, there followed a brutal edict: Those who continued to hold on to their Anabaptist errors, those that baptized others or had served as leaders should be burned at the stake; those that had been rebaptized but had turned back or had given protection to Anabaptists should be executed, the men to be decapitated and the women drowned. Confiscation of property and banishment also took place. There was no discrimination made between those who held to the use of violence and the peaceful Anabaptists. At a meeting close to Haarlem there were thirty-two preachers; the great majority of these opposed all forms of force and espoused the original Anabaptist refusal to use the sword.

It seemed as if the brutal persecution by the Catholics would root out the movement in the Netherlands. It has been estimated that approximately 1,500 persons were put to death during the following decades, the last one in 1574. Mystic traditions from the late Middle Ages had survived in some parts of Holland, laying a good groundwork for the Anabaptist message and church polity. Emden in East Friesland was the starting point of the movement, and the work went on under the joint ministry of a number of the outstanding leaders in Holland after 1540.

In most of the cities in Holland the movement won a place, and in many instances it was able to remain in spite of the difficult persecution. Very early Amsterdam became the chief center of the movement. After the martyr's death of Trijp-maker in 1531, many difficulties arose, largely due to the radicals like Jan Matthys. Matthys was in Amsterdam, and he had a number of followers. Thirty soon suffered martyrdom. Finally, difficulties eventually vanquished the radicals, and the congregation was led on a sound course by Menno Simons, who visited there about 1542. In a few years several hundred persons were baptized, even though the risk was very great. When the city was taken over by William of Orange in 1578, the Anabaptist congregation, together with others, enjoyed religious freedom. From that day until the present, Amsterdam has been an important center for the Mennonites; located there are a place of higher learning, a library, and an archives collection.

Another active center for the Anabaptists was established at Leeuwarden, the capital of the province of Friesland. Hundreds were baptized in a few years in spite of the threat of death. It was here that two brothers lived, Obbe and Dirk Phillips, the former a doctor and the latter a Franciscan monk. Within a few years these two men were the leaders in the peaceful Anabaptist movement. Hoffmann had even won adherents in Leeuwarden, and the martyrdom of some had caused a great sensation. This was the factor that drew the two Phillips brothers to the movement. Their affiliation with the Anabaptists at this time does not imply that they accepted all of Hoffmann's fanatical writings and eschatology. Instead it can be concluded that these brothers became the real foundation of the sound Anabaptist movement in this area. The followers were also called "Obbenites" after the more prominent of the two brothers. This was before the term "Mennonite" became common. In order to separate themselves from the Anabaptists who had gained such an unsavory reputation because of the Münster disturbance, a group of the Anabaptists in Holland called themselves by the term "Baptism-minded" (*Doopsgezinden*) .[1]

Obbe Phillips wrote a book in which he described the difficulties as well as the progress which he and his brother experienced trying to establish the movement. Even Menno Simons a little later related some of the same things. It does not seem that Obbe Phillips remained very long the leader of this work. About 1540 Obbe gave up and left the catacomb congregation which he had built up. His brother, Dirk, and the most important elder or bishop, Menno Simons, took up the work in earnest. Dirk Phillips made long trips in northern Germany and visited congregations and Anabaptist groups there. He remained a long time as the Anabaptist leader in Danzig and ministered to the growing free church movement in the entire Vistula territory. He died in 1568.

It was, however, Menno Simons' introduction into this movement which marked the beginning of a new epoch. It was primarily Menno's spirited ability as an author which gave this branch of the free church movement great stability. He was a theological teacher and a richly endowed leader who should be placed beside such men as Hübmaier, Hutter, Riedemann, and Marbeck. He surpassed all of these men in that his influence has remained continually within the tradition of a denomination until the present day. To be sure, the free church movement was already in progress with a ten-year martyrology when Menno Simons appeared on the scene, but none the less, he became the pioneer of the peaceful branch of the Anabaptist movement in Holland and accompanying territories. He was able to bear up under persecution and for twenty-five years worked untiringly for his concept of the truth and the church. This lengthy service was very unusual, especially in a time when death was always lurking for the Anabaptists and in particular for their leaders. Most of the Anabaptist leaders were only able to work a few months or years for the cause of the free church movement.

---

[1] This term is difficult to translate into English. Another name often used for the Mennonites in Holland was *Doopers*. This is equivalent to the German word *Täufer* (Baptizers or Baptists) , which was in general use in Germany.

It is believed that Menno Simons was forty years old when, as a Catholic priest in his home province of Friesland, he came in contact with the upsurging movement of Anabaptism. Early in the decade of the 1520's some Reformation literature had come into his hands, and he began to doubt the transformation that was said to take place in the Mass. The execution of an Anabaptist in 1531 also compelled him to make a closer study of the baptismal question, and even at this point his Catholic convictions began to waver. In the beginning, Menno Simons preached against the Anabaptists. This is easy to understand, for at that time the only type of Anabaptism he knew was that which was represented by Hoffmann's radicalism. In the meantime, he explained, he was disturbed over the demand that the Brotherhood expected a complete, separated life. But he took the step—he accepted the new baptism administered by Obbe Phillips in 1535, or at the beginning of 1536.

Menno's own brother joined the Anabaptist group that believed in force, and consequently he lost his life close to the birthplace of Menno, in Witmarsum. It was in this city that Menno Simons served as priest, so this incident gripped him deeply. He decided to take those who had been led astray and direct the movement back into a sane path. He warned and admonished; he published a booklet opposing Jan of Leiden, which was the first of a long series of theological books. When he renounced his well-remunerated position, Menno Simons married and then he started his life of dangerous travels. For a period at the beginning he remained in seclusion, perhaps in East Friesland, to study the Bible and write. He received many urgent invitations to become the pastor or the presiding bishop among the Brethren, and in January, 1537, in Groningen, Menno Simons was set apart to be an elder or bishop by Obbe Phillips. These original designations of the leaders in the congregations were used in the Anabaptist movement.

Not much is known about the travels of Menno Simons. He had to move in the deepest secrecy, and his meetings with the Brethren were held in the woods, in barns, and in remote farmyards, often at nighttime. The new martyrs' songs were sung, Menno Simons preached and instructed, baptism was conducted, and the Lord's Supper was observed. These underground revival movements were filled with dramatic episodes, and through all of it Menno Simons was able to slip through the snare of the persecutors. Mention has already been made of the fact that Simons visited Amsterdam and that he ministered for a period in Cologne in the middle of the 1540's. A price for the imprisonment of Simons was set by the emperor, and those that took the evangelist into their homes were threatened with the death penalty. He also remained for a period at Wismar, and he made trips along the coast of the Baltic Sea, even as far as Danzig and the territories of West Prussia. This was the time when there was a large-scale emigration of Hollanders. In the decade of the 1550's he made trips to Cologne to consider and discuss the points of difference among the Brethren. Important Anabaptist conferences were held in Lübeck and Wismar. However, it appears that he resided mainly in Holstein, because here he was protected and found refuge on an estate, Wüstenfelde. A printing press was available, and consequently many of Simons' books were sent out from there. Here Menno Simons died in the year 1561.

The latter years of Menno Simons were darkened by the inner dissensions within his movement. Simons maintained a strict point of view in regard to church discipline, and this problem was the basis of many difficulties which led to correspondence and deliberations. In matters of doctrine he disagreed on a few points with other Anabaptists—for example the doctrine concerning the humanity of Jesus. In opposition to the mystics, he demanded an organized congregation which practiced church discipline and recognition of the authority of the Bible above that of the "inner word." He opposed the practice of community of goods, but he also strongly emphasized the need of mutual assistance. He was also opposed to taking an oath, and he dismissed the doctrine of predestination as held by the Swiss reformers. He was positive in his attitude toward a "Christian government," and with the exception of Hübmaier's followers, he did not go as far as the earlier Anabaptists in repudiating the sword or the magistracy. He strove for truth and religious freedom. There is no opportunity here to analyze the many writings of Menno Simons. They have meant much to the Mennonites throughout the years, and they have been translated into both German and English.

At least two other names should be mentioned in the Dutch movement, men who were active in the latter portion of the sixteenth century. One is Leonard Bouwens and the other is Hans de Ries. The former was ordained to the ministry in 1546 and became an elder or bishop five years later. He was undoubtedly the most successful of all the preachers. He recorded that he baptized no less than 10,378 persons in 142 different places. He was also an ambitious traveler. He died in Hoorn, Holland, in 1582. Hans de Ries was one of the second-generation men, baptized and ordained to the ministry in 1577, but because he made his major contributions to the cause of the movement before the close of the sixteenth century, he bears mention in this connection. He was the important man of the "Waterlanders," and he ministered in various places in Holland and northwest Germany, particularly in Middelburg where the English refugees resided. He lived until 1638. During the decade of 1590 he was the leader of the congregation in Emden, East Friesland. He was also at home in the art of medical science. He was the author of several books, one of which was a doctrinal statement containing forty articles. In this statement he collaborated with one of his close friends, Lubbert Gerrits. He edited a well-known hymnbook for his friends in the faith. Finally, one more name should be mentioned, Peter Janz Twisck (d. 1636), who was bishop of the Friesian congregation in Hoorn. He wrote a confession consisting of thirty-three articles which was published about 1600.

The study of the Bible was central among the Mennonites, and it is not surprising that they made their own Bible translation. The entire Bible was published in 1560, and this indicates that there were scholarly adherents who were well acquainted with Latin, Greek, and Hebrew. This Dutch Bible appeared in thirty editions from 1562 to 1600. Among the theological writings, which were available to, and accepted by, most of the Mennonites, were the books of Menno Simons and Dirk Phillips.

This movement in Holland was able to withstand all of the difficulties, and at the end of the Reformation century it had a well-organized group of many congregations. The freedom which was made possible through the new regime of William of Orange during the period of the 1570's increased the possibilities of an effective ministry. In no other country, Catholic or Protestant, did the "sects" have such a recognized position, because elsewhere severe measures of punishment were employed in order to bring about a uniform state or national church. But within the various groups of the Mennonites there arose disputes and cleavages, which as always hampered and harmed the work. Similar occurrences within the history of the free church led to a weakening of the movement in Holland and the accompanying areas.

The foremost cause of strife was discipline. One group opposed the strict discipline which was proposed by Menno Simons, Dirk Phillips, and Bouwens, and they were reluctant to place a formulated confession of faith alongside of the Bible. They also thought that the elder or bishop had received too much authority in the congregation. This free-minded group was called "Waterlanders," named after the place from which this opposition arose, Waterland. They called themselves "the baptism-minded." This separation took place during the decade of 1550. At the same time, it also became clear at a conference in Strassburg that there was a break between the west German and Dutch Anabaptists. Other divisions followed in Holland, and the weakness in the zealous advocacy of individualism was revealed to all. Several times Mennonites met to discuss unity, as they themselves recognized the problems in their schisms. But as always, it is easy to divide but difficult to unite.

The Free Church in England Late in the Sixteenth Century

All of the reformation churches began as minority groups within the established Roman Catholic Church institution. Even Luther's, Zwingli's, Calvin's, and Cranmer's churches, which soon became state or national churches, had their origin in small opposition groups. However, when these churches became the dominant church in their respective countries, they no longer tolerated the assembly of independent groups or the preaching ministry of independent persons.

This was the condition in England during the time of Henry VIII and his Tudor successors. During the reign of Henry VIII, uniformity was maintained by means of repressive compulsion, but during the reign of the young successor, Edward VI (1547–1553), there were increased possibilities for a more thorough reformation of the English church, as well as a greater amount of freedom for individuals with other religious affiliations. Religious refugees even came from the Continent. During Mary's bloody and brutal policy of reconversion to papal leadership, 1553–1558, many Protestants fled to other countries, particularly to Holland and Scotland, and even to Switzerland. These refugees came to have great importance in the future church development in England. Many staunch Protestants remained in England and started to conduct conventicles in secret, conducting their own worship services.

During Elizabeth's long rule, 1558–1603, the Anglican state church was established, and compulsory uniformity in religion once again became the practice. The young queen was sharply opposed by the pope and the entire Catholic Church, primarily since the pope maintained that Elizabeth was illegitimate because she was a child of the unlawful union of Henry VIII with Anne Boleyn. According to the pope, Henry had never obtained a legal divorce from Catherine of Aragon. As the queen struggled for the Anglican church and against the Roman, she had to vindicate herself and her throne. The danger was not over until the Spanish Armada was destroyed in 1588.

Under the leadership of Elizabeth, the English national church was established. In the meantime, the queen not only had opposition from Rome and the native Catholics to contend with but there were also dissatisfied men from the other wing of the Reformation. These were the men who during the Marian reign had gone to the Continent for security. Some of these men in Switzerland and Holland were strong in their Protestant zeal against Romanism. They had received a taste of both Calvin's theology and his order of society. They had learned that the altar and vestments were an abomination, that the episcopate was a Roman innovation. They believed that theology ought to be corrected according to the great Genevan reformer's dogmatic work, the *Institutes*. Even a number of the new bishops had sympathy with these radical Protestants, and if they tolerated the Prayer Book, it was only because they hoped for an early revision. The new generation of ministers in England had, to a degree, been educated in this type of spirit. Calvin's *Institutes* was the standard work of theology even for the men of the English reformation. The theological textbooks from the Middle Ages had been laid aside, and no one within England had, up to this time, written any theological work of any great significance. The only volume which was known, which gave a clear and consistent theological system, was Calvin's popular work. Thus it was that the *Institutes* came to be within a few decades the recognized theological textbook in the universities of England. During half a century it formed the theological opinion of the new English ministry. This is an important fact that must be kept in mind, especially when those in Germany and Sweden at the close of the seventeenth century and later counted the English church with the Reformed. This was not incorrect, as the Anglo-Catholics of later periods have claimed.

The radical stream also received support from the remnants of the old Lollard revival, especially when the radicals directed their attacks against the Church liturgy, demanding its revision. This group came to be known by the historic name "Puritan." This movement reached out across the land against Rome; especially among groups of laymen anything was detestable that was associated with Rome. Every place where there was some evidence of popery there was conflict. Men were encouraged in this revolutionary attitude from places outside of England, especially Geneva. Associated with this radical stream was a tie with the democratic and parliamentary freedom which directly opposed the absolutism of the princes and the aristocrats, which was especially obvious during the seventeenth century.

Against this Puritanism, there stood from the very beginning a more conservative segment within the reformed Elizabethan church, which wanted to hold to those traditions and customs that could not be considered contrary to the reformation which had already taken place. The new archbishop, Matthew Parker, (1559–1575) was predisposed to this conservative position, and he had several within the episcopate who sided with him, and foremost he had the support of the queen. The leaders of the church had to try to steer between Rome and Geneva, and it soon was going to be evident that when Rome was clearly rejected, the question regarding Geneva was going to be more serious. The more Catholicism pressed its demands, the more irreconcilable grew the Puritan opposition. The moderate men of the Reformation, such as Archbishop Parker, had a difficult time in remaining neutral. Many of the bishops had active associations, if not with Geneva and Beza (d. 1605), then with Zürich and Bullinger (d. 1575). The latter reformer was more cautious with regard to the established and traditional forms in England, while Beza stirred up the radical Puritans. These Puritans had a distinct advantage, partly because of the previously mentioned influence of Calvin's *Institutes* and partly because of the fact that they had been the most clear-cut opponents of Romanism in a time when Rome was threatening the nation.

The Puritan opposition within the remodeled Anglican church directed its attention primarily against the clerical vestments and the details of liturgy. During the decade of 1560 this characteristic of the Reformed churches was the main question. The demand for a simplification of the worship services was based upon the Bible, which for this group was the decisive factor both for the cult and the order. These radical Protestants repudiated much which the revised Prayer Book prescribed, such as bowing the knee at the observance of communion, the sign of the cross at baptism, certain practices at marriage services, and, above everything else, the altar robes. The Puritan preachers, *i.e.* the radicals, did not use the prescribed altar robes, definitely opposing such attire. Other Puritans accommodated themselves to the State Church when the archbishop gave in on a few points. These individuals became the Conformists and were the largest group among the Puri-

tans. The former ministers, who definitely rejected these ac-
commodations within the Church, were called "Nonconformists," a term that later came to be synonymous with dissenters
and free churches. The Nonconformist Puritans led the battle
within the world of English Protestantism, which later was
filled with much dramatic action, and it divided the national
church from its very beginning into two important divisions:
the Church of England and Nonconformity. From the beginning of the decade of 1560 until 1689, this was a conflict of
great significance. At times there were periods of intense outbursts, and at other times the Nonconformists were suppressed
as an underground movement.

Radical Puritanism was for Elizabeth an unacceptable phenomenon. Her Renaissance interest led her to detest those
who zealously reacted against church music, paintings, sculp-
ture, and beautiful stained glass windows as something evil and
dangerous. Elizabeth's political calculations were also disturbed
by the radicalism which threatened to break sharply with tradition. If reform should become too radical, Romanism might
gain support because of the accepted conservatism of the large
masses of people. As did Luther before her, Elizabeth feared
that the entire cause of the Reformation would be compromised
by some radicals. Consequently, she took measures to stave off
the influence and the work of the Puritans. Because of the great
amount of arbitrariness on the part of the established leaders
and irregularities within the religious order, there was growing degeneracy of the church system. Much of this was the
result of the fact that there were few suitable recruits for the
clergy. The disorder, however, which threatened the worship of
the church, was increased by the radical Puritans. Many of
these ministers preferred dismissal rather than submit to a
form of worship of which they disapproved. Many ministers
were discharged from their office. When the Nonconformists
began to conduct meetings outside of the church, police measures were taken against them. Hundreds were imprisoned. The
campaign against the unlawful gatherings of Nonconformists
in England now began. The role of the conventicles in the
Protestant world has a long history. It gradually became evi-

dent that even during the period of the 1560's this movement of piety was winning adherents from the highest stratas of life, both from the court and the clergy. In this latter group there were many Puritans of a milder type who thought that these severe measures imposed upon the radicals were inappropriate. At times it appeared as if these Puritans might be able to win control, but the Queen's determined attitude and orders hindered this action.

At the close of the 1560's, Rome again became a serious threat for Elizabeth. This situation considerably promoted the cause of the radical Puritans. The uprising in northern England for the benefit of Mary Stuart and the advance of the Duke of Alva in the Netherlands were indications of anticipated events. When the pope's interdict and the bull of excommunication of 1570 was published, Elizabeth realized she would need all of the strength she could command to oppose Rome. She was also aware of the fact that those who were most bitterly opposed to Rome were the radical Puritans, who now would have to stand by as reliable auxiliary troops. This fact was a boon to the Puritan movement. However, this advantage was neutralized somewhat in that the conflict with Rome also brought about a drastic demand for religious conformity. Primarily intended to stifle the Catholic remnant, this also struck at all types of nonconformity.

Gradually there was a change in the Puritans' position. From the beginning of the 1570's the matters of church order became acute. In the meantime, details pertaining to liturgy became less important, at least as far as an open struggle was concerned. One of the Puritans began to be occupied with the structure of church organization as found in the book of Acts. He was a professor at Cambridge, Thomas Cartwright, who in his lectures on the book of Acts raised the question regarding the position of elders in the congregation. According to his studies, he demanded that all ministers be on an equal level; he could find no graduated organization of hierarchies in the New Testament. Further, the congregations should be led by elders and pastors. In this way Presbyterianism began to develop in England. Church administration and discipline now became imperative. Episcopal church administration was now being threatened all the more because the church in Scotland had at this time accepted the Calvinism of John Knox. From the north there came strong influences to aid the cause of Puritanism. The conflict broke out into the open when Cartwright showed himself to be a zealous promoter of Puritan ideas. He was removed as a professor and banished from the university. In the meantime, Puritanism had gained a hold in the Parliament, and Cartwright and his friends were now able to gain a closer relationship with these groups. Cartwright, because of a booklet he published in 1573, became the theoretical father of English Presbyterianism, and within a few years there were attempts to establish his ideas within the framework of the existing church system. The consistent Calvinists could not adapt themselves to an order of bishops nor to Roman Catholic forms of worship. Calvinism and Episcopalianism are basically incompatible, even if in some instances they have been tried out together. Privately, English Puritans began to organize classes and synods. In this way the Presbyterian church started in England, and its supporters hoped that it would eventually become the dominant church.

There were even a few Anglican bishops who were sympathetic with the Puritan conventicles and the Presbyterian polity as a means of reaching the people and extending responsibility within the church. After Archbishop Parker died in 1575, a person sympathetic to Presbyterianism, Edmund Grindal (1576–1583), was appointed to the chair at Canterbury. Grindal was one of the Marian refugees who became a Calvinist when he was on the Continent. However, as Bishop of London, and later as Archbishop of York, Grindal had outwardly tapered his opinions to be conformable to the Anglican establishment. When Grindal became Archbishop of Canterbury, he appeared to be bent on patronizing Puritanism, so much so that he took it upon himself to point out to Elizabeth which direction she ought to take in church policies. It was evident, however, that the queen had her own definite opinions on these matters. Shortly thereafter, in 1577, the archbishop was relieved from official duties, and consequently his influence was immaterial in the church. Elizabeth expected that the bishops would suppress the assemblies and organizations which were leading to separatism. After the disposal of Grindal, the queen acted against the conventicles. During the period of the 1580's, Rome and Spain threatened England, and this situation gave rise to a new wave of Protestant enthusiasm over the nation. It has been stated that Puritanism now was able to gain some real advantages.

It should be pointed out, however, there was no great opportunity for expansion among the Puritans at this time, for after the death of Grindal there came to the archbishopric in Canterbury a straight-laced Episcopalian whose love of pomp and position was diametrically opposed to plainness and simplicity of the Puritans. He was John Whitgift. Whitgift was also Calvinistic in his theological dispositions. He satisfied Elizabeth, who was influenced by the Renaissance and was convinced that neither a deviation from the Prayer Book nor a Presbyterian system could be advantageous for her kingdom. She consistently maintained her anti-Puritan course, even though she had to make temporary adjustments due to the conflict with Rome. Whitgift was not slow in doing the bidding of the queen. Earlier, as chancellor in Cambridge, he had denounced the errors of Cartwright, and as Archbishop of Canterbury he was firm in his opposition to Cartwright and his co-religionists. Parliament was subjected to pressure by the anti-Puritan policies of the archbishop and queen. When an effort was made in Parliament, in the middle of the 1580's, to introduce the Presbyterian church system, Elizabeth and Whitgift both worked against it.

At the close of the 1580 period, aggressive Puritanism began to lose its influence among the people. Meanwhile the danger from Rome had been averted. The Puritans endangered their cause by publishing some libelous tracts, causing the queen and the archbishop to take sterner measures against the movement. The five years following the defeat of the Spanish Armada in 1588 were difficult for the Nonconformists. Many were imprisoned; some were executed. Cartwright was imprisoned, but he escaped and made his way to Holland, where he became a preacher in the Mercantile church in Middelburg. Parliament received a request from Elizabeth to take up measures against the Nonconformists. One law that was passed made it clear that all who would not conform, or those who attended the prohibited assemblies, would be banished from the realm. Scores of people returned to the regular program of the state church, but in their soul and heart they continued to be Puritans, merely biding their time. Many others, who were eager for a free order, chose to escape from the country; on the Continent they established free churches.

It was at this time that the radical free church movement increased. This movement went farther than Cartwright. It was nothing new. The communications with Holland had brought results. Between these two nations there existed an intimate relationship because of the well-traveled sea lanes and because of the commercial exchange. It is known that small groups of Anabaptists came over to England even during the reign of Henry VIII. This is ascertained from the restrictive actions which were taken at that time. In 1534 an edict from the king was announced which opposed these Anabaptist strangers, and the impression is given that they were a sizable number. The year following, twenty-five Anabaptists from Holland were tried in London. They were condemned to die at the stake. At the same time, there were other similar measures taken in an effort to exterminate these foreigners—and thus it continued.

At an Anabaptist conference in Bocholt, Westphalia, in the year 1536, two Hollanders from England participated. The conference expenses were underwritten by an Englishman. Relations between England and the Continent were lively from other points of view, and in some respects they reflected similar problems. For example, when Cochläus wrote to Erasmus in 1528 asking him to write a pamphlet against the Anabaptists, he also explained that he was going to ask John Fisher, the English bishop and a good friend of Erasmus, to do the same. The baptismal question was thus early considered among the English churchmen. The Hessian Anabaptist preacher Peter Tasch was mentioned for his connections with England. There

142

is a record of a letter from this period which relates how Tasch communicated with his friends in the faith in Germany about the Anabaptist progress in England. When this letter was uncovered in an investigation in 1538, Philip of Hesse joined with the electoral prince of Saxony to write to the king of England to make him aware of the widespread growth of this dangerous movement in his kingdom. Even Luther and Melanchthon were aware of the situation. Melanchthon was charged with the responsibility of writing a letter to the king of England, which he did. He wrote about the "Anabaptist pest" in the districts where the pure doctrine was not clearly proclaimed. In England, Henry VIII and his chancellor, Thomas Cromwell, immediately set about to break these "stiff-necked rebaptizers."

Menno Simons personally had been in contact with the English refugees, particularly during his stay at Wismar, when large numbers fled there in 1553 during Queen Mary's Catholic reaction. Refugees came continuously to Holland, and they became acquainted with the Dutch Anabaptists. John á Lasco, the friend of reform in Poland who in the 1540's organized the Reformed church in East Friesland, was also in close contact with them. As a national church leader, he then opposed the movement. In 1550 á Lasco went to London. Refugees from Holland to England increased, due to the furious regimentation of the Duke of Alva in the Netherlands during the 1560's.

During the time of Elizabeth many Anabaptists were found in England. During the 1570's a large number of them were imprisoned, most of them from Holland. Eleven were sentenced to die, two were burned at the stake, others were banished. The immigration of Anabaptists into England during the sixteenth century is confirmed by the many edicts and legal measures drawn up against them. The many writings of refutation, designed to warn the people of the Anabaptists, also give witness to the fact that England dreaded their influence. That these free groups had an influence on the separatist viewpoint among the Puritans is self-evident, and it must have been due to this that the discussion about baptism became current in the

Puritan fermenting period in England at the close of the century. The lively exchange of refugees in the realms on either side of the Channel implies a reciprocal influence, which naturally is not recorded in the minutes nor preserved in the documents, but by analogy with similar phenomena must be regarded as a historical fact.

Other foreign churches also arose. Conventicles and groups emphasizing freedom in worship advanced even during the time of Bloody Mary, and later these groups became powerful fermenting agents within the life of the English church. The Foreigner's church, which John á Lasco established in London in 1551, was accordingly organized on a voluntary basis and was a free church in the essential idea of this term. Á Lasco began to make use of "prophesyings" (cf. 1 Cor. 14:31), which soon developed into conventicles among the Puritans. To be sure, this church disappeared during the time of Mary's Catholic reaction, but it became a pattern for later free churches. Such congregations remained independent with separate existence parallel with the revived English Catholic Church. Apparently there were other emigrant congregations as well. Mention is made of a group which came out of Scottish Presbyterianism in 1566 and later developed into a Congregational church. A few free churches in London at the close of the 1560's were dispersed because of persecution.

These foreign congregations, as well as conventicle groups among the English, arose out of necessity, and they did not always build on the principles of the free church concepts, such as the Anabaptists did. In the struggle of Calvinistic Puritanism against uniformity and the high church ideas there also lay a tendency toward separatism. The dealings with Cartwright and his striving for Presbyterianism unleashed the radical powers. Now the question was not basically over the liturgy and vestments but the administration of the church and the order of the congregation. Therefore, it was not altogether a surprise when Congregationalism appeared in the 1580's.

The man behind this Congregational free church concept was Robert Browne. At about the age of thirty, together with a friend in the faith, he founded a voluntary congregation in

Norwich. During his studies at Cambridge, Browne had listened to Cartwright, who was there for a short period as a theology professor. When Browne was graduated, he became an assistant to a Puritan clergyman for a brief period, and thus his interest in the Nonconformist movement increased. In Norwich at this time there was a group of Anabaptists from Holland, and it is evident that Browne learned about their doctrine concerning the church. Consequently, Browne came to a congregational point of view, which resulted in the organization of a church in Norwich in 1581. The church of believers ("gathered church"), according to Browne, was to be autonomous, following the pattern of the New Testament. The members of this free church united themselves together in a solemn vow and covenant in the presence of God, a custom which became characteristic of the separatist Puritans, both in England and in North America. Such a "contract," signed by the believers, was also used by the Anabaptists. Browne became the pastor of the congregation, and he spent much time in traveling, spreading his particular ideas. In this way the first free church practicing infant baptism emerged in the post-Reformation period. Browne's activity, of course, led to his arrest and stay in prison. When the congregation in Norwich had hard opposition, the majority of the members emigrated, and as for many others, Holland became the new homeland. Settling in Middelburg, these members were followed by Browne in 1582. Here he was again influenced by the Anabaptists; here he devoted himself to writing. Because of conflict within the congregation, Browne left. The church remained for only ten years.

Browne, however, did not become the great pioneer for Congregationalism. His separation ideas were not established on clear principles; consequently, he soon left the way of separatism. Browne went to Scotland, and here he even had to experience imprisonment. Soon after he returned to England he surrendered to the Archbishop of Canterbury in 1585 and was once again received as a priest in the Anglican church. He lived until 1633 a life filled with many varied experiences. However, the Brownists became rather numerous, even though there were not many separatist congregations.

Henry Barrow was more consistent than Browne in his struggle to establish a free church. He, too, was a Cambridge man; however, he studied law. He soon came into contact with the Puritan preacher John Greenwood, who conducted conventicles within the church. Barrow led the movement into the separatist position, and in 1586 this forbidden assembly was discovered close to St. Paul's Cathedral in London. Greenwood was put in prison, but Barrow, who was not present when the raid was made, was able to be at liberty for about a month. During the time of imprisonment, Barrow wrote several significant pieces of literature in which he presented the principal lessons concerning the free church, which he championed. He was fortunate to be able to smuggle the manuscripts out of the prison. Later these writings were printed by his friends in Holland. Here again is another clear testimony of the close association between those on either side of the Channel.

At the several hearings, both Greenwood and Barrow frankly aired their criticism concerning the prelates and the state church. Their time had run out; Greenwood and Barrow were sent to the gallows in 1593. The same punishment was meted out to another separatist during this same time, John Penry, who had been careless and printed some fiercely anticlerical pamphlets, such as the Martin Marprelate tracts. He was also accused of having written these tracts. Even for many of the Congregational adherents his witticism and satire was offensive.

Barrow had laid a basis, however, that stood. In 1589 he set forth the principles of his free church concept in a book, *A True Description*. In the very beginning of this book, he established this fact: Conformity should not be demanded in any form by the state church. The church should never be associated with the state, nor should the state have anything to do with the affairs of religion. The state should attend to secular matters, but the citizen's conscience should be left alone. In the second place, there ought not to be a centrally controlled and authoritative free church that attempts to create uniformity. Every independent congregation should be of equal status. The New Testament *ecclēsia* shows that devotion, doctrine, and practice should be autonomous. Certainly congrega-

146

tions could voluntarily associate in common tasks and fellowship, but in this fellowship there is no church authority that can take charge and direct the free churches. Furthermore, Barrow emphatically stated that in each autonomous free church all of the members are granted equal rights. The pastors have no special positions in the church, but they serve as they are fitted for the task. Laymen may also attend to all of the religious functions in the church, even the interpretation of the Scriptures.

Also remarkable for Barrow and his followers was the radical dismissal of the rigid liturgical forms. No formulated or authorized prayers were to be used. Bible study and voluntary prayers in the conventicles, together with a radical simplification of the ordinances of baptism and the Lord's Supper, were identification marks of these free congregations. The Barrowists, like the Brownists, practiced infant baptism.

It is obvious that this radical free church must have irritated the Anglican bishops and the despotic queen who demanded submission to the church regulations which had been established by law. The Barrowist movement, in spite of everything, continued. Several similar congregations could be traced which consistently followed out the separatist tendencies within Puritanism. The leadership in Barrow's congregation in London was taken over by another man of importance, Francis Johnson. He, too, had studied at Cambridge University, where so many separatists had been stimulated. After having been in prison several times, Johnson left England, and in 1590 he lived in Middelburg, Holland, serving as the pastor of the Mercantile church. At this time Johnson was still Presbyterian in his opinions, rejecting the writings of Barrow in Holland. These writings did make a deep impression, however, for when Johnson returned to London, he visited Barrow in prison. Later, in 1592, Johnson became the pastor of the Barrow congregation. Johnson and his church suffered persecution. He was imprisoned until 1597, after which he followed his congregation, which earlier had emigrated to Holland, settling first in Campen, then in Naarden, and finally in Amsterdam.

Both Presbyterian and Congregational Puritanism seemed

147

at this time to be nearly exhausted in England. The coercive enactments of 1593 were neither ambiguous nor flexible. They required that anyone who refused to attend the worship services of the prevailing state church, or by word or writing encouraged another person to do so, or who participated in some other worship service, should be put in prison and kept there until submission. If after three months imprisonment such culprits did not repent, they should be exiled, lose all their possessions and their citizenship. They would be forever shut out from all of the territories of Britain. If such a one should get back to England without proper permission, he would be threatened with the death penalty of a traitor. This draconic decree was even in force when the great Puritan exodus began in the beginning of the 1630's. After the end of the sixteenth century there was no alternative in England for those who were convinced in their faith of separatism and the free church. They could either flee as refugees or suffer marytrs' deaths.

Church life in England at the beginning of the seventeenth century was very complicated. Anglicanism had started to find its way in formulating theological convictions. The foremost leader in this respect was Richard Hooker, whose celebrated work appeared during the 1590's. Hooker had been in debate with the Puritans while he was at Oxford, and this engagement had settled his theological convictions. Another leading theologian was Richard Bancroft, who later (1604–1610) became Archbishop of Canterbury. Before he became archbishop, Bancroft had battled with the Puritans and laid the foundation of the Anglican high church theology. The basic kernel of this theology was the doctrine of the divine origin of the existing episcopate. The Anglican theologians were gradually abandoning Calvinism, which had been the controlling concept in the universities. This situation made the cleavage with the Puritans even deeper. The Anglican high church became more and more theologically independent and self-confident. More and more it opposed Puritanism within the church, and even much more opposed the Puritan Presbyterianism which was propagated by Cartwright and others. The conflict against separatist Congregationalism was especially severe. The Anglican theologians also had to be on the watch for a crypto-Catholicism, which in defiance of all that had occurred was still in force in some areas. When Queen Elizabeth died in 1603, church uniformity had been established; but behind the solid façade of the Anglican state church were many serious problems.

Evaluation of the Sixteenth-Century Free Church Movement

This chapter has sought to trace the development of the peaceful, biblical free church and the leading personalities in this movement. That phase of the movement referred to as "spiritual" or "mystical" has only been mentioned occasionally, as has the eccentric, revoluntionary parties. These groups lie outside of the defined borders of the free church movement presented in these pages.

The one-sided, severe criticism of the peaceful branch of the Anabaptist movement has depended to a certain extent on confusion between the revolutionary groups within the Lutheran Reformation—such as the Zwickau prophets and their followers—and the free church movement which broke out of Zwinglianism. This attitude was dependent also upon the fact that Anabaptist teaching regarding baptism shook the foundations under all the established churches, which existed on the inherited mode of infant baptism. The Anabaptist doctrines were a threat both to the Catholic Church and to the Protestant state and national churches. The latter group of churches were aiming at a closely knit religious uniformity, which was supported by the princes and the government because of their interest in political unity. By the means of laws and prosecution, this enforced uniformity made progress. Furthermore, the Protestant princes and estates feared that the Reformation might be compromised, giving the Catholic reactionaries opportunity to regain power. This explains the simultaneous oppression of the Anabaptists and other free church movements and the brutal attempts to uproot them. These persecutory measures can never be defended. From Protestantism it would be expected that there would be something other than this inconsiderate trampling down of the free conscience and contempt for the lives of individuals.

In the meantime, no attempt is made here to prove that the peaceful free church movement is beyond the scope of criticism. On the contrary, it is comparatively easy to point out weak points in Anabaptist doctrines and ministry. First of all, it should be asked: Did the Anabaptists have any real understanding of the historical situation? Did they ever at any time try to view the situation from the other side; in other words, did they ever consider what might have happened if the entire leadership of the Reformation—Zwingli, Luther, Calvin, and their associates—had forsaken all consequences to advocate the way of the free church? If this had been the case, it is certain that in many places the civil authorities would never have united with the Reformers to advance the new order. Consequently, the old Church system would have retained controlling power. The Anabaptist leaders perhaps should have considered their movement as a complement to the national church Reformation, but this was not easy when they were threatened and hunted as destructive devils who were subverting the gospel and the true church and considered a danger to society.

Another question can be asked: Was it not possible to build a free church without insisting on the baptism of believers as a primary prerequisite? If this could have been accomplished, then the movement would have escaped much of the threats and contempt which it had to bear. In other words, would not a pure Congregational plan rather than a Baptist pattern have been less offensive? This is a rhetorical question in which a historian has little interest, because the actual situation never came to pass to warrant such a solution. For Anabaptist leaders, the concept of the free church was logically bound up with the baptism of believers, and even if they might have perceived that it would have been easier to establish a free church without believers' baptism, they did not dare attempt this nor even reflect upon this because of their conscience.

There is a certain historical tradition, especially among some

Mennonite writers, which presupposes without any further consideration that the Anabaptists represented the highest form of Christian discipleship. Consequently, nearly every form of criticism of the Anabaptist movement is rejected. This viewpoint is not historically correct, and nothing is added to the present investigation by such a view.

Even if the basic doctrines of the Anabaptists are correct, yet a historian may scarcely evade the fact that correct principles and doctrines may often be applied in a faulty manner. The Anabaptists' zeal in supporting the individual's personal acceptance of faith, personal justification through faith, could lead to a loose type of spiritualism or mysticism, as has been seen. Dependence upon the Holy Spirit's leading always has been a delicate question, especially when it deals with the individual, autonomous conscience. The Anabaptist movement does not have to be studied very thoroughly before it is evident that at the point of the individual's relation to the Holy Spirit there is a weakness and a danger. A corrective to this defect lay in a closely ordered congregational life. However, a well-organized congregational life, centered in responsible leaders, was difficult when the groups had to work underground, as many did.

Moreover, unceasing dependence upon the Bible could easily degenerate into an extreme literalism. This situation became a problem, not only during the time of the martyrs but in later periods as well. An illuminating example of this extreme biblical interpretation is found at the second disputation at Zürich at the close of October, 1523. Konrad Grebel desired that the Bible should be followed in all matters; so much so, that the Lord's Supper should be celebrated in the evening only because Jesus and his disciples did so, that the bread should be whole and unbroken, that the communicant should take the bread for himself and not have the piece put in his mouth by the priest. The same reasoning was used regarding the use of the cup in communion. This was a type of biblicism that drifted into unessential details. This attitude toward the Bible, as could be expected, led to strife and misunderstanding regarding the interpretation of incidentals.

151

Church discipline, expressed in the ban, was a central question for these churches. Their demand that true faith should produce fruit in a Christian's life was one of the basic matters which separated them from the national church. This naturally led to a system of strict discipline within the free churches, which could lead to ironclad regulations of the way of life for the members. This matter became a tender point in the entire history of the free churches, and because of this rigorism many divisions resulted. Exclusion and avoidance of any intercourse with those who had been put out could be hard and absurd. At times it was demanded that there should be a complete separation (*Meidung*) from those who had been excluded, whether the cause was doctrinal or moral. Even family ties should be broken, as well as associations between husband and wife. There should not be any eating with one who had been excluded. Such demands naturally were only found among the most rigorous groups, but it indicates how hard some could be in holding a line of separation between the church and those who were outside of the fold.

If it is conceded that individualism, when rightly understood, is a true Christian attitude and that biblicism and church discipline are likewise correct, it is evident that these concepts could be faultily applied. But the Anabaptists also had some doubtful opinions, which in practice naturally could not lead to good results. Foremost among these concepts was their exclusiveness (*Absonderung*), which was so characteristic of every congregation and every member. When the Anabaptists withdrew from society as embodied in the national churches, there also was a cleavage on the other side of society—the civil municipality and the state. The free church movement was not in opposition to the state, but the religious competence and functions of the state were denied. "The Christian government" which played such an important role in Luther's, Zwingli's, and other reformers' point of view had no place among the Anabaptists. Consequently, they remained passive to the state, and they refused to serve in any capacity, whether as an official, administrator of justice, or soldier. This summary opposition to any collaboration with the state or its officials was based upon understanding of the New Testament, for in the New Testament there was no union between the Christians and authorities of government. One aspect of this position was the Anabaptists' refusal to take an oath, and here they again pointed to the words of Jesus when he forbade his disciples to swear.

This negative position toward the rulers of government was not accepted by all Anabaptists; however, this idea dominated during the sixteenth century. Hübmaier was the only great leader among them who clearly taught that a Christian could be a magistrate and act as a Christian to make the government more honest. The preachers were warned by Hübmaier not to take on strange offices or be burdened with worldly occupations. But "the sword" was accepted as necessary. This idea of Hübmaier was espoused definitely for the first time by Baptist groups in the seventeenth century as an essential Baptist principle.

Another aspect of this exclusiveness was the passive attitude of Anabaptists toward culture and social problems. This is revealed in the matter of making a living. The Hutterites and the Mennonites believed at first that Christians should be restricted to natural sources of livelihood: agriculture, related tasks, and handicrafts. They were warned to keep away from such occupations as business and public service. Urban culture was regarded as essentially dangerous. It was at this point that the Dutch Anabaptists showed some departure from the older ideas. During the sixteenth century, however, when the Anabaptist movement generally was forced out into the rural areas to find shelter, it soon developed into a movement of farmers and craftsmen. University-trained men soon disappeared as martyrs. It was in the English free church movement that educated leaders once again came to have important significance.

This exclusiveness, in many instances, was strict even in the marriage relationship and the rearing of children. When the young people wanted to establish their own homes, they were required to select partners from their own group, and it was not uncommon that the selection was dictated by an elder in the congregation. If anyone dared go outside the prescribed

153

borders, it was common practice that such a one should be excluded. Exclusiveness was even forced on children, in order to hold the children in the family and away from strangers. Hutterite children were brought up in established children's homes away from the parents. This discipline became altogether too narrow an upbringing for the children, and it gave them a warped view of life and society. Consequently, many fell away from the faith of their fathers when they learned to understand life as it really was.

Even the teaching concerning the community of goods must be considered as an unsound requirement among the Christian brotherhoods. In an undeveloped society based upon the feudal system one could till the soil and work with the hands and follow through this idea of community of goods. In the new day which was dawning, alive with commerce, sea travel, and urbanization, this was not practical. It was only among the Hutterite rural brotherhoods in the villages that it worked. On the other hand, there is evidence that the Christian maxim which other Anabaptists held, namely that the brotherhoods had an economic responsibility for one another, functioned well in the western European Anabaptist movement.

Even in such a point of doctrine as foot washing of believers there arose a serious question which only led to strife in the groups. This humble act of service was based, to be sure, on the example of Jesus in John 13:4–15. It was practiced among the Swiss Brethren and later among the Anabaptists of Holland. Menno Simons and Dirk Phillips gave directions concerning this service. Foot washing was mentioned in some of the articles of faith, while others omitted it.

It is also important to remember that the Anabaptists, who were so severely criticized and persecuted, also were very critical of others in times of strife. Often in the heat of battle they did not hesitate to make use of derision and sneer. This attitude was often interpreted by others as self-arrogance. Not a few times did they treat both their own and others without differentiation. The Anabaptists did not seem to have practiced any psychology in the art of the cure of souls.

More criticism could be brought against these men who

were martyred, who because of their sufferings often were led to rigorism, and who were strengthened in their convictions that the world was in the power of the evil one. But with all their faults, they cleared a way for a new period in the history of Christianity, where tolerance and religious freedom would be known. They were also the pioneers of a more faithful adherence to the Bible and of a greater comprehension of the distinctiveness in Christian living.

IV

The Seventeenth and Eighteenth Centuries

The Older Anabaptist Movement

The Swiss Brethren.—In the former chapter it has been pointed out that the Swiss Anabaptist movement was not a mere episode which quickly passed away. This movement continued to live and develop during the entire sixteenth century. At the beginning of the seventeenth century the Swiss Brethren were active but found it difficult to carry on their ministry because of continuous coercion and restraint. During the following century even more difficult times came.

Within the canton of Zürich, compulsory church attendance was maintained, and the order of worship prescribed by law was considered sufficient. When some of the inhabitants wanted to assemble on a Sunday afternoon for Bible reading, they were refused permission, even though they intended that the conventicles should be led by a clergyman. Strife continued over church discipline, and one of the standing criticisms by the Anabaptists was directed at the poor moral life in the church. Among some of the groups in the population there was expressed an apprehensiveness about taking communion with those who were living in open sin. This problem was even a matter of discussion with the magistrate. It was then explained that church discipline was unnecessary if the civil authorities would punish the guilty. In such situations the Anabaptists won sympathy. When compulsory baptism was carried out, there were many people who sided with the Anabaptists. For pious Christians the moral demands and the rigorous life of the Anabaptists was manifestly something worthy of imitation.

The Anabaptist movement in the canton of Zürich, as in

Bern and Basel, had been driven out into the rural areas during the sixteenth century because of persecution. As a consequence farmers and craftsmen replaced trained clergymen and other persons of high culture in the leadership of the movement. It is natural that the Anabaptists continued as small minority groups, not only in the canton of Zürich but also in the other evangelical cantons such as Bern and Basel. That their numbers did not increase is natural because of the severe persecution and the emigration which resulted. As has been pointed out before, there was a perpetual, fairly strong flow of emigrants to Moravia. The possibilities of migrating to this asylum continued even until the Thirty Years' War. This migration took place in other areas as well.

During the early portion of the seventeenth century there was generally an active relationship between Switzerland and Holland. Learned men, businessmen, and students traveled between the two countries on various tasks, and there even developed an active reciprocal mission in the life of the church. Zürich, like the rest of Switzerland, more and more relinquished its association with the German Empire. This break also resulted in the fact that the country was not involved in the Thirty Years' War. The association between the Swiss Anabaptists and the Mennonites in Holland became stronger and more meaningful, as was revealed later in the century.

During the regime of the great statesman and church leader, Johann Jacob Breitinger, the religious climate in Zürich became more austere. After he assumed leadership in 1613, there followed a rigid church policy with an increased demand on uniformity. It then became impossible to tolerate the Anabaptist free churches, their mode of baptism, and the performance of their own marriages. The mandate of 1585 was again revived; this threatened the Anabaptists with the death penalty if they defied the order. This attempt to force the Anabaptists into the Reform church failed; consequently, brutal measures followed. One of the Anabaptist preachers was condemned to death and was executed in 1614—the last-recorded execution for heresy of an Anabaptist in Switzerland. This action was a terrifying thing, and that it could take place

157

so close to the time of the great Counter Reformation against all Protestants indicates how blinded the Reformation leaders were in their attempt to bring about uniformity.

Although the death penalty was not enforced after this, there was no cessation of the rigorous persecutions. Heavy fines were exacted from those who resisted the edict. The abominable practice of condemning people to work as galley slaves was now applied to the Anabaptists; shocking incidents are recorded about it. Confiscation of property also occurred at the same time, and even those that migrated were deprived of their own property. Marriage ceremonies conducted before their own congregations were not recognized by the state, and civil authorities therefore made it clear that the children of the Anabaptists would be given no right of inheritance, even being deprived of their own property. Stripped of everything and threatened, the Anabaptists found it difficult to exist. Their numbers decreased, but the movement by no means disappeared.

Switzerland was almost drawn into the Thirty Years' War, and tension between Catholic and evangelical cantons increased greatly. Anabaptists were largely left alone. At the close of the 1620's, and especially at the beginning of the 1630's when the Swedes advanced into southern Germany, this war tension was acute. There were many problems in the country, including conscription, exorbitant taxes, inflation, and even crop failures. When the immediate external dangers of war were over, attention was again focused on domestic problems, and once again the subject of the Anabaptists and their position in the country came to the foreground. This was the period of Breitinger, who was just as inflexible in campaigning for his opinions regarding church uniformity as was William Laud in England at the same time.

A little earlier there was a gradual relaxation of restrictions so that the death penalty and the judgment to serve as a galley slave were not employed. However, there remained the penalties of high fines and other economic harassments for those who refused to attend the church or who were baptized. Breitinger and his men also concluded that there must be a reform in church discipline and in the behavior of the preachers.

Therefore, a government commission was appointed to expedite all of these reforms. In 1630, Breitinger wrote a memorandum to the commission in which, among other things, he enumerated the reasons why the work of the Anabaptists must be stopped. This program of extermination should be accomplished primarily by means of preaching and instruction; only the stiff-necked who segregated themselves in their free churches should be punished by the authorities. A declaration signed by five congregations was presented, but there was nothing new in it. The most difficult point to approve was the fact that the Anabaptists stated they would not attend the state church until church discipline and the exclusion of notorious sinners had taken place. This was directly opposed to the reformer's policy on uniformity. The Anabaptists made no demand for themselves except that they should be permitted to maintain their own congregations and their own worship exercises in peace.

Later, in 1633, there was an attempt to compile a census of the Anabaptists. This indicated that there was a rather small number in the movement, even if the count was unreliable. Only persons who were over twenty years of age were recorded, and even this classification was highly uncertain. None the less, it was taken for granted that the Anabaptists would have to be rooted out. At first the authorities began with milder measures. The clergymen were instructed to attempt to correct the wayward; however, the Anabaptist leaders were to be imprisoned and their property confiscated. The government commission was active, and Breitinger presented a lengthy account of his view regarding the situation. The report was replete with complaints and abusive invectives. He laid great emphasis on the fact that the Anabaptists refused to bear arms and therefore denied the right of national defense. The divergent articles of faith were briefly considered because they were sufficiently understood earlier. Breitinger wanted above everything else for the Anabaptists to observe regular attendance at the state church. He demanded uniformity in worship. He was primarily concerned about the children who did not receive correct doctrinal instruction. Consequently, methods of punishment had to be applied to the parents, commanding them to attend the church regularly. Breitinger in this way attempted to show that the Anabaptists were themselves to blame for their own difficulties and their unfortunate situation.

After this attack by Breitinger, the case against the Anabaptists could be prosecuted to the full. A large number were imprisoned in the summer of 1637. There were long trials, imprisonments, confiscation, and other persecutions. In a few years most of the Anabaptists had been imprisoned. Prisons became so crowded that inmates had to be released. The movement continued in spite of everything. Once again connections with the Mennonites in Holland were revived. Various forms of assistance came from Holland, and some Anabaptists emigrated to this northernly haven. Of special interest is the intervention in behalf of these persecuted brethren by the Dutch government in 1660. A similar move had been made by the Dutch in the early part of the century. It now became necessary that the Swiss government explain its position, and consequently the chief emphasis was upon the necessity for loyal citizenship. The Anabaptists refused to pay the tithe, to swear oaths, to render military service, and to obey the state. They were considered as anarchists and consequently had to be apprehended. The state and the church, after all, were one and the same.

When Breitinger died in 1645, the Anabaptist movement in the canton of Zürich had just about been crushed. The scattered remnants were not numerous, but even at the end of the century refugees were still coming from this area to Alsace and to the Palatinate. Several colonists who came to Pennsylvania during the years 1710–27 were from Zürich, and even in 1750 it was reported that a few solitary Anabaptists were found in the canton. In the canton of Bern the movement was able to hold out longer, with some Anabaptists existing there even to this day.

Zürich, during the sixteenth century, had been the leading evangelical canton, both in the widespread development of the Anabaptist movement and in the persistent resistance to this movement. The canton of Bern became, in the meantime, the other headquarters for the Anabaptist movement, and there the persecutions did not lag behind those in the Zürich canton. Like Zürich, the Bernese canton severely enforced the mandate of 1585, with the consequence that the emigrant numbers increased. It was the Brethren in Moravia that received these Bernese refugees, who came stripped of everything because all of their property had been confiscated. At the beginning of the seventeenth century the government sought to put a stop to these secret escapes to Moravia. Children were disinherited if their Anabaptist parents had been married in their own religious group. This sharpened the economic problems considerably.

During the decade of 1640 a new attempt was made to control the Anabaptists in Bern, but again the insurmountable problem beside baptism and separation into free churches was resistance to the use of the sword. The result was another strict mandate, in 1644, which was definitely designed to uproot the movement. All of the Anabaptists were to be imprisoned and censured. If the "stiff-necked" continued to hold firm to their opinions, they should be escorted to the boundary and banished with the threat of the death penalty if they returned. In the year 1659 another period of difficult persecution began which culminated in 1671. A "Commission for Anabaptist Affairs" was established in 1659, and it declared, after conferring with the authorities in Zürich, that the death penalty or condemnation to be galley slaves would no longer be used against the Anabaptists. Banishment, however, which had been an earlier decision, was still in effect. The reason given for this act was that the Anabaptists opposed governmental regulations: they preached, baptized, and practiced church discipline without obtaining the permission of the authorities. Besides this these heretics neglected to attend the worship services on Sunday and prayer days, which the authorities had legalized as being mandatory. The mandate of 1659 expounded these points of view, and it also clarified that the Anabaptist leaders and teachers would be searched and imprisoned. In the meantime, the church officials were commissioned to go from house to house, recording everyone, inquiring whether the people attended the preaching services, instruction classes, and the communion service.

When persecution rose to its peak at the beginning of the 1670's, imprisonment, banishment, and confiscation of property were no longer sufficient measures, for now even in the Bernese canton, contrary to the 1659 mandate, Anabaptists were again sent to work as oarsmen on the galleys. This persecution increased the migration out of the country to such places as the Palatinate, where a new center of the movement developed. As it was with Zürich, so here protests and interventions came from Holland, some from the Mennonites who for years had sent love gifts, some from certain cities and academic groups, and finally some from the very authorities of state (the States' General). Religious freedom was highly respected in Holland. The States' General again sent letters of intercession, in 1661 and in 1668. The authorities in Bern answered this appeal, but otherwise it had little effect on the situation. Brutal persecution continued; even up until 1717 Anabaptists were condemned to the galleys. It is natural that their literature was censured and prohibited; all of their writings which could be obtained were destroyed. The writings spread just the same, and the Anabaptists continued to exist, even though probably most of them were put in prison.

At the beginning of the eighteenth century, the government at Bern tried a project which indicates the impossibility of curbing the movement. A great plan was projected in which all of the wayward people would be assembled and shipped over to America. The plan failed, however. Nor did the Anabaptists accept the generous invitation from the Prussian king, Frederick I, to pick out a free place to dwell within his territory. Instead, they were more interested in going to Holland where their friends in the faith had made great contributions to help them during their difficult experiences of persecution. Similar to the counsel from the Dutch government suggesting tolerance and amnesty for the Anabaptists, there came an admonition from Frederick I in Prussia. The government in Bern finally came to grant some amnesty. The Amnesty Proclamation of 1711 stated that the Anabaptists should be set free from the prisons and that they would have the privilege of migrating and retaining their property. During earlier banishments, all of the property was confiscated, as has been already mentioned. There was no relaxing of difficulties in the Amnesty Proclamation for Anabaptists who wanted to stay in the canton of Bern. It was expressly declared that no Anabaptist assemblies could continue, and serious punishment would threaten those individuals who returned to the canton.

A migration to Holland now took place and also to the territories of Prussia, where the movement has lived on even to the present day. That some Anabaptists remained in the canton of Bern is evident. The earlier "Commission for Anabaptist Affairs" was reorganized, and it remained in operation until 1743. The special people who had been appointed to imprison Anabaptists continued their work. In many places in the canton the populace aided the persecuted, giving them protection and assisting them in various ways. Especially in Emmental this situation occurred, where to this day the movement lives on. Again in 1714 the government was forced to issue another mandate against the persistent Anabaptists, indicating that in spite of the forced migrations with the amnesty, the movement was still a concern for the government. Thus it went on during the eighteenth century. The oppressive measures did not diminish. Penalties alternated in forms of fines, imprisonments, banishments, confiscation of property, deprivation of inheritance, compulsory military service, prohibition in holding meetings, and using books. This final category is illustrated by the manner the authorities opposed an edition of the New Testament printed in Basel, a translation which they considered was infiltrated with the Anabaptist heresies. Its publication was flatly prohibited.

The governors in the canton of Bern were exceptionally intense in their persistent and despotic persecution of the Anabaptists during the seventeenth and eighteenth centuries. Partial explanation of this is found in the fact that in no place in Switzerland was this movement so full of life and so progressive as in Bern. The Reformed church, stressing unity and uniformity, would not tolerate any divergence, and the governmental authorities regarded it a matter of prestige and order to maintain the identity between the state and the church. Consequently, this sordid history of oppressive, compulsory proceedings continued. Only after the middle of the eighteenth century did another spirit begin to be felt. When Switzerland came under the jurisdiction of France for a short time during the Napoleonic Wars, there was supposed to be full religious freedom, but the application of this idea was slow in materializing. In 1810 the Anabaptists presented an appeal to the government soliciting recognition, but they were denied their request with the explanation that they grew out of the Thomas Müntzer movement. Later during the nineteenth century, freedom increased, but the Anabaptists did not increase, largely because of the great emigration to the United States. Emmental and the western portion of the Bern canton now became a center for them. The Brethren here became more influential than in any other place in Switzerland, maintaining a continuous history since the time of the Reformation.

The third important evangelical canton in which the Anabaptists had a long history was Basel. As has been mentioned, in the development of the Anabaptist movement during the sixteenth century Basel was in many respects the center of divergent opinions for the entire Reformation. It is understandable that this active city of culture became the gathering place for radical humanists and also the "baptism-minded." However, the story is the same here as in other places. Because of the severe oppressive measures, the Anabaptist movement retreated into the rural areas, and here the tillers of the soil and craftsmen became the leaders. Earlier the movement had been led by scholars and converted priests.

About 1600 there appears to have been a bricklayer who was the teacher and leader for the scattered Anabaptists in the territory of Basel. Similar to the pattern in Zürich, the Anabaptists in Basel canton were condemned to banishment with the confiscation of all property. This brought about aggravation. Conventicles were held in the homes, sometimes in the woods, and those that attended were always threatened with the fear of being discovered. In Basel there was also an exodus, primarily to Moravia, and the old families died out. In this canton the movement was obviously much weaker during the first part of the seventeenth century than in Zürich and in Bern.

The Anabaptist movement, nevertheless, lived on and later became stronger in these territories, due to the fact that agriculturists immigrated into this area. This type of Anabaptist made important cultural contributions. A rural estate then became the headquarters for them. Such places are spoken of during the early part of the eighteenth century. However, it appears that the movement in Basel had less dramatic experiences than those which befell the Anabaptists in Zürich and Bern. In the records of the state archives of Basel, there are, however, testimonies concerning oppressive measures which were employed at the close of the seventeenth and the beginning of the eighteenth century. This persecution gradually diminished. After the revolution in France and during the nineteenth century, religious freedom was realized in Basel as well.

It appears that in the territory of Basel there was a shifting composition of immigrant strangers. Inner theological and practical problems crippled the Anabaptist congregations here more than in other places. At the close of the eighteenth century there were two Anabaptist groups, which were sharply opposed to each other. One of these groups came to be known as the Amish Mennonites. This group has continued until the present day.

The Amish Mennonite group originated through the influence of an elder in an Anabaptist congregation in Switzerland. His name was Jacob Ammann, and he began his activities in 1693. He insisted on a more exacting form of church discipline, recalling the rigorous demands laid down by the Anabaptists of the sixteenth century. He called for a complete separation from those that had been excluded from the congregation and insisted that the members should not even eat at the same table with one excluded, even if he were a member of the family. If one of the parties in a marriage were excluded from the congregation because of sin, a complete separation must take place. Foot washing was mandatory, and strict regulations were laid down concerning food and clothing. Buttons were not to be used on the clothes, but instead hooks and eyes. This branch of the movement has had an active existence, and even today there are stalwart congregations in the United States.

Ammann traveled around Switzerland and gathered many followers, which caused an irreconcilable opposition to increase. In the area of Basel the movement divided into the old type and the Amish. Basically, the Amish followed the established, well-known principal articles of faith: faith in the Scriptures; preaching by laymen; conversion; baptism; the free church; separation of church and state; and refusal to swear an oath, to bear weapons, and to assume the responsibilities of a governmental official. This is true of the entire Swiss movement, as well as for the Amish. In the summer of 1952 the Basel Anabaptists were hosts to a Mennonite world congress. The Swiss Brethren have had a number of intimate associations with various Mennonite groups.

As has been said before, there were only a few of the original Swiss Anabaptist congregations which were able to outlive the persecution and emigration and continue in their history to the present day. In the meantime, emigration had spread the Swiss Brethren widely. Already during the sixteenth century, as has been indicated, the Brethren made their way northward to the German territories, but as has been seen, this branch of the movement was largely destroyed. During the seventeenth century the Swiss emigration continued. This time it was primarily to the territories in southwestern Germany, especially Alsace, Baden, and the Palatinate. During this time there was both a voluntary and a forced emigration, so that a new and an active movement arose in these territories. It is reported that at least five Anabaptist congregations were found in Alsace during the 1660's. These were migrant congregations, for the older Anabaptist movement had almost disappeared. Strassburg, which had been an active center for the movement, was no longer important, although there was a little group that continued to carry on in a weak manner even until 1875. However, as in Switzerland, the Anabaptists of Alsace and other German provinces were driven out of the cities and became farmers and craftsmen who continued to exist in the rural areas. It was these Swiss refugees who here became renowned because of their skills in agriculture and animal husbandry. When the tempo of the persecution in Switzerland increased, migration also increased. An edict in 1712 was leveled at the Anabaptists in Alsace, and they were ordered to leave the country. Because of this edict many made their way to the colonies of Holland, to America, or back to Switzerland where they met with new persecutions. During the eighteenth century there were many Mennonites who still existed in Alsace, living very unobtrusively. During the nineteenth century these Mennonites, like others, obtained a greater degree of freedom. At the close of the century the congregations once again began to assemble in conferences. In 1896 the first of these "Old Evangelical" Mennonite conferences was held in Alsace-Lorraine.

Even in the Palatinate the Anabaptists had restrictive laws imposed upon them about 1600, for in a decree of 1603 the electoral prince reminded the men of authority regarding these restrictive regulations. Only weak remnants of the earlier movement were able to outlive this oppression. In the meantime, new groups of refugees came from Switzerland, and a number of these came to the Palatinate. After the Peace of Westphalia in 1648, this migration increased. The worship services often had to be conducted in the woods, and if the conventicles were discovered, there were heavy fines. In the year 1661 all of such worship services were forbidden, but soon the government tried another policy: worship services would not be hindered, but every attendant would have to pay a tax for participating in the service. In the entire German Empire there was an uncertainty and inconsistency, even in the courts, for the old governmental laws against the Anabaptists still stood on the books. These laws demanded the death penalty for rebaptizers.

Later, during the 1660's, a concession was granted for the privilege of conducting worship services. In this connection, in an official business document in southern Germany, the term "Mennonite" was used for the first time instead of "Anabaptist." One of the basic reasons for granting tolerance to the

Anabaptists was a need of skilled agriculturists to help restore the land which had been ravaged by the long war. A number of established restrictions, however, restrained the movement from making any progress. During the latter part of the seventeenth century the stream of migrants from Switzerland increased, and because of this it was necessary to increase freedom and privileges established by laws. The authorities, however, were on their watch, and the circumstances varied according to the personal disposition of the electoral prince. During the 1690's there was a renewed persecution, and the government in Holland made another appeal. At the beginning of the eighteenth century there was another restrictive mandate which encouraged a great migration of Anabaptists to America. It has been estimated that by 1732 three thousand Mennonites from the Palatinate had made their way to America. Forty years later, over thirty thousand Palatinate names were recorded on the immigration register.

The Swiss Brethren also came to other territories in southern Germany, especially Baden, and in this way the Anabaptist movement was able to rally in areas where it had largely been destroyed during the sixteenth century. On the other hand, it was not to be expected that a strong movement would develop in southern Germany.

The Hutterites.—The Hutterites, as has been pointed out before, became the major Anabaptist representatives in Moravia after the original assembly divided—that is, when the congregation, which had been led by Hübmaier up until his martyr's death in 1528, lost its leader. The Hutterite Brethren also divided, but they found new support through the constant flow of immigration. At the beginning of the seventeenth century the Hutterites had a very important position in Moravia, which is revealed in an article written by a Catholic opponent in 1607. In this writing it is even mentioned that the Hutterites were outstanding farmers, managers of property, servants, and craftsmen. It was the noblemen and other important property owners who protected these heretics, taking advantage of their skills. During the war against the Turks at the turn of the century, 1599–1600, and the later Thirty Years' War, the Hutterites suffered disastrous reprisals, and several of their villages were devastated. Many people were murdered and others were carried off to slavery, but through it all these heroic people remained steadfast to their basic ideal of not defending themselves with the sword. Nor would they pay taxes for the purpose of supporting war; however, the government forcefully extracted taxes from them by confiscating their livestock.

During the Thirty Years' War the scourging of the Hutterites increased, especially when the Catholic troops ravished the land. According to a contemporary cartographer, the number of the Hutterites was supposed to be about seventy thousand, but this figure is certainly too high. Their farms were destroyed, many were murdered, and the burden on the group became nearly unbearable. Shortly before, there were great immigrations because of Moravia's generous offer of freedom. Consequently, the ravages of war seemed all the more bitter. It was Franz Cardinal von Dietrichstein who led the assault against the Hutterites, a man who knew no mercy. In September, 1622, an imperial decree ordered that the Hutterites should be completely exterminated. All of the Anabaptists were ordered to leave the country because, as it was said, the movement was daily expanding, drawing in simple-minded people, creating manifold difficulties. Furthermore, they would not give any obedience to authorities. No less than twenty-four villages had to be abandoned, including all permanent as well as movable property. This time the migration of the Hutterites went to Hungary and to Siebenbürgen (a part of present-day Romania). In these places new Anabaptist centers sprang up which persisted for about 150 years. Many difficulties and hardships came, and then, as with the Anabaptists of Switzerland and western Germany, the Mennonites of Holland came to the aid of these believers.

The end of the heroic saga of the European Hutterite Brethren was migration to the United States, but before leaving Europe, the Hutterites made another move farther east. This move was encouraged by Catherine II of Russia, who at the end of the eighteenth century invited the Brethren to take up residence in her country, promising freedom from any military service. The group stayed in Russia less than a century and then began to make its way to America. From the year 1874 the emigration to America can be marked. Thus the Hutterites left Russia, closing their specific history in that part of the world. This fellowship of believers still exists today in South Dakota and Canada, where there are approximately fifty villages (*Bruderhöfe*) with more than five thousand members.

The organization of these villages is about the same as that prescribed by Jakob Hutter over four hundred years ago. Each collective communal has a pastor and a steward or superintendent who is responsible for all of the working conditions and the economic welfare. The superintendent has four or five assistants who are called elders. These men are responsible for all that takes place within the congregation, and they can hold their position as long as they fulfil the requirements in a satisfactory manner. Only the superintendent takes care of the congregation's finances, and the foreman within each branch of activity must answer to him for the entire administration of the work. There is no private ownership, but the land, buildings, implements, and household utensils belong to the colony as such. Community of goods is practiced within each separate village, and at the present time one colony is composed of between fifteen and twenty families. The demand for great frugality and asceticism is impressed upon this Christian communism. The basic principle is that of mutual help and trust.

The Mennonites.—The strongest and best-known branch of the original Anabaptist movement in Europe is the present-day Mennonite denomination from Holland. Much has already been told about their earliest history. During the seventeenth and the eighteenth centuries the Mennonites were well established; and, as has already been set forth, they were of great assistance to the persecuted brethren of the household of faith in Switzerland and western Germany.

The Anabaptist movement which grew up in Holland and northwest Germany, to which the term Mennonite has been given, had a secure position at the beginning of the seventeenth century. The relative acceptance which they enjoyed, by contrast to Anabaptist fellowships in other countries, was due to a great measure of religious freedom. This is the reason why the Mennonite movement had a stronger social and economic position and therefore could aid fellow believers in other places. The movement in Holland had, through zealous preachers and elders (bishops), been established over a wide territory with central points in northern and southern provinces of Holland, besides East Friesland, Holstein, and West Prussia. Amsterdam, Leeuwarden, Emden, Hoorn, Dordrecht, Krefeld, Hamburg, Danzig, and Elbing were focal cities. Dutch refugees had established congregations in Germany early in the sixteenth century.

The religious freedom which had been granted to the Mennonites was strengthened considerably in 1672 when the group was formally recognized as a religious body with the right of free religious exercise under the protection of the state. The Dutch movement was led by two distinguished men, Hans de Ries and Peter Janz Twisck, who actively labored for many years in the seventeenth century. Their writings and their leadership long gave the Mennonite movement a real stability in the Netherlands. The schism which had occurred during the sixteenth century between the Friesians and the Waterlanders still remained, however, and it weakened the Mennonite movement. The Mennonites won an important leader and writer in Tieleman Janz van Braght, who compiled the renowned *Märtyrerspiegel* [*Martyrs' Mirror*], a historical chronicle related to the martyrdom of thousands of Anabaptists. Van Braght was from Dordrecht, a city known in history for the Calvinistic confession adopted at the synod there. Here van Braght joined a Mennonite church. In 1648 he was ordained as an elder, and he was soon recognized as one of the competent apologists and teachers in the movement. The catechism written by van Braght was reprinted several times, and after his death in 1664 there appeared a volume of his sermons. His great accomplishment, the Anabaptist martyrology, has been translated both into the German and English languages, and it has been an important, if not always reliable, historical source for the study of the movement. Ma-

171

terial was collected and arranged without any critical evaluation.

During the early portion of the seventeenth century, the Mennonite movement enjoyed increasing acceptance. The Dutch movement, especially among the Waterlanders, was not as strictly ascetical as that of the Hutterites, and it was more adaptable to the culture of the times. Because of this liberal attitude, scores of people were won to the Mennonite cause in the early part of the century. The records indicate that there were about 160,000 Dutch Mennonites in 1700. The possibilities for persecution were not lacking, however. The synods of the state church looked with considerable displeasure upon the growing Mennonite movement, and they found opportunities to warn and also interfere with the group in spite of the regulations concerning religious freedom. State church officials were able to create an unfavorable opinion against Mennonites by means of sharply worded pamphlets. In some instances, local governments interfered by prohibiting their meetings. For all marriage ceremonies prior to official recognition in 1672, the Mennonites were compelled to use state church clergymen.

The Mennonites early indicated an interest in setting forth their opinions in a confession of faith. During the Thirty Years' War they were much concerned about this matter, and it was at this time that they attempted to bring about a uniform confession of faith. This was the case of three of these compiled confessions which were written in Dutch or Latin at the close of the 1620 period. One of these statements was presented to the authorities in order to show the right of the Mennonites to obtain full religious freedom. The most commonly used confession of this time was one drawn up at a unity conference in Dordrecht in 1632. The church in that city, which belonged to the Flemish group, deplored the schism between congregations of the same faith and practice. Consequently, the bishop of the congregation, Adrian Cornelius, wrote the first draft of a confession of unity.

Accordingly, at the same time there was a convocation of a large number of elders and preachers who organized a "gen-

172

eral union," which was ratified with the "kiss of peace," the celebration of the Lord's Supper, and the acceptance of the eighteen articles of this confession. Among the fifty-two signers of this confession were men from western and southern Germany. This Dordrecht Confession of 1632 was soon translated into German, being printed in Rotterdam in 1658. This document even won recognition among the Anabaptists in Alsace. Already by 1712 this confession was printed in English, and it has since this time been generally accepted and used by the conservative Mennonites in America.

While some in the two Mennonite groups sought fellowship in this manner, conservative groups within both movements held their established positions. The Waterlanders had the more liberal point of view, and they already had their own confession of faith. In their theology they were conservative; however, they were not as strictly dogmatic as the other groups, considering the Bible as their only basis for faith.[1] The Waterlanders were tolerant in practice; this is illustrated, for example, in the matter of church discipline and in the attitude toward those who had backslidden. The three leading groups in the Dutch-German Mennonite movement remained the same as they had existed, in spite of the attempts to establish a confession of unity. Not even the Waterlanders' invitation to Christian peace and understanding in 1647 was able to bring any agreement.

In fact, there was yet another division. This schism took place in Amsterdam, and it arose over a personal disagreement between two leading preachers, Samuel Apostool and Galenus Abrahams. This situation reveals again the weak point in the free church.

Bishop Apostool (d. 1699) was the leader of the right wing in the congregation, for he was dissatisfied with the tendencies

[1] The Bible translation by the Mennonites during the sixteenth century, which had a successful distribution, continued during the following century. It is said that from 1602 to 1650 there were over twenty-four editions published, and up until 1725 this Bible translation had been printed in at least ninety editions. During the same period there were sixty-four editions of the New Testament alone. The Mennonites were zealous Bible readers and generally gave less consideration to written confessions.

173

of an increasing liberal attitude toward other churches which were held by his colleague, Galenus Abrahams (d. 1706). Abrahams was a practicing physician as well as a preacher and leader of the Flemish congregation in Amsterdam. He attempted to establish relationships with other churches, and it is stated that he was influenced by Socinian points of view. He did not maintain the established ideas that the only true church was the Mennonite free church. Abrahams and his followers developed a friendly relationship with the "Collegiants," a spiritualistic movement within the Reformed state church. Together with another preacher, he published a defense of some of the Collegiant opinions. This was too much for Bishop Apostool, who, with approximately seven hundred other conservative members of the congregation, withdrew and established a new congregation. They called their new church "the Sun," and from this they received their name, "Sunnites." The older group was called the "Lammists." This division spread, and the majority of the congregations joined the conservative Sunnites. However, Galenus Abrahams continued to progress with his work. He established contact with the Quakers in England, and both George Fox and William Penn visited him with the expectation of winning him to their spiritualistic position. This, however, did not occur.

The successor to Galenus Abrahams in this church, after a few years, was the distinguished teacher and preacher, John Deknatel (d. 1759). Together with others, Deknatel founded a seminary in Amsterdam in 1735. Deknatel also was known in England. John Wesley recorded in his journal that he visited Deknatel and was well received in his home. Wesley also heard Deknatel preach, and he received a very good impression of him. For many years Deknatel also maintained a close personal relationship with Zinzendorf. Thus the Mennonites of Holland were sympathetic with the leading personalities of the eighteenth-century revival movements.

Deknatel wrote many books and pamphlets, among them a catechism which was translated into German and often reprinted both in Holland and Germany. In the year 1753 he published a volume of selections of Menno Simons' writings, which was also translated into German and reprinted in several editions. A volume of his sermons was published in Dutch and German. This Mennonite leader of the early portion of the eighteenth century was a spiritual personality who exerted an influence far beyond the church in Amsterdam. Although this was a period of relative weakness in the Dutch Mennonite movement, there were strong leaders who preserved some of the best principles of the Anabaptist movement.

A man of a conservative disposition was Herman Schijn, a physician and bishop who ministered in Rotterdam and Amsterdam (d. 1727). He wrote several publications which defended the conservative position and demanded loyalty to the established Mennonite standards of faith which were in accord with the confessions and the Bible. He also disapproved of open communion, which most of the Mennonite parties practiced. Schijn became especially renowned because of two Mennonite histories which he wrote, printed both in Dutch and Latin. In these volumes he presented a study of contemporary theology and history in different countries.

The Dutch Mennonites generally had a good reputation for leading truly Christian lives, as well as for helping a needy mankind. Even the opponents in the state church, who contested the ideas of the Mennonites, admitted that in this respect they surpassed others. Their temperance in food, drink, and clothes was noticeable, especially when many of the Mennonites at this time were beginning to win fortunes and social prestige. When the Dutch government intervened in behalf of the persecuted Anabaptists in Switzerland, reference was made to the Mennonites of the Netherlands. In a similar governmental communication to the canton in Bern at the beginning of the eighteenth century, it was pointed out that the Mennonites in the Netherlands had enjoyed tolerance and freedom for many years, and as loyal citizens they lived in peace and humility and were obedient to the government in all things that they did not regard to be in conflict with God's Word. Dutch Mennonites also sent economic help to the Anabaptists in Prussia, Poland, and Lithuania. Their ministry of help was widespread, reaching as far as the persecuted Waldenses in Italy and to the French Huguenots after the Edict of Nantes was revoked in 1685.

The ability to give large sums of money to aid foreign groups was possible because of the special character of the Dutch movement. Members had become established in the urban middle class, which resulted in a rising economic prosperity and at the same time threatened the original ideal which insisted upon a break from the ways of the world. This flowered into a greater acceptance of the world and accommodation to the milieu. As Holland became more and more characteristically commercial, the Mennonites soon became a fellowship within the cities and among the mercantile groups. Consequently, typical Anabaptist pattern of the social establishment in the rural economic order did not prevail, and social standards became quite different from what they had been previously. This situation lies behind the eighteenth-century transformation within the Mennonite movement.

Swiss Anabaptists who came to Holland, directly from their homeland or by way of various German territories, could not escape noticing the liberal attitudes of the Dutch Mennonites. During the early part of the eighteenth century these refugees came in large numbers, some to settle in Holland and others to continue on to North America. They thought that their Dutch friends in the faith had departed from the good old paths. These emigrants felt that the Mennonites were not strict enough in doctrine or practice, for as far as the Swiss were concerned, the Dutch did not measure up to their separatist standards. It was evident that the zeal had diminished among many of the Dutch Mennonites. The time of relaxed attitudes had taken possession of the Mennonites.

Tension between the "Lammists" and the "Sunnites" continued through the entire eighteenth century, although there were several attempts to bring about a reconciliation and unification. The Lammists rejected confessions, remained freer of traditions, and maintained relationships with friendly groups within the Reformed state church. In their individualism and free relationships they followed the Waterlanders. The Sunnites held closely to the authority of the church, its confession,

176

and its discipline. New confessions also appeared. The conservative Sunnites felt that they had more in common with the Reformed church than with the Lammists; consequently, many of them went over to the Reformed church during the closing part of the eighteenth century. In fact, there were ministers who directly worked for this union.

The Dutch Mennonite movement had the same difficulties as other Christian groups during the early part of the eighteenth century. The spiritual decline was evidenced in the steady reduction in church membership. Many of the congregations completely disappeared, and even the larger churches declined numerically. As has been mentioned, the Dutch Mennonites in 1700 numbered about 160,000. A hundred years later only 27,000 members could be listed. The reasons for this decline were many. Some of these reasons have already been mentioned, such as the inner oppositions and schisms, the loose discipline, indifference to doctrine, and the acceptance of riches and luxury. In some of the smaller towns where there were Mennonites, there also was a gradual degeneration in economic and social ideals. The new generations pulled loose from the Christian standards held by their fathers, and in many instances they joined the national church. Socinianism and Unitarianism also exerted their influences. During the latter part of the eighteenth century, the spirit of the enlightenment was evident.

Church discipline became more and more liberalized, the strict demands disappeared, and exclusion from a congregation was all but forgotten after the middle of the eighteenth century. No longer was the old Anabaptist insistence on refusing to bear weapons generally upheld, and even more remarkable, the demand for baptism of believers was no longer chiefly maintained by all of the churches. In spite of this, several large church buildings were built during this time. This can be attributed to the rising economic prosperity among the Mennonites, in spite of the recession in spiritual power and numbers. This prosperity made it possible for the Mennonites to develop a large social work program among the churches, such as care for the aged, sick, widows, and children. Various enterprises in the area of general welfare were initiated, and various cultural institutions were established.

The Mennonite movement in the areas of northern Germany developed much the same way as it did in Holland. The movement depended much upon its Dutch roots. The preaching services were conducted in the Dutch language, and even in the nineteenth century the German congregations obtained their ministers from the seminary in Amsterdam. Crefeld, a city in the Rhine region, northwest of Cologne, became an important center where well-to-do merchants were the leaders within the movement. The most prominent man in the early generation was Hermann op den Graeff (d. 1642), whose name appears as one of the signers of the Dordrecht confession of faith. Because of the severe persecution in Cologne, and for a time also in the Palatinate, many refugees fled to Crefeld, where they found employment and opportunity, as well as an established congregation. It was the Mennonite textile weavers who primarily brought the city distinction in the field, making it flourish industrially. During the early portion of the eighteenth century, when the city came under the jurisdiction of the Prussian kings, the rights of freedom were increased. In approximately a hundred years, Crefeld became a center of religious movements, including the Quakers and the Moravians. Both the radical pietist, Gottfried Arnold, and the mystic, Gerhard Tersteegen, were associated with the Mennonite church in Crefeld.

The church at Crefeld, with its prosperous mercantile class, followed much the same natural development as that in Holland. The strict rules and ideals were overthrown when members began to become established in the affairs of this world. A loose church order soon prevailed, and the association with the existing culture became more active. More and more the lay preachers were put aside in place of the academically trained spiritual guides.

In Emden, where the Mennonites existed from the early days of the movement, and in Hamburg, Mennonite preachers from Holland ministered continuously. The church in Emden has experienced varying fortunes in its long history since 1530, continuing to the present day. In Hamburg the conservative element was in control during the seventeenth century, and most of the Mennonites here aligned with the Dutch Sunnites. Dutch Mennonites early came to Hamburg and to the neighboring village of Altona. The senate of the free city of Hamburg took note of the fact that it was an advantage to have such able craftsmen and businessmen in the city; consequently, the Mennonites obtained a degree of religious freedom as early as 1605. Refugees came to this neighborhood, some from the Spanish Netherlands and others from various places in western Germany. The Dutch people were the most dominant, and the Dutch language was used in the worship services even until the 1830's. One of the foremost leaders of this church was Gerhard Roosen (d. 1711), who for sixty-two years held his pastoral post of leadership in the church. This ministry Roosen rendered without any compensation, for he was a wealthy ship owner. Roosen was the author of a widely used catechism which was translated into English, being reprinted several times in America. He also wrote a Mennonite history, and through his extensive travels in Germany, the Netherlands, and Poland he was able to exert a strong influence over the Mennonite churches in these areas.

The Quakers visited Hamburg-Altona, and consequently several of the Mennonites were won over to this point of view. Among them was one of the leading deacons. Roosen sought to meet this threat by writing a book in which he pointed out the meaning of the sacraments and defended other Mennonite doctrines in counterdistinction to the Quaker spiritualism. There was considerable prosperity within the church, and large sums of money were given to fellow believers in other countries. The membership roll, however, was comparatively small, as it is even to this day.

Mennonite churches in West Prussia and Poland divided into various parties as those in Holland. The Dutch language was used in the Danzig territory even until the end of the eighteenth century. The Danzig churches obtained their elders and ministers from Holland, and it was to Holland that the parents sent their children for education. Amsterdam was the center for higher education. The West Prussians were under the jurisdiction of the Polish kings, who permitted the Mennonites freedom to maintain their teachings. Even in Poland proper there were some congregations of which a few remain even to this day. Many of the Mennonites in this territory lived off the soil, and therefore they held to the traditional Anabaptist source of livelihood. During the decade of 1770, Danzig and West Prussia came under the jurisdiction of the Prussian kings, and the freedom of the Mennonites was confirmed.

A few years later, the Mennonites experienced difficulties because the state demanded military service, and it was at this time that Czarina Catherine II of Russia invited the Mennonites to move to southern Russia. Several hundred families accepted this invitation, so that many Mennonite colonies grew, and new ones were established during the next hundred years. However, from these Mennonite groups in Russia there was a great emigration to America during the latter part of the nineteenth century. In spite of this, it is recorded that in the year 1914 there were approximately a hundred thousand Mennonites still remaining in Russia. This estimate includes even the unbaptized children. Thus the western movement of the Anabaptists had curved northward and through an eastern offshoot entered the same territory where the eastern branch, the Hutterites, had settled after wandering from Moravia and Hungary. Many remained in Danzig and West Prussia. It is interesting to note that the meetinghouse at Elbing, which was built by the Dutch refugees in 1590, still remained and was used by the congregation even until 1900. However, there was a new congregation in Elbing founded in 1852, which also erected a church building.

In the entire northern German and Polish territories the Mennonites were exposed to permanent difficulties created by church and the civil authorities. It is true that the Mennonites enjoyed tolerance and obtained the permission from various princes to stay on; however, there were serious limitations. They were supposed to remain in their own groups and not to expand their work too much. They were subjected to the arbitrariness of local authorities, and above everything else, they were put under pressure by the churches surrounding them whether they were Lutheran, Calvinistic, or Catholic. The Mennonites often had a good economic position, and therefore taxes and imports of various kinds were levied against them. The tribute money which was demanded because the Mennonites refused to bear arms was collected in an arbitrary way. In general, it was easy to subject them to harassments without ever giving them a chance to receive justice, and this continued not only during the seventeenth century but even later.

There is one question of great consequence that should be considered before leaving the history of the Mennonites during this period. This problem pertains to the significance the Dutch and the German Anabaptist movements had to the development of the Pietist movement, which began with Spener, a German Lutheran, about 1670. This is a very involved question. Undoubtedly the subject has been touched upon in various discussions without giving any clear-cut appraisal. Recently a study has been made of this subject that advocates the view that there is a relationship between Anabaptism and Pietism. This is the work of Robert Friedmann, an Austrian historian, now working in the United States, who for many years has made a thorough study of Anabaptism based upon primary sources. In 1949 the result of his research appeared, *Mennonite Piety Through the Centuries: Its Genius and Its Literature*.

At the very beginning Friedmann stresses the importance of the situation in Germany, a stream from the sixteenth century which can be called "pietism before the Pietist movement." In many instances this was characterized by the same features which distinguished the Anabaptists. Friedmann also points out that Pietism became most securely established in the very same class of merchants and city people in which the Dutch Mennonite movement had its deepest roots. Therefore, it would be clear that the Mennonites, because of their influence in Germany, were the most natural group to build the bridge over to the Pietism of the seventeenth century. The demand of the Anabaptists for a Christlike life, their conventicles, and lay preachers undeniably resemble the early basic views of the Pietistic reform movement.

Friedmann also points out that the scattered groups of Anabaptists in Germany during the seventeenth century gave up the old ideas of a radical imitation of Christ in every detail and became satisfied with a more quietistic tendency.

However, the question of a possible connection between Pietism and the early Anabaptist movement is not solved yet. No documentary proofs can be found to show that the Württemberg Pietism, which also spread out over the countryside, was a continuation of the earlier Anabaptist movement in this vicinity. There are many similarities, and the fact that Pietism established its central headquarters in a place where the Anabaptists had been strong has given the scholars cause to conclude that possibly an Anabaptist legacy remained in these territories. The observation is interesting, but in this treatment it is impossible to deal further with this subject. Irrespective of the hypotheses of the geographic spread of the movement, one can establish that a great amount of Anabaptist literature was widely circulated.

The radical pietist, Gottfried Arnold, together with others, revealed a great interest in the Anabaptists, which is indicated in his book, *Unpartheiische Kirchen und Ketzerhistorie* [*An Impartial History of Churches and Heretics*]. In the early part of the seventeenth century some Anabaptist literature was reprinted in new editions. Friedmann gives examples of these writings, which were reprinted both in Amsterdam and Halle, and he points out that this literature, then a hundred and fifty years old, was much esteemed by the Pietists. It was a spiritual affinity which developed the renaissance of these old Anabaptist writings. From the other point of view, Friedmann shows how the Mennonites had a high regard for the books of Johann Arndt, so much that they even incorporated Arndt's prayers in their own devotional literature. By itself this evidence does not mean too much, for the demands of a pious life can be satisfied with devotional literature irrespective of church affiliation. The Protestant can be satisfied with the works of Thomas á Kempis or Francis of Assisi, and the Catholic can be satisfied with Bunyan's *Pilgrim's Progress* or Arndt's *True Christianity.*

One thing is certain. The ideal of the free church continued to be maintained on the Continent of Europe during the seventeenth and eighteenth centuries, and those Anabaptists who had proclaimed the evangelical teachings concerning conversion, a regenerate church membership, and a fruit-bearing Christian life had thousands of followers who in many places had to suffer assaults and martyrdom for their faith. There has been a continuous succession of this free church ideal.

It has been indicated that some of the persecuted refugees from several Anabaptist localities ultimately made their way across the Atlantic to find freedom. Already in the 1640's Dutch Mennonite businessmen occasionally went to New Amsterdam (New York), but the first colonization resulted from the migration of the Mennonite church in Crefeld during the 1680's. It was natural that these immigrants would settle among the Quakers in Pennsylvania in the neighborhood of Philadelphia; in fact, a section of the city is called Germantown. After this, the Mennonite immigrants came in waves from Europe—the first groups came during the first half of the eighteenth century from the Palatinate and Switzerland where great numbers left a difficult environment in the old country. It is estimated that perhaps five thousand Mennonites came to America before the War of Independence, which began in 1776. After the Napoleonic Wars there was another new move of emigration, and after the Civil War, 1861–1865, the modern Mennonite emigration movement took place with emigrants coming from many parts of Europe, including Russia. After World War I there was a large-scale migration out of Russia to the United States, Canada, and even to South America. In the meantime, in America the free church policy had already been introduced, even before the arrival of the Anabaptists.

The Early Free Church Movement in England and North America

Anglicanism.—After the death of Queen Elizabeth, James, the king of Scotland, came to the throne of England as James I, reigning over two kingdoms which had formerly been hostile to each other. During the time of Henry VIII and his successors, Scotland had been in alliance with the enemies of England, an old role for the Scottish. James I had great weaknesses, and he had grown up during abnormal times. As an one-year-old child, in 1567 James succeeded his mother, Mary Stuart, to the throne of Scotland and was early declared of age. He was baptized as a Catholic with all of the display of Scottish Catholicism, which was still strong. The church system of John Knox, with its very strict form of Protestantism, also made a deep impression upon the growing boy-monarch. By the time James came to the throne of England, he had already gone through a rigid training in his homeland. His training in the classics and theology was good; he was a learned man. However, he also saw the variations of Calvinistic zeal, and besides he was compelled to see the strife within the old families and the bitterness among his own people which attracted him little to the new religion. In reality, no one knew for sure just where the Scottish king stood in matters of his church opinions. The Catholics placed their hopes in the king on the basis that he was the son of Mary Stuart and that he had received the legitimate baptism. On the other side, the Puritans anticipated better times because the new king had been grounded in Calvinism and had received an anti-Roman upbringing. The Protestant leaders on the Continent considered England a fortress against Rome during the time of Elizabeth. Now these leaders anticipated a more clearly defined policy when this Scottish Presbyterian came to the throne. All of these parties miscalculated the situation.

When James I came to England he soon revealed which way he was going to take, especially between the choices of Presbyterianism or Anglican episcopalism. He discovered that episcopalism in England gave him a better answer to his claim to the divine right of kings than the stern Presbyterianism which insisted on its special divine right even in the question of politics. He did not thrive in the theocratic government which the Scottish theologians and churchmen pursued and in which he was reared. In England James encountered the new Anglican stream with its Renaissance ideas, its assent to worldly culture orientation, and its sentiments of submissive loyalty toward the sovereign on the throne. This was a different atmosphere from that of Scotland, where there was a suspicious watchfulness concerning the king's words and deportment. It was natural, then, that James came to hold obstinately to the idea that the sovereign monarch and episcopalism must belong together. Puritanism in one form or another was a danger, especially in that it was united with the difficult opposition in Parliament. These opposing factors characterized the entire Stuart regime of the seventeenth century.

At the very beginning of his reign, James I found it possible to assume control of the church policies. The king seemed to have planned to build a wide base within an Anglican framework to allow for a variety of opinions, and because of his wide theological knowledge he intended to reach farther than Elizabeth, who regarded church problems as simple political, administrative questions. Therefore, when James was on his way from Scotland, he was met by many Puritans who presented him with the Millenary Petition, so called because it was supposed to bear a thousand signatures. This petition demanded a revision of the Common Prayer Book to be made conformable to the accepted concepts of Puritanism. The king consequently invited the Puritans to a conference at Hampton Court. James issued a proclamation that he desired to abolish all of the inconsistencies in the church, and therefore the Hampton Court Conference was to be held at the beginning of January, 1604. Now, however, the king revealed his ambiguity and double-mindedness, his uncertain administration of affairs, and his inclination to put aside matters, qualities that would characterize his reign. In the very composition of this meeting it was evident that the Puritans could not look for much consideration. Against the nineteen church leaders who represented the Anglican church, only four Puritans were invited. The king himself attended the meetings. There was a decision to make a new revision of the Bible (King James Version). At the mention of conventicles and presbyteries, however, the king became irritated. He declared that Presbyterianism and monarchy were no more compatible than God and the devil. Such a theological thesis on the part of the king was at that time not easily refuted. No arguments could convince him; he did not want to hear anything further concerning the matter. In fact, he angrily stated that he would make these Puritans conform or otherwise harry them out of the land. Even stronger measures were taken, but the hard-pressed clergymen had their friends in the Parliament. It now became apparent that because of the king's behavior at the conference there were awakened misgivings concerning the monarch among the subjects, especially among those who were well represented in the Parliament. They suspected, and correctly so, that back of the king's action there was a struggle to increase his own power. Because of this, the rights of the Parliament became an important factor in the religious struggles and oppositions in the early part of the reign of James I.

It was at this time that the new, rigid Anglicanism accepted the *Book of Canons,* a church discipline, which clearly set the church above all attacks and objections. This was a new way of compulsion to conformity, and it was especially favored by the new king. It was on the authority of the king that the High Commission Court based its repressive judgments, and this implied a civil supremacy in the jurisdiction of church matters which went much farther than Bancroft and the new Anglican church leaders would otherwise allow. These men, in the meantime, were satisfied with their progress made against the Puritans. Most of the Puritan clergymen subscribed to the new church constitution, but about three hundred refused, leaving their pastorates to go to the Continent and other places. This completed the first phase of the Puritan struggle.

On one point, in the meantime, the most loyal Anglican subjects of the king and the most rebellious Puritans could unite—the treatment to be given Catholics. These groups were united in preserving the severe criminal code against the Catholics drawn up during the time of Elizabeth, even though the situation was completely changed after the death of Philip II of Spain and the coming of Henry IV to the throne of France. There could be no question now of any threat from Rome against their country, and even less from any English Catholic refugees on the Continent. Because of this situation and because originally the king desired to establish a broad church foundation in his country, he sought to inaugurate a milder treatment of the Catholics. But on the other hand, he certainly did not want to see them grow or make any encroachment on the prevailing general structure of the church organization. The hard laws were now henceforth to be applied only against the Catholic priests.

This policy promoted by the king met with disapproval from every direction: Catholics were dissatisfied with the halfway measures, the Puritans visualized this as a compromise with the antichrist, and the leaders within the Anglican church considered this matter to be a muddled and arbitrary ordinance. It did not take long before the king became concerned about the growth of the Catholics, for even in the spring of 1604 he complained to the Parliament about their establishment in the realm. The old laws against the Catholics were again revived and enforced. After the Gun Powder Plot in 1605, which was designed to blow up the Parliament with the king, government, and both houses, strict measures were taken against the Catholics. This insane project had been arranged within a Catholic group, and the revenge against the Catholics was severe.

In this manner the new king, during the first years of his reign, executed a hard policy for a national church conformity. The Puritan leaders were brushed aside, and the Catholics and their friends were forced into submission. One would suspect that now the king would be inclined to follow a more positive Anglican course, but it was soon evident that surprises were not over. It is true that the Anglican theologians and the Episcopal leaders with Bancroft, Andrewes, and some favorites of the young Laud came into the center of leadership, but on the other hand, the king did not want a clericalism that would rise above his leadership. Therefore, he surprised the English people, after Archbishop of Canterbury Bancroft died in 1610, by appointing a Puritan-inclined churchman to fill the vacancy, George Abbot (1611–1633). Once again the

Puritans returned from the Continent. Abbot was not able to accomplish much against high-church Anglicanism, which now not only pressed forward demanding its liturgy but also advanced its anti-Calvinistic theology. Anglicans now began to sense a closer relationship with the old churches, Roman and Oriental, than with the Reformation churches with their inner strife. The Puritan tendencies of Abbot finally led him to suffer disgrace, for during the 1620's, his last decade, he lost all of his influence with the court. Within Puritan circles, however, it was considered an important matter that the archbishop of Canterbury had an understanding of the Low Church movement.

In 1625, James I was succeeded by Charles I, who fell heir to an inheritance which proved to be a real problem. Because of the weak policies of James I and his uncertain attitude in various questions, the Puritans had become a significant power in Parliament. The House of Commons was on guard to maintain its rights against the autocracy of the king, and the Puritan element kept a sharp eye on the Catholic danger. The Parliament demanded that the penal law against the Catholics should be carried out: priests should be exiled and others forced to submit through fines and imprisonment. When Charles I had married the sister of the king of France, a Catholic princess, the French rulers had obtained a secret document signed by James I, Charles, and the prime minister, which secured religious freedom for the Catholics in England. The new queen came with a French Catholic court, all of whom demanded their freedom, a challenge both to English nationalism and to Puritanism. Charles did not dare go against his own people, so he did not keep his secret promise and enforced the penal laws once again. However, the queen's court continued to conduct Catholic worship services until 1643.

The growth of Puritanism during the final years of James I, mentioned above, increased Parliament's opposition to the absolutist tendencies of the king. The Puritan-minded Archbishop Abbot was gone, and the king was carrying on active negotiations with Spain. All of this only incited the Puritan powers to gather together and to rally opposition. When

Charles I acquired a Catholic queen with her Catholic court and showed himself hostile to Parliament, the Puritans aroused themselves to battle. Politics and religion were united during the entire seventeenth century.

Puritanism now came up against a strong man's unyielding position, a firmness which did not yield except to force or revolution. This man was William Laud.

At the close of the decade of 1590, Laud began his teaching duties at Oxford, where his strong anti-Calvinistic position got him into a feud with George Abbot, who was then master of the University College. At the same time that Abbot became archbishop of Canterbury, Laud became the president of St. John's College in Oxford. These two opponents were thus separated, but it was Laud with his lower post who advanced to be the powerful leader in the church, while Abbot in his high post was not able to maintain the leadership. Even while Laud was at Oxford, it was realized that the high-church concept had a strong advocate of its ideas. He regarded association with Rome more important than that with the Protestant churches on the Continent. The Roman Church had an unbroken episcopate since the days of the apostles, and therefore to Laud, it was a true Church, while the nonepiscopal Continental churches had lost all claims to be considered a part of the true Church. Laud's influence was one reason for the slowness of the Stuarts to help the Protestants during the Thirty Years' War.

When Laud powerfully set forth his viewpoint during his time at Oxford, where he clearly championed for ritualism, he was openly charged in the University as a popist. He became a friend to one of the bishops, who was a favorite of James I. In 1611 the strange young king James I, who had named Abbot as archbishop, took Laud, the opponent of the archbishop's theology and church policy, to be his chaplain and court preacher. Laud quickly grew in favor and influence with the king, while Abbot's position gradually diminished. Laud had personal qualities which enabled him to win success, and furthermore, the king prepared him quickly for advancement. In the year 1621, Laud became the bishop at St. David's, and he already at that time had a position of dominant influence with the court. From this time on until his imprisonment about twenty years later, Laud was unequaled as the foremost person in the Church of England. He must be identified with the rigid high-church policy, which during this period came to be the primary form, and through persecution and arrogance he tightened the bow to the breaking point.

Laud believed that the church was threatened by two dangers: first, the decline in church discipline which prevailed among both the clergy and the laymen, and secondly, the Puritans' efforts to establish their own worship and organization. Laud was a fanatical conformist. Prohibition of dissent from the forms and formulas, whether it be breaking of bread, liturgy, or church organization, became articles in the law by which people would be judged. He was going to try to silence the Calvinistic preachers. It was this high church which now with embittered rage turned against the harsh and pure cult on which the Puritans insisted. There was no possibility of reconciliation. A state and church police force was developed which drove thousands of Puritans across the Atlantic, while others were put in prison and in some instances were tortured and died. This severe regimentation could not continue, even if the taskmasters were convinced that they were rendering the right service to the church and to God. The convictions of the high church had hardened into bitterness and strait-laced fanaticism.

That this spirit was met by a Puritan fanaticism did not make the matter any easier. It was at this time that the High Commission functioned as an inquisition court. During the early years of Charles I, Laud gained greater heights of prominence, and he became all the more severe against his opponents, even against those who championed the right of Parliament over the growing boldness of the kingly absolutism. When Charles I made Laud bishop of London in 1628 and chancellor of Oxford University in 1630, this despotic power in church matters had reached his zenith, as was confirmed when he was appointed to be Abbot's successor in 1633. The decade of the thirties produced restrictions of a type that under any circumstances can never be justified.

Congregationalism.—The separatists and the free churches were very sparse in the beginning of the seventeenth century, but they represented a tendency which had inherent powers and which made a powerful impact during the subsequent revolution. Preceding sections have indicated how this separatism, at the close of the sixteenth century and at the beginning of the seventeenth century, progressed simultaneously with Puritan presbyterianism. The names of Robert Browne and Henry Barrow were mentioned in this connection.

Barrow, as it has been pointed out, had to suffer a martyr's death in 1593, but the movement of which he was the pioneer lived underground and waited its time for expression. This free congregationalism stood in conscious opposition not only to the Anglican high church and to the Puritanism within the church but also to presbyterian Puritanism. It is possible, therefore, to distinguish these four streams in the life of the English church during the early part of the seventeenth century. In addition to these, there should be mentioned crypto-Catholicism.

The severe persecutions during the time of Elizabeth hindered the radical Puritans from developing a congregational type of organization in England. However, when these radicals were forced to flee from England, especially to Holland, the free church was a natural form for church government. There is also a parallel in this situation to the earlier churches of refugees which had attempted to remain in London and maintain fellowship until their members were forced to scatter. Their affinity in language and nationality, as well as their spiritual type of piety, made it natural that these refugee Englishmen would become members of the free churches. The ideas of Browne, Barrow, and Johnson could not be dispelled. These refugees had lived in separatist Puritan circles, and when they came to the Netherlands they translated these ideas into a practical organization. It was the Anabaptist congregational system which now had an opportunity to be employed, even among the English-speaking groups.

During the decade following the strict Conventicle Act of 1593, several assemblies traveled to Holland and augmented the multitude of Puritan separatists in the free churches. A famous congregation was established in 1609 in Leiden under the leadership of John Robinson. He was an educated and respected man from Cambridge who aligned himself with the Barrowist free church movement, defending this concept with a well-written brochure. It was from this congregation from which the so-called Pilgrim Fathers in 1620 left to cross the Atlantic on the *Mayflower* and settle in New England. These English refugees faced difficulties theologically as well as materially, which hindered the English free churches in the territories of the Netherlands; but by means of writings, as well as their example of church life, they were able to disseminate their new ideas far and wide. They treasured dearly the freedom to order and arrange their own church community, and this practice of self-government stimulated their friends in the faith in England.

It was this congregationalism just mentioned which was practically developed in Holland in the organization of churches, and the concept was soon transplanted to the North American colonies. It therefore can be stated with assurance that these refugee separatists made a contribution to Christian polity which began to have important repercussions on English church life even during the seventeenth century. These separatists, in their new environment in America, were able to show their fellow believers in England how to organize a free church and develop its organization. Reports that were sent, as well as visits that were made to England, all became very meaningful. It is of great significance that the congregationalist pattern of church organization was already established in North America when the great Puritan stream in the 1630's came from England to New England. For the greater part, these Puritans broke completely with their own low church Anglicanism and accepted the free church idea. These Puritans had no desire to be associated with Laud's church, and when they now saw congregationalism already in operation on the North American coast, it was natural for them to accept it.

One of the most important pioneers for English congregationalism at the beginning of the seventeenth century was Henry Jacob. He was a student at Oxford, and he was recognized as one of the foremost leaders among university men who worked for the free church ideals. At the beginning of his career, Jacob opposed the consistent free church concepts of the Barrowists, which at that time were being led by Francis Johnson. After Jacob had been in prison for some time because of his activities, he left England to go to Holland, where he found a position with a merchant's church in Middelburg which formerly had been served by similar Nonconformist clergymen. Jacob also came under the influence of Robinson and his congregation in Leiden. All of this strengthened his understanding of the free church. There were similar free churches in Delft, Haag, Utrecht, and Rotterdam.

In 1616, when Henry Jacob returned to England from Holland, he organized a Congregational church in Southwark, London. This was the period when the mild Puritan, George Abbot, was archbishop of Canterbury, and it was during these years that the Nonconformists found it easier to visit and work in England. This Congregational church was the first of its kind, and its organization became the starting point for Puritan congregationalism, which during the latter portion of the seventeenth century developed into the strongest free church denomination. After Jacob's death in 1624, there was a succession of noteworthy men who served as pastors of this congregation. Several of them were educated university men, and a few of them had previously been Anglican priests. During the time of Archbishop Laud, John Lathrop was singled out for persecution, whereupon he, together with a congregation of about thirty, emigrated to North America in 1634. The talented Cambridge man, Henry Jessey, assumed the leadership of the Southwark church, which continued to develop.

This original Congregationalism in England did not have any great expansion until the time following Cromwell, when the Stuarts and the Anglican policy of oppression were again restored. Baptist ideas began to win approval in this Southwark church. It is estimated that at least five Baptist congregations stemmed from this Congregational church, and even this mother church finally accepted the Baptist principles, first maintaining an open membership and then later a closed membership. Open membership was the practice of accepting members into the fellowship of the church who had not been baptized as believers. This was before baptism became the door into the church. The questions of open communion and open membership were soon prevalent among the free churches.

Baptists.—Among those refugees who arrived in Holland was one who would become the first leader of the English Baptists. He was John Smyth. Like Robinson, Smyth was a highly educated man, coming from Cambridge University, where at the close of the sixteenth century free church ideas had many exponents. Smyth obtained a good position as a preacher in the city of Lincoln, but because of his separatist leanings he was removed. This took place in 1602. Later Smyth worked as a physician, but he continued to hold to his separatist ideas. In northern England there were many with these ideas, so Smyth organized a church after the congregational pattern and became its pastor. Robinson and two men who became Baptist pioneers, Thomas Helwys and John Murton, joined this congregation. Persecution soon struck, and migration became the way of escape for these separatists.

In 1608 the Smyth congregation was in Amsterdam, where it took an independent position from that held by the earlier Johnson congregation. At first Smyth practiced as a physician, but soon he became the leader of the congregation. Smyth was an especially impressionable man, zealous and thorough in his seeking. He began to do a lot of writing, and in 1608 he published a book in Amsterdam, *The Differences of the Churches of the Separation.* This work gives a good clarification of the origin of the free church movement and its development into a radical concept. Smyth wanted to revive completely the primitive life of the New Testament church, including the charismatic gifts. It can be expected that a man like Smyth could not help but be impressed with the Dutch Anabaptist movement with which he had come in contact in Amsterdam. It was generally believed that the Mennonites were an example of the radical free church ideas to which many of the English refugees were drawn. However, Smyth came into conflict with churches led by such men as Francis Johnson and John Robinson.

It was in a writing published in 1609 in which Smyth clearly set forth his Baptist faith. The publication is called *The Character of the Beast,* and it is here that Smyth testified that infants should not be baptized, because such a baptism cannot be found recorded in the New Testament. The order in Jesus' command was first preaching and winning disciples, then baptizing. Smyth now went from word to action. He baptized himself, after which he baptized Helwys and other members of his congregation, since each one had given a personal confession of faith. Later Smyth became uncertain about the validity of his self-performed baptism and consequently became interested in the Mennonite church in Amsterdam, attempting to become a member there. In the meantime, only a few of Smyth's congregation followed him, finally seeking affiliation with the Waterlanders. This separation became final when Smyth died in 1612, leaving the group without a leader.

Among those who did not follow Smyth into the Mennonite movement was Thomas Helwys, who like Smyth had accepted the ideas of Arminianism and had separated from English Puritanism, not only on the matter of baptism but also in his attitude toward the Calvinistic doctrine of election. Here it is possible to see an influence from the Mennonites. Helwys wrote some significant theological works in which he clarified his doctrinal position. He also represented a departure from the old Anabaptist movement in regard to his ideas of state and community. Helwys gave the future English Baptists a positive position in questions concerning the oath, the sword, and the holding of civil positions. This position became the basic expression of the modern Baptist movement.

In spite of severe laws of England, Helwys decided to return home. One ought not to withdraw from persecution by fleeing to a foreign land. It was in this way that the first Baptist church was established on English soil, when Helwys organized this congregation in 1612 at Spitalfield, near London. It seems that Helwys was soon thrown into prison, where he died either in 1613 or 1614.

John Murton took up the leadership of this first church after Helwys. This church continued until the end of the nineteenth century. Murton proceeded by means of writings to motivate as well as to defend the practice of requiring baptism to be the door of the free church. Among the Congregationalists there was the so-called covenant that constituted the free church of confessed believers. Soon several similar Baptist congregations were established in England. When Murton died in 1625 or 1626, it is believed that there were at least five congregations with approximately 150 members. In 1644 there were forty-seven churches. During the time of Laud's regime these congregations were persecuted, and many of the members left the country. All of these churches were Arminian in theology. The usual mode of baptism evidently was aspersion, not immersion, although already in 1613 there was a booklet in which immersion was set forth as the correct mode. These first English Baptists embraced the idea of "general grace," which differed from the Calvinistic concept of election or "particular grace." Because of these differences, the names "General Baptists" and "Particular Baptists" arose. The attempts to bring about a closer relationship with the Dutch Mennonites did not succeed, primarily because of the English Baptists' positive viewpoint concerning community and state.

These early Baptists were the first ones to present the concepts of full religious freedom in the English language. Even in John Smyth's confession of 1612 it is stated that the authorities, because of the power of their office, should not interfere with the religious establishment or in the matters of conscience, nor compel any person to one or another form of religion or doctrinal teaching. According to Smyth, Christ alone is the king and judge of the church and the conscience. All Christians must respect the rights of the religious opinions of others, for each person must be considered as seriously committed to his own cause. Helwys furthered this idea of religious freedom when he maintained that each person must choose for himself the way he should take in matters of religion, seeing that every person must stand before the judgment seat of God to answer for himself. If the king or anyone in authority uses his power to force one to submit regarding "heavenly or spiritual matters," then it is better to become a martyr and maintain his conscience inviolable before God. The king is not God; he does not have the power to enforce laws and ordinances upon immortal souls. This writing provoked James I, and he gave the order that Helwys should be thrown into prison, which has already been mentioned.

The third man among the Baptists who clearly expressed himself on the subject of religious freedom was Leonard Busher. In 1614 he presented a tractate entitled *Religious Peace or a Plea for Liberty of Conscience* in which he, like Milton later, pleaded that it ought to be lawful for any person, even Jews and Catholics, to write, discuss, print, and publish any matter concerning religion. In this he also avowed that true religion comes only through faith and the new birth, and therefore the true religion can only be justified by the Word and the Spirit. All persecution is diametrically opposed to the merciful principles of Christ, and therefore persecution has never really worked. It is thus meaningless when the aim is considered. It is also a danger for the security and the welfare of the state, for it can drive the subdued conscience to conspiracy. Consequently, religious oppression is dangerous for both the prince and the people, while the freedom of conscience not only furthers the gospel but also guarantees security for both parties. In this tract he appealed to the king and the Parliament, stating that as they did not desire to be compelled into conformity by the pope, so they ought not now attempt to subdue the conscience of others. No church which compels people to join is a true church. The writer attacked the bishops as the instigators of the Anglican policy of compulsion and therefore advocated abolition of their official position with the state and their power to punish. In this way the freedom of the conscience could be upheld and religious freedom could be formed in the land.

The Baptist movement which grew out of the previously mentioned Puritan congregational church in Southwark was another type than that which arose out of the emigrants from Holland. The latter group, as has been stated, was influenced by the Mennonites and maintained an Arminian point of view, while the Puritan Baptists, which arose during the 1630's,

197

were committed to the Calvinistic stream which governed not only those Puritans within the church but also the Nonconformists without. Already it has been mentioned that the Calvinistic Baptists went out of the Congregational church during the decade of the 1630's. Henry Jessey became a Baptist, and another important leader was Hanserd Knollys, also from Cambridge University, as well as the prosperous businessman and able preacher William Kiffin. By 1644 there were seven of these churches. These so-called Particular Baptists soon began to surpass the earlier General Baptists. They did not have the same opposition in the Puritan circles as the General Baptists, who had thrown overboard the typical Puritan doctrine of election. Among those who later were counted among the Particular Baptists were Roger Williams, the father of the American Baptists, and John Bunyan, the most celebrated Baptist of the seventeenth century. The doctrines pertaining to total depravity and "grace abounding" were the principal diet of the Particular Baptists. It was among these Particular Baptists that there developed zealous insistence that the mode of baptism be by immersion, not aspersion or sprinkling.

The Cromwellian period.—When William Laud became archbishop in 1633 and the primary administrator for Charles I in church matters, there followed, as has been mentioned, a ten-year persecution of nonconformists of all kinds. The purpose here was that by means of law and punishment people would be driven into the church, especially into liturgical conformity. This church struggle paralleled the king's autocratic political regimentation, which even sought to set aside the Parliament. This brought the Puritans into the political struggle to preserve the established legitimacy of the Parliament over against the absolutism of the king. In this way the church struggle was also a preparation for the uprising among the people, the revolution which occurred during the 1640's. The Scottish people came to play an important role in national events. Between them and the nonconformist Puritans in England was a congeniality of mind which evoked a crusade in the struggle against the policies of the Stuarts.

The Puritan spirit was hard and uncompromising. Laymen

pressed to the fore when the preachers were silenced, and separatism grew when Laud attempted to restrain Puritanism within the church. In spite of all of the persecution measures against nonconformists, the separatist congregations continued to spring up, which usually meant a strengthening of the political forces against the king's autocratic strivings. It is impossible here to draw any clear line of demarcation between the religious and the political fields of action. Soon such men as Cromwell, Milton, Hampden, Pym, and others were in the leadership of the revolution and later in the nation. For these men the religious opposition against the Stuart demands was as apparent as the political. These men, like a number of others, championed the rights and privileges of the people, for the freedom of churches and citizens, and in some instances they sought complete toleration. In 1641 John Milton published three antiepiscopal brochures, and later a skilful treatise dealing with religious freedom and tolerance. Within Puritanism a tradition of opposition had arisen which reared a group of stern and brave men. The logical way out for many of these men was separatism.

It is impossible to speak of a clear and easily interpreted situation during the next two decades, 1640–1660. The Parliament designated as the Long Parliament (from 1640) and the victories of the Cromwell army brought about a new regime. The presbyterian Puritans, in their theological conclave called the Westminster Assembly, planned a new church organization. But the congregationalistic stream became too important, especially when the migrants came from Holland as well as from America, encouraged by the Parliament's gatherings and measures taken against the persecutors, among them Archbishop Laud. The execution of Laud in 1645, and of Charles I in 1649, seemed to be the blow which completely abolished the episcopal order. The old fear for the pope and Rome was behind the radicalism which now appeared in church affairs. Charles I had definite sympathies for the Catholics. Dissention against the king and against Laud's demands for a high-church uniformity had grown. Now there developed also an aversion against the Scottish influence in the power-demanding Presbyterians. This led to an increased success for separatism and congregationalism. Cromwell and his army's interests were in this regard so strong that the Westminster Assembly's decisions at the close of the 1640 decade could not be realized.

In the place of presbyterianism came Cromwell's experiment with the autonomous congregations within the old parochial system. The congregationalist idea now had an opportunity for expression, in that it was possible for nonconformist preachers and Puritan separatists to gain positions as preachers and spiritual guides in the parish churches and other Anglican sanctuaries. It must be remembered, however, that there was an abnormal situation during the two decades until 1660. This period was too short to make possible a needed consolidation of the newly won victories of the radicals. There were uncertain compromises, loose experiments, and many times there came forth measures from the outside which had no anchorage in the local customs and the church methods. Therefore, reaction to this new way also became very strong.

The loose organization of the Cromwellian movement showed up in the development of several apocalyptic and chiliastic groups. The war and the difficulties give an explanation of this. The radical movements such as the Seekers, Familists, Fifth Monarchy Men, and the Quakers came to life just at this time. Some of these were considered as revolutionary, others had only a brief existence, while others developed into established organizations. This latter fact was especially true among the Quakers, who with George Fox arose during the 1650's. It is estimated that during the time of the Protectorate over three thousand Quakers were imprisoned.

The Congregationalists and the Baptists often intermingled because both open communion and open membership were to be found among the Baptists. The positions of these groups won adherents from many directions. Even John Milton, who accepted the Congregational form of organization, spoke out in behalf of believer's baptism by immersion. It was also at the beginning of the 1650's that John Bunyan joined the Baptists and became one of their most talented and independent leaders. There is a record stating that before 1660, 297 Baptist churches had been established. With the acceptance of their confession in 1644, the particular Baptists progressed as the leading group among the English Baptists. There were soon occasions to compose new confessions, which were basically revisions of the 1644 confession. Even during the time of the restitution in 1660 it was deemed necessary to present another confession. In 1658 the Congregationalists formed the so-called Savoy Declaration, of which John Owen was the chief designer. The new Baptist confession was not written until 1677.

The composing of confessions of faith among the General Baptists was started during the time of John Smyth and with his assistance. These confessions came to be a basis for understanding with the Mennonites. Helwys even wrote a confession in Holland which was printed in 1611. In 1651 a number of General Baptist churches united in a new confession. At the time of the Restoration this same group drew up its standard confession in 1660, accepting it at a general conference in London. It also was presented to Charles II the same year. In this confession the General Baptists agreed to practice baptism by the mode of immersion.

Migration to North America.—The struggle which the Stuarts, and especially William Laud, carried on against dissenters and the free church movement became disastrous for themselves. The revolution was partly a result of this brutal policy. Another result of great significance in world history was the migration to North America. Puritans, who became weary of the vexations, set out across the Atlantic to win freedom in the wilderness regions in the West. It was in North America that the free church had its great opportunity. There were no domineering church organizations which demanded subservience, but here the thousands of immigrants built their own church organizations according to their own convictions. It is estimated that during the decade of 1630 twenty thousand immigrants came over, and the numbers continued to increase.

In American history the romanticized voyage of the *Mayflower* in 1620, upon which the first important group of English Puritan refugees from Holland came to settle in a territory close to Boston, was the beginning of a great Protestant development on the new continent. Earlier, in the south a group of businessmen had established a colony. Here the official Anglican church functioned as a part of the life of the colony. However, it was the Puritan tradition in the north, New England, that pointed out the path for the future. Here people wanted their own church organization, and they would not tolerate any other besides their own. Because of the difficulties and inner unrest in England, these Puritan colonists had freedom to arrange their community affairs as well as their own church life. No involvement with the motherland in civil or in church authority could take place; however, certain difficulties could arise because of the request for concessions made by the colonists.

While England was writing its history with civil war and the Cromwellian interregnum, the Puritan pioneers were establishing a new community and a new church fellowship in North America. Before 1660 it was the Congregationalists in New England who led this development. However, other individuals and groups made their contributions. Already by 1638 there was established a denomination which was destined to become the largest Protestant body in North America, the Baptist. An Anglican priest, Roger Williams, came to the new settlement at Boston with a radical attitude regarding church matters. He soon was persuaded to the Baptist point of view. But then he discovered that the Puritan fathers were not willing to permit religious freedom in their communities. Williams, together with others, had to flee to a place farther south, and here he established the colony known as Rhode Island, which established a policy original and unique in the Colonies. Full religious freedom was proclaimed—an unusual experiment at this time of history. Rhode Island became the headquarters for the Baptists of North America during the entire seventeenth century. A physician, John Clarke, was one of the foremost leaders here.

Other Protestants, some of whom followed the free church concept, came to the New World on the American Atlantic coast. Swedish Lutherans established churches in the Delaware territory under the watchcare of the homeland. These Swedes made an insignificant impression in Colonial life. Of greater note and importance during this period was the Calvinist Dutch colony which was established as New Amsterdam (later called New York). The Reformed and the Presbyterian free churches developed from this place. In the middle colonies, north of Virginia and south of New England, the Presbyterians were the leading church at this time. They were strengthened in some ways by the Huguenots who fled to America during the persecution by the French government.

In the south the Anglican church held forth, and during the time of the Cromwellian interregnum, many Anglicans had to leave England, strengthening the official Anglican church in Virginia and in other southern colonies. This church was organized as a branch of the English state church, and because of this the free church movement here met great difficulties for a long time. After 1660 the state of affairs became even more varied.

Growth of the Free Church Movement

England until 1689.—After the death of Cromwell in 1658, there followed a period of weak leadership by Cromwell's son Richard. The great masses of the people had no serious hesitations concerning the monarchy; it was only the radical Puritans who had republican sympathies. Furthermore, the great majority of the citizenry was dissatisfied with the new church order. It was not only the Anglicans who were looking for a new day but also the presbyterians who believed that they had been wrongfully robbed of their position in the life of the English church. They were afraid of these radical groups, both from political as well as religious reasons. The peculiar church regime during the decade of the 1650's was built on a political minority power, and in principle it opposed the intrinsic congregational idea and its teachings concerning the separation of church and state. In the very organization of their church program, leaders of the new regime had made a mistake.

At first the presbyterians were zealous for restoration of the monarchy, accepting the recall of Charles's son in 1660 to become Charles II. In this way, naturally, this church group sought to strengthen and fortify its own position. The young king led the presbyterians to believe they had his favor, but when the monarchy became established, the presbyterians soon began to sense the real position of this new Stuart descendant. His aim was to revive the Anglican church and drive hard for the principle of uniformity. Also, the young king's sympathies for the Catholics became apparent, and it is understandable that it was the high-church Anglicanism which triumphed. In the spring of 1661 the Parliament decided to reinstate the church with its established privileges.

The line of conciliation which the presbyterians chose brought no lasting results. Soon strict decrees were issued which would force all nonconformity to be subdued, including that of the presbyterians. The so-called Corporations Act denied the free church people the right of holding public office, and the Act of Uniformity in 1662 screened out all of the preachers in the state church who did not accept the Anglican Prayer Book and the prescribed order of worship. A public declaration was required from all those who held any positions within the church and the universities that they would yield to the Uniformity Act and never carry arms against the king.

The result of this compulsory law was twofold. Approximately two thousand preachers were relieved of their parishes, among them such important men as the presbyterians Richard Baxter and John Howe, the congregationalists John Owen and Peter Sterry. This naturally was a fateful draining of the spiritual power and life of the established church. On the other hand, some who had never belonged to free churches now joined them, and this meant that the free churches made real progress. Presbyterianism was not in its basic principle a free church, for in Scotland it had formed a very strict state church. In England during the period of the 1640's the presbyterians expected that they would achieve a similar position. This expectation was not realized, and the attempt as royalists in 1660 to win an advantage in the newly revived Stuart regime completely failed. After 1662 even the presbyterians became free church exponents. This brought about inner strength to the Presbyterian church as well as to the entire cause of free churches, for now there was new numerical strength and a new alliance in the struggle for religious freedom.

There was by no means any real religious freedom for the various free church groups. On the contrary, the cleavage in the English religious world caused the authorities in the state and in the Anglican church to adopt forceful measures intended to compel uniformity of all nonconformists. In 1664 the Conventicle Act was issued which prohibited the assembly of any free church groups with more than five people in attendance. The first offense against this decree brought either a five pound fine or three months in prison. At the second offense the fine was doubled, and the third offense demanded a fine of a hundred pounds. If offenders could not pay, they would be exiled for seven years to one of England's colonies. (The Swedish Conventicle Act of 1726 was similar, with its three grades of punishment.)

A special act, the so-called Five Mile Act of 1665, was designed to restrict independent preachers. Every preacher who would not conform to the laws of uniformity was forbidden to come within five miles of his former congregation. Disobedience was punishable with a fine of forty pounds. In this way the nonconformist pastors' influence—and income—would be cut off. At times there was some relief during the Stuart period up to 1689, but this was a time of real suffering for the free church in England.

For the older free churches, the Congregationalists and the Baptists, the new laws had less effect. They were free churches in principle, and only in rare instances had members held public offices which were curtailed. Nevertheless, these free church groups suffered much through persecutions which were going on at this time. Multitudes were deported to the "world's dark areas," as Baxter wrote. It was during this time that Bunyan was forced to sit in the Bedford prison twelve years, and even Baxter was imprisoned for a period. The Quakers emerged in this stormy period. Fox and other Quakers were often in prison and mistreated. However, their numbers increased. William Penn, a man from a respected family, created a sensation by joining the Quakers in 1668.

In the meantime, Charles II retained his Catholic sympathies, and on the basis of this he was interested in making possible some alleviations for those whom the strict Anglicans were persecuting. The association of Charles II with Louis XIV in France increased his desire to aid the Catholics in England. Thus he pronounced an edict of toleration in 1672, which declared that the king with his divine right could suspend the penal laws against the dissenters. Freedom was given to great numbers of imprisoned free church members, among them John Bunyan. A number of licenses were issued which permitted preachers and worship services in the local communities. This seemed to be a good time for the nonconformists. In ten months about 2,500 licenses were issued for those within such denominations as the Presbyterians, Congregationalists, Baptists, and Quakers.

It soon became evident, however, that Charles's purpose was an attempt to aid the Catholics, and therefore when the Parliament reconvened, opposition against the king's policy of toleration had grown. It was stated that the king had assumed rights which he did not possess. The free churches revealed an unusual idealism, for they despised the freedom for their own part if the Catholics were to gain benefits for their point of view. They had expected some special privilege, but in its conflict against papism the Parliament made a summary of the whole cause. The result was the famous Test Act of 1673, which led to much strife in the following century, even until its abolishment in 1828. The Test Act was basically a revision of the former Corporation Act of 1661, declaring that all citizens in civil or military services were required to celebrate communion according to the Anglican service and at the same time were to make a declaration against the doctrine of transubstantiation. This final clause was directed at the Catholics.

A new period of persecution followed. Bunyan, Fox, and others were again put in prison. William Penn, who was the most outstanding man among the Quakers next to Fox, was compelled to go to prison in spite of his important connections. It was while he was in prison that Penn wrote the well-known *No Cross, No Crown.* Fox and his successors encouraged the cause of spiritualism by their teachings of the "inner light" and the immediate experience of God without any assistance of clergy or sacraments. Fox emerged as a preacher of repentance and revival, and he criticized sharply the existing state church and all organized Christianity. Fox's sharp opposition against every type of war and force caused him to be considered a danger to state and community. His refusal to have any association with social affairs in the community brought him disgrace and opposition, even by persons who were spiritually associated with him. John Bunyan had a serious controversy with Fox. This conflict resulted over the fact that Fox also attacked the organization of free churches. It soon became evident, however, that the Quakers had to form some similar type of organization in order to continue as a group.

In 1685 the brother of Charles II succeeded to the throne, and he reigned for three years under the name of James II. He openly espoused Catholicism and was resolute on crushing the free church movement. The king obtained gruesome assistants, and death by burning was instituted. But the king pulled the bowstring too hard, and it broke. The revolution at the close of 1688 swept him away, and the Calvinist, William of Orange, the son-in-law of James II, was invited to be the king of England. Consequently, the Protestant policy was secured, but the matter of the free church activity was not hereby solved.

One of the results of this change in administration was the celebrated Toleration Act of 1689. This act was not a definite law granting religious freedom, but it did grant that the free churches would no longer be judged and condemned to punishment and that they would be permitted to have their own congregations and conduct their own worship services. They must, however, continue to pay the tithe and other taxes to the state church. Tolerance also was only for the Protestants who swore allegiance and fealty to the king and subscribed to a declaration against transubstantiation. Catholics, Unitarians, and Jews were excluded from the Act of Toleration. A free church preacher was required to subscribe to at least thirty-four of the thirty-nine articles of the Anglican church. Articles concerning church organization and ceremonies were exempted. For Baptists the article concerning infant baptism was exempted, and the Quakers were allowed to give solemn assurance in place of taking the oath. Many were dissatisfied with the parsimonious attitude of this Act of Toleration. It was at this time that the great philosopher John Locke began writing and made a real impact for full religious freedom, the same which the free churches had demanded earlier.

Through all of these difficulties the free churches had sensed a bond of oneness. Some even sought union between the Congregationalists and the Presbyterians. In 1691 an agreement on a number of articles that was drawn up seemed to gain approval from some quarters. It was, however, obvious that the time was not ripe for such a unification of the two denominations. Not only in the organizational points of view but also in doctrine there were differences. No workable union was concluded among these two Puritan denominations, of which Congregationalism was more strictly Calvinist.

The Baptists were fewer in numbers, and they continued as two groups, the General Baptists and the Particular Baptists. The Baptists also experienced inner difficulties over the question of the practice of the Lord's Supper, to which earlier reference has been made. The Quakers, like the Baptists, were exclusive and radical in their attitude against the state church; they were opposed to all interference of the state in the life of the church. The Quakers had no fellowship with the other free church groups, but they made very good progress. After William Penn returned from his sojourn in America, he played an important role in the development of the Quaker movement.

Nevertheless this limited freedom, which was granted by the Act of Toleration of 1689, lead to a new epoch in the history of England and the Protestant churches. The old idea which had dominated since the time of the Reformation that political unity in the country was dependent upon religious unity was now abandoned. England presented an example of a cleavage in church opinions which did not hazard political unity or strength, and down through the centuries this fact has been confirmed. The old epoch of persecution was at an end. Even from some other points of view the old era had disappeared, for this time saw the passing of some of the greatest men of the free church movement. John Bunyan died in 1688, as had John Owen five years before. George Fox died in 1690 and Richard Baxter in 1691. Fox left diaries of great interest, and Baxter in an autobiography had described his life.

North American developments.—The extension of the English free church movement, which found opportunity to expand in the new territories of North America, had a comparatively peaceful development during the latter portion of the seventeenth century. These churches were not much disturbed by the restoration and the persecution back home in England. In the north the Congregationalist churches reigned in New England, and the Baptists continued to build their colony in Rhode Island and to spread into other territories. The Presbyterians settled largely in the middle colonies.

The greatest occurrence in the religious life of North America at this time was the coming of William Penn and the Quakers. At the beginning of the 1680's, Penn had obtained from the English crown the permission to lay claim to the great territory which now makes up the state of Pennsylvania. Penn established the city of Philadelphia, where he announced there would be complete religious freedom. Large numbers of immigrants came here. The expansion of the Quakers led to the fact that the Swedish Lutheran churches came under the jurisdiction of the Quakers. Previously, the English had occupied this territory. The Lutheran churches maintained their own organization, being tied with the church in the homeland, a relationship which continued until the 1780's.

The religious freedom which was proclaimed in Pennsylvania resulted in the fact that many religious groups sought freedom in this area. Congregationalism had its establishment in New England in the north, and those of like-minded faith went there at this time. English Baptists went to various territories, but soon Pennsylvania became a haven for them. The Baptists had earlier stood with the Quakers in the struggle to win freedom to express their own religious convictions. A Baptist church was established in Pennsylvania in 1684, and later several others were organized. One of the well-known

Baptist leaders from England, who visited America for a brief period to do the work of a pioneer, was Elias Keach. However, he soon had to return to his homeland. Pennsylvania became a second American center for the Baptists, whose forces were augmented by the English immigrants, as well as by fellow believers from Rhode Island.

In the year 1698, the first Baptist church was established in Philadelphia. New immigrants came from England, and soon this city became the center for the Calvinistic Baptists (Particular Baptists). During this same period other groups established a firm footing in this territory, such as the Mennonites from Holland and the so-called Dunkards from Germany. Life in the colony was marked by freedom as long as Penn's Quaker ideas and toleration continued, for as proprietor of the colony he was the highest in command.

At the close of the seventeenth century the free church movement had reached a meaningful goal—religious freedom for which it long had struggled. There can be no doubt that the development of freedom and independence in America's frontiers made a significant impression on the homeland and influenced and determined the movement there. This church influence continued throughout the following centuries.

Eighteenth-century England and America.—During the reign of William III, which was comparatively short (d. 1702), the free church naturally made great gains. The new freedom opened new opportunities, and the formerly persecuted nonconformists took advantage of this fact. During the twelve years preceding 1700 the free church movement moved forward with great strides. It was now that the prayer-meeting houses began to play an important role in the lives of the English people. It is reported that no less than 2,418 such places of worship were licensed and opened for services during these years. Naturally all of these buildings were not new, for some of these had existed before as unlawful or unlicensed. Many were also temporary. This powerful new development made for greater inner problems for the free church groups. One of the most serious problems was that of trying to find qualified leaders for the rapidly growing movement. Within the older fellowships, such

210

as Congregationalists, Presbyterians, and Baptists, there had been instituted some time before a plan to train preachers, but the Quakers were opposed to such education.

As in America, the training of pastors was a humble and simple process. Often a few young men would gather together with an older pastor who would attempt to teach them in his own home. This was, however, the beginning of the "academies," which soon played an important role in the life of the English free churches. It is estimated that in 1689 about twenty such small schools existed. Members of the free churches were not allowed to attend the universities, even until the latter portion of the nineteenth century. The free churches were also interested in the secondary school training program, and their contributions in this area later proved to be of a pioneering nature. This was especially the case at the beginning of the nineteenth century.

During the reign of Queen Anne (1702–1714), the free churches went through another period of difficulties. She was the daughter of James II, and she was occupied with prejudices against the strong, growing free church movement. She was a conservative of the high-church type, and consequently there was an entirely different atmosphere in the life of the church during her reign. During this time the political parties, the Whigs and the Tories, began to play their parts in English politics. The Tories were the conservative party, and therefore they followed the strict Anglican church line in their politics, while the Whigs were the forerunners of an emergent liberalism. The free churches had their great share in the liberal movement and began now to associate with the exponents of the liberal political ideas. It was the Tories, however, that came to power in the Parliament during the time of Queen Anne's reign, and consequently there followed hard times for the free churches.

The Test Act and the Corporation Act were still in force, so that the free church members were excluded from all official positions and services. In the meantime, a method was initiated that could auger nothing but difficulty. Some free church members accepted a "temporary conformity," which meant that in order to hold an office a well-qualified free church member went to communion once a year in the Anglican church. He continued, however, to participate in the worship of the free church. Many free churches opposed this compromise; others were convinced that they were entitled to use this middle way. This practice, however, was prohibited by a law of 1711. No person could hold an important office or responsibility if, after assuming the position, he continued to visit the conventicles or a free church meeting. If such a person were found guilty of this infraction, he would lose his position and be fined forty pounds, which would go to the informer. This statute became especially hated. It was at this time that Daniel Defoe, author of *Robinson Crusoe,* wrote satirical brochures against the Anglicans. Defoe was the most disputed apologist among the free churches at this time.

The year that Queen Anne died (1714), the so-called "schism interdict" came into force, through which an attempt was made to destroy the free church schools and seminaries. One of the most bitter opponents of these institutions was the father of John and Charles Wesley. He was a zealous high-church priest. All teachers, according to this law, should receive a license from some bishop, accept the Anglican liturgy, and take communion in the state church at least once a year. Such teachers were not allowed to visit any worship service but the Anglican. If the teacher did not heed this warning, he could be condemned to three months' imprisonment and declared to be unsuitable as a teacher for the rest of his life. During these years there were several mob insurrections against the free churches. Houses of worship were destroyed, fixtures were broken, and pastors were abused.

After Queen Anne, George I came to the throne of England, and the new Hanoverian dynasty was in to stay for a long period. The Whigs soon came to power, a position which they held until 1760. The new law against the free church schools and seminaries and the law against "temporary conformity" were abolished. Pastors of the free churches, at the accession to the throne in 1714 by George I, alerted him with an address of loyalty. These free church leaders maintained an active relationship with the Whig party. The bitter opposition against the Anglican church continued, not the least because the church's representatives in office so ruthlessly attacked the ever better-equipped men and movement of the free churches.

Punishment could constantly be meted out to those who violated the Test Act and the Corporation Act. When George II came to the throne in 1727, a law was passed that took away the punishment levied against the free churches yet permitted the original laws to remain on the books. This was a humiliating ordinance, for the free church people who served as officials and servants in government were stamped as criminals by law, considered a lower class of citizens, primarily because they did not take communion in the Anglican church. But the free churches were not silent in this matter, for in 1732 the three older denominations—Presbyterians, Congregationalists, and Baptists—organized in a unified effort by appointing a representative committee, the "Dissenting Deputies." This was the first step for the free churches to set up a unified defense for their rights as citizens and strive together for complete religious freedom. It was the beginning of a great unified struggle that continued through most of the next two centuries.

The great interest of the new dynasty in the free church led to a unique procedure, which in the long run proved to be unfortunate. The king began to give gifts of money (regium donum) to various free church pastors to be used for the aid of preachers' widows and poorly paid pastors. This was regarded by both friends and foes as a method used to silence the free church. This situation created a great sensation, as it seemed that the nonconformists ought to have opposed the system of public bribery in order to be consistent with their earlier relationship to the state as well as to the mismanagements in the community in general.

When the men of the free church submit to the state and its mercenary inducements, the reason often proves to be an inner spiritual deterioration within the movement. This condition was unmistakably evident in the entire religious condition of England's churches during the first decades of the eighteenth century. The degeneration within the Anglican state church

213

was alarming, and even the free churches experienced a time of weakness. Unitarian concepts won wide acceptance, especially among the Presbyterians. Many of their churches became Unitarians. It was not long before English Presbyterianism had almost disappeared. The Unitarians also made headway among the Baptists, but the congregations which seemed least affected by these ideas were the Calvinistic Congregational churches. Skepticism was spreading widely within the cultural life of the nation, and it was at this time that "free thinkers" made great headway. In many areas among clergy and laity, a moral decay prevailed.

Nevertheless, certain features within nonconformity witnessed to spiritual power and farsightedness. The licenses for houses of worship increased during the years 1701–1740 by nearly three thousand. Within Congregationalism were two men who were especially renowned, Isaac Watts (d. 1748) and Matthew Henry (d. 1714). Watts has been considered the pioneer of modern psalm and hymn composing in the English-speaking world. Until this time the Puritans had opposed any psalm which did not come directly from the Scriptures. In 1707 Watts published *Hymns and Spiritual Songs* and thereby made the English free church members a singing people. Watts also had an interest in philosophy and theology and was considered a patron of higher education.

The other distinguished person, Matthew Henry, made his influence felt in an entirely different area. He was a son of one of the preachers who was expelled in 1662. As a free church pastor, Henry set himself to the task of writing a commentary of the Bible which was of great significance. He labored on this project for twenty years and was able to complete five volumes, to the close of the Acts of the Apostles, before death concluded his ministry in 1714. This commentary became a pattern for similar projects for a long time. A third man of importance was a friend of Watts, Philip Doddridge (d. 1751), noteworthy author of hymns and inspirational literature. One of his helpful books was *The Rise and Progress of Religion in the Soul*.

The great Methodist revival, which began in the 1730's, was a turning point in many respects. Even if one must admit that

214

the usual dark description of the conditions in the Church of England about 1730 are somewhat overdrawn, yet there is no doubt that the spiritual movement in which John Wesley and George Whitefield were the leaders broke with the existing religious calm and inertia. It is necessary to confine the present treatment to the main features of this remarkable movement on both sides of the Atlantic. Numerically speaking, there was no tremendous influx into the Methodist societies. At the death of Wesley in 1791 there were approximately 72,000 members in Great Britain, but the influence went much wider and deeper than numbers indicate, affecting Anglican church life as well as that of the free churches.

The attempt to reform the moral life of the nation by legislation and punishment had not succeeded. One historian explains that England now was "less in need of law than grace." It was a clear exposition of grace that Wesley so forcefully proclaimed. Wesley, an Arminian, presented the doctrine of "universal grace." On the other hand, Whitefield was a Calvinist and proclaimed the gospel in the same spirit. As is well known, theology led to a division between the two great revival preachers. Whitefield's extended ministry among the Puritans in North America was well suited for his Calvinistic theology. Both Wesley and Whitefield were primarily concerned about "saving souls from the great coming judgment," for both were clearly aware that all men were lost in sin and stood in need of grace abounding.

As has already been mentioned, Wesley came from a high-church preacher's home, and his inherited prejudices against the older free church groups never seemed to have left him completely. His mother, however, came from a well-known free church family. Wesley did not want to be classified with the free churches, nor did he want to be called a dissenter or a separatist. In reality, however, Wesley was a separatist, and his entire movement with its deep consequences went into separatism. He had been trained in his home and in the high-church atmosphere of Oxford, where he became a preacher and academic teacher. Because of this situation, Wesley had many possibilities to extend his influence farther than the

215

average pastor, and he was also free to travel to different parts of the country. Together with the young Whitefield, his brother Charles (the gifted hymn writer), and others, John Wesley during his time at Oxford developed a strict form of piety, which must be characterized as being legalistic yet with an undertone of mysticism. Wesley's ideas as a minister had a good opportunity to be tested when he went to the newly established colony of Georgia in 1735. It appears that he did not pass this test, for when he returned to England he was disappointed and depressed. With this experience the first period of his life was concluded.

In a Moravian meeting in London, May, 1738, an experience took place which changed the entire future for Wesley. After this conversion experience, the concentration and intensity of his preaching ministry was radically different from that of his earlier life. Wesley frankly testified of this experience in which his faith "for the first time" was realized in his inner being. This was the beginning of a new epoch, not only in the life of Wesley but in the religious history of England. It was the influence of Moravianism, an interpretation of Lutheranism, which brought Wesley to this new experience. Even when it came to the organizational structure, Wesley was influenced by the Moravians. Wesley's zeal for revival and evangelization was heightened considerably when he heard and read what was going on in America. Ever since his return from America he had been well acquainted with Jonathan Edward's remarkable ministry in New England.

Whitefield soon joined Wesley in his revival ministry. They preached against the indifference and worldliness of the day and also attacked the free thinkers, but above everything else they proclaimed the need for everyone to be converted. A writer for the high church has stated that Wesley added two statements of faith to the doctrines of the Anglican church, namely the doctrine of the new birth and of entire sanctification. By baptism the church had implied the new birth, and infants were also made church members. Now with the revival preaching and the declarations by these preachers it was made clear that conversion was a personal act of the consciousness which brought about the new birth. The teaching of holiness came to be a special doctrine among the Methodists, and the often misunderstood doctrine of "entire sanctification" has had much influence, even among various free churches. During the nineteenth century there was much talk about the "second blessing," and in later years the Pentecostal groups accepted the doctrine concerning the baptism of the Spirit. In both of these emphases there is an indication of a departure from Wesley's emphasis admonishing a life of holiness.

It soon became apparent that Wesley and Whitefield were directing their own work, which was not approved by the bishops and clergymen. Churches were closed to these revivalists, so that their meetings had to be conducted out in the open. This is the way the open-air meetings came into being. Soon, however, there appeared the need for chapels, and in 1739 the first Methodist chapel was erected in Bristol. This was the first step on the way to the free church position, as the nonconformists had already been building their own meetinghouses.

As was mentioned previously, Wesley developed the ideas of his organization from the Moravians, which was acceptable for the masses within his movement. Each society was organized and divided into classes, and it was not long before the development to the free church position could be traced. In the 1740's Wesley, together with a group of clergymen and lay preachers, began conducting annual conferences. The conference, which included all of the Wesleyan preachers, became the steering organization of the entire movement. At the beginning there was no fixed number of members in the conference, but later when the movement developed, Wesley as the undisputed leader appointed one hundred pastors to his conference who became jurisdictional leaders. This took place in 1784, and for all practical purposes, Wesley's movement clearly became a new free church. The Methodist confession of faith was a revision and abbreviation of the Thirty-nine Articles which was drawn up by Wesley.

The number of Methodist chapels continued to increase, and all progress was wholly independent of the bishops and other appointed leaders of the established church. The Anglican clergyman, John Wesley, went his independent way, and it was a simple consequence that he later ordained preachers. Independent administration of the sacraments was the ultimate step in a complete break. The demand for complete church life was especially strong in North America, and it influenced the Methodists in the homeland. In North America the Revolutionary War broke out in 1776, and the years that followed shaped an indefensible position for the Anglican church. The clergymen were pro-British and consequently despised. Most of the ministers were driven out, fleeing as refugees, or they were placed in prison. Consequently, it was impossible for the Methodist churches in America to continue to uphold the sacraments if their own preachers could not officiate. In 1771 the powerful leader Francis Asbury came to America to take over the leadership of the Methodists, and it became apparent that the Methodists considered themselves an independent church. In addition, they called their leading men bishops, marking the beginning of the strong Methodist Episcopal Church's great history. The Wesleyans in England maintained their original organizational pattern for a long time, and they have never adopted episcopal church polity.

The great revivalistic preaching of Wesley and Whitefield reached far beyond the Methodist societies. Within the Anglican church there was a stir of revival among the low-church groups, the so-called evangelicals, and the older free church groups received a spiritual renewal which bore fruit at the close of the century and the beginning of the next. Congregationalism was strengthened, as it had been earlier by a number who had come from the Presbyterians. At the beginning many took a "wait-and-see" attitude toward the Methodist revival, and there were some instances of complete repudiation. This attitude was especially true in regard to Wesley, who was an anti-Calvinist in his theology. It was easier to accept Whitefield, who with his virile Calvinism was acceptable to the Puritans. Whitefield was also more agreeable to co-operating with the free churches. The emotional phenomena of the revival drove some within the older dissenter movements away, in addition to creating some crises within Anglicanism. The revival in Wales led multitudes away from the state church, and the free churches became the dominant order, a situation which remains to the present day.

The revival also had a great significance for the Baptists. The General Baptists had been weakened through the Unitarian influences, but a new fellowship, the New Connexion, was organized in 1770. The Particular Baptists stood in a better position, and they made steady progress. It is without a doubt that Wesley's influence had a strong effect on tempering the rigorous Calvinism within the most active Baptist group, the Particular Baptists. The outstanding theologian, Andrew Fuller (d. 1815), was one of the instrumental persons in this theological shift. He was a close friend of William Carey, and he became the first leader of the Baptist Missionary Society, which was organized in 1792. This was also a fruit of the Wesleyan revival. Thus the Baptists showed the way in the missionary epoch which stàrted in the 1790's. Besides their own group, two other societies were organized, the Congregational London Missionary Society in 1795 and the Church Mission Society in 1799. At the close of the century there was within the Baptist movement a long list of notable preachers and spiritual leaders. Robert Robinson (d. 1790) had unusual success at Cambridge, where people from the University and many others attended his services. Another outstanding pastor was Andrew Gifford in London (d. 1784), an educated man with associations in the highest classes of society. John C. Ryland (d. 1792) was well known as a strict Calvinist and consequently was not very interested in Carey's missionary plans. There were many outstanding well-to-do laymen who supported the Baptist undertaking, the best known of these being members of the Hollis family. One of these men contributed a significant amount to endow two professorships at Harvard University in North America.

Advancement of the free church movement during the eighteenth century is recorded in the following information given by an Anglican church historian. He states that at the beginning of the eighteenth century the ratio of members in the free churches and in the state church was one to twenty-four. At the beginning of the nineteenth century it was one to four. The explanation of this great shift lay in the revivals.

The development of the free church movement continued in North America during the eighteenth century. Migration into, and within, the Colonies changed considerably the geographical distribution of the various churches. German immigration increased during the middle of the eighteenth century. A Lutheran church was established in Pennsylvania under the leadership of Heinrich Melchior Mühlenberg. Even others, such as Huguenots, Reformed, and various Anabaptist groups, settled in this territory as well as in other parts of the Colonies. In connection with the War of Independence, the question of the future constitutional position for the churches became acute, and it was at this time that the characteristic clause including religious freedom was formulated in the United States. The states as such took a neutral position and did not engage in the affairs of the churches. Consequently, the concept of the free church was accepted as a general principle in a great nation.

Among the various churches there was a consolidation process taking place during the eighteenth century. In the old Congregational territories in New England, Jonathan Edwards (d. 1758) became the first great revival preacher. Besides this, Edwards was a renowned philosophical and theological writer. Through the ministry of Edwards and George Whitefield the old doctrines of conversion and confession as prerequisites for membership were revived. The Great Awakening from the middle of the 1730's was influenced by Edwards' Calvinistic teachings and clear theological thinking. It is possible to speak here of a "pre-Wesleyan Methodism," and as stated above, Wesley soon became acquainted with this movement and was influenced by Edwards' description of the Awakening. Later Whitefield came not only to New England but even to southern colonies, where he became the great preacher of the Awakening, uniting all of the denominations and hundreds of thousands of people around him.

The effects of the revival in America were extended long

into the future, and it made an imprint of emotional revival spirit on the life of the American free churches that is noticeable even to the present day. The Whitefield theory of the mass meeting became a pattern, and soon the camp meeting became the usual phenomenon among those who were moving west on the new frontier. Congregationalism in New England did not participate much in this "inner mission," but instead it was the Presbyterians which took an active part in this ministry and won great advances in competition with the Baptists and the Methodists.

The Methodists' role in America was comparatively insignificant until after the War of Independence. Mention has already been made of the great Methodist pioneer and first leader, Francis Asbury (d. 1816). For forty-five years Asbury worked untiringly in the same way as his great patron leader, Wesley. It was through the efforts of Asbury that the Methodist Episcopal Church foundation was laid. He gathered a number of evangelists around him, and it was these men especially who employed the camp-meeting style to which thousands of people gathered for several weeks of protracted meetings. The number of churches as well as the number of members grew rapidly to the close of the century.

Baptists in America, as has been previously mentioned, had their centers of activity in Rhode Island and Pennsylvania. In the latter place the Particular Baptists expanded into a strong movement, and it was in this area that the pioneer district association was organized in 1707. The Baptists during this same period made rapid gains in the southern colonies, especially because of the English immigrants. Before 1730 the Baptists had made little progress in Virginia, for the Anglican church dominated here and vigorously opposed other denominations. In adjacent North Carolina the Baptists were able to expand during this period. As in Virginia, so here the General Baptists were the most prominent. Also in the middle colonies, Baptist churches were organized, the first one in New York City during the 1720's.

It was the Calvinistic Particular Baptists, however, which made the greatest advancements and dominated the expansion

221

during the following 150 years. This was dependent partly upon the stable organization of the Pennsylvania Baptists and partly on the Calvinistic-Puritan character of the Great Awakening. The Particular Baptists were able to co-operate in this movement and therefore were able to reap a rich harvest. Baptist principles won wide acceptance in New England, and through the influence of a leading Calvinistic revival preacher, Isaac Backus, there occurred a separation from Congregationalism. Backus became a highly respected personality among the Baptists as an apologist and historian. His work for the establishment of religious freedom after the War of Independence was of great significance. He also held to the view of closed communion within the Baptist fellowship.

For the training of ministers the previously mentioned English Baptist, Hollis, gave large sums of money, not only to Harvard University but also to individual Baptist students and to libraries. The question of beginning a Baptist school, like the Congregationalists' Yale and Harvard and the Presbyterians' Princeton, arose during the 1760's. This resulted in the establishment of Rhode Island College, which later obtained the name of Brown University after a generous donor, a name which it carries to the present day.

An American church historian has estimated the membership figures of the North American denominations about the year 1800 in the following ways: Baptists, 100,000; Congregationalists, 75,000; Methodists, 65,000; Presbyterians, 40,000; and Protestant Episcopalians (Anglicans), 12,000. These figures are naturally only approximate, but it does give a general idea of the strength of the various groups at the turn of the new century.

The Last One Hundred
Fifty Years

General Orientation

The free church movement of the modern period begins its history simultaneously with Lutheranism, Zwinglianism, and Calvinism. As long as the movement was confined to the German and Dutch territories of Europe, it was not very extensive nor did it exert a strong influence upon the community or the nations. It was a different situation, however, when the free churches were able to secure a position in the English-speaking world. The movement grew rapidly, and it became a powerful factor of influence in political as well as social life. It blazed a trail for democracy and people's rights by advocating equal rights among church members, together with responsibility and co-operation. The inflexible Puritans resisted the authority of the king and defended the idea of representative government, and at the same time they fought against hierarchy and the coercive powers of the church. A passion for education and social betterment clearly developed, especially in the free church world of North America where cultural and economic freedom made it possible.

The older free church movement on the Continent (the Anabaptists) had started to dwindle, partly due to persecution and partly due to its own strict ascetical requirements. Its history in Europe and in America has been traced up to the present day. There are seventy thousand Dutch and twenty thousand German Mennonites in Europe. In the United States there are two hundred thousand, in Canada over eighty thousand, and in Latin America some sixteen thousand. Over one hundred thousand are still in Russia and Siberia.

During the nineteenth century there was a remarkable development. Throughout the century the ideas concerning the free church, the gathered church, won wide acceptance throughout the entire world; tens of thousands of new churches were organized with millions of new members joining. This free church march of victory during the last 150 years has been favored both by the irresistible process of secularism developing in the cultural areas of the nations of the Western Hemisphere, with a tendency for a real free church within the established state churches, and the giant expansion of Protestant world missions with the building of the minority churches (younger churches) in the non-Christian countries. This has given strong support to the free church advance for the past 150 years. This appears to be the principal line for the future, because all of the so-called Christian nations are missionary countries where the true Christians must voluntarily seek their own fellowship and work for the conversion of the world. Consequently, a policy of religious freedom, which is a part of the present-day culture, has been necessary.

All of these ideas have not been accepted without a struggle, nor did they find acceptance early in the nineteenth century. It was only in the United States where the free church ideal at that time was acknowledged and established. Otherwise these concepts met severe opposition. But gradually this idea of the free congregation developed into the free church. The new free church was far removed from the narrow view of culture and circumscribed society characteristic of the Anabaptists of the sixteenth century. Dutch Mennonites already had broken from their isolationism, as already mentioned, and in the English-speaking world the free churches built purposefully in the community, assuming the civic responsibilities, not withdrawing from the tasks of industrialization nor the hardships of political life. This development can be discerned both in the United States and in England during the eighteenth century, and during the nineteenth century it became increasingly evident.

Now when an attempt is made to give a review of the free church movement's development during the last 150 years, the writer is faced with such a mass of material and historical details that he is nearly compelled to give up. An attempt must be made, however, to outline a lucid presentation of one of the most remarkable phenomena in this period of church history. The ramifications are so many, the fields of operation so changing, the personal and economic contributions so great and variable that only through a very careful winnowing process is it possible to present a coherent treatise within a limited space.

The arrangement of the material is most suitably effected when the original motherland of this world-embracing free church movement—England—is considered first, followed by the United States where unique conditions were created for it. Following this is a summary of the free churches on the European Continent and Scandinavia, and finally mention may be made of missions in the various countries and its bearing upon this subject. It is natural that the free churches of the English-speaking world should receive the major attention, in part because the free church is much greater here, in part because it has been so missionary-minded during the last 150 years that all other free church movements in comparison are recipients and their size comparatively insignificant. A suitable dividing point to break up this period of history is 1865.[1]

The Period from 1800 to About 1865

Great Britain.—At the turn of the new century, the free church fellowship in England had grown to be a power in community and state. The Methodist revival had resulted both in the establishing of a new free church denomination

---

[1] All division of history is, of course, debatable. My choice of this date is dependent upon the fact that in the main countries of the free church movement, England and the United States, there were certain epochal events which transpired. In England it was the time of Gladstone's liberal policy of religious freedom, and in the United States it marks the end of the Civil War and the beginning of the enormous development of the central and western parts of the nation where millions of immigrants streamed in and built free church history. It was during the decade of the 1860's that liberalism and efforts of reform were winning acceptance in many of the European nations. Industrialism grew in power, and communications made surprising strides from this period on. These facts also had their influence on the evangelical free church movement in various countries.

as well as a shaking up of the older denominations. Even within the Anglican church there had been a stir of revival, called evangelicalism, which built a strong establishment whose theological viewpoint and practical work was influenced by the Methodist and free denominations. The evangelicals were distinguished from the Wesleyans in that they were Calvinists. They proclaimed the doctrine of total depravity, individual conversion, personal reception of the witness of the Holy Spirit, together with a personal missionary responsibility to "save souls." Like the Puritans, these evangelicals were opposed to all worldly amusements, such as the dance and theater, and their clergymen were zealous revival preachers of the gospel, warning people of the awfulness of sin. In this evangelical stream there were such men as August Toplady (d. 1778), composer of the song known all over the world, "Rock of Ages"; William Wilberforce (d. 1833), the untiring champion against slavery; Robert Raikes (d. 1811), the man who initiated the Sunday school movement; and William Cowper (d. 1800), one of the greatest poets of his time.

These indications of the continuing power of the revival within the fold of the church made a congenial atmosphere for the free church movement to continue its ministry. It should also be pointed out that at the beginning of the nineteenth century there was a conservative reaction that set in, a result undoubtedly of the French Revolution. All of the thoughtful citizens abhorred the excesses of the uprising across the Channel. The people of England desired a secure defense against the new revolutionary ideas and against the armies of Napoleon. People engaged in Christian missions felt a special call to check this anti-Christian current which was progressing in the French Revolution.

The opportunities for home missions also grew without cessation when the rapid growth of the cities and industries created new social and church problems. The industrial revolution had already started in the eighteenth century. This brought about a radical advancement in revising the methods for producing and distributing food products, clothing, and other necessities. In the same connection, technology made tremendous advancements in the acceleration of new inventions and the operation of machinery. Against the reversals in North America, the British power had made great gains in other parts of the world, especially in India, Australia, and South Africa, which became more important during the nineteenth century. Even before 1800, England had become the leading industrial nation in the world; this was noticeable especially in the textile business.

Because of the rapid increase in industrialism, great numbers of laborers were released to work in the factories. The spinners and weavers, the coal miners and machinists, all those who made up the working classes, lost their relationship with the home village, church traditions, and even a family consciousness. It was at this time that the cities grew powerful, that the slums arose, and that there was the development of the proletariat. The people migrated from the good farming land in southern England to the coal mines in northern England where the steam engine received its first good test. Numbers of people started business establishments in the cities, for industrialism gave commerce and sea transportation new possibilities. This advancement was associated with a rising standard of living.

This remodeling of the social structure had meaning for the life of the church. It became noticeable in two directions. A new middle class of entrepreneurs and merchantmen emerged, and these people often exhibited an independent spirit and interest in reform which was willing to break with the revered traditions. Alertness and initiative distinguished these men, even when it came to the affairs of the church and religion. They often were economically independent, well able to handle things themselves; they expected results from an enterprise. It was among these groups that political liberalism gained its strongest support, which often resulted in a break with the church traditions. The free churches experienced some of their best times when some of these businessmen were won over to their cause, and they helped advance the mission of the free churches by their personal enlistment as well as their financial support.

Another factor in the development of the church was the collection of unattached workingmen in the new city sections and new communities, who in a large degree were won over to the Christian ideals, as exemplified within the free churches. The British labor movement was from the beginning strongly imprinted with Christian ideals, and throughout the years it has been influenced by the national religious foundations since the time of the great nineteenth-century revivals. The social dangers of the gathering of workers in the great cities and the industrial slum quarters were often overcome by the alertness and encouraging work of the free churches.

The political situation was this: the Tories had been in power since the ascendancy to the throne of George III in 1760, with only a brief break until 1830. After 1806 the Tory regime became more stern, basically because of disturbing events in France. In the years of reaction following the Vienna Congress in 1815, the conservative trend became increasingly clear, and after a milder period during the 1820's there followed a brief time with the Duke of Wellington as the head of the government. The victor of Waterloo was a man of the old school, and he did not tolerate the free ideas of the time. The Whig opposition was working industriously all during these years but was not able to accomplish much. Much of this was dependent upon the fact that the unreformed Parliament was basically not a representation of the people. The question of reforming the Parliament, therefore, was a burning issue even until the early part of the 1830's, but in the reactionary proceedings that were carried on, those that were in power feared every point of discontent and every demand of reform. The liberal Whig opposition finally won a victory when the Parliamentary reform in 1832 was accomplished. This change of situation in Parliament shifted political power from rural communities to well-to-do businessmen, the middle class in the industrial centers. Along with this, evangelicals and free church people won new political influence. This was of importance in the struggle for religious freedom, which now became more active.

The Anglican church had in evangelicalism a stimulus, and

228

several experiments in home missions were started. But the church as such did not have power to advance its own cause in competition with the needs of the growing population, nor was it able to take up the church work in the many new centers of population. The activity of the free churches under these same conditions was of much greater importance. Gradually a church building program was established, but by this time the free churches had already taken over a strong position in many of the large cities as well as the new communities. Parliament voted large sums of money for new Anglican church buildings, and the proposal of dividing up the old parishes won approval.

There was a tendency within high-church Anglicanism which began to grow beside the low-church evangelicalism, and this movement advanced extensively during the 1830's through the Oxford movement, whose best-known leader was J. H. Newman, later a Catholic cardinal. This high-church movement gave the Roman Catholic Church in England powerful encouragement; many pastors transferred to the Catholic Church. This development gave the Protestant free church denominations important material for propaganda. Enthusiasm for the "Bible alone" and the free churches increased. From the middle of the century new great advances for the free church movement can be marked. New reforms came in with Gladstone's policies during the 1860's, which gave increased freedom and legal privileges to the growing multitudes among the free churches.

The earlier survey of the free fellowship of believers in Great Britain treats the struggle for religious freedom. Representatives from the older denominations, the "Dissenting Deputies," had the privilege of making their demands known before the throne, and this was not neglected. During the long reign of George III, 1760–1820, the Conservative party was unfavorable to the free churches, and in Parliament there had been little progress. Especially strong was the reactionary spirit in the House of Lords where the bishops vigorously opposed every measure to ease the position for the free churches. The demand that the free church pastors and schoolteachers should sign the Anglican Church Confession, the Thirty-nine Articles, had been nullified by a Parliament decision in 1779. In this struggle the Unitarian, Joseph Priestley, and the Baptist pastor in Cambridge, Robert Robinson, had made great contributions.

There was still a long way to go before the free church people were able to obtain full rights and freedom as citizens. Even at the beginning of the nineteenth century there remained the unjust Test Act and the Corporation Act. The free church members were deprived of the rights to hold office in the state, to serve in the municipalities, and to study at the universities. Besides this, the order still remained that they should pay a tithe as well as other church taxes to the Anglican church. The state had sanctioned the free churches by the Act of Toleration in 1689; however, all of the various religious bodies did not benefit by this tolerance. Among those who were excluded was the Roman Catholic Church, and its struggle for freedom was simultaneous with the work of the free churches to gain full rights and privileges as citizens. Reactionary men, however, kept their eyes on all dissenters, especially since the French Revolution had frightened them. Consequently, the free churches remained somewhat peaceful, especially after their attempt at the close of the eighteenth century to repeal the Test Act had failed. There was a degree of relaxation when there was a closer association between the evangelical group of the Anglican church and the free churches, but this condition abruptly changed after the Napoleonic War when the reactionary stream within the church grew stronger.

Much excitement was stirred up over a law proposed in the House of Lords in 1811 which aimed at checking the rapid increase of licenses for free church preachers and the free church houses of worship. The Conservatives agitated much for this development. The free churches protested violently, for they foresaw that this was an attempt of the state to interfere in the internal matters of their own churches. Opposition movements were organized, and resolutions and protests literally flooded the Parliament. Also, the Methodists took part in this campaign, although they normally did not want to have anything to do with the dissenters. After lengthy debates, the proposition failed. The threat was averted, but a few days later the Protestant Society for the Protection of Religious Liberty was established. This organization was greeted with enthusiasm by the free churches. After only a year this organization was able to announce its first victory.

The case was this: the old Conventicle law of 1664 still remained on the law books, and this law meant that the freedom of worship in the homes or in temporary meeting places was forbidden unless a formal dissenter congregation had been established which, according to the original Act of Toleration of 1689, had obtained a lawful license for having a place of worship and a preacher. Certain authorities attempted to prevent the work of conventicles if the preachers did not have the call of a lawfully established congregation. The free church people and revivalists started an active agitation against this discrimination. In 1812 Parliament was forced to repeal both the Conventicle Act and the Five Mile Act. The year following, the Unitarians were awarded religious freedom, which up to this time they had not enjoyed. They even established a society for the protection of their rights as citizens.

The previously mentioned Protestant Society enlisted even greater interest, and the circles around this group had a significant share in advancing political liberalism. At the head of this movement stood an influential member of Parliament, John Wilkes, who thrilled thousands at mass meetings. During the 1820's this society came into a close alliance with the Whig party, which was the beginning of a valuable association between the free church movement and liberalism throughout the century. At the annual meetings of the society on religious liberty, important men from the political world served as chairmen, among them the aged champion of freedom, Lord Holland, and the young Lord John Russell. The latter came to play an important role in English liberal politics.

The free churches first concentrated on having the Test Act and the Corporation Act repealed, but they also aimed at a change of the laws pertaining to marriage, burials, and university studies for their members. They were alert to all infringements against the free churches and took legal actions, if such were necessary. During the 1820's conditions were more favorable, for the reactionary waves had ebbed away and the violent struggle for the freedom and rights for Catholics and the reform of the Parliament was under way. It seemed as if it would be possible to drive forward and have the Test Act nullified. It was through the instrumentality of Lord Russell that the case was brought before Parliament at the beginning of 1828. Hundreds of petitions came in, and a special periodical was initiated in behalf of this cause. The demand that a person must take communion in an Anglican church in order to hold office in the state or the municipality was out of date, for the majority of the officials had never submitted to the old clause. Lord Russell gave a great speech in behalf of this case, and he said that he spoke on behalf of the rights of three million citizens. When the motion was approved and when in May, 1828, the king sanctioned the action into law, it was still a result of a compromise. All of the Test Act was not repealed but only certain parts. The repeal was attached to the provision that all the free churchmen who got into office were to agree not to injure or weaken the English state church. The opponents interpreted this to mean that the dissenters were bound not to work for any separation between state and church. This loyalty pledge to the English church met with great dissatisfaction in certain areas among the free churches.

Civil rights were granted to the Catholics in 1829, and through the reform of Parliament in 1832 important changes took place in that body. The Catholics, as well as a growing number of free church people, now entered into this political assembly, which even legislated matters for the Anglican church. The abolition of some of the episcopal offices in Ireland and the withdrawal of income to the state increased the unrest among the conservative churchmen, and this uneasiness because of a growing liberalism and free church opinions helped to advance the high-church Oxford movement.

From the beginning of Victoria's reign in 1837, it is possible to see a shift from the one-sided revival activities in the free churches to a greater interest in social questions and practical co-operation in community affairs, but this did not mean that the evangelical ministry was neglected. The Whigs and the new liberals were, in general, quite suspicious of their free church brethren in politics, but they were united against clericalism and in the demand for the freedom of the individual, both in matters of the church and economic questions. The privileges of the state church and its position of monopoly in the state were opposed by both the free churches and the nonchurch liberals. The cry for a separation between the state and the church was becoming stronger. This situation caused the conservatives to make careful concessions on the more reasonable demands.

The people of the free churches organized themselves into an active campaign to distribute information and develop opinions, and this took much time, money, and personal sacrifice. A series of publications was launched to help advertise free church principles and justifiable claims and to increase influence in politics. An unexpected help for the free church concept came from Scotland when a minister published a sermon in 1830 in which he vigorously attacked the state-church system as being against the Word of God. This sermon stirred up a great debate in Scotland, and it was followed in England with interest. Voluntary church associations were organized in several of the cities of Scotland, meetings agitating this cause were conducted, and a special periodical was issued to further this idea. This energetic struggle for the separation of church and state eventually bore fruit. It especially became important when Thomas Chalmers, in 1843, stepped up to defend the cause of the Scottish free church.

This struggle in Scotland had its reverberations in England, and it strengthened the faith of the free churches in their attempt to advance their concepts. Special campaign organizations and young men's societies were established. The so-called Chartist movement, a radical labor movement with strong Christian influences, came into being during the 1830's. The free churches were not beguiled into rash action but worked purposefully. An antistate church society was organized in 1844; later it was called the Liberation Society. A number of

the foremost men in the free church movement here champ-
pioned for their ideas. The result of all of this strife and
debate brought about a partial reform in the questions which
had been discussed earlier. After the middle of the century the
free church movement and liberalism in general united and
began their victorious progress, which lasted until World
War I.

After the middle of the 1830's, the repeal of the church
taxes for free churches was a standing question which appeared
repeatedly in Parliament. It took thirty-four years, however,
to put this reform measure through. It was in 1868 that Gladstone led in achieving repeal of compulsory taxation to benefit
the Anglican church. In 1836 Lord Russell's recommendation
of a uniform civil registration of births, deaths, and marriages
was approved so that the civil officials listed these in the
records. The same year, Russell's motion of a new marriage
law was accepted. This allowed for three possibilities: marriage
in the state church as previously; marriage without any religious ceremony but in the presence of a recorder, whose function was official; and marriage in a registered free church
chapel according to its peculiar ceremony. One other fact of
great importance occurred during 1836: the government
accepted free church pastors as qualified army chaplains. In
1880, for the first time, free church pastors obtained the right
to perform burial services in national church cemeteries.

In regard to the school question, the free church advocates
made little progress. It was a very complicated problem, and
this situation has remained in England with its strong private
school programs alongside of the state and municipal educational institutions. The campaign to open the doors of the
universities to the students from the free churches did not
come to any satisfactory conclusion. Leading men of the free
churches worked together to start a free university in London
during the 1830's. At Oxford a young man was required to
subscribe to the confession of faith of the Anglican church, the
Thirty-nine Articles, when he matriculated and again when he
took the examination. It was not so strict in Cambridge, but

the members of the free church could not obtain grades unless they could declare that they were bona fide members of the Anglican church. Both Oxford and Cambridge, from a practical point of view, excluded free church members from the colleges. In 1854 Oxford accepted free church students, followed by Cambridge two years later; however, there were still some restrictions. Among other things, the free church students were not able to pursue theological studies. In 1871 Parliament abolished the remaining confessional barrier, but conservatism seemed to dominate. The free church students were not able to take theological degrees or follow courses in order to become teachers, and besides this, the dominant Anglicanism was able to maintain a strict hold on the various colleges as well as the worship conducted in them.

During all of these struggles from the beginning of the nineteenth century, the free church movement had made great progress. The various denominations had fought together: Congregationalists, Baptists, Presbyterians, Unitarians, and Quakers. The foremost champion in Parliament against the resistance of the bishops was the dreaded debator, Quaker John Bright (d. 1889). Bright was for several years a member of Gladstone's Liberal cabinet.

It was not only the high-church leaders that looked down on the free churches but also intellectual Whigs who had close political connections with them. The educated and socially superior classes looked down on the free church people as groups of illiterates and enthusiasts. None, however, could fail to see that the free church movement was a significant social movement among the people. During the first fourteen years of the nineteenth century there were issued on the average 518 new licenses each year for free church chapels. When an account was made of the seating space, it was estimated that in the free church chapels there had been an increase of no less than 1,950,000 seats during the years 1801–1831, while at the same time the Anglican church sanctuaries had added seating facilities for only 412,600. This fact reveals something which has already been mentioned, that the free churches made rapid inroads with their ministry in the new industrial and growing centers of population.

Of the older free church denominations, the Presbyterian was the weakest during this period, and it played an insignificant role in the spiritual life of the nation. As has been pointed out, the condition of the Presbyterians was largely due to Unitarian inroads. In many instances, some of the older Presbyterians had made their way back to the Anglican church, where the evangelical wing satisfied their Calvinistic position. A number of Unitarian groups were, on the other hand, prepared for a closer relationship with the intellectual phalanx within the Anglican church. The older type of Presbyterianism had almost disappeared at the beginning of the nineteenth century, except in northern England where a few congregations held to the Puritan faith and to the Westminster Confession. Present-day Presbyterianism in England is an outgrowth of Scottish groups in England which founded free churches. These groups organized into a solid denomination in the middle of the nineteenth century.

In the early part of the nineteenth century there was a resurgence of power within Congregationalism. This denomination took a position of leadership among the free churches, mainly because it was the largest. It maintained the Puritan inheritance with a greater care than the Presbyterians, and its leaders exercised important influences in many directions. The Congregationalists held to the local autonomy of the free churches; they were dedicated to the work of evangelism, which at that time was called Methodism. In the basic points, the Congregationalists definitely repudiated the Unitarian-Presbyterian point of view, rather holding to the older theological positions. They were also suspicious of the numerous illiterate preachers with radical points of view.

However, Congregationalism had to give way to the revival movement, and in many places this denomination lost its old character, where intellectual training and ethical character molding were the leading motives. At the same time, the Congregationalists made rapid progress among the masses during the early part of the nineteenth century. It is recorded

that in 1812 there were approximately eight hundred congregations, but in 1836 there were over eighteen hundred. This
expansion among the masses, by means of the usual methods
of revival, resulted in losses among the higher social classes
and the established middle class. This same situation was true
even for some other denominations. The split away from the
higher culture became wider, and in some instances it was
possible to perceive a certain tendency toward free church
isolationism, which had been characteristic during the sixteenth
and seventeenth centuries.

Congregationalism, however, had won a significant number
of adherents from among the new economic middle class, as
well as from the Presbyterians. The great masses of the new
members lacked appreciation for the traditions and doctrines
of Congregationalism. On one side an enthusiastic wing
emerged, while on the other side there was a rather sluggish
indifference. Many criticized the enthusiastic group, and by
the 1830's the educated classes largely had left this free church
movement. One serious objection was to illiterate preachers,
who in their Bible interpretation depended upon imagination
when they lacked knowledge. The celebrated American evangelist, Charles Finney, exercised a great influence over his
Congregational brethren in England during the decade of the
1830's. His *Lectures on Revivals* went through thirteen editions in a comparatively short time.

Critics naturally overstated the inner degeneration of the
Congregational denomination, but criticism was not entirely
without reason. The foremost denomination of the dissenters'
movement now stood in danger of losing its essential convictions. As long as the revival leaders could point to the growing
membership, however, they were not interested in talking
about cultural matters. This does not mean that the entire
period manifested only weak tendencies. A number of distinguished men led the denomination during this period, and the
great gathering of funds for such causes as foreign missions
(London Missionary Society), home missions, and Bible and
tract distribution gave witness to satisfactory co-operation as
well as a great willingness to contribute. Several new semi-

naries, as well as the older academies, were in full operation with courses of studies which could be followed for six years. The recruitment of pastors was not confined to men with such training. Because of Congregational independency a church could call a young man without any training for his calling.

English Congregationalism was at this time moderately Calvinistic, with the emphasis on the word "moderate." Wesley, as previously mentioned, had undermined the old Puritan doctrine of election to such a great extent that even orthodox Congregationalists could not maintain the traditional view. Still holding the final authority of the Bible, however, they sought to justify their position in church polity and their principle of voluntary membership. Opposition to the state church was sharp, remaining throughout the entire century. The evangelical revival, which was disputed so much, kept Congregationalism from the spiritual decline and inner disintegration to which Presbyterianism fell victim, nearly causing its dissolution. If the revival had not brought the farmers and the laboring families into Congregationalism, then "its own dignity would have killed it," states one historian. The foremost leaders, however, held energetically to the established cultural traditions and their faith in the importance of a well-trained corps of preachers.

In the meantime, the feeling of denominational fellowship was not strong, for this fellowship did not easily adapt itself to independent congregations. A denominational paper, the *Congregational Magazine,* was founded 1818, and in the next year the Home Missionary Society was organized. An interdenominational publication, the *Evangelical Magazine,* had already been issued for about two decades. Preparations for the development of a national organization of churches continued until 1832 when the Congregational Union of England and Wales was founded. Since this time, the representatives of the churches to this convention's annual meeting have had charge of their common mission. At the first annual meeting a confession of faith was adopted, a declaration which indicated that Congregationalism had removed farther from Calvinism than the Savoy Declaration of 1658. The new confession was naturally not binding for individuals or congregations. It is distinguished more for its edifying form than for its theological character.

A number of the leading men within Congregationalism deserve mention. David Bogue (d. 1825) exercised great influence in his day. For a succession of years he was the president of a seminary. However, Bogue is most prominently known because he initiated the London Missionary Society. His zeal for missions was great, and he was able to inspire others so that most of the more important missionaries were soon brought into this fellowship. Some of these missionaries had received their training from Bogue. As a preacher and writer, Bogue championed the cause of full rights for citizenship among the free church people. One of Bogue's closest associates was George Burder (d. 1832). He was secretary of the London Missionary Society and editor of the *Evangelical Magazine*. Earlier he had been spoken of as an outstanding revival preacher.

A distinguished pulpit orator was William Jay (d. 1853), who for over sixty years was the leader of the church at Bath. Every year Jay preached a few weeks in London, and he was able to draw large groups of people from all classes of society. Jay is analogous to Robert Hall and C. H. Spurgeon among the Baptists. Mention should be made of school men and exegetes such as John Pye-Smith (d. 1851) and Ebenezer Henderson (d. 1858). Pye-Smith was the rector of Homerton College for some time, and therefore he trained hundreds of preachers. Henderson was a good Hebrew scholar and translator, serving as a teacher at Highbury College. There were a number of other training establishments for prospective pastors, such as Spring Hill College, which in the 1880's moved to Oxford and took the name of Mansfield College.

Together with these men was John Angell James (d. 1859), who received his higher training at Bogue's seminary and for over half a century was a great free church leader in Birmingham. He promoted school training and publication and also wrote. His best-known writing is *The Anxious Inquirer*, which was translated into several languages. His successor in the pastorate was the no less influential R. W. Dale (d. 1895), who stayed in this church until his death. Dale won great influence in the political and cultural life of the city and nation. He was also an able author of theological subjects, and he gave new inspiration to the adherents of Congregationalism.

Two more names among the denominational leaders should be mentioned, Edward Miall (d. 1881) and Josiah Conder (d. 1855). Miall as a pastor was heavily engaged in the struggle for religious freedom. One of the members in his congregation in Leicester refused to pay the church tax and consequently was placed in jail. This so stirred Miall that he decided to be a newspaperman and take up the fight against the compulsory ordinances of the state church. He started a newspaper, the *Nonconformist*, in 1841, moved to London, and vigorously campaigned against the Anglican church policies. Miall was a member of Parliament during the years 1852–1857 and 1869–1874, where he fought for the rights of the free church people, including educational training. Conder also was a newspaperman and preacher. He edited the monthly paper the *Eclectic Review* from 1814 until 1837. In 1832 the newspaper the *Patriot* was founded, and Conder was its editor until his death in 1855. Both of these organs fought for the ideas of the free church. Conder wrote a number of books and published hymnbooks, among them the *Congregational Hymnbook* of 1834.

Among the Congregational laymen was none who became more famous than George Williams (d. 1905), who is considered the founder of YMCA, organized in 1844. Williams was supported in this project by his pastor, the great London preacher, Thomas Binney (d. 1874). The most noteworthy missionaries among the Congregationalists were Robert Morrison (d. 1834), missionary to China; Robert Moffatt (d. 1883) and David Livingstone (d. 1873), missionaries to Africa; and John Williams (d. 1839), missionary to the South Sea Islands.

The third of the older free churches was the Baptist denomination, a comparatively loose fellowship at this time. It can be observed here, as with the Congregationalists, that a careful guard was kept over the independence of the local churches. As was pointed out previously, in the larger group of the Baptists, the Particular Baptists, there was a breaking up of the rigid theology, largely through the efforts of Andrew Fuller. As the secretary of the Baptist Missionary Society, he had close association with William Carey (d. 1834), whose remarkable missionary exploits in India should be considered as the most notable undertaking among the Baptists during the first part of the century. A remarkable result in the homeland was that the independent churches decided to work together for the mission, which prepared the way for a closer union between them. In 1813 the General Baptist Union of Great Britain and Ireland met for the first time, but this union was of no great importance until 1831 when, after the example of the Congregationalists, it began a purposeful ministry. This organization gained adherents from the New Connexion (General Baptist). A few years earlier a Home Mission Society had been formed, which later had an effective ministry. The Baptists obtained their own denominational organ when Thomas Smith in 1811 began to publish the *Baptist Magazine*. This paper became the foremost spokesman during the century.

The Baptists harbored inner theological difficulties which now began to appear. The foremost problem was Calvinism. Fuller's book *The Gospel Worthy of All Acceptation* was attacked from many areas within the fold of Calvinism. However, as a theologian Fuller won wide acceptance, not only in England but also in the United States. The conservative Calvinists were dissatisfied with this trend, and so they established their own union in London in 1845. The communion question continued to be a matter of strife. The Particular Baptists were known for their position of closed communion, advocated even by Fuller, while another leading man, the previously mentioned John C. Ryland, a teacher at a Baptist seminary, took the position of Bunyan and held to open communion. Ryland's son, John Ryland, Jr. (d. 1825), who was pastor in Bristol and rector of the seminary there, took the same position as his father. This question of the Lord's Supper became a major issue between two of the prominent preachers, Robert Hall (d. 1831) and the learned Joseph Kinghorn

241

(d. 1832) , who for forty-three years served as the pastor of the Particular Baptist church at Norwich, the center of the old dissenter movement.

Robert Hall was the foremost preacher in the dissenter movement during the early decades of the nineteenth century. He became well known because of his ministry at Cambridge, but the most radiant part of his life's work was his ministry at Leicester, 1809–1826. His extraordinary ability as an orator and his industrious activity in writing brought him recognition even in foreign countries. In 1793 Hall published his work *Apology for the Freedom of the Press and of General Liberty,* which came out in several editions. It was an appeal for political freedom, especially for the rights of dissenters. Hall's apologetical work, *Modern Infidelity,* created great interest. He built up a prestige for the Baptists which they had never fully enjoyed before. His battle for open communion awakened a lively discussion among the Baptists, especially after his book *Terms on Communion* appeared in 1815. In this book he definitely opposed the idea that the reception of communion must be preceded by baptism based on confession of faith.

Kinghorn, the foremost opponent of Hall, had a good reputation as a Hebrew scholar and was highly respected as a preacher. The battle of words which broke out between these two men revealed that each one had multitudes of followers, but Hall's opinion was destined to be followed in the future. Kinghorn's theory in this matter was that position maintained by the conservative Particular Baptists: all Christian churches are united in holding that only baptized believers should partake of the Lord's Supper. The Baptists recognize only one form of baptism, namely the baptism of a confessing believer. The consequence must be that only those who, after their own confession of faith, have been baptized are allowed to participate in the communion service in a Baptist church. Kinghorn was supported in this struggle by the pastor and Baptist historian Joseph Ivimey (d. 1834) . The reputation of this man of letters was great, and his book *History of the English Baptists,* which came out in several volumes, was highly respected.

However, not even Ivimey's campaign for closed communion could hinder the development of the practice of open communion. Later in the century this strict practice of closed communion was quite generally ruled out by the English Baptists. Not only open communion but even open membership was introduced in several places. This move led to the later development of organizing "union churches," such as federated churches in the new sections of the cities.

In Scotland the practice of open communion among Baptists received support from the Haldane brothers, who joined them in 1808. Robert Haldane (d. 1842) owned much property but sold it all and gave his money to be used for missions. Among other things, he built a chapel in Edinburgh for his brother, James Alexander Haldane (d. 1851), who was pastor at this place for a number of decades. Both brothers were instrumental in winning great numbers to the Scottish Baptist fellowship. One of the associates of the Haldane brothers was John Paterson, who became an outstanding promoter of the spread of the Bible on the Continent. He is well known in Sweden. Many churches were established, but the influence of English Baptists, who required closed communion, made itself noticeable in Scotland.

The Baptists, like the Congregationalists, devoted themselves to disseminating literature and newspaper publication. Many of the more or less occasional newspapers were popular during this period. The Baptists established a new tract society to help spread their own ideas. The older hymnbooks were replaced by new ones. Hymns were closely scrutinized to see if they contained the true doctrines, for this was one of the easiest ways of presenting ideas to the congregations. Because of a special situation, the Baptists were constrained to establish their own Bible society in 1840. The case was this: When the Carey Bible was to be revised, one of the missionaries had translated the Greek word *baptizo* with the word in the Bengali language which means immersion. Other missionaries looked upon this as partisanship, and they protested the translation. This situation caused the British and Foreign Bible

243

Society to refuse to print this translation, whereupon the Baptists established their own Bible society.

Although there were a number of outstanding men who appeared among the Baptists in the middle of the century, especially in London, the Baptists were marked by a rather languid conservatism and obvious calm or inertia. Then there came upon the scene Charles Haddon Spurgeon (d. 1892), a twenty-year-old man who in 1854 became the pastor of the old Southwark church in London. He became the evangelist above all others. For nearly forty years he was London's most outstanding preacher. Regularly he had six thousand attendants in his great church, the Tabernacle, which was built in 1861. Even this large building was not able to house all of the people at times. In special halls often over ten thousand people gathered to hear him preach, and when he was twenty-three years old he preached to nearly twenty-four thousand people in the Crystal Palace during a national day of fasting and prayer. Spurgeon won world fame because of his sermons, which were printed and distributed in many countries, even printed in the newspapers. He founded a theological seminary, although he had never obtained formal higher education, and his philanthropic ministry aroused others concerning the social issues of the day. During the 1860's Spurgeon entered a debate with the Anglican theologians over the question of baptism. In his theology he was generally a conservative and a mild Calvinist.

The old Baptist academies developed into theological seminaries; however, in England they are called "colleges." The colleges of special significance at this time were Bristol, Rawden, and Regent's Park.

The Quakers (Society of Friends) diminished numerically during the entire nineteenth century. Much of this was conditioned by the strife which divided the Quakers into two groups—the so-called Hicksite controversy in the United States. There was also a constant drain of members because of migration to North America. It was through their ideas and their good representatives more than their numerical strength that the Quakers exerted their significant influence. The original stormy character of the movement, when Fox and others were extremely aggressive, was followed shortly after the Act of Toleration in 1689 by a relapse into a humanistic philosophy and a critical intellectualism which later often dominated the movement. Strict individualism was maintained, but the responsible fellowship among the Quakers brought unity in humanitarian procedures of various kinds. The Quakers also became economically self-sufficient. Like the Dutch Mennonites, they became more concerned with worldly things than in earlier days. The old ascetical ideals no longer held the primary position in their concepts.

During the middle of the eighteenth century, a certain contraction took place when the older rigorism was revived. It does not always follow that this brings about a deeper type of religion or power, but often the old customs merely become external observances. Because of their basic principles, the Quakers had failed to educate any preachers and leaders; consequently, the movement lacked stability and there was no purposeful missionary program. Neither were there any real criteria for liturgy or church organization, and the absence of any material "means of grace" placed a greater demand upon personal spiritual maturity. Not even at marriages or funerals were there any ceremonies. The union within the movement was maintained by quarterly and annual meetings, together with diligent correspondence. The meetings were predominated with silence and quiet prayers. Sometimes there would be some reading of the Scriptures and audible prayers, sometimes an exhortation when a person was "moved by the Spirit."

The most noteworthy persons among the Quakers at the beginning of the century were Joseph Lancaster (d. 1838), a zealous worker for popular education and originator of the Lancaster schools, and Elizabeth Fry (d. 1845), the reformer of prisons and prison discipline. Mention has already been made of the great accomplishments of John Bright as a member of Parliament. Lancaster's work suffered much opposition. Earlier, the zealous acceptance of the Sunday school work by the free churches was watched with disapproval by the Anglican high-church clergymen, who could not free themselves from the idea that the children of the nation belonged to the spiritual watchcare of the Anglican church. Now when Lancaster appeared at the head of a school program, which became popular even outside the borders of the nation, there was increasing unrest and opposition among many church men. The popular method at that time was teaching by monitorial instruction, which Lancaster used and to which he won a great following. In his own school he soon had a thousand children, and he could operate with little expense by using the older children as monitors. Others had also used this system, but Lancaster's enthusiasm made the plan work. A great organization was built up, and its influence was felt in many countries.

Soon there developed considerable opposition and strife about this free church school method of instruction. Lancaster attempted to form nonconfessional schools at which no particular church creed would dominate. This was a challenge to the Anglicans, who placed their catechism and prayer book at the top of their school scheme. A church school system was established on the basic principles of the established church, and the battle against the nonconfessional schools came into full force after 1806. Lancaster was forced to experience many misunderstandings and much opposition, but he had given a tremendous boost to the popular education which had been largely neglected thus far.

Elizabeth Fry was a member of the famous Quaker family, Gurney. Her brother, Joseph Gurney, was a zealous Christian who indefatigably worked for the Quaker ideals, and her brother-in-law was a faithful co-worker with her in many projects. Elizabeth was married at the age of twenty; she became the mother of several children, but in spite of all the work in a large family she had time for persevering social work, chiefly in reforming the prisons.

Alongside the older free church denominations, there developed the new Methodist church, which became a real power in the lives of the people. By the end of John Wesley's life the Methodist revival had developed its own format. The authorized Conference was the highest authority in this free church. The Methodist chapels and Methodist preachers gathered more and more people around themselves. Two years after the death of Wesley, the Conference decided by a great majority that the congregations (societies) could, after they individually decided, celebrate communion in their own gatherings. Soon they had developed their own ceremonies. Only gradually, however, did the separation from Anglicanism take place, for they had such a great respect for the advice of Wesley that they should not separate that they tried to convince themselves that Methodism was not a dissenter denomination. In the 1890's, however, the Conference made its first formal acknowledgment that the Wesleyan denomination was a separate church. Many who had been won to Methodism without any earlier ties with the Anglican church looked upon this uncertain attitude as unjustifiable. Therefore, several separations occurred from the main Wesleyan denomination. This church was able, however, to retain its strong position.

The Wesleyan advance was imposing. The organizational structure stood secure in all kinds of storms, and it became extremely well established. The membership had increased from 72,000 at Wesley's death to about 211,000 twenty-five years later. The number of ministers had increased during the same period from 294 to 868. The same characteristic spirit was evident in England as on the American frontier, where Methodism won great victories by means of camp meetings and fiery evangelists. Many preachers were lacking in schooling, but they were lay preachers who needed nothing more than the Bible and possibly Wesley's main works when they set out as circuit riders. The Methodists took an active part in the struggle in the industrial cities and the newly developed centers of population. The Methodist chapels grew rapidly in numbers, and they became important religious and social centers.

Outstanding among the Wesleyan preachers and leaders was Thomas Coke (d. 1814). Both because of his association with Wesley and because of his unusual gifts he was able to secure this position of leadership. Coke was a zealous promoter of missionary expansion, and through his influence the Wesleyans increased their missionary giving so that they became one of the leading missionary denominations. The Wesleyan Methodist Foreign Missionary Society was organized in 1813. Coke, like Wesley, was an Anglican clergyman and did not approve of separatist ideas. But the generation from the eighteenth century gradually died out; the last of Wesley's ordained ministers died in 1842. The generation following Wesley had such men as the commentator, linguist, and preacher, Adam Clarke (d. 1832); the learned Bible expositor and author, Joseph Benson (d. 1821); and the celebrated preacher, Samuel Bradburn, "the Demosthenes of Methodism" (d. 1816).

At the beginning of the 1830's and in the initiation of the Victorian period, the course was determined by such men as Jabez Bunting (d. 1858), Richard Watson (d. 1833), Robert Newton (d. 1854), and Thomas Jackson (d. 1873). It was at this time that a very conservative attitude developed toward the state church, in open opposition to the other free church denominations' energetic work for a separation between the state and church. Especially Bunting's strong leadership and conservative position caused discussion within his own fellowship. Within Methodism was found much social interest with great sympathies for underprivileged people in the community. At the same time, there were a number of leaders who agitated for preachers' training; however, it took time to develop these ideas. In 1834 the Conference decided to establish a theological school in the vicinity of London. This school was under the leadership of Jabez Bunting. A new seminary was founded in 1842 at Manchester, and the third in 1868 near Leeds. The leading denominational newspaper among the Wesleyans was the *Methodist Magazine,* which was a successor of the *Arminian Magazine,* which had been founded by Wesley in 1778. The name changed to the *Wesleyan Methodist Magazine* in 1822. Later the paper the *Watchman* had a great influence.

Inner struggle had been a part of Methodism from the beginning, and this expressed itself early by demanding a more democratic order within the movement. One of the first leaders of this radical Methodism was Alexander Kilham (d. 1798). As one of Wesley's traveling preachers, he believed that Methodism ought to avail itself of all of the privileges which the gospel afforded by breaking completely from the Anglican church. Methodists should pay no attention to the worship and sacraments of the church. Still more serious, it seemed that Kilham wanted a decided change in the constitution of the Methodist church. Above everything else, Kilham wanted the laymen to have a greater influence so that they could, consequently, become members of the steering organization, the Conference. The Conference made short work of Kilham, declaring that he was unworthy to be a member of the Wesleyan denomination. Kilham's answer was building a new fellowship —the New Connexion. This was the first separation, but it was not large. This group later joined the United Methodist church.

Ten years later there was another separation which was precipitated by a demand for less prejudice regarding new types of revival meetings and a more spontaneous order of service than that which was controlled by the closely organized denomination. The circuit riding, zealous revival preachers, who often received inspiration from the frontier revival men in the United States, broke all regulations which were viewed as being a hindrance to an active spiritual revival. When the American camp meetings really began to be promoted in earnest, the leading Wesleyan men became concerned about ecstasy and mass suggestions. Two leaders of the revivals were excommunicated, and in 1810 the Primitive Methodist church was organized, made up of those who were excluded. This new separatist Methodist group followed without any hesitation the revival emphasis which Wesley and Whitefield had advanced, but now the Wesleyan denomination repudiated this as American innovations. This new church organization had a greater degree of democratic organization and accepted women as preachers. Its preachers exercised a great influence over the lower classes in the industrial and coal mining districts, where they often championed the cause of social righteousness. In this point they separated from Jabez Bunting's conservative Tory position. This Methodist organization had a wider adherence than the first separation.

A number of other separations also took place: one in 1828, another in 1834, and another in 1849, all of which united in

1857 to form the United Methodist Free Churches. In the very name there was an acknowledgment that these churches considered themselves part of the free church movement. During all of this inner schism and separation into new groups the main Wesleyan group marched steadily forward, maintaining its dominant position both within the country and on the mission fields.

Another movement in England which had a measure of progress during the eighteenth century was Moravianism. It had great significance in its homeland, Germany, and for the entire free church movement on the Continent. However, the original intention was that it should never develop into a separate church. Through Zinzendorf and his faithful co-worker, Peter Böhler, Moravianism had become established in England by the time of the 1740's. It was at a Moravian meeting in London, of course, that John Wesley experienced his conversion in May, 1738. Even in another way Methodism was influenced by Moravianism.

Zinzendorf had accepted the title of bishop, and he was anxious to be recognized in England. Through acts of the Parliament in 1747 and 1749, Moravianism was sanctioned as a Protestant Episcopal church, its doctrines differing little from the Anglican church. Consequently, Moravianism was a recognized dissenter church in England, and as such it made its imprint upon church life. At the beginning of the nineteenth century there were Brotherhood colonies in Bedford, Bristol, Dukinfield, Bath, and Devonport. The polity of Moravianism was similar to Presbyterianism's board of elders, in spite of its episcopal designations.

The Moravians in Great Britain have always been a very small group, but through their missionary activities they have exercised great influence. The Anglican church's Lambeth Conference has more than once considered the question of how this old religious body (the remotest history goes back to the Hussites during the fifteenth century) might be recognized by the English church, and yet there has never been any official intercommunion established between the two religious bodies.

Two smaller religious bodies which exerted an influence

even abroad developed out of an apocalyptic movement during the 1820's. The Catholic Apostolic Church had as its background the ministry of the Scottish preacher, Edward Irving (d. 1834), who was an assistant pastor to Thomas Chalmers in Glasgow and later the pastor of a Scottish Presbyterian church in London. Because of his great oratory, Irving won many followers. During the 1830's, the advocacy of prophecy and speaking in tongues gave strength to the preaching of Christ's second coming. Crowds grew considerably. Irving was excommunicated from the Scottish church, and it was natural that his own movement would become a separate church—an "apostolic church." This name inferred the apostolate, so twelve men were selected for this service. Several congregations were established, and the movement even reached over to the Continent. These churches were characterized by a rich liturgical order of service.

The fellowship which goes under the name Plymouth Brethren was not much larger than the group just mentioned. The movement had its first center in Plymouth, but a preacher from Ireland, John Darby (d. 1882), became the prominent leader of this movement. The Plymouth Brethren are like the Baptists regarding the question of baptism, and in organization and worship they attempt to return to the simplest primitive Christian forms. They do not recognize the official office of pastor in their congregations, but every member may go forth as a preacher. They take a negative attitude toward the cultural expressions of the day. They founded small groups, but they were able to win a number of outstanding men, among them a brother to Cardinal Newman and the celebrated George Müller of Bristol, who in social work did an unprecedented service. Like the Irvingites, the Plymouth Brethren were able to establish groups and win followers in a number of places on the Continent.

It may be of interest to mention another free church with international connections which made headway in England, namely the Swedenborgian, or New, church. Swedenborg did not have many followers in his homeland, Sweden, but a few years after his death a group was established in London. From

251

this time, 1787, this movement has continued, but it has made little progress. Some members have been won in the United States.

In conclusion it should be mentioned that no attempt has been made to give an account of all of the denominations or fully describe the denominations mentioned and their mission in Great Britain during this period from 1800 to the middle of the 1860's. Scotland and Ireland could provide material for a more extensive coverage of these groups but no significantly different characteristics.

It may seem as if the free church movement in Great Britain during two-thirds of the nineteenth century was especially divided into strong, rigid denominations which zealously continued to maintain their individuality in opposition to one another. This was undoubtedly more the case at the end of this period than at its beginning. It must not be forgotten that during the early years of the nineteenth century interdenominational fellowship developed with unusual strength. It was not only foreign missions that created interest but there was also a great expansion of home missions. For mutual efforts to promote common tasks this was a day of triumph, whether in their current struggle against slavery or drunkenness, in their Sunday school development, Bible and book publication, popular education, philanthropy, and prison reform.

Of the new co-operative enterprises two especially seem to have enjoyed a lengthy international significance. One was the tract distribution fellowship in London, the Religious Tract Society (1799), and the other, the Bible fellowship, the British and Foreign Bible Society (1804). They were supported by both the low-church movement and the free churches. Among the latter group were the Congregational pastors, Bogue and Burder, who have been mentioned previously. The ministry of these societies soon reached far beyond the borders of their own country. In 1808 these groups extended their printed services to Sweden, and tract and Bible distribution through the efforts of these societies increased in a remarkable way. This was the result in many countries. The Bible Society especially grew in an extensive ministry, receiving much assistance from auxiliary societies. Without a question, it became one of the most remarkable Protestant enterprises. This society has given assistance to revival movements in many countries in addition to Bible translation and linguistics for foreign missions. William Wilberforce was the first vice-chairman, and a Baptist by the name of Joseph Hughes (d. 1833) was secretary in both of the societies just mentioned.

It is natural that the extreme high-church leaders would make sharp objections against alliances which developed within these fellowships, but the evangelical clergymen and laymen took part wholeheartedly. Differences in opinions within the groups engaged in such union efforts led to some hardships, but in spite of this the cause pressed forward steadily. It was the Sunday school cause to which strict Anglican leaders gave the most serious opposition, because they demanded that all children in England should be enrolled in their catechetical training and their worship services. But even in this cause the free churches and the low-church revival leaders united in a mutual fellowship, and in 1803 they established the national organization, the Sunday School Union, which was a great influence in establishing methods of teaching.

This inclination for union in great Christian enterprises continued. One of the most meaningful co-operative movements in the middle of the century was the Evangelical Alliance. This organization began in London in 1846, and this new union from the very beginning was not only interdenominational but also international. The significance of this organization in various countries in the matter of religious freedom cannot here be described. But it should be mentioned as an example of the co-operation that took place within England's free church world during the period under discussion.

In conclusion, a few statistics should be given from the middle of the century in order to give an appraisal of the strength of the free church movement in comparison with the English church. In 1851 England and Wales had a population close to eighteen million. There were 34,476 houses of worship, of which 14,077 belonged to the Anglican church. The total seating capacity of these churches was not less than 9,467,000, of which the Anglican church had 4,922,000. At a morning worship service in March, 1851, there participated altogether 4,428,000 people, of which 2,371,000 were in attendance at the Anglican churches, while the others were in one or another of the free church chapels. Of such church buildings the Wesleyans had the most, followed by the Congregationalists and then the Baptists. It has since been estimated that about 50 per cent of those attending Protestant worship go to the Anglican church, and 50 per cent go to the free churches.

The United States.—After the War of Independence, which was concluded with the Peace of Paris in 1783, there arose a new political and church situation on the North American continent. This introduced a new phase in the progressive history of the free churches. The Constitution of the United States completely separated the new government from engaging in any concerns of the churches and directed the autonomous churches to depend upon their own resources and directives. Gradually this principle was accepted in all of the states of the great Union, although it took some time in some of the older states. It was easier to apply this principle in those new states which quickly formed in the Union during the first part of the nineteenth century. Consequently, the free church idea began to be generally practiced. This, however, does not mean that the voluntary principle, earlier designated as characteristic of the free church movement, was always followed.

When the free church movement made its initial modern advances during the sixteenth century, these requirements for a free church were always present: the church should be free in its relationship to the state, free from any authoritative super-church control, and free in matters of personal commitment of faith, which ultimately through baptism led a person into fellowship, or by means of a covenant bound him together with others. These three distinguishing characteristics were maintained during the entire time of the Continental free church movement, while within Great Britain's free church world a change soon took place. This occurred, for example, when churches with presbyterian government arose as free churches in England after 1660. In its basic principle the

Presbyterian church is a national church, not building its membership on voluntary commitments but on infant baptism. This church also has a central type of government which does not allow the local church an autonomous position, such as was true among the early free churches.

In the United States there were many such free churches which became large. Through immigration the national churches in Europe had many branches in the United States, and even if these American organizations became free churches in intent, in that they were completely free from the state, yet they were not free in their personal membership affiliation nor in their constitutional order regarding the local churches. At the same time, it became evident that the strongest and most progressive Protestant churches were the free churches which held strongly to free-will admission to the church by confession of faith and evidence of a Christian life. The Methodists and the Baptists were the leaders in growth during the nineteenth century and soon became largest in membership.

There was a long period of peace during the nineteenth century in the United States, favorable to population growth and material development. The tremendous population movement to the west, "the westward movement," and the steady stream of immigrants from the various countries in Europe constituted a remarkable influence in this church development, creating an inner source of power and upbuilding. The life of the frontier was simple and the social conditions were common, and this way of life had its influence upon the life of the church. In this territory the colporteur and the circuit rider had important tasks to perform, and the free and robust struggle for existence minimized the demands for the forms of worship. There was also an inner struggle which disturbed the young life of the nation, and this increased to a high pitch between Northern and Southern attitudes toward slavery. The Southern states looked upon the slaves on the plantations as an economic means of livelihood, while the states in the North more and more opposed slavery as a social evil. Prior to the Civil War, some of the largest denominations had been divided over this question, and it had caused much conflict.

Enormous population growth began immediately after the Civil War. In 1800 the population of the United States was approximately 5,300,000, and after thirty years it had more than doubled, to 12,800,000. About 1850 there came a great wave of immigration, and after 1865 there was another great influx of immigrants, so that the population in 1870 had risen to 38,500,-000. In 1900 there were over 75,500,000 inhabitants, and during the important half-century since, the count has more than doubled. In such an enormous and mobile population the possibilities of the free churches came into their full rights. Millions of immigrants were members of the European church system, and they often held onto the old church customs transferred from the homeland, although their churches were now independent of the state. As the various denominations no longer received privileges from the state, all had the same potentialities to use their authority to the extent of their power to carry on their activities.

Because this rich church life in the United States during the nineteenth century developed its resources and inner strength within the form of the free church, a discussion of the American ramification of the free churches would take in nearly all of the religious affairs of the Union during this time. Such a comprehensive treatment cannot be handled in this volume. Major emphasis will be given to the denominations which represent the free church concept in principle. The rich church life in the United States is a powerful testimony of the capacity for survival of the free church ideal and its practical superiority. The martyrs from the persecuted separatist churches of the sixteenth century could never have dreamed that their struggle for the voluntary church made up of believers would ever attain such results. However, history certainly has vindicated these pioneers.

Those denominations which at the end of the eighteenth century were most receptive to revival continued in this course. This was especially true of one branch of the Presbyterian church and the Baptists, together with some of the Congregationalists from New England. Methodism was entirely in the revival movement and during the nineteenth century zealously devoted itself by means of revival meetings to the winning of the people on the new frontiers and the rapidly growing cities. In New England the old Congregational church appeared as two opposing streams: a revival tendency centered at Yale University and a Unitarian, intellectual line with strong support from Harvard University.

The revival movement even went in two different directions. One branch of "the second revival," to be compared with Edwards' and Whitefields', began with local revivals at the close of the 1790's and was in the beginning confined to the frontiers of Kentucky and Tennessee. It was the Presbyterians, Baptists, and Methodists who carried on the campaign against evil and won new victories. The religious ferment and ecstasies were more sensational than anything else, and the aggressiveness among them which went with it increased. The revival spread over several southern states and even to the north. This type of evangelism came to be characteristic during the nineteenth century in the United States. There is no doubt that the revival in its beginning became extremely significant for the masses of people where it was most needed and won its greatest following. In this way in the western frontier movement the revivals became, with the development of the free churches, a powerful combination which could release significant cultural forces of various kinds, not the least in education.

In the cities of New England and the old cultural centers the revival took on quite a different character, as can be expected. It was not as tumultuous nor as emotional as the other type of revival, and it was directed more to counteracting a growing intellectualism. It was strongly anchored at Yale University. In many places it was a reaction to original Congregationalism, a return to Jonathan Edwards and his concepts about God and man. There was therefore a question of rehabilitating Calvinistic theology. The important man in this revival movement was Edwards' grandson, Timothy Dwight (d. 1817), who became president of Yale in 1795 and who formerly had been involved in a struggle with French and English skepticism. Partly as a theologian and preacher, partly as a teacher and spiritual guide, Dwight helped develop several generations of

257

students. Great revivals resulted among these students at Yale, and important results were seen both in home and foreign missions.

One of Dwight's followers was Lyman Beecher (d. 1863), among the best-known Congregationalist pastors of his time. Beecher carried on the ministry of revival set out by his patron teacher and also became known as a great champion for temperance. His participation in the campaign against intoxicating liquor also had significance in Europe. Besides this, Beecher's importance was enhanced by the fact that he was the father of one of the greatest American preachers of all time, Henry Ward Beecher (d. 1887), and Harriet Beecher Stowe (d. 1896), the celebrated author of *Uncle Tom's Cabin*.

New England Congregationalism obtained new strength because of the revival which was evident already during the early decades of the century. It was among the Congregationalists that the first great missionary enterprise started, and it was among this group that the American type of revival had its best model. A number of educational institutions were established, and extensive united undertakings for the dissemination of Bible literature and opposition to intoxicating liquor and slavery were started. Besides this, a series of religious newspapers and periodicals were established. New England Puritanism in this modified form of revival experienced a renewal.

At the beginning of the 1830's, the fires of revival burned at the camp meetings of the West, in old churches in New England, and on the plantations in the South. Now a new great name was beginning to be noticed. Charles G. Finney (d. 1875) was born and reared under the humblest of circumstances in New England. When he was twenty years of age he began to study law. When Finney was thirty years of age, he experienced a violent spiritual crisis; he obtained a "powerful baptism in the Holy Spirit" in 1821 and began to preach. As Finney had associations with the Calvinistic Presbyterian church, he obtained a preaching license within this church, where at this time the "new school" revival inclination was growing strong. But in the theological seminary of the church, Princeton, Finney was not accepted. Finney soon left his secular work in law and became the foremost evangelist of the century before Moody.

Charles Finney directed his ministry primarily to the large cities of the East, and here there arose movements which without a doubt had not appeared since the days of Whitefield. The revival spread in many different directions, resulting in thousands of conversions; new churches were built and the older churches saw their membership increase to great heights. It is estimated that in a short period more than a hundred thousand persons were added to the churches. Finney soon felt altogether too bound by the regulations of the Presbyterian church, so he founded his own Congregational church in New York, for which a new place of worship was built, the Broadway Tabernacle. Here Finney was pastor for some years. In the middle of the 1830's Finney published his *Lectures on Revivals,* the book being published in several editions in the United States and England, as well as being translated into several European languages. A publisher in England alone had printed eighty thousand copies of this book before 1850. Finney's autobiography, which is a glowing propaganda for revivals, later spread in great quantities. In 1835 Finney was called to be a teacher at Oberlin College, Ohio, and at this educational institution he remained to the end of his life, first as a teacher and then as the president. Finney conducted evangelistic meetings in various parts of the country. He also made two extended visits to England, and everywhere he went there was a great spiritual movement.

In these revivals in the United States significant preachers and leaders appeared. One of these was E. N. Kirk (d. 1874), who in 1856 received into his church in Boston the nineteen-year-old D. L. Moody. Another was the celebrated Methodist evangelist, James Caughey, who during the middle of the 1840's ministered in England and was instrumental in influencing a young man by the name of William Booth, the founder of the Salvation Army. The Baptists had a newly established school, Hamilton College in the state of New York (now called Colgate University after the great donor, William Colgate), and there was also a seminary in this school of higher learning in which the revival took hold. Several of the alumni from this school won great achievements and contributed much to make the Baptists, even during the nineteenth century, the greatest Protestant denomination in the United States alongside of Methodism.

Another wave of revival swept over the United States in 1858 and the years following. Henry Ward Beecher, who was the leader of a Congregational church in Brooklyn, now enjoyed his greatest period, and his Presbyterian neighbor in New York, Theodore C. Cuyler (d. 1909), who was a well-known preacher and theological author, partook wholeheartedly in the revival. This "Prayer Revival," as it has been called, continued even after the Civil War had broken out in 1861. The largest auditoriums could not contain the crowds in the great cities where the movement was especially strong. It was at this time that D. L. Moody actively entered the evangelistic ministry. When Moody was a shoe salesman in Chicago, he was gripped by the call of evangelism as a layman.

In the middle of the century, several denominations in the United States, including the older English Puritan groups such as the Presbyterians, Congregationalists, and Baptists, went through a time of serious divisions. The Presbyterians divided into two sections, of which one, "the old school," held securely to the older pattern of Calvinism while "the new school" was open to revivals. Especially in the central and western territories this group made great progress. This situation led to an inner break, for many were dissatisfied with the congregational opinions which began to make inroads within the Presbyterian church. A union with the Congregationalists had been in force since 1801, but now the conservatives demanded that this agreement should cease. In the General Conference in 1837 the new school was expelled. More than a hundred thousand members, nearly half of the entire membership, were excluded. The year previous, 1836, the Presbyterians and the Congregationalists had united in establishing a new seminary, the renowned Union Theological Seminary in New York. Originally this new school was considered as a counteraction to the "old school" of the conservatives, Princeton Seminary. The new men worked

closely with other denominations in various alliance fellowships, especially with the Congregationalists. In mid-century
there developed a conscious fellowship in the various denominations, and even among the new-school Presbyterians there
developed an organization for home missions and for publication.

Among the more important men within Presbyterianism at
this time were William B. Sprague (d. 1876), who edited the
great work *Annals of the American Pulpit* in nine volumes,
and Robert Baird (d. 1863), who is best known for his work
on temperance, his visits in Europe and Sweden during the
1830's and 1840's, his work with George Scott in Stockholm,
together with his support of C. O. Rosenius there. He wrote a
church history, *Religion in the United States,* and when he
visited Sweden he held lectures about the religious conditions
in the United States. Baird was the first American who, together with Scott, established a firm relationship between the
revival fellowships in America and the Swedish *läsarirörelsen*
[reader's movement].

The German Reformed church should be considered along
with Presbyterianism. This church had its headquarters in
Pennsylvania. In the city of Mercersburg a theological seminary was established in 1825, and it became a real center of
the work. This church had two distinguished theologians, John
W. Nevin (d. 1886) and Philip Schaff (d. 1893). Schaff, who
was Swiss, became best known as a church historian and as an
editor of the well-known Schaff-Herzog religious encyclopedia.
Later he came to the Union Theological Seminary, and he was
the founder of the American Society of Church History.

In the old stronghold of Congregationalism, New England,
great unrest prevailed during the early portion of the nineteenth century. It has been mentioned that there were two
lines in the church development in New England—the revival
group and Unitarianism. The important leaders of this latter
group were the Congregational pastor William E. Channing
(d. 1842) and those who went even further, Ralph Waldo
Emerson (d. 1882) and Theodore Parker (d. 1860). Channing
and his co-workers turned their energies against the old Cal-

vinistic Puritanism and the new revival movement under the influence of Methodism. Unitarianism grew at this time to be a strong and influential movement which extended far beyond New England and the old territories of Congregationalism.

In this treatment Unitarianism has not received much attention. It is true that during the seventeenth and eighteenth centuries it made an impression on the free church movement, but it did not supply any unique strength to the movement. It had ramifications among churches that already were in existence. It was called Socinianism during the sixteenth century, when it was associated with certain Anabaptist groups, where it arose out of Italian humanistic groups. Lelio and Fausto Sozzini with others carried it to Bohemia, Moravia, and Poland. Unitarianism in England at the close of the seventeenth century and the beginning of the eighteenth century has already been mentioned. There it divided the Presbyterian church and influenced the Baptists and Congregationalists. The situation in England encouraged the development of Unitarianism in the United States. The Unitarian preacher, Joseph Priestley, came to the United States when he had to leave England in 1794 because of his opinions. When the Enlightenment ideas spread out more and more, Unitarianism made its greatest progress in the United States during the first half of the nineteenth century.

Channing's parental home was in Rhode Island, the first home for religious freedom in North America, and he obtained his academic training at Harvard. This renowned seat of learning had its important share in the advancement of the deistic Unitarian point of view, and it continued in this line. In 1803 Channing became pastor of Boston's foremost Congregational church. His severe criticism of revivalistic Calvinism brought him sharp conflict with the newly organized Andover Seminary and the men from Yale University. The old Congregational church now definitely divided in New England, and in 1825 there emerged a new organization which was built with the direction and leadership of Channing, the American Unitarian Association. This association was joined by many churches with Unitarian pastors. Many of the foremost men of culture belonged to this group. Later this Unitarian association divided through the radicalism of Theodore Parker and his followers.

During the time of the 1830's, the venerable Puritan denomination began to gain strength after the Unitarian upheaval. Although many of the oldest, most cultured and foremost congregations followed Channing, the division was largely confined to certain territories in New England. The orthodox and missionary-minded Congregationalists turned their energies to the new possibilities for aggressive evangelistic effort in reaching the western movement of population. Union with the Presbyterians had in some instances hindered this expansion, but after 1830 the Congregationalists began their own aggressive ministry in western states. They organized state conferences, and in 1860 there were ten of these organizations. Their work extended all the way to California and Oregon. In the year 1826 the American Home Missionary Society was organized to be an ecumenical fellowship for home missions, in which the Congregationalists had great influence, but now they did not think that it was sufficient for advancement of the denomination. Consequently, the question about home missions was discussed at a great conference in Albany in 1852, and the result was the establishment of the American Congregational Union. This new denominational consciousness among expanding Congregationalism was strengthened all the more when theologians and historians began to publish works dealing with the doctrines and organization of old Puritanism. Men like Leonard Woods (d. 1878) from the Andover Seminary and Leonard Bacon (d. 1881) from Yale, who was also pastor in New Haven, made tremendous impressions in this respect. Bacon also held the post as the first moderator of the newly established Union.

Even within this active Congregationalism there arose doctrinal disputes, which as usual were caused by conservatism on the part of many and new tendencies on the part of others. This occurred over such a fundamental question as the Calvinistic doctrine of election, and the result of this discussion, which continued a number of decades, was that Congregationalism

discontinued its official Calvinistic position so that even Arminians could be recognized as fully qualified members. The question concerning the meaning of conversion and the place of
infant baptism within the Congregationalist churches was another question of dispute. An outstanding pastor, Horace
Bushnell (d. 1876), gave a powerful blow against the basic
essentials of the Edwardian church concept: demand for conversion. Bushnell wanted to establish a stronger denominational consciousness founded on infant baptism, and he was
desirous that children should be so reared in Christian homes
that they would never need remember the time when they
"began to be religious." This writing did not have any immediate effect in winning over those who held to the revival
point of view, but it did have significance in establishing a
closer denominational point of view.

In spite of the weakening effect that the Unitarian struggle
had occasioned, Congregationalism continued to advance in
the middle of the century. New permanent congregations were
organized, churches were built, schools and seminaries were
established, and by means of newspapers and books new groups
of people were reached. The membership of the Congregationalists had risen to 457,000 in 1860, while thirty years earlier it
was only 140,000. The largest increase had come during the
1850's.

Of the older denominations, the Baptists made a greater
progress than those already mentioned. This becomes especially true later on during the eighteenth century. The mildly
Calvinistic group soon became dominant, even in the areas
where the General Baptists had spread out earlier. The Separatist Baptists, which have been mentioned before, also united
with the Particular Baptists, who later were often called the
Regular Baptists. Especially in southern states these Baptists
made great gains because of the revivals. The autonomous
churches in the South were served to a great measure by
laymen, while in the North the churches exerted themselves
by raising the training standards of preachers in the old and
new seminaries. In New England there was a strong cultural
demand on the Baptists, and in this area there were organized

seminaries, one in Hamilton, New York (1819), later called
Colgate Seminary, another in Newton, Massachusetts (1825).
The former is now Colgate-Rochester and the latter Andover-
Newton, after a union with Andover Seminary. It was also in
New England that the Baptist foreign mission fellowship
started in 1814 for the primary purpose of supporting Adoni-
ram Judson's mission in Burma. Because of this common task
in the cause of missions, some of the strongly independent
churches were gradually drawn together in a closer fellowship
of organization.

During this period even the Baptists experienced inner divisions. Apart from a number of smaller groups which have no
numerical significance, such as the Seventh-Day Baptists and
the Free Will Baptists, there was a great schism which took
place under the leadership of a number of zealous revival leaders in the South. The foremost of these was Alexander Campbell (d. 1866), who came to the United States as a Presbyterian who had withdrawn from the state church of Scotland.
He had been influenced by the Haldane brothers' Baptist
movement, and when he came in contact with the emotional
revivals in the interior sections of the United States and saw
the various church splits, he received the inspiration to form a
new fellowship which would not be a church denomination.
Both Alexander Campbell and his father, who also was a
Presbyterian preacher, were baptized by a Baptist preacher in
the summer of 1812, and consequently the movement began
to take on a more definite form. At the beginning, both of
these men joined their movement with the Baptists, and consequently there developed within the Baptist denomination a
seceding group, led by the eloquent and educated Alexander
Campbell, who zealously advanced his ideas of separation.
Campbell taught that baptism is a part of the process "of
forgiveness of sins" and that no written confessions should be
acknowledged outside of the Bible alone. All human organizations and denominational distinctions should be abolished.
Campbell's followers called themselves simply Disciples. Later
the movement came to be known as the Disciples of Christ.

Alexander Campbell was an unusual agitator, and he was

265

able to make great progress. Large numbers of people followed him wherever he traveled to deliver his severe criticism against organizations of all types which were not mentioned in the Bible, such as missionary societies, Sunday schools, synods, conferences, and district associations. Especially during the 1820's Campbell had great success, winning adherents not only from the Baptist churches but also from other denominations. This loose movement had inner difficulties, and in order to stabilize the movement Campbell founded a theological seminary in 1840. This Baptistic denomination became one of the largest in the United States, but it has never been able for any period to keep up with the advance of the Regular Baptists. The Disciples' negativism in many points hindered their development.

The original Baptists had at the beginning of the 1830's increased from about a hundred thousand in 1800 to over three hundred thousand, and at the beginning of the 1860's the Baptists had recorded over a million members. The Baptists' denominational sense was strengthened because of the consciousness that their progress had been great in spite of the widespread division. They early realized what the struggle in the West implied, and they did not join in any alliance in trying to win this territory. The home missionary program was carried out with zeal by the establishment of the Home Missionary Society in 1832. As in England, the American Baptists established their own Bible and tract society, and this developed over the translation of the word *baptizo*. The older American Bible Society refused to designate money in 1836 for the printing of a translation into one of the languages of India. The Baptists then built their own Bible society, and this also was a factor which increased the exclusiveness of the denomination.

Even in the matter of foreign missions the Baptists went their own individual way, primarily because of the ministry of Judson. The division between the North and the South over the question of slavery also led to a division among the Baptists so that a separate denomination was organized in the South among the Baptists, called the Southern Baptist Convention.

In the North the Baptists rebuilt the earlier denomination and called it the American Baptist Missionary Union. Foreign missions in Burma, India, and China went forward with great strides. Of significance for the free church movement in Europe was that this society and the Baptist Publication Society began to underwrite home mission work in the various countries, such as in France in 1832, in Germany in 1834, in Sweden in 1855, as well as in Norway, Denmark, Russia, and in other countries on the European Continent.

In connection with this widespread expansion the Baptists also established in the United States from 1830 to 1850 no less than seven theological schools. Of these, Rochester in northern New York state soon became the best known. In 1859 the Southern Baptist Theological Seminary was founded, which in 1877 was moved to Louisville, Kentucky, and there grew to be Protestantism's largest theological graduate school. Because of the work of these seminaries it could be foreseen that the Baptist churches would be supplied with well-trained pastors, which gave an increasing sense of solidarity to the denomination. From these schools there went an increasing stream of trained missionaries to foreign countries, where the Baptist free church ideas were applied and theologically motivated. After the Civil War the Baptists increased with even greater activity.

During the nineteenth century there were none of the principal free church denominations which had as large a following as the Methodists. As it has been mentioned before, it was after the War of Independence that the Methodist church under the leadership of Francis Asbury advanced to the foremost position. Methodist traveling preachers now began to compete with the Baptists and the Presbyterians. Circuit riders covered western territories. The Methodists made more effective use of the camp meetings than the other churches. The camp meetings were an outgrowth of the open-air meetings of Whitefield, and they were a welcomed change in the hard daily life of the pioneer. An entire family could settle at one of these camp meetings and stay for several days. The emotional phenomena, the numerous and often dramatic conversions, the lively testimonies, and the strong sense of fellowship at these meetings attracted the masses, and this meant much to the growth of the Methodist church.

In the wake of the camp meetings new congregations grew up, church buildings were erected, and the campaign for members in the older churches was great. It is natural that it was not only on the Western frontier that the Methodist church advanced its successful mission. In the great cities of the East and in the more closely settled communities the Methodist preachers did not stand behind others in evangelistic preaching. But in the United States, as in England, Methodism had inner difficulties of various kinds. Foremost was the problem of organization. The organization among the English Methodists was controlled by a one-sided pastoral authority, and this had led to energetic attempts to make room for laymen as leaders. This same problem existed in the United States.

During the decades there was an attempt among the Methodists to discover a middle way between episcopal control and the influence of the laymen. The laymen were long refused the right to voice their opinions in the conferences, and finally in 1824 there was organized a society in Baltimore which was designed to influence opinions. Soon a newspaper was founded to campaign for this cause. At the General Conference in 1828 there was a serious attempt to grant laymen their due rights within the church, but all of the efforts were in vain. In the meantime, they continued to fight for this cause, and the consequences were that many of the zealous reformers were excluded from the church while others left the church on their own free will. Two years later there was a conference which met in Baltimore, attended by pastors and laymen, which organized the Methodist Protestant church. This church made good headway, but it was no serious threat beside the growing membership of the mother church.

The Methodist Episcopal has enjoyed steadily increasing numbers. At the beginning of the 1830's the church had approximately 470,000 members, more than seven times as many as it had thirty years earlier. During the following ten years the numbers continued to increase rapidly, so that the number went well over the million mark, an average accession of nearly sixty thousand a year. The slavery question was the occasion of difficult times during the 1840's, and it divided the Methodist church into separate Northern and Southern organizations. This cleavage checked the advance of Methodism for a period, but just before the Civil War broke out in 1861 it was reported that there were nearly a million members in the North alone, while in the South there were approximately 750,000. During the war the Northern Methodists aided President Lincoln and his armies in various ways, and the President announced that Methodism, in comparison with other churches, because of its great numbers was "the most influential of them all." There was no other church at this time that could keep pace on all fronts with far-reaching Methodism.

It was natural that the Methodists' zeal and successful evangelism would absorb major interest, and therefore it was some time before they began a program of higher education. Even the training of ministers was weak at the beginning. By means of evangelistic preaching, Bible studies, and Sunday schools, they conveyed to their constituents only the necessary essentials. In 1831 the Methodist church started its first school of higher education, Wesleyan University in Connecticut, and later new colleges and universities followed in quick succession. Several were insignificant and some quickly passed off the scene. The largest and most renowned is Northwestern University in Illinois, which was founded in 1851 and at present is one of the best-known universities in the United States. In connection with the university Garrett Biblical Institute was founded in 1855. Another well-known seminary is Drew Theological Seminary in Madison, New Jersey, established in 1866. Just before the Civil War there were twenty-five institutions of higher learning under the direction of the Methodists. The Methodists did not have the same interest in theological graduate studies. The only theological graduate school before 1850 was the one established in New England in 1839. It was moved to Boston in 1867, and it became the theological department of Boston University.

The great advances of Methodism in the United States

corresponded to the expansion in new territories in other parts of the world. The American Methodists assumed their first missionary responsibility in Africa during the middle of the 1830's, and after a few years they had gained a secure entrance in China and South America. Like the Baptists, the Methodists also soon opened up missionary fields in European countries, and in both instances the emigration movement played a significant role. The American form of Methodism with its evangelistic ministry rapidly made entrance in Norway, Sweden, Denmark, Germany, and Switzerland. From the middle of the century the Baptists and the Methodists were actively engaged in the old Protestant state and national churches to "win souls" and build free churches—"gathered churches."

In North America the Quakers had small numerical success, but they had now become a well-organized denomination. By means of traveling preachers, annual and quarterly meetings, and a regular correspondence, they found it possible to work together, even though they maintained their aversion for highly organized groups. When the earlier form of enthusiasm had passed, the loose regulations and the extreme individualism was an evident weakness, and other closer knit organizations with regular use of the sacraments could easily win members away from the Quakers. Not even in their old central headquarters of Pennsylvania could the Quakers maintain their position, and when they gave up their original qualifications, that only confessing believers should be admitted to the membership of the congregations, then there appeared an evident decline in the movement.

As in England, it was through their humanitarian ministry and their social concern that the Quakers became renowned, not through their numbers nor through their missionary methods of winning the public. Not the least was their campaign against slavery and intoxicating liquors in which the Quakers made outstanding contributions, and their work would have been even greater if a serious division had not enfeebled the movement. In many places the religious life was weak, and many were members simply because of tradition more than because of a conviction and a personal experience. One of their most popular preachers was Elias Hicks, who against the formal and loose connections began to make the old ideal of the "inner light" dominant. Hicks maintained views concerning the life and ministry of Jesus that were quite radical, and he opposed all external usages in religion. He wanted to revive the original spiritualistic ideas, and his theology was close to Unitarianism. Against his ideas there arose orthodox Quakers, resulting in a serious conflict in 1822. The two parties continued in a stubborn struggle until 1827, when a definite division took place. The followers of Hicks—Hicksites—went their own way with their own annual conference and took members into their own congregations. They had great success and after a few years were nearly twice as large as the orthodox group. About 1830 both of the groups together had about 85,000 members. There was no great numerical advance later.

The same things can be said concerning the Moravians: small numerical gains but fine contributions to humanitarian and evangelistic missionary tasks. Zinzendorf had visited Pennsylvania in the 1740's, and he took part in establishing headquarters for the movement. New Moravian settlements chose biblical names. Bethlehem was the center of the movement for the future. Even the Swedish Lutherans in Delaware were influenced by this active, sincere revival movement. The movement, however, was rather isolated and made little progress. The Moravians had been pioneers in foreign missions, and they continued in this course. In the United States this group was largely tied up with the German immigration to Pennsylvania, and it remained completely under the leadership of the older conference in Herrnhut. This was by no means satisfactory for the development of the fellowship in the new land of freedom, all the more because the movement lacked qualified pastors.

The Moravians did a small but significant missionary work among the Indians. One of their foremost missionaries was David Zeisberger (d. 1808), who spent more than sixty years in energetic and self-sacrificing work. As inspiring examples the Moravian missionaries meant much, and in the new settlements —with biblical names like Bethlehem, Nazareth, and Emmaus

271

—they stood guard over the free grace in Jesus Christ and expounded their theology of the cross, even when "enlightened" ideas crowded in and the doctrine of propitiation was shoved into the background in several churches.

Under influences from Methodism there occurred a simultaneous flowing together of reforming revival movements with Mennonite circles at the beginning of the nineteenth century. A confession of faith was accepted that recognized the Mennonite adult baptism and foot washing. Organization followed the Methodist episcopal order, and the name of the denomination became the United Brethren of Christ. It has always had a small membership.

Another denomination was established among the Germans, namely the Evangelical Association. This was a break away from the Lutherans, and it obtained its greatest following in Pennsylvania. In 1807 this group held its first annual conference where the delegates were to a great extent lay preachers. Even this body was greatly influenced by Methodism. It continued to use the German language in worship services for a long time; even at the close of the nineteenth century this was the situation in two-thirds of the denomination.

Two denominations of somewhat great numbers and with international outreach were established at this time. They can be termed genuinely American. One was Mormonism and the other Adventism. Both are zealously mission-minded and have reached over to Europe with their activities. Mormonism's first prophet was Joseph Smith (d. 1844), and the foremost leader in establishing the new state of Utah was Brigham Young (d. 1877). Smith, who lived in the central part of New York state, published the *Book of Mormon* in 1830, a unique compilation of Bible passages and pseudohistorical fantasies which was soon believed by followers and accepted as a sacred writing. This resulted in a new denomination, the Church of Jesus Christ of Latter-day Saints. Emphasis on a millennial kingdom was an important point in this new gospel, drawing large numbers of people to the movement. Even a number of preachers joined and worked for Mormonism. This group claims to be Christian but adds to the Holy Scriptures the authority of the *Book of*

Mormon. Mormons preach the necessity of conversion, practice of baptism by immersion, and reception of the Holy Spirit by the laying on of hands.

When Smith died, Brigham Young, one of the "twelve apostles," came forward to take over leadership, and he ruled the group with a hard hand. At the close of the 1840's caravans had gone as far west as the Salt Lake Valley, and here the center of the movement arose, Salt Lake City. From this place their mission has extended to many countries. In 1837 they had their own preachers in England, and about 1850 they had won followers in Denmark and in Sweden.

The origin of Adventism was dependent wholly upon the expectancy of the return of Christ, which during the 1830's was the subject of many speculations. A Baptist by the name of William Miller (d. 1849) was not satisfied with the general exhortation that "Jesus is coming soon" but set a date for this great occurrence. In the books of Daniel and Revelation he found material for his calculations, declaring that the Lord would return about March 21, 1843. Soon this movement swept over a great territory, and the Millerite groups were closely knit. Great conferences were conducted, but the movement was later divided into several smaller groups; among the most important are the Seventh-day Adventists. Their missionary enterprise has gone over the world.

It is natural that many other examples could be given of the division in the denominations. The status of freedom in the United States, the loose order in the westward population movement, and the enterprises of individual leading personalities made such divisions more possible than in other countries. If this appears to be a weakness of the free church as a basic type of historic Christendom, it is not historically confirmed that the national and established churches within Protestantism are better able to hold their people together. In reality the modern free church movement has grown up in territories with legally protected state and national churches.

As in England, a tendency to come together in united fellowship and organization developed among American churches. This is an observation which completes the picture. In most instances the schools of higher education were supported by the churches, and in this respect the denominational lines were followed very well. However, a united effort of support developed, first embodied in the American Education Society in 1815. Other organizations followed, some maintaining the confessional distinctions. Richly endowed universities and colleges have grown up in the United States. Liberal and free-will giving became one of the outstanding characteristics in American church life.

The Sunday school won great recognition and made unusual progress. In order to advance and stimulate this ministry, several associations were established, and in 1824 negotiations led to the development of the American Sunday School Union. This was an interdenominational fellowship led by laymen, and soon it became one of the special Christian virtues to teach in Sunday schools. The great businessmen here found an outlet for their desire for service. John D. Rockefeller and John Wanamaker were among those that could be named.

As a consequence of the immigration, there were hundreds of thousands of foreigners who went into western territories, which increased the significance of home missions. A national central organization was established in 1826, the American Home Missionary Society. This, too, was a union fellowship in which the Presbyterians and Congregationalists dominated. Several hundred missionaries served through this organization. In the West it began to make important contributions in behalf of the immigrants, and it was this society that subsidized the Swedish clergymen, L. P. Esbjörn and T. N. Hasselquist, who in the 1850's started the first Swedish Lutheran congregation in Illinois.

In the rapidly growing cities a special type of ministry was established, the city mission, and it was in application of this idea that C. O. Rosenius, in co-operation with the American and Foreign Christian Union, was supported as a city missionary in Stockholm. A mission for sailors was established on a co-operative basis, the American Seamen's Friend Society, which came to play a part in the revival history of Sweden. As in England, the various denominations united in an enterprise of publication in an interdenominational organization. In 1814 such a publication society was organized, and since 1823 this group has been called the American Tract Society. In 1816 there was a centralized organization for the purpose of Bible distribution, the American Bible Society, which not only attempted to place a Bible in every home and give a copy to every immigrant but extended its work to other countries as well. At the beginning it was the object of foreign missions to work together in an alliance. In 1810 the first step of the creation of such a group took place in the famous American Board of Commissioners for Foreign Missions. Later there appeared missionary societies with a more confessional imprint, but the American Board continued its strong position on the same basis as the London Missionary Society.

Two issues of great importance, both of which united and divided, should be mentioned—the cause of temperance and the Negro slave traffic. It was during the revival of the free churches when the battle against the liquor traffic started with full force. Among the Quakers and the Methodists great importance had been placed on this subject even before the nineteenth century. It was not until the 1820's, however, that the American Temperance Society was established in the old stronghold of Puritanism, Boston. Now the demand was for total abstinence from intoxicating drinks. The movement rapidly spread over the States, and very soon its influence reached Europe. One leader was Robert Baird. His book about the temperance societies in the United States was translated into several languages, and it became an influential factor in the development of the temperance movement in Europe. Thousands of societies were organized in the United States, and the revivalists took the leadership.

This was also the case when in 1851 the Independent Order of Good Templars was organized in the state of New York. The Good Templars spread out widely, even in Europe. From the beginning it was primarily a religious temperance organization, and a Methodist pastor was one of the founders. Even later, temperance organizations appeared through the activities of the men and women of the free churches.

The slavery question was both a dividing and unifying factor. In Northern states the propaganda went out against the Southern defense of slavery as a matter of economic importance. Several alliances for abolishing slavery were established, and in 1833 a national society was organized, the American Anti-Slavery Society. In this way Northern churches united in a battle against the unchristian managing of other humans, while at the same time, because of the attitude among the theologians and church leaders of the South, the tension of the entire nation embraced also the fellowship of believers. In the middle of the 1840's proslavery denominations were established in the South among the Methodists, the Methodist Episcopal Church, South, and among the Baptists, the Southern Baptist Convention, both organized in 1845. A decade later a similar division took place among the Presbyterians. In 1852 *Uncle Tom's Cabin* appeared, written by Harriet Beecher Stowe. In 1861 the four-year war for the preservation of the Union and the emancipation of the slaves broke out, and Abraham Lincoln's position finally won the victory in this epic conflict.

The European Continent.—The appearance and development of the modern free church movement on the Continent took place rather late. It was not a fruit of the older free churches, the Anabaptist movement, for these, even when they did continue to live on, did not have the active missionary spirit nor the power of recruiting which could have led to an expansion in new territories. Instead it was the Anglo-American denominations which came to make the great and abiding impressions. This took place during the nineteenth century, especially after the dividing point of this period, which has been established in this writing at the close of the 1860's. It was after the Civil War in America and the mass emigration which then started, after Gladstone's first advance for increased religious freedom in Great Britain, after the Franco-German War, and the following development of industry, commerce, and communications. Anglo-American free churches felt called upon to make a special endeavor in evangelizing Europe.

However, during the first half of the century there had been a preparatory work going on, and this stood in close connection with the powerful development within the free churches in England and America. It was the voluntary society movement which preceded the building of the free churches on the Continent. Free church mission organizations in the English-speaking world gave encouragement to great international activities. In this way the "old world" became the recipient, and it was characteristic that as time progressed it was the United States, "the new world," which took the leadership in the support of this European ministry. This was intimately connected with the countless family connections across the Atlantic which had developed with the emigrants. Millions of people were connecting links, and by means of letters, literature, and visits to the homelands, Europe was influenced.

This fact must be emphasized emphatically: the English-speaking world's free church leaders did not plan an evangelistic campaign to conquer the ground from the state and national churches in Europe. Emigrants from these churches by tens of thousands were won to the active and progressive free church movement in the United States. It was these who felt called to a work of evangelism in their homeland with its static, legally bound church life and its masses of nominal Christians. The emigrants especially felt led to establish the religious freedom which existed in the United States against the religious oppression and persecution which was characteristic of the policies in the European countries. Thus it was that Swedes, Norwegians, Danes, and Germans, after a visit and conversion in the United States, returned to their native countries glowing with zeal to preach revival and establish groups of believers.

Organized mission societies added support to such work. Pietism and Moravianism already had disturbed the Protestant churches in Europe. It is not necessary to study Pietism and Moravianism long to find that the foundation principles within these movements during the eighteenth century essentially agree with the central emphases of the free churches. It is to Pietism's everlasting credit that against Continental orthodoxy it placed the Bible and Bible studies in the center for private and church spiritual life. It further insisted that not only correct doctrine but also a righteous Christian life must characterize those who bear the name Christian. Pietism demanded conversion, even of clergymen who did not live a Christian life but satisfied themselves with "sound doctrine." Furthermore, the Pietists had worked for conventicles on the Continent and at the same time gave laymen a spiritual, authoritative position which orthodoxy did not recognize. All of these are tremendously important factors in the life of the Protestant churches on the Continent and in Scandinavia.

The basic principles of the Pietists and Moravians lay along the same lines which the free churches formerly preached and demanded, even if they did not go as far as some of the earlier groups. There is no necessity of reviewing here these doctrinal distinctives. It is enough to affirm this: True believers are different from the masses of people; they have the need and the right to come together for their own edification and spiritual care; they are not dependent upon ordained pastors for conventicles and separate gatherings; each one who is converted and is a believer can read and interpret the Holy Scriptures for himself; and the Bible is superior to all human interpretations, even the confessions of the church. At the same time, emphasis was laid on communion with God (*unio mystica*) and fruits from a life of faith. With such a chain of tradition reaching back to the seventeenth century, pious people on the Continent could at the beginning of the nineteenth century be accessible to the influences from the free church movement of the English-speaking world.

However, Pietism did not form free churches nor did it become a separate organization. In this respect it clearly differed from the free church movement. In contrast, the Moravians showed the way even to a separate organization; in this respect they became the pioneers in Protestant Europe from many points of view. Both Pietism and Moravianism had a zeal for missions in foreign countries, and even this circumstance led to the development of a form of united fellowship. The Moravians went farther by organizing societies among the established state churches. Eventually Zinzendorf and his associates saw the need of gathering all of "God's children" in a super church fellowship without regard to denominational lines, an ideal brotherhood above man-made church boundaries. This produced the usual result of such plans. Before long there was a new, well-organized denomination. The episcopal polity with the Saxon Count in the leadership has already been mentioned in connection with the demand for recognition by the English Parliament.

It is therefore significant to note that the fellowship which the Moravians had developed in Germany and which spread to many countries became in its practical development a type of a free church—"a gathered church." When the Moravians were sending out lay preachers, "Diaspora workers," in various directions and likewise built houses of worship, "fellowship halls," where services were regularly conducted, they only continued the free church tendency, which had followed the "Bohemian Brethren" even from the time of the fifteenth century. The type of work among the Moravians became a pattern for the Continent and Scandinavia and prepared the way for conventicles and congregations of believers. The Moravians also influenced great numbers of people with their universal opinions about free grace, the assurance of divine kinship, and the gospel as glad tidings. The Moravians won followers not the least by their songs of fellowship—Zion's songs.

However, this movement with societies, preachers, meeting halls, and literature did little to organize people in a succession of new local assemblies. The entire Moravian movement from an organizational standpoint was very limited, and besides this, in the Lutheran countries it had an uncertain position. It accepted the Augsburg Confession and wanted to be recognized as Lutheran, but it carried on its own ministry alongside the legal state church worship. There was thus a restraining element in the Moravian free church and its ministry.

It was a different situation when the ministry of the societies from British and American church life extended across Europe's mainland and a net of new organizations was laid over the countries. By means of liberal donations from the leading organizations in Great Britain and the United States, the work of these societies became established as a promising enterprise. A rapid and comprehensive expansion took place from the

279

growing bases in Great Britain and the United States. By 1815 the tract and Bible societies had been established in the Scandinavian countries, Germany, Switzerland, France, and Russia. Later they continued with new establishments in several other countries. By means of personal agents and an active correspondence, the Anglo-American societies were able to exert a great influence. Some time later, the American temperance movement came with an active society organization.

The type of piety, which especially the booklets and tracts advocated, was revival-centered; conversion was the primary interest. To this concept was tied the permanent doctrinal position that the Christian life should give evidence of the fruits of faith and that to follow Christ led to happy results for a person. It was the circle of believers which stood at the center of the message in millions of small booklets. European church life was permeated by a leaven of individualism which gradually had great revival results both within old churches and in separatist groups.

The society movement was an opportunity for the free church movement to make an entrance and develop in several countries. Here are only a few examples. Of the Anglo-American free churches the Methodists and the Baptists were most active in their contact with the European mainland. The need for colporteurs and traveling distributors for the tract and Bible societies soon created a new class of teachers and preachers, and among these men there were those who were linked with the revival movement in the English-speaking nations. What took place in Sweden is of great significance, and similar situations occurred in other countries.

It was a branch of Scottish and English Congregationalists and Baptists which became influential in Sweden when the *Evangeliska sällskapet* (Evangelical Society) in 1809 began a ministry in Stockholm. Missionaries John Paterson and Ebenezer Henderson had come out of the movement of the Haldane brothers, who carried on an energetic ministry in Edinburgh. The work in Sweden was of the same quality. When these men had some Moravian Brethren join them, a new era of a Christian voluntary movement started in Sweden. To describe their contributions in their work of tract and Bible distribution cannot be undertaken; it is important now only to show the meaning of the society movements for the development of the free church situation in this Scandinavian country. The translation and distribution of thousands of small pamphlets written by such men as Doddridge, Fuller, Angell James, and others was a sowing that brought forth fruit. But above everything else, the awakening of individual interest and the organizing into societies became the model for future free churches. Consequently, Henderson started his own free work in Göteborg, which resulted in an actual free church organization after the pattern in Scotland and England. The English Wesleyan mission achieved greater recognition, because from 1826 it had an established work in the capital city due to the ministry of J. R. Stephens among the workers of the English industrialist Samuel Owen, as well as others.

The ministry of George Scott in Stockholm, 1830–1842, had a direct free church character when he, with the typical Wesleyan Methodist missionary zeal, extended the cause of revival in Sweden. He organized Methodist classes and established a society according to the order of original Wesleyanism. This, naturally, did not become a permanent church, primarily because Scott was forced to leave the country. The work in his new church building ceased, but the ice was broken and the pattern was given. At the same time, there was a co-operative work by two Uppsala students, C. O. Rosenius and Anders Wiberg, who were to mean much to the spiritual life of Sweden. Scott's ministry in furthering tract and Bible distribution had enduring significance, and his contribution for the cause of temperance and foreign missions was decisive. He worked for ten years in behalf of the British and Foreign Bible Society and the Tract Society. Because of his travels in the United States in 1841 he was able to get the American societies to direct some of their activities to Sweden in support of tract and Bible distribution. It was especially significant that he could appoint some colporteurs for this work and could supply economic support for C. O. Rosenius. It was through colporteurs that the Baptist point of view won an entrance into this country. The best known of these men was a sailor, F. O. Nilsson (d. 1881), who was converted in the United States and became a Methodist. Later through various influences he began to question the validity of infant baptism, being baptized in Hamburg in 1847 and joining the Baptists. He also founded the first Swedish Baptist church in the province of Halland in the year after his baptism. During the 1840's, and even after his affiliation with the Baptists, Nilsson served as a colporteur for the American Seamen's Friend Society. This work came to an end when Nilsson was exiled from Sweden in 1851, but after he was pardoned by the king of Sweden in 1860 he returned to Sweden to be the preacher in the Baptist church in Göteborg during the 1860's. The Baptist movement was the first principal free church organization in Sweden, and at the close of the 1860's it was reported that there were 207 churches with 8,100 members.

The Anglo-American free church movement expanded in this manner. It was through the progressive ministry of the societies for tract and Bible distribution, for agitation for temperance, and for missions that the common people learned to gather together and listen, learned to organize, and at the same time were aroused by reading a new type of literature.

Through the organization of the Evangelical Alliance new channels were formed in the English-speaking world, and when a branch was established in Sweden in 1853, colporteurs were appointed for this cause. The Evangelical Alliance gave important assistance to the cause of religious freedom in Sweden, and its colporteurs were appointed irrespective of denominational affiliation. Baptists were among these, such as Carl Möllersvärd and C. M. Carlander during the 1850's. By means of this association the Baptists were able to make considerable progress in Sweden. Anders Wiberg (d. 1887), after he had left the priesthood in the state church and before he traveled to the United States in the summer of 1852, had given the budding Baptist movement a theological treatise of basic significance, namely the book *Hvem bör döpas och Hvaruti består dopet?* [*Who Should Be Baptized, and What Is the Meaning of Baptism?*]. This book appeared in the latter part of 1852, and by this time Wiberg had already gone to America. In the United States Wiberg stayed for three years, working with the Baptists. He returned to Sweden in the fall of 1855 when he was promised support for himself and the colporteur ministry. Because of this the Baptist work in Sweden received a real lift under the leadership of Wiberg. The year before Wiberg returned a few churches were organized, among others those in Stockholm, Örebro and Norrköping. The Americans continued to support others in Sweden who had accepted the new convictions in the question of baptism and who worked for revival and the upbuilding of free churches. An important boundary line was the year 1866, for then Bethel Seminary in Stockholm was founded for the training of preachers for the young Baptist denomination. It was Wiberg with American support who was behind this enterprise. The leader in the seminary, K. O. Broady (d. 1922), a colonel in the American Army, received similar support for decades. Broady received his education in the United States, and he held to a strong reformed and anti-hierarchical theology. With Broady was Adolf Drake (d. 1906), who had completed his theological studies in Uppsala during the 1850's. By 1858 he was converted to the point of view of the Baptists. In 1868 he founded the periodical organ *Vecko-Posten,* which besides Wiberg's theological periodical *Evangelisten* was the voice of the Baptist denomination at this time.

While the Baptists were developing a free church movement in its original concept, the work of the societies continued with an increased tempo. Above everything else, the free missionary societies within the state church became many and influential. The greater majority united in the Evangelical National Foundation, which was organized in 1856. This organization became an important factor in the dissemination of literature and Bibles, together with the development of the colporteur's ministry. These missionaries laid the foundation for a later free church program in many areas of the country.

At the close of the 1860's Methodists appeared as an organization, but not in the American format. The Swedish brothers O. G. and Jonas Hedström, who had been converted among the Methodists in the United States, had become preachers and during the 1840's exerted a strong influence upon the Swedish immigrants. O. G. Hedström's long ministry as a preacher and seaman's missionary at the Bethel Chapel in New York harbor especially was of great significance. Several sailors and emigrants were converted and became enthusiastic for the mission in their native lands. Several of these men returned and became revivalists. This also happened in Norway and Denmark. One of these converted Swedes was a clergyman's son, Albert Ericson, who returned to Sweden in 1866 for further studies, for he was going to be a teacher in the Methodist seminary in Chicago. In Stockholm Ericson was instrumental in stirring up a real spiritual awakening by his preaching. Another emigrant who returned as a Methodist preacher was Victor Witting. In 1868 the first two churches were established in Stockholm and Göteborg, and Victor Witting, after a twenty-year stay in the United States, became the leader of Swedish Methodism. Stockholm, Göteborg, and the island of Gotland became the principal centers.

In Germany Johann Gerhardt Oncken (d. 1884) came to be called the "Father of the Baptists on the Continent." He was an untiring worker for the free church convictions which he had acquired as a young man. Through the visit of a Scottish businessman in Oncken's home town in Oldenburg, Oncken was encouraged to become a businessman, and so he accompanied his employer to Scotland. Oncken was fourteen years old when he left Germany. For nine years he worked for this businessman, and he was deeply impressed by the Scottish piety. It was, however, after Oncken came to London that he was actually converted. In London he came under the influence of the Congregationalists and Methodists, and after his conversion Oncken began as a missionary by passing out tracts. Oncken was soon noticed, and he was called to proceed to his native country and minister in behalf of a society which had especially taken the Continent as a mission field, the Continental Society.

Oncken now began a ministry of several years in Hamburg, Germany. The singular fact was that this young Lutheran joined the English free church in the city. His ministry as an agent for the dissemination of tracts and Bibles was along interdenominational lines. He soon began to preach, although he was threatened with punishment, and in order to establish a base for his ministry he started a modest book store and became a citizen in the city. At this time he was a representative of the Edinburgh Bible Society, and he also received support from the Sunday School Union in London to open Sunday schools. It has been said that the well-known founder of Rauhes Haus, the university professor J. H. Wichern, taught in this school. During this time, Oncken was traveling and preaching, and through his own personal Bible study he began to doubt the validity of infant baptism. He corresponded in regard to this question both with Haldane in Edinburgh and Ivimey in London, but it was not until 1834 that he was baptized in the Elbe by an American professor from Hamilton College. The American Baptists had found out about Oncken's situation. Several were baptized at this occasion, and the first Baptist church was established in Germany. The American Baptist Foreign Mission Society called upon Oncken, and later he enjoyed their support for many years.

At first Oncken endured hardships as a Baptist pastor in Hamburg. As in most countries with a state church, there were prohibitions, prosecution, imprisonments for shorter or longer periods, as well as fines. Finally the authorities had to cease their persecution, and from the 1840's the German Baptists had an unhindered progress. Oncken received many associates in the work, and many new churches were established. In 1847 another center for the Baptist movement was built in Berlin, and the third center was established in 1857 in Königsberg in East Prussia. Oncken's influence reached even to neighboring countries. Oncken was the one who baptized F. O. Nilsson in 1847, as well as another Swedish Baptist pioneer, P. F. Hejdenberg, who was baptized and ordained at Hamburg in 1854. Oncken made many preaching missions to several countries, even down to the Balkan countries and to Russia. Repeatedly he visited Great Britain, and in 1853–1854 he made a long trip to the United States. As a preacher, publisher of books, writer, and organizer, Oncken was a good representative for the

Anglo-American inspired "inner mission" on the European Continent.

Leading men beside Oncken were Julius Köbner (d. 1884), son of a Jewish rabbi in Denmark, preacher and song writer, and G. W. Lehmann (d. 1882), who became the leading man in Berlin where he was a pastor and organizer. The Baptists in Germany, as in Sweden, received aid from England and the United States, and in their struggle for religious freedom they were supported by the Evangelical Alliance, of which a German branch was organized in 1853. One of the Alliance's secretaries and editor of its periodical, *Evangelical Christendom,* Dr. Edward Steane, who was a Baptist, visited Germany in 1851 and spoke in behalf of religious freedom. Steane also visited Sweden in 1858 on the same errand of religious freedom, taking part in the annual conference of the Baptists. Oncken and Köbner also visited the Baptist conference in Sweden at the same time.

One of Oncken's young associates, Friedrich Maier, went to Switzerland, and in the summer of 1849 he baptized eight people at Zürich and organized the first Baptist church. Consequently, there had been a complete circle from 1525 to 1849. Even at this time in Zürich there were persecutions of the Baptists, punishment and banishment. The first Baptist church to be organized in Holland was in 1845 after a baptism performed by Julius Köbner. It was through the activity of Oncken's group in Hamburg that the Baptist work was started in Holland. There was no connection with the older Anabaptist movement, the Mennonites. It was through the work of the British societies that the Baptists were able to get started also in Austria. Edward Millard lived in Vienna as a representative of the British and Foreign Bible Society and supervised a Bible depot. Through his ministry the first Baptist church in the country was organized in Vienna in 1869.

The German Methodist church origin and development was in intimate relationship with both Wesleyanism in England and the Methodist Episcopal church in the United States. At the beginning of the nineteenth century there was a young resident from Württemberg by the name of Gottlieb Müller who went to England. He came from a Moravian home, but he was converted in a Methodist chapel and became a lay preacher. Müller returned to his home territory in Winnenden, Württemberg, preaching and winning adherents. He again returned to England, but from the new converts there came a letter in 1830 to the missionary leaders there praying that Müller might be sent back as a preacher to the homeland. The cause had so developed that a number of Methodist Germans were returning home. The year following, Müller came back to his home territory. He distributed pamphlets, preached, and assembled groups of believers. Like Scott, who at the same time was a Wesleyan missionary in Sweden, Müller did not intend to establish a new church, but nevertheless this eventually took place. At the close of the 1830's Müller could report approximately six hundred members, but it was obvious that it was still a loose organization. Several of the associates became pioneer preachers within German Methodism. One of these was J. G. Steinlen (d. 1884). He had been in the United States where he was converted, and in 1848 he joined Müller.

After Müller's death in 1858 there was no leader of Methodism in Germany, whereupon the Wesleyans in England sent John Lyth to fill the responsibility as superintendent. He soon found that during the twenty-six-year ministry of Müller the organization had been rather loose, and the relationship with the national church was not clear. The Conventicle Act of 1743 was in force and was employed against the Methodists and Baptists. Fines were imposed and opposition was hard. Trying to maintain a relationship with the national church seemed impossible. After a ministry of six years, Lyth had a congregation of nearly eight hundred members. This was considerably less than earlier, but these were actual members. Now the Methodists became an independent church, and it was no longer possible to maintain the fiction that they were a movement within the established church. This situation became clear to all in the middle of the 1860's.

After Lyth, John C. Barratt came in 1865 to lead the German mission. There were new revivals, and a few young men were trained by Barratt to serve the movement as preachers.

The mission widened considerably when in 1867 a preaching hall was rented in Stuttgart and a new successful ministry was inaugurated. Earlier the Methodist movement had been confined to small towns and villages in Württemberg. In 1868 there were over a hundred preaching stations, and the membership roll was close to sixteen hundred.

While this Methodist work had been going on in southern Germany up unto the close of the 1860's, there was another work of the same type in the north. It was the emigration to the United States that played the decisive role there. From America emigrants returned, representing the Methodist Episcopal church, and they preached revival among the German Protestant people. In a few decades there were five million Germans who went to the United States, many of whom were converted and gripped by missionary zeal. Lengthy American letters described both the meaning of conversion and the free country's free church life. The leaders of the mission in United States received letters with the request that preachers be sent to Germany. In 1844 an American missionary leader made a personal visit to Germany, and when he discovered that there existed no legal freedom for the Methodist work, he was dissuaded from starting a mission. After the February Revolution in Europe in 1848 it seemed more feasible to start a work, so in 1849 the American bishops decided to take up the work in Germany with the help of German immigrants.

Thus it developed that L. S. Jacoby (d. 1874) became the first preacher and leader. In 1849 Jacoby established his headquarters in Bremen. In this free imperial city religious freedom was respected, which was not the case in much of Germany. Jacoby had a great influx of followers, and he followed the usual practice of appointing colporteurs for distributing Bibles and inspirational literature. He had some tracts printed as well as some of Wesley's sermons. Already after a year the first Methodist church in Bremen was organized, and the same year Jacoby started a paper, *Der Evangelist*. Also during this same year, 1850, two new preachers came from the United States, and Jacoby was appointed superintendent. This newly established work appeared promising.

The Methodists came to Saxony in the usual way, via emigrants. An emigrant by the name of Erhard Wunderlich returned at this time to his home area, Rüssdorf in Saxony. He had been converted in the United States and revived many by his preaching. In Saxony he met with the usual persecution, imprisonment, fines, and banishment. When Wunderlich returned to America, a number of fellow believers went with him. His brother Friedrich continued the work in Saxony, and in spite of fines and warnings he was able to hold out. He was ordained in 1865 and took charge of the little congregation in Rüssdorf, where the chapel was a stronghold for Methodism.

Under the leadership of Jacoby the ministry developed, new preachers came from the United States, work was taken up in such cities as Hamburg and Frankfort on the Main as well as in several other places, especially in northwest Germany: Oldenburg, Hannover, and Braunschweig. Many, however, tired of the persecutions and emigrated to America.

It was natural that this Methodist Episcopal work should be noticed by the Wesleyan men in Württemberg, and it is equally natural that they should be drawn closer together. Jacoby visited Müller in 1851, and a certain association was established. He also obtained a place in Württemberg for his American church. A preacher was stationed in Heilbronn, but opposition was strong and the usual penalties were inflicted on the Methodist preachers. A chapel was dedicated in 1864, making the free church character of the work evident, and the movement spread to other sections. Through meetings between the northern Episcopal Methodists and the southern Wesleyan Methodists an association resulted which after a few decades led to the unification of one Methodist church in Germany.

Methodism as an actual reality started in Switzerland during the decade of the 1850's. The work began as a mission in Lausanne through the instrumentality of a young preacher who was associated with Jacoby's ministry. The work grew and made good progress. It was concentrated in three centers: Lausanne, Zürich, and Basel. This development had already taken place before 1860. It was in the German section of Switzerland that the Methodist Episcopal church won new adherents, and this mission was organizationally related to the German Methodist group. Consequently, the Swiss took part in the conference at Bremen in 1857, which an American bishop attended. The great conference of the Evangelical Alliance was held the same year at Berlin, and one of the American Methodist representatives brought a presentation of his church.

An important step was taken in 1858 when it was decided to erect a seminary in Bremen. From this time on there was greater security in the continuity of the Methodist mission in Germany. Another important development for this church was the opening of Methodist work in Berlin in 1859. In spite of a great resistance, the Methodist movement made progress from the very beginning. At this early period the Methodist work was divided into four districts, each with its own superintendent. Annual conferences were now held. At the conference held at Frankfort on the Main in 1863, the Swedish emigrant missionary O. G. Hedström came from New York to visit, underscoring the strong connection between the United States and the Methodist mission in Germany. At the annual conference in Berlin in 1868, Jacoby resigned his post as leader and soon returned to the United States. At this time there were about 4,800 members in Germany, not counting 1,500 who were on probation.

From the German areas of Europe the Baptist and the Methodist missions spread to several other countries, but during the time under consideration this missionary expansion was of little significance. The situation in Denmark and Norway should now be mentioned. Denmark early came into contact with the German free church movement by means of the Baptists. Oncken's associate, Julius Köbner, made a visit in 1839 to his homeland, where spiritual revivals were in progress. Köbner wanted to know more about these revivals, and in Copenhagen he met a group of believers who were beginning to doubt the validity of infant baptism. In Köbner they found an apt teacher, one for whom they had been waiting. When Köbner again returned to Germany, he maintained his connections with the group by means of correspondence. Because of this, Oncken and Köbner were encouraged to go to Copenhagen in the fall of 1839, where they baptized eleven persons and organized the first Baptist congregation in Scandinavia. This expansion was motivated by the church in Hamburg, which was only five years old. The following year the two preachers from Hamburg revisited Denmark and baptized a number of others. When the movement began to expand considerably, severe persecution was leveled against the Baptists. Members were apprehended by the police and repeatedly thrown into prison. Petitions in behalf of the persecuted came from both England and the United States. After ten years, in 1849, a law providing religious freedom was enacted, but by this time the worst of the persecution had subsided. Now there were six churches with a membership of approximately four hundred.

Until the middle of the 1860's progress was slow among the Danish Baptists, but the work in Copenhagen was beset by difficulties, primarily because of the "mission" carried on by the Mormon representatives. It was at the church in Copenhagen that the exiled Swede, F. O. Nilsson, labored a few months from 1851 and on. It was here also that Nilsson baptized Wiberg in 1852. In 1864 the entire membership of the denomination was approximately sixteen hundred, and it continued to grow steadily. The following year Köbner came to the church in Copenhagen to assume the leadership. A new church building was erected, being completed for dedication in 1867. When Köbner left his country in 1879, the Baptist movement had been organized and stabilized in several respects.

Methodists arrived later in Denmark. The Danish-born C. Willerup came from America to go to Norway in 1856 to organize a Methodist work there, but by 1858 he moved to Copenhagen to serve as superintendent of the northern missionary work. Because of the lawful establishment of religious freedom, the Methodist preachers did not fare as badly as the first Danish Baptists or the Methodist preachers in Germany. Willerup was aided by a colporteur who came from the United States. It was in 1866 that the Methodists erected their first church building in Copenhagen, with American financial support. At this time there were only four established points for Methodism in Denmark. In all, their membership was only 170.

Up until 1868 Willerup had charge of the entire Scandinavian mission, but during this year Sweden obtained its own superintendent in Victor Witting. Even Norway was furnished a similar leader. After the 1860's Danish Methodism made good though not rapid progress.

In Norway, Methodism preceded the Baptists. There were also contacts with the United States in this country because of emigrants and returning sailors. In this respect, O. G. Hedström played an important role, for there were conversions again and again in the famous Bethel Chapel in New York. In 1849 one of these converted Norwegians, O. P. Petersen, made a trip back to his native land. He began to preach, and there were many conversions. His stay was lengthened over a year. At the close of 1853, Petersen in the meantime returned to Norway as a missionary, and Willerup came from the United States to help in 1856. These two built the first congregations, one in Sarpsborg and the other in Fredrikshald.

Several preachers were sent after this, but soon there appeared leaders among those who had been converted in Norway. The first man of importance in this group was Martin Hansen, who later became a district superintendent. He also became known as a writer, and he was the leader of tract distribution. However, most of the preachers in the first generation were emigrants who returned to their native land with the glad tidings. In the capital city, Oslo, the work was started in 1864, and in 1869 Petersen became the superintendent for the Methodists in Norway.

The first Baptist preacher in Norway was a Dane, Fredrik Rymker, who settled in Porsgrund, close to Skien, in 1857. He, too, was converted and baptized in America while he was a sailor. It was just at this time that the so-called Lammers movement created attention in the country. A state church clergyman, G. A. Lammers, had rejected the doctrine of the new birth by means of baptism, and he even held adverse views regarding the relationship between church and state.

In the summer of 1856 Lammers left the state church, together with a number of followers, to build a free church. In this congregation some members practiced the baptism of believers. Rymker appeared on the scene just when this question was the great sensation in Norway. In 1860 two Baptist churches were established, one near Skien, the other in Larvik. A third church was started in 1862 at Kragerö. F. O. Nilsson visited and preached in Norway for a time.

There was no rapid progress for the Baptists in Norway. This was largely due to want of leadership. Already by 1863 Rymker had left his post, but then another preacher who had been converted and baptized in America arrived. He was G. Hübert, who in 1862 returned to his native country and began his preaching ministry. He had also taken part in the Civil War for a period. For several years he was supported by the English Baptists, and in Bergen he organized a congregation and erected a chapel. At this time a few preachers came from Sweden who later became good pastors. At the close of the 1860's only a few congregations had been established, and even by 1877 the entire membership was only a little over five hundred.

Actually the free church movement on the Continent and in Scandinavia inspired by the English-speaking world was very weak at the close of the 1860's. To be sure, there were smaller advances which took place in other countries besides the ones we have already mentioned, such as in Holland, France, Italy, and Bulgaria, but there was not much progress in these places. It was after this period which we have been treating that this free church movement was able to be of some significance in these countries.

A free church movement in the Congregational mold started on the Continent as a direct indigenous phenomenon. In this respect the Anglo-American Congregationalists differed from the Methodists and Baptists in England and America who strongly supported the missions in the European countries. There was some support, however, from the American Congregational missionary society.

Spiritual movements arose early in the nineteenth century

in Switzerland. Robert Haldane exercised a great influence; for a while he was detained in the area of Geneva in 1817 where he did missionary work. In Switzerland, like in other parts of the Continent, the spirit of the Enlightenment predominated in the churches, but Haldane had an entree as a preacher among the students as well as others. Among those who experienced conversion were such men as Frédéric Monod (d. 1863), the great free church man in France, and Merle d'Aubigné (d. 1872), known also as a writer of church history. A chapel was erected, and the separate celebration of the Lord's Supper led to the formation of a free church. Leaders of the national church raised much opposition, but the development into a free "evangelical church" was fully realized in 1849. Already by 1831 a theological school had been established, where Merle d'Aubigné was among the teachers. The work of societies and the distribution of Bibles and literature increased rapidly, and the association with the English-speaking world was strengthened.

There were revivals in other Swiss cantons as well, more or less under Anglo-American inspiration. Consequently, in Bern, Zürich, and Basel free churches were established during the 1820's and the 1830's. In the canton Waadt, in the middle of the 1820's, all gatherings of this nature were forbidden. Now the well-known Alexander Vinet (d. 1847) took up the cause of the independents and began his campaign for religious freedom. Vinet had been a clergyman in the Reformed state church. When the conflict came to a peak, he left the church in 1840. In this respect he became an example to others. In 1845 there were no less than 147 clergymen who left the state church to establish free churches. The same thing happened in the canton Bern. Vinet's struggle bore fruit in many parts of Switzerland as it did in other countries. Even in Sweden Vinet drew much attention.

As a professor in theology in Lausanne, Vinet exercised great influence in the literary and theological circles, primarily among the French-speaking population. His writings were translated into several languages. The principles were the usual ones maintained by the free churches. A person is not a

Christian because his name is written in a parish book, for Christ did not come into the world to establish parishes and pastorates but congregations made up of true believers. To such churches belong only those who have joined of their own free will, for the church is a spiritual body made up of spiritual people, not all the people in the community. A Christian church is only conscious of its true character when it is aware of the fact that it is composed only of believers.

The revival in the French section of Switzerland spread with remarkable success in France through the ministry of the Monod brothers, Frédéric and Adolphe. Both of these men had studied at Geneva and came under the influence of the growing spiritual movement among the students, which was led by Robert Haldane. Frédéric called Haldane his "spiritual father." When Frédéric came to Paris after his ordination in 1818, he began to work for a Bible society. Later he became the great and eloquent preacher among the reformers in this city. As for his general theological position, he was, like the other revivalists, a biblicist and consequently came into conflict with some of the leaders of his church. He was outspoken in favor of the free church idea, and in 1849 he resigned from his pastoral position in the chief Reformed church in Paris. He immediately began to build a free church, and later during the same year there was formed an association between his church and ten other free churches in various parts of the country where the revival had made headway. With help from Great Britain and America he was able to erect a church building in Paris for his congregation. Here Monod served until his death in 1863. The Free Church Association continued its tie with the free churches in the country. By 1873 there were seventy-three congregations.

Adolphe Monod (d. 1856), after his ordination, served a free church in Naples and at the close of the 1820's became pastor of the Reformed congregation in Lyon. Here he won a great reputation as a preacher, but since he, like his brother, had a conservative point of view on several theological questions, he was removed by the Consistory in 1831. He then organized a free church in the city, and from this congregation there went forth an active mission program. In the meantime, Monod became a professor on the faculty in Montauban, the only Reformed faculty in the country. During the last decade of his life he was the preacher in the chief Reformed church in Paris.

Perhaps Vinet's most prominent pupil in France was Edmond de Pressensé (d. 1891), who in a free church in Paris demonstrated both religious and political eloquence. He was a member of the senate and fought against the policies of Catholic clericalism. As an editor for many years of the *Revue Chrétienne,* he was able to extend his influence in a wide circle.

The German Congregational movement stood in close relationship with the Swiss-French free church movement. In the middle of the century this arose in Wuppertal (Elberfeld-Barmen-Ronsdorf), and became the cause of free church foundations in the Rheinland, Westfalen, and Hesse. A businessman by the name of H. H. Grafe (d. 1869), who belonged to the Reformed church in Elberfeld, had become acquainted with Monod's free church there during a visit in Lyon in 1841–1842, and he had seen in this group the picture of the primitive congregation. Julius Köbner worked in Elberfeld in 1851–1852, and a Baptist church was established there in 1852. This Baptist influence must have also impressed Grafe. Grafe was critical of his own church in Wuppertal. He left the church in 1854 to build a church similar to the free congregation. This was the first of its kind in Germany, and it can be considered the pioneer of the new type of Congregational church on German soil. A theologian by the name of H. Neviandt (d. 1901), who was ready for service in his church, had begun to doubt the correctness of the state church order. He now joined the free church and became its first pastor. The motivating principles were about the same as those set down by Vinet, and an active association was maintained with the free churches in Switzerland and France. The Calvinistic confession of the Genevan free church was translated and became the foundational doctrinal points for the Wuppertal church. Several groups grew up in various parts of western Germany, and societies for communion were established which developed into free churches.

During this period under discussion, the Congregational free churches made no great impression in other European countries, even though the foundation was laid through a society movement. Of greatest importance were the missionary societies, which for example in the Scandinavian countries meant an organization of revival people within the state church. It was during the final third of the century that the founding of free churches developed extensively.

The Period from 1865 to 1950

Great Britain.—In England as in the United States, the phrase "the second awakening" designates the spiritual revival of the 1860's and 1870's. The latter decade was especially a period of advance among the free churches in Great Britain. It was at this time that D. L. Moody (d. 1899) was so successful as a revivalist. Ira D. Sankey (d. 1908) sang himself into the hearts of awakened European people. These men made the greatest personal contribution to Europe in behalf of American revivalism. The influences that issued from Moody's labors and the spread of the "Sankey songs" quickened the entire free church world, not only in Great Britain but also in other countries. There were also a number of revival preachers within the free churches of England, so everything did not depend upon the campaigns which Moody and Sankey conducted. Until his death in 1892, C. H. Spurgeon continued to be a central figure in the awakening, and with him there are several who could be mentioned from among the various denominations. It is estimated that nearly a million persons affiliated with the various church groups during this period.

In this generation which bridged the centuries, from the close of the nineteenth century to the beginning years of the twentieth, there were a group of influential preachers and church leaders who in various ways made special impressions, for example, Congregationalist R. W. Dale (d. 1895); the famous Methodist, Hugh Price Hughes (d. 1902), who was

297

noted for his social work; and the esteemed Baptist Bible commentator, Alexander Maclaren (d. 1910). Younger than these men were such preachers and Bible expositors as Campbell Morgan, J. H. Jowett, and A. E. Garvie among the Congregationalists; Dinsdale Young and A. E. Whitham among the Methodists; and F. B. Meyer and John Clifford among the Baptists. Leaders of the present period among the free churches in Great Britain are numerous and well known.

From this awakening the Salvation Army emerged, along with the missionary enthusiasm for Hudson Taylor's China Inland Mission. Of far-reaching significance, too, was the work of the physician, Thomas Barnardo, in the interest of children's homes and the achievements of the layman, Robert Wilson, in behalf of the famous Keswick Conferences, as well as the work of Timothy Richard in China.

As has been mentioned before, the Protestant church population in England was approximately evenly divided between the Anglican church and the free churches. This even balance prevailed in 1910. The number of communicants at the Lord's Supper was about the same in the two groups. However, the seating capacities in the churches were 8,788,000 for the free churches against 7,236,000 for the Anglican. The struggle for religious freedom on the part of the free churches continued even during this period. A school law of 1870 precipitated a lively controversy. In this contest, the Anglican church won a great advantage. The attempt to develop a state school system without confessional religious instruction did not win much approval.

In 1902 the so-called Balfour Law promised state support for the church schools. The great majority of such schools belonged to the Anglican church, and consequently it was this church which benefited most by tax support. This law occasioned sharp protests from the free churches, and, in some instances even the refusal to pay taxes. This entire question led to an intensified opposition between the free churches and the Anglicans, which compares with the situation which existed early in the nineteenth century.

This strife stimulated the free churches to erect several of their own schools of various types. Among the seminaries and the institutions of higher learning, the following can be mentioned which became affiliated with universities: the Congregationalist Spring Hill College, which was moved to Oxford in 1886 and renamed Mansfield College. Its great leader was A. M. Fairbairn (d. 1912). The Baptists moved Regent's Park College to Oxford in 1928. Their outstanding man was H. Wheeler Robinson, the great Hebrew scholar (d. 1945). The Methodist Wesley House was established in Cambridge in 1926, and the Presbyterian Westminster College earlier was situated in the same city. The Congregationalists moved their Cheshunt College to Cambridge, that source of so many leaders in the beginning of the English free church movement. The Unitarians have higher schools of theological training in Manchester and Oxford. Several of the learned men of the free churches have won distinction, Baptists and Methodists in Old Testament research, while the Congregationalists distinguished themselves in the field of systematic theology. Likewise, within the areas of New Testament research and in church history men from the various free churches have made valuable contributions. Besides those who have been mentioned a few others should be listed, such as W. B. Pope, J. Scott Lidgett, T. R. Glover, W. B. Selbie, C. H. Dodd, H. H. Rowley, and R. Newton Flew.

The English free churches during the first part of the nineteenth century were one-sidedly engaged in the ecclesio-political struggles, but they turned their attention during the last part of the century to social matters. This took place partly because of the practical developments, such as when William Booth (d. 1912) and his Salvation Army pioneered in practical Christianity and partly in a theoretical and political struggle for justice for those in the lowest strata in the community. As has been mentioned, the Methodists above all the others took the lead in these social matters. The early history of trade unions and co-operatives is closely associated with the free church movement, and free churchmen were the first Labor representatives in Parliament. The trade unions and the Labor movement in Great Britain, even to the present day, bear the imprint of this Christian support, even though during the latter years indifference and open opposition to Christianity has found a place in the leading groups where there is no association with the free church movement.

The old association with the Liberal party continued, and it gave great opportunity for advancement. During the election in 1906 this party gained control of the government, and it was after this period that important men came out of the free churches, such as H. H. Asquith (d. 1928) and Lloyd George (d. 1945), who rose to the summit. When the House of Lords opposed the liberal reform policies, its privileges were pared down; the free churches regarded the House of Lords as being antiquated, and they fought against it. Among the social reformers two names should be mentioned, one within Parliament, the other without. The former person was a Congregational pastor, C. Silvester Horne (d. 1914), and the latter leader was the Baptist pastor, John Clifford (d. 1923). Silvester Horne is also known for his *Popular History of the Free Churches*. His outstanding gifts as an orator gave him great influence. Clifford was the great orator and agitator for social policies, who from his pulpit in Westbourn Park Chapel made his voice heard so that it sounded over the entire English-speaking world. It was the old convictions of freedom and righteousness which sparked this work of social reform.

The Methodists, possibly more than other denominations, had a political-social interest, especially in the Primitive Methodist church, which had early espoused the cause of laborers. No person among the Wesleyans made a greater impression in the social question than the London pastor, Hugh Price Hughes. His book *Social Christianity* is considered a historic event within Methodism. In 1885 Hughes started the *Methodist Times;* the year following, the foremost free church newspaper, the *British Weekly,* was initiated and rose to prominence through the leadership of William Robertson Nicoll. In several newspaper organs a liberal campaign was waged in behalf of protective labor laws, better social advantages, the cause of temperance, the care of prisoners, the establishment of children's homes, and the care of young people. Some homes for children became world renowned, such as those established by George Müller, Thomas Barnardo, C. H. Spurgeon, and T. B. Stephenson.

In the greater and more influential free church press, the liberal concepts were predominant, and until World War I, progress was made in the areas of social policies. It was also a free church leader, a Unitarian by the name of C. P. Scott, who for a time was the editor of the influential organ *Manchester Guardian*. The free churches exercised a great influence in Parliament in behalf of social matters. For example, because of the energetic ministry of the Congregational pastor, Benjamin Waugh (d. 1908), the legislation of a number of laws for the protection of children was effected. There is no denomination that did more for the cause of temperance than the Methodist, and in this cause Hugh Price Hughes played a leading role. Both in the matters of legislation and in the practical work of temperance among the masses, Hughes was a driving power.

World War I completely upset the political balance in England. Liberalism divided and was weakened. The Labor party consequently became the alternative to the Conservative, the old Tories. By tradition, the free churches were associated with the Liberal policies, but when this party ceased to play any important role in Parliament, its political influence soon diminished. To be sure, many free church politicians had close associations with the Labor party, and several of their members during later years have been members of the cabinets. The best known of these personalities was a Methodist, Arthur Henderson (d. 1935). Today the Labor party is under the leadership of men who have no association with the free church movement, which means that the free churches can hardly be said to have a representation in British politics in proportion to their outreach and significance in the culture of the nation.

It is possible from another point of view to point out a change in the free church situation. The struggle for religious freedom had held the free church movement together. When the goals in the ecclesio-political situation had largely been achieved, confusion prevailed in regard to new objectives, especially in the matter of upholding free church ideas in opposition to the Anglican church. Then too, a cultural leveling process took place which created a new fellowship with the Anglicans. During the present century the membership of the free churches has been declining. The new generation within the free churches has become preoccupied with secular activities.

The weakening of the dissenter consciousness became especially marked after World War I. At this time there was a strong movement for reunion with the Anglican church, as well as a striving for unification among all of the free church denominations. The former plan of union has now come to an end, but the latter movement has resulted in the union of like-minded groups and in an international fellowship which crosses denominational and national lines. Participation in the ecumenical movement since the Stockholm meeting in 1925 is an expression of this development. This fellowship and the debates at the ecumenical meetings and conferences have, in reality, gradually awakened once again the dissenter consciousness within the free churches of Great Britain. During later years the movement has become engrossed in its own theological presuppositions and the basic position of the free churches.

Other problems which cause difficulties are also found among the free churches in Great Britain. Early they had to take a position regarding natural sciences, rationalistic philosophy, and the historical-critical study of the Bible. The last-mentioned problem was especially relevant to the free churches where the basis of existence rested on the older method of biblical interpretation. Many viewed new trends as a serious threat. When Spurgeon began to suspect the "new theology" within the Baptist Union, he protested by withdrawing from this fellowship. This was during the 1880's when the "downgrade controversy" was in progress, and it was at this time that an attempt was made to effect a union between the two older groups among the Baptists. This new organization was finally completed in 1891. A controversy, similar to that which ravaged the American denominations regarding rationalism, did not occur in England, even though "fundamentalists" from the United States have had some influence in Great Britain. There have been conflicts, but in many cases they have been overcome.

Another controversial question related to the one just mentioned was the emphasis which was given such outstanding attention in the United States, "the social gospel." It has already been pointed out that many free church leaders applied the gospel to the social questions of the day. In some instances they went too far, so that they reduced the gospel to a social-political instrument. One person representing this type was the silver-tongued Congregational pastor of the historic City Temple in London. His name was R. J. Campbell, and he was an exponent of an immanent interpretation of Christianity. It was a "new theology" which made Jesus Christ more a social reformer and philanthropist than a Saviour. His book *The New Theology* came out in 1907, presenting an extreme human optimism. "Sociology is put in the place of soteriology," as one historian evaluated it. This social movement did not have the same power as the movement for reform which has been mentioned above. Campbell's position within the Congregational denomination became unacceptable so that he left his post as pastor of the City Temple and went to the Anglican church.

Optimism in many quarters came to an end after World War I, and even in the British free church movement one could soon observe a return to the older theology. British thought was influenced by Karl Barth and Emil Brunner. Later the advance of Communism, Nazism, and Fascism revealed the depraved nature within man, and a return to the Pauline interpretation of man and the evangelical teachings of salvation became even more marked. In regard to the social questions, the free churches in Great Britain continue in their course toward the left. The American professor in social ethics and theological interpreter, Reinhold Niebuhr, has exerted a certain influence.

Concerning the separate free churches, much could be

written, but here there is room only for a few facts to be recorded. The Congregationalists have, during the period under consideration, strengthened their position in the social and cultural life of the nation. One of their foremost preachers was Joseph Parker (d. 1902), who attracted great crowds to the central sanctuary, the City Temple of London. Parker was twice president of the Congregational Union. The denomination built a new headquarters in the Memorial Hall in the heart of London, which was occupied in 1875. When the Congregational Union celebrated its fiftieth anniversary jubilee in 1881, it had become well established under the wise leadership of its secretary, Alexander Hannay (d. 1890). Hannay was able to widen the perspective of his denomination by making trips to the United States, Canada, and Australia, where he was instrumental in developing a new spirit of fellowship. These measures resulted in the planning of a Congregational World Congress. The first Congress was held in London in 1891. It took the form of an advisory meeting with three hundred invited delegates. The chairman was R. W. Dale, and in the presidium there were representatives from the United States and Australia. Relations with America became especially active, and such men as Henry Ward Beecher and historian Henry M. Dexter had attained great respect in England. At this international free church meeting, P. P. Waldenström created interest with his account of the development of the strong free church movement in Sweden. During the 1880's American Congregationalists visited Sweden, and they became acquainted with the Swedish Mission Covenant.

After 1891 six similar world conferences were held in various places in Great Britain and the United States, the last one taking place at St. Andrews, Scotland, in 1953. After World War II, international contacts were once again revived. A new constitution drawn up in 1904 has effected a closer organization with a central leadership. The organs which during the last decades have been the spokesmen for the denomination are the *Christian World* and the *Congregational Quarterly*. The Congregational movement in Great Britain is divided into four branches, of which the union for England

and Wales is the largest in size with approximately 236,500 members, according to the records of 1948. The Scottish fellowship had about 36,000 at the same time, while Ireland had only 1,600. An independent Welch-speaking fellowship in Wales (established in 1872), listed approximately 125,500 for the same year.

Within the Baptist denomination, after the downgrade controversy during the 1880's and the reunion of the General and Particular Baptist fellowships in 1891, there was a peaceful and smooth development. As has already been mentioned, the Baptists were zealously engaged in the social-political controversies. The best-known politician was Lloyd George, and by means of his books the best-known university man was the classicist in Cambridge, T. R. Glover (d. 1943). Among the laymen within the business world only one needs to be mentioned, Thomas Cook (d. 1892), the founder of the world-famous travel bureau which bears his name.

The acquisition of a new headquarters building in 1903, the Baptist Church House in the central part of London, helped the Baptist denomination to increase its position and influence. The denominational organ, the *Baptist Times,* also took on increased significance. Interest in the denominational history was maintained primarily by the *Baptist Quarterly.* Behind this inner development was the general secretary, the highly gifted J. H. Shakespeare (d. 1928). He was also the spokesman for the free church reunion with the Anglican church, but this did not win acceptance. By means of participation in the ecumenical program, the older Baptist point of view has become clarified for the English leaders. Shakespeare's significance, however, is acknowledged by all.

Shakespeare was the one who organized the first Baptist World Congress, which was held in London in 1905. Seven such congresses have been conducted. The Jubilee Congress was held in London in 1955. One of the Baptist World Alliance's most zealous champions was J. H. Rushbrooke, who was the first general secretary. When he died in 1947 he was president of the Alliance.

The English Baptist denomination reported at the beginning

of the 1950's a membership of approximately 340,000. Besides, approximately eighty thousand belong to the Baptist union in Wales, established in 1866, and nearly twenty thousand belong to the Scottish union, which was organized in 1869. A small number of congregations are also found in Ireland. As a consequence of the strong free church movement in Wales and through the efforts of Lloyd George, separation between church and state there was made possible more than forty years ago.

The principal Methodist group in Great Britain after the 1860's was the Wesleyans, even though both the Primitive Methodist church and the United Methodist Free Churches had a considerable and growing work. Even the Wesleyans now made some approach to the other free churches. Because of this, there followed a liberalizing of the policies both within and without the denomination. As mentioned before, Hugh Price Hughes stood as the central figure in this development. The older conservative spirit was to a great extent won over, and the new direction was also united with a wider program of evangelism. The Wesleyans especially have members in the large middle classes. As in the other denominations, there took place a widening of the sphere of activity and an inner revival when personal and economic contributions of great significance were made. Schools were erected, both of higher and elementary learning, and the theological seminaries increased in their significant ministry.

The old controversy regarding the status of laymen continued within the Wesleyan denomination. The conference composed of pastors ruled the entire movement. Gradually the laymen were able to become active in the local congregations, and therefore it seemed self-evident that even the highest controlling body would ultimately be opened to them. In 1877 a plan was introduced giving laymen representation, and the following year it was formally put into action. The plan prescribed that the pastors would assemble first in their own session to consider urgent matters, then later the great conference was conducted when an equal number of delegates of pastors and laymen took part. This united representative conference has, since 1901, met before the pastors' assembly; consequently, the latter group has lost much of its importance as far as church leadership is concerned.

During the 1880's an "Advance Movement," appeared which may be interpreted as having released new-won powers among the laity. There were a number of men in the generation of Hugh Price Hughes who pressed to the front. It was at this time that the Methodist denomination began its ecumenical conferences. The suggestions came from the United States, but it won a quick response among the Wesleyans. The first of the world conferences was held in London in 1881, and since then they have continued every ten years, alternating between England and America. The last of these worldwide conferences was held in Oxford in 1951.

More than any other free church group, the Methodists have during the recent decades concentrated on inner movements of unity. There were major divisions during the nineteenth century, but the Methodists were able to overcome these, setting an example to others. By 1907 the preparatory work had progressed so far that three of the earlier schismatic groups united. They were the Bible Christians, the Methodist New Connexion, and the United Methodist Free Churches, all of which were united under the name, the United Methodist Church, which embraced approximately 160,000 members. However, this was only the beginning. After World War I, arrangements were continued with other groups of Methodists, and in 1932 there was the great union when the Wesleyan Methodist Church, the Primitive Methodist Church, and the United Methodist Church were brought together in one strong organization, which is simply called the Methodist Church. This is the strongest free church in Great Britain with a membership of nearly 900,000.

Although reintroduced into England during the nineteenth century, the Presbyterian church has never been able to win large support. The Presbyterians have also joined together in a world alliance, but since several of the Reformed churches in this group are state or national churches, they fall outside the limits of this investigation.

Likewise, the Quakers have not been able to win any great support, but their reputation in humanitarian enterprises, especially during and after both of the world wars, has won the admiration and wonder of the entire world. Their head-quarters in the central part of London is comparatively new. The Quakers have also made an important imprint on forging the chain of unity. The remarkable experiment at Birming-ham, Selly Oak, with its five colleges for the various free church denominations, is unique in church history. The Quaker's Woodbrooke College (established 1903) is the center. The remaining schools train missionaries and Sunday school teachers for various denominations. The significance of the Selly Oak institution for interdenominational and interna-tional fellowship can hardly be overrated.

The co-operation which the free churches initiated in the early period has continued. A closer unity was attempted when the National Free Church Council was organized in 1896. It is natural that the first president should be Hugh Price Hughes. A closer organization based on a representative system was organized in 1919, the Federal Council of the Free Churches, and it started to function under the leadership of J. H. Shake-speare. Both of these organizations for a number of years existed side by side, but in 1939 they united in one council.

The United States.—The United States became the "prom-ised land" for the Christian free churches. From 1620 to 1914, the year World War I started, many millions of Euro-peans crossed the Atlantic to the new country with its great opportunities of liberty. The immigration stream became especially heavy after the Civil War, and in unbelievable proportions houses of prayer, chapels, and church buildings were erected in thousands of new communities. It was the time of the great expansion for the voluntary congregations, con-quering and cultivating the interior areas of the continent. The simple matter is that in this treatise it is impossible to write a comprehensive report of free church expansion. A few principal features of developments within the United States and from there to various parts of the world can be mentioned.

The American voluntary system has proved itself suitable to

the winning of new consciously active members for the congregations. There has been a marked increase in the number of church accessions during the last decades. As far back as 1800 only 7 per cent of the population belonged to any church, while corresponding statistics for the year 1850 indicate 12 per cent, a significant increase. But more noticeable was the great increase during the last half of the nineteenth century. Population rose greatly, but church membership grew even more rapidly. Church membership included 35 per cent of the population in 1900 and over 60 per cent in 1956.

The church development in the United States up to the close of the 1860's was pioneered by the left wing of Protestantism. This has continued to be true. It was the revival groups, the Baptists and the Methodists, which won the greatest number of adherents, and this took place without any appreciable gain by winning members through immigration. Other denominations, such as the Catholics, Lutherans, and Episcopalians, have won millions of adherents because of the influx of immigrants. It was also the free church denominations which attracted the great masses of the population stream going west on the American continent. The Baptists report 17,470,000 church members, while the Methodists have 11,665,000. The Lutherans in the United States now have 6,313,000 church members, and the Presbyterians record 3,535,000.

More than ten million foreign-born were living in the United States in 1903, and the number of children born of foreign parents surpassed 26,000,000. From a religious point of view, these millions of immigrants were a checkered group. Some came as conservative adherents of the European state or national churches, and others in great numbers came as opponents to their native church system, taking advantage of their new freedom to organize their own congregations. Other immigrants who came in great numbers considered themselves completely separated from the European church system, and they united with the American churches, especially those which provided a spirited revival ministry for the immigrants. In this regard the Methodists and the Baptists were the leaders. Naturally there were those immigrants who considered them-

309

selves free from all church affiliations and employed religious freedom to be free from all religion.

It has already been indicated that religious oppression in Europe played an important role in emigration during the seventeenth century and later. In the middle of the nineteenth century there are several testimonies of similar instances of religious persecution, including some from Sweden. It is natural that when these immigrants came to the United States they would take full advantage of the opportunities offered in the free church to express their own worship and desire for service. In this way several thousand new free congregations arose, and the voluntary system was capable of functioning even for immigrants who were not opposed to the state churches of their homelands. For example, the Swedish Lutherans established their own voluntary system in the Augustana Synod without any administrative or economic dependence on the church in the motherland. The successful operation of the free church system for the immigrants was dependent to a great extent on the fact that these smaller, homogeneous congregations found it easier to preserve their faith and their mother tongue. Even in the 1916 church census it was reported that there were still 132 church denominations which in their ministry continued to use in some form a language other than English. There were no less than forty-one languages used.

During this period of growing immigration and active sea travel, the various American church denominations set up mission chapels at the harbors and industrial cities in the United States and other parts of North America, Europe, and Asia. For a number of years there was a real concern in America for the great stream of foreigners, and this led to increased efforts to gain a secure footing for the American democratic ideal in foreign countries. There was special concern over the great masses of Catholics which arrived. The denominations within the United States increased their efforts to convert the immigrants to the free spirit which was the pride of America. The tremendous increase of immigration after the 1860's increased the activities in the churches. The various home mission societies purposefully pressed on to the west, erecting stations, building churches, and sending out colporteurs and preachers. It was often arranged that these colporteurs and preachers were stationed among their own countrymen in the immigrant settlements. In this way the free church ministry was supported and greatly enhanced, although both personal and economic resources were often rather meager. This entire story is a remarkable history of the voluntary mobilization of Christians in a struggle for moral ideals and religious awakening.

It has previously been indicated how the interest in the sailors and the immigrants led to the development of missions in the European countries. For example, the energetic support that Scott and Baird gave to Rosenius' ministry in Sweden has already been mentioned. It was the American and Foreign Christian Union which stood behind this work. This society supported missionary activities in several European countries. A large number of letters and reports from missionaries have been published in their news organ. This newspaper carefully observed the progress of religious freedom in the Old World, and it carried on an active campaign against coercion and persecution. The same situation was true in the newspapers among the Baptists and the Methodists: continuous reports, vigilant communication of religious coercion, and sharp criticism of Europe's intolerance. For a number of years Baird edited his own paper, which also was the voice of the Evangelical Alliance, and it was replete with news from the mission and the spiritual struggle in Europe.

From a European point of view, it is interesting that the American statistical reports considered Europe as a mission field. They published information about the mission stations, missionary workers, and communicant members. It was especially the Baptists and the Methodists who in this way made known their concern about the modern European free church movement. But other denominations had similar experiences to relate. In the middle of the 1890's the American Board of Commissioners (Congregational) reported in this same fashion about their mission in such countries of Europe as Turkey, Spain, and Austria. The Baptist Missionary Union related its ministry in Sweden, Denmark, Norway, Germany, Finland, Russia, France, and Spain. The Methodist Episcopal Church at the same time published information concerning stations and missions in Germany, Sweden, Norway, Denmark, Finland, Russia, Switzerland, Italy, and Bulgaria. The Seventh-day Adventists gave accounts of work in England, central Europe, Denmark, Sweden, Norway, Germany, and Russia. In the middle of the 1890's the number of missionary workers in Europe in the American missions was 2,745, and there were 153,500 communicants, including 92,000 Baptists and Methodists in Germany and Sweden. In 1850 the number of communicants in these same missions was only 5,400; consequently, the Americans could rejoice over the progress of the free church ministry which they supported in the European countries.

The American free church life was strengthened, not only by the European immigration and by its attending results, but there was also another factor which had a similar effect. This was the group of liberated Negroes. Already great numbers of slaves had been won to the revival groups. It is estimated that in 1860 there were no less than 207,000 Negroes who were members of the Methodist churches in the Southern states, while at the same time there were over 250,000 who belonged to the Baptist churches. After liberation, the Negro churches made rapid increase, for the church became the central, secure haven for the liberated. The social functions for the Negroes were concentrated in the churches, and here the Negro preacher became the teacher, counselor, and supervisor. The great denominations, especially in Northern states, dug into their resources and supplied schools and education for the liberated. Both in the matter of pure spiritual influence and in the matter of higher and lower education, great results were achieved. In the meantime, it is natural that there was a spirit of independence that arose among the Negroes. They formed their own organizations, both congregations and denominations, and they personally took the leadership in educational institutions. The best known among the leading educators was Booker T. Washington (d. 1915), who in 1881 pioneered in the work for a remarkable development, the Tuskegee Institute in Alabama. Large donations were made by men from the Northern states for the erection of school buildings for the Negroes. Some Negro universities have secured academic recognition.

From a religious point of view it was natural that even the Negroes would divide into several denominations. They have readily held to the congregational independence, and they have consistently stayed with the left-wing of Protestantism. Of the eight or nine million Negroes who are church members, more than half of them are Baptists and nearly three-fourths of the remaining are Methodists. Both within the Baptists and the Methodists the Negroes have their own denominational organizations, giving evidence of good harmony and unity.

In the early part of this period under consideration, the cause of temperance became a great social question. With the great immigration and the liberation of Negroes, many saw the need of pressing the battle against intoxicating liquors with renewed vigor. In 1865 several organizations were united into a national society. On the other hand, the invested capital of the liquor industries increased enormously, and the new wealthy class from these sources of production became a powerful influence in society. The Puritan spirit was awakened to a new activity, especially among the revivalist denominations. In 1869 the National Prohibition Reform Party was organized, which was directed against the brewery and tavern interests. The famous women's organization of 1874, the Women's Christian Temperance Union, was led for many years by a Methodist woman, the highly gifted Frances E. Willard (d. 1898). This women's movement soon became international in its outreach.

Pastors and preachers championed for temperance, and revivalists such as D. L. Moody were clear on this point. President Hayes and his wife, who were Methodists, abolished intoxicating drinks from the White House and even refrained from having wine at the dinners of state, which increased interest in the question concerning alcohol's position in the life of the community. When the political prohibition party did not succeed, the famous Anti-Saloon League in 1893 came into being, and this organization too, had promoters and leaders from the churches. The prohibition movement gained force, and in 1917 the American Congress approved the Prohibition Amendment. Two years later it was formally ratified. This law was retained for about twelve years. The desire of a large part of the American population achieved its repeal.

As in Great Britain, this era was characterized by the distinctive great spiritual movements which were especially related to D. L. Moody and a like-minded ministry. As Finney dominated the first part of the century as the great revival preacher, Moody put his imprint on the latter part of the century. Moody was from New England, and in Boston he came under Congregational revival influence. He soon came to the Middle West, and in 1856 he was a shoe salesman in Chicago. He began to work in a Sunday school, won proficiency as a speaker, and was so gripped by the evangelistic opportunity of the laymen that in the beginning of the 1860's he quit selling shoes and put all of his energies into the neglected areas of rapidly growing Chicago. Soon Moody had a large group gathered around him, and so he built a church where he served as a lay preacher. During the years 1865–1869, Moody was also the secretary of the YMCA in Chicago, and he was instrumental in elevating this program to a high level of effectiveness. It was a clear ministry of revival which was promoted, and for the YMCA's history in the United States Moody's ministry was of great significance. At these conferences for young people, Moody met the singer Ira D. Sankey, who from 1871 was Moody's faithful co-worker.

The greatest period of advance was achieved by Moody after two years' stay in Great Britain. Sankey's *Gospel Hymns* were such a pronounced success that perhaps no other song collection has ever won such worldwide distribution. Moody and Sankey returned to the United States in the fall of 1875, and now they were world-renowned men. There followed a succession of extensively planned campaigns in the leading American cities, when hundreds of thousands of persons were converted and joined churches. For over twenty years Moody continued

314

his travels in all of the sections of the United States and preached continually the gospel of salvation and piety. Chicago became the center of his ministry, and here a new great church building had to be built for this colossal movement—"a Pentecostal visitation"—which stirred up the entire Middle West. Ecstasy and tumults did not take place in these meetings, for Moody proclaimed love and grace and gave assurance of salvation and peace. Moody was a sound and practical man of organization, who in his work with young people had learned to appreciate life's realities. Consequently, he began to conduct congresses for his supporters and those who ministered in the revivals. These congresses became an important part of his ministry. At these assemblies, advice and instruction were given, and here Christians experienced the riches of religious unity and fellowship. Moody had a firmly established reputation as an honest and honorable servant of the Lord, and this meant much for him as a leader of a great movement.

Moody was a Congregationalist and Sankey a Methodist, but the entire spiritual movement surrounding them was built on an ecumenical basis. Possibly the Sankey songs contributed more to its interconfessional character than anything else. Other hymn writers and composers were associated in this movement, and the various denominations naturally employed the methods and general directions of the movement. Moody secured an abiding influence through the Moody Bible Institute, which he established in connection with his church in Chicago in 1889. R. A. Torrey (d. 1928) came to this school and made a deep impression as president, serving for many years. Moody also planned for the future when he established schools for young men and women in the city of his birth, Northfield, Massachusetts. The same can be said concerning the conferences for Christian mission workers, which Moody initiated in the same city in 1880, as well as student conferences which began in 1886. Nathan Söderblom, from Sweden, participated in the student conference of 1890, and he received an enduring impression. It was out of this latter group that the Christian Student Volunteer Movement for Missions began. This movement became one of the most remarkable enterprises in the Protestant world under the leadership of John Mott.

Moody inaugurated a high point for revival emphasis in the United States. Many people followed the evangelist, some of whom were gifted and independent while others were simply imitators. The best-known leaders in revival were Gipsy Smith, Sam Jones, and Billy Sunday. In our present day the name of Billy Graham is known around the world. Graham's ministry, together with the great influx of people who come to his meetings, indicate that the old methods of mass evangelism still function remarkably well even in the strange world of the 1950's, in spite of the claim of some that new conditions demand new methods of evangelism.

It would be completely erroneous to conclude that everything has been said concerning the last eighty years about American free church life with an account of revivalists and great numerical advancements. Increase during the period of 1870–1890 was not entirely due to revival campaigns. Much of this growth resulted from the fact that the denominations developed their own activities for youth and Sunday schools, making them more effective than heretofore. The various denominations started youth organizations, and in these, similar to the Sunday schools, the laymen were active in the leadership. Courses in adult education and conferences have also served the cause of Christian youth. Out of this type of activities there arose the famous Chautauqua Institution. John Vincent, later a Methodist bishop, arranged for short educational courses at Chautauqua Lake in the state of New York during the 1870's. The courses of instruction at Chautauqua have been a pattern for similar programs reaching out beyond the borders of the United States.

The Christian Endeavor movement, which grew to international proportions, led young people to work together for definite objectives. The founder was a Congregational pastor, F. E. Clark. At the close of the 1890's this youth movement reported nearly three million members in various parts of the world. In the struggle to keep the young people, and in an effort to win the outsiders, the larger cities especially have developed church social centers—"the institutional church." This is a ministry that is similar to the YMCA and other similar institutions. Great sums of money have been given for buildings and equipment. It is certain that these institutions have had great significance.

At the beginning of this period, which was the time of "big business," many private schools of higher education were established. Great donations made possible the development of new universities and colleges. Most famous of these was the University of Chicago, which in a new form began its great history in 1892. In the early years of this school's history, John D. Rockefeller donated $35,000,000. The University of Chicago during the early days was definitely under Baptist leadership, but at the present, like so many other schools, it has become rather secular. The theological department for many years has been a point of dispute among fundamentalists. Quaker donations made possible the establishment of Cornell University, Ithaca, New York, in 1868 and Johns Hopkins University, Baltimore, Maryland, in 1876. These universities held to science and research independent of the teachings of the church, and this was the general tendency after the turn of the century with institutions of higher learning.

Controversies over doctrine became a problem in free church life in the United States during this period. There was a real struggle over the question of instructional freedom in the schools and the pulpits. In some states the teaching of biological evolution was challenged and forbidden. This new naturalistic science, often more simply termed "Darwinism," caused much unrest and strong opposition. The so-called Dayton trial a number of decades later was a testimony of this fact. The old seats of learning have gradually adjusted themselves to the new times, often as a consequence of the fact that in the newer states much of scientific research and instruction has been carried on in state universities which stand outside the control of religious denominations. Even many private institutions of learning have turned into the same independent direction.

It is not possible to illustrate further this tendency at American seats of learning, which became quite general in the latter decades. It is clear that at least in the Northern states the churches lost control of these higher institutions, but theological schools associated with these universities have tended to maintain their denominational connections. These seminaries or theological faculties have not completely withstood the change of the times. The conservative church people soon took notice of these tendencies and reacted in various ways. Support was often withheld, which did not greatly affect those schools which were already well endowed. The conservatives also warned young men not to study at seminaries which did not conform, leading to a type of boycott. At times new schools proclaiming their loyalty to the Bible have been started in the neighborhood of older seminaries. This has occurred within several denominations.

Against "modernism," which accepted biological evolution and interpreted the Bible in the light of historical criticism, stood a strongly united church group with pastors in the leadership. This was especially true of the denominations arising out of revival, who with full consciousness widened the division between themselves and modern science. This set of circumstances gave rise to the so-called "fundamentalism," which energetically and often fanatically fought all forms of modernism or that which was suspected as such. The fundamentalist movement began in 1910 when *The Fundamentals: A Testimony to the Truth* were published in twelve small instalments with over 2,500,000 free copies given to clergymen, ministers, and other Christian leaders. During the next three decades vicious personal attacks were made by fundamentalists on liberal theologians and suspected modernists in the various denominations. This struggle has sometimes led to schism in the denominations and missionary societies, and many personal injuries have been inflicted.

It is of course true that there has been cause for watchfulness and, in some instances, good reason for complaint. In some of the theological schools and seminaries extreme views have been advanced. This condition began early in New England, and it spread to other sections of the country. As in Great Britain, some teachers and educated men zealously espoused the "social

318

gospel." Among the pioneers of this movement were Washington Gladden (d. 1918), a Congregationalist pastor, and Walter Rauschenbusch (d. 1918), a Baptist pastor and professor. In line with this liberal position in theology and active ministry for social betterment there were also the Baptist pastor and professor, Harry Emerson Fosdick, and several Methodist bishops, including G. Bromley Oxnam. Many of the university and seminary teachers, pastors and editors, as well as leading laymen from various fields of endeavor, continue to follow this new line. Recently, however, such concepts have become modified in many circles, and there is a closer approach to the more conservative ways of thinking. Several theologians have made contributions to this relatively conservative trend of recent times, undoubtedly the most notable being under the influence of European Barthianism. Professor Reinhold Niebuhr of Union Theological Seminary is perhaps the foremost representative of this "neo-orthodoxy."

As far as the separate, principally free church denominations are concerned, a great deal could be related about the last eighty years. Very little space can be given to this discussion now. The revivalist denominations have steadily increased in numbers. During the decade of 1870–1880, the number of communicants in all churches increased nearly three and one half million, which was considerably more than the corresponding statistics for the entire period from 1800 to 1850. This increase continued during the decade of 1880–1890.

It was during this enormous period of expansion after the Civil War that free thinkers made their great attack against the churches. The foremost assailant was the lawyer and politician, Robert G. Ingersoll (d. 1899). Once when Ingersoll was speaking and asserted that the church was dying out, a Methodist secretary sent the following telegram to him: "We are building more than one Methodist church a day, and we aim to increase to two a day."

In the cause of foreign missions, giant strides were taken during these last decades, so that the churches of the United States became the leaders in the missionary enterprise in foreign countries. The Methodists and Baptists have everywhere been in the lead in home and foreign missions because of their larger membership. In the Methodist Episcopal church, laymen were given the right of representation in the general conference in 1872. In 1869 the Presbyterians united their two branches, the Old and the New School, and the Congregationalists spread westward from New England. After 1871 the Congregationalist National Council convened every third year. The Southern Baptist Convention continued to grow, and today, along with the Methodist church, it is the strongest of the Protestant denominations in the United States with more than eight million members. The Baptists in the Northern states reorganized their fellowship in 1907 and called themselves the Northern Baptist Convention, which was changed in 1950 to the American Baptist Convention. Both among the Methodists and the Baptists are also a number of smaller groups, constituting denominations with various national language backgrounds.

In the United States the Quakers have gradually organized like the other denominations with permanent pastors and the prevalent forms of worship with preaching. The Salvation Army, which in this treatise receives bare mention on the ground that it can hardly be called a free church, appeared in the United States in 1880. Several new denominations have arisen, many of the pentecostal variety. Some denominations lacking the strongly biblical basis of the classical free churches —such as Christian Science, Jehovah's Witnesses (Russellites), and Theosophy—are passed by in this writing.

The weakness among the free churches which has been pointed out before, that of breaking up into new groups and denominations, naturally found expression in the United States with its full religious freedom and a voluntary system. But it should not be forgotten that the leading denominations are great and dominant, and the number of members in these separate organizations is relatively small. As an example, the Methodist church may be mentioned. This great and dominant church reports 9,180,000 members, while the entire number of Methodists in the United States is 11,665,000, and this surplus of two and one half million is divided into not less than twenty-one different denominational groups. The same can be said for the Baptists with twenty-four organizations, the Lutherans with twenty, and the Presbyterians with eleven.

The conditions that exist in Great Britain are also the same in the United States, in that there is a definite tendency toward unionization, the joining together of several denominations. Some of this union effort has taken place among related denominations; other mergers have occurred across confessional lines. The most remarkable merger among denominations of similar points of view took place when the negotiations, carried on during a prolonged period between the Methodists of the North and the Methodists of the South, were crowned with success. A third denomination joined this union, the Methodist Protestant church. Thus there was formed in 1939 in the United States the largest Protestant church, and it was simply called the Methodist Church. At the time of the merger it had 7,590,000 members, and since then the church membership has increased to over nine million.

Similar situations have occurred in smaller proportions in other denominations. The old Congregational denomination joined with a smaller denomination in 1931 and within a few years has reached a membership of approximately 1,175,000. Two Reformed churches followed the example of merger in 1934. In 1918 three Lutheran churches united to form the United Lutheran Church. For several years the American Baptists and Disciples talked about a merger, but little has come of this.

The interconfessional fellowship has in later years had an established council in matters of home missions, such as earlier was formed for foreign missions. Since 1908 there has been a large, effective organization which has existed in the Federal Council of the Churches of Christ in America. In the leadership of this organization there were men who zealously worked together in the interest of ecumenicity. In social and ecclesio-political matters this organization has made a great impression. This group has recently been reorganized and is now called the National Council of Churches. This program of working together has been sharply criticized by the fundamentalists and strict confessional groups. The attempt after World War I to develop an interchurch world movement with dollars and organizational means met with violent and justified criticism from many places. The great plan undertaken fell short of the mark. Against this there developed a growing interest in the cause of ecumenicity among most of the leading denominational groups, even though opposition still exists.

Many of the American free churches took part in the organization of the World Council of Churches in Amsterdam in 1948.

The European Continent.—The free church movement in Europe outside of Great Britain had a good beginning during the first two-thirds of the nineteenth century. This movement did not arise out of the older free church groups on the Continent but, as has been pointed out earlier, was inspired and supported by the churches in Great Britain and America. In a number of countries revival came within the movement around 1870, especially in Germany and Sweden. There was progress in the other countries as well, and in Russia a strong, distinctive movement developed, which because of the conditions during the last thirty-five years has not been easy to appraise. It is possible that in the future the full significance of this free, voluntary movement in Russia, in contrast to the weakened national church, will appear in its true light.

In the meantime, the European church system did not offer any favorable conditions for a free church work of this type. It has already been shown how coercive measures and persecution met the first free church pioneers and how these conditions continued until the period under consideration. Neither the Protestant state churches nor the Catholics would tolerate any sects within their monopolized territories. Eventually religious freedom was won in these places, even though it was limited. Now it is only in totalitarian and strongly Catholic countries with their political hierarchies that the free church movement is persecuted. However, even until the present century severe penalties could be imposed upon the free church work in Protestant countries.

The Anglo-American free church alliance with the free

church movement on the European mainland continued and increased. Especially after the two world wars, which caused spiritual and material impoverishment among the European folk, desperate needs aroused the Christian philanthropy and helpfulness of the American people. The tremendous mobilization of relief forces among the American churches helped blaze new trails into the homes and the communities on the Continent. Together with the sister churches in America, the denominations in Europe co-operated in finding new possibilities for reaching the people. The noble example of the Quakers in this respect has attracted the attention of the entire world. Other denominations have not been far behind in this struggle against want. This relief work was carried on in several forms. This ministry is a new characteristic of the Anglo-American influence on the churches in Europe.

As has been mentioned in the foregoing section, the Baptists and the Methodists, who were the most prominent in the United States, maintained the support and co-operation with their newly won co-religionists in Europe. In the reports of the churches in the United States, the designation of help and aid was placed on a level with missions among the Negro, and this met with protest in the European countries concerned. Over against this, the American mission magazines and annual reports maintained that the support was given to the evangelistic work in the countries where "popery" or rationalism had extended their power. Because of this situation, the Americans felt justified in conducting their mission, and this interpretation was endorsed by thousands of immigrants and sailors who had experienced conversion as well as the active manifestations of piety in the United States.

The free church movement received its first impetus among the Baptists in Germany. From 1870 and on, the Baptists continued to grow steadily in the three strong centers which had been established, Hamburg, Berlin, and East Prussia. Baptist influence spread from Germany into Russia, Poland, and Hungary. Publications and newspapers developed. The theological seminary in Hamburg was opened in 1880, and soon it had a four-year course for students from the various countries of eastern Europe. When in the 1880's the old triumverate of Oncken, Köbner, and Lehmann had passed off the scene, the denomination was well organized, owned a good theological school and a progressive publishing house. The latter was moved from Hamburg to Kassel. This great publication building was completely destroyed during World War II.

By 1887 the Baptists of Germany had started the deaconess organization with a ministry for the sick, which later grew to be an extensive operation. At the present time there are five deaconess houses with over eight hundred sisters who work in three of their own hospitals. This work bears a strong element of a social mission, which has been greatly needed, and it has helped to further the cause of evangelism in the Baptist movement. Baptist work was handicapped during World War II. Part of the seminary building in Hamburg was destroyed (now reconstructed), and seventy-four of the 335 churches were totally destroyed, while 190 were damaged. However, the work of the Baptists continues in spite of hardships such as the difficult problem of helping refugees from the east.

Shortly before World War I, the membership of the Baptists in Germany was 45,600, but at the present time it is about a hundred thousand. This advance is dependent partially upon the union of two smaller denominations in 1940 with the Baptist denomination, the Plymouth Brethren and a group which was oriented toward Pentecostalism. At the same time, it should be observed that the various groups in the adjoining countries, which earlier belonged to the German Baptist denomination, have established their own organizations. The young people's organization grew, a great interest in foreign missions developed, and the active work in spreading literature advanced considerably.

Baptists came to other German-speaking countries quite early. An off-shoot of the Baptist work in Germany was in Switzerland, and it was the preachers from Hamburg who labored there after the first church was established in Zürich in 1849. These few churches in Switzerland for a long time belonged to the German denomination, maintaining a separate district within this fellowship. The Swiss pastors studied at the Ham-

burg seminary, and all of the news periodicals and other literature that the Swiss needed were obtained from the German denomination. During the Hitler regime there was a break in this
association, and at the present time the Swiss Baptists exist as
an independent denomination with its own literature ministry.
However, the entire membership of the Swiss Baptists is only
about fourteen hundred, so it is not an extensive movement.

The Baptists in Switzerland have experienced severe persecutions for a long time; imprisonment and banishment, as well
as compulsory baptism of infants, have been among the repressive measures. It was not until 1875 that new legislation was
enacted which lessened the oppression in the Swiss cantons.
During and after World War I, the climate for Baptist work became difficult. Undoubtedly much of this was due to the fact
that the work was allied with the German Baptist work. Recently a new center of influence has been established in the
vicinity of Zürich. This is the European Baptist Theological Seminary which the Southern Baptists from the United
States organized at Rüschlikon. Although this school has been
in operation only since 1949, it has already become a most influential factor of Baptist life in Europe, not least through its
many annual summer conferences. This school also means
much for the Swiss Baptists. In the original stronghold of the
Anabaptists, the principle enunciated by Balthasar Hübmaier
has seen confirmation: "It is impossible to kill the truth." In
this connection it should also be mentioned that in Waldshut,
where Hübmaier preached and baptized multitudes and where
a Catholic reaction destroyed his work, there is now a Baptist
church which was erected in 1953. In this church most of the
communicants are refugees from eastern Germany. This program is also primarily a ministry of the Southern Baptists in
the United States.

The Baptist movement in Austria, started in Vienna in
1869, progressed even more slowly. The founder of the first
church, E. Millard, remained there until 1887. In this city
where Hübmaier was burned at the stake in 1528 there are
now two churches with suitable chapels. Since the last world
war, several chapels have been built with assistance from the

Americans, such as in Salzburg. Even in other districts where the original Anabaptists had congregations, such as in Linz, Steyr, and various places in Tyrol, there is now some form of a Baptist witness. The membership is only a few hundred. This group has also been intimately connected with the German Baptists.

In the old German territories in Poland, the Baptists advanced after the period of the 1860's; however, until World War I it was only among the German-speaking people that the Baptists had any success. This fact was true of those Polish sections which were under Russia as well as under Germany. After World War I, Poland became independent, and there was a period of religious freedom when many Poles were won to the Baptist cause. At this time the Baptists were organized into three conferences, two German and one Polish, and all three were united in one union with about fifteen thousand members before World War II. The Polish Baptists have received support for many years from two sources, partly from a Baptist church in Edinburgh and mostly from the American Baptists. The condition of the work after the last war is not clear.

The Baptists of Holland, whose work in the beginning was also closely allied with the Germans, have in these latter years made noticeable progress. Both the general church situation in Holland and the church divisions have been unfavorable for a revival of the free church type. The work in Holland grew very slowly after the first church was established in 1845. The denominational organization was not formed until 1881, and since then the work has progressed slowly. At the present time the membership is estimated at about seven thousand, which indicates that progress has been good during the last thirty years. The training of the pastors has taken place partly in Hamburg and partly in the English seminaries.

In eastern Europe the German influence also made itself felt. It was among the German colonists in southern Russia that the Baptists started their work. There the Stundists and the Mennonite movement were known earlier. Preachers who came from Germany during the 1860's collaborated with the Mennonites, which did not happen elsewhere. Beside this movement among the German people in Russia, an indigenous Russian Baptist movement began about 1870. It was in the south and southeast that this group advanced, with headquarters in Tiflis. The "All-Russian Baptist Union" was organized in 1884 under the leadership of Vasili Pavloff. Another branch grew up which existed in St. Petersburg (now Leningrad), and this branch grew out of the revival with which the English Lord Radstock was associated. It was among these people that Ivan Prokhanoff became the uncontested leader. This group called itself the "Evangelical Christians," and it was clearly baptistic. In 1922 it was announced that this group had about 250,000 members, while the older Baptist Union had nearly a hundred thousand. A union organization was formed in 1922. The extent and organization of the Russian Baptists during the latter years has been obscured. The Baptist Union reports its membership to be about 520,000.

Even in Hungary the influence of Oncken's ministry from Hamburg was felt. A permanent work was started in 1873 when a German preacher by the name of Heinrich Meyer settled in Budapest as an agent of the British and Foreign Bible Society. In 1875 he baptized the first Hungarians. Earlier work had been limited to the Germans. Success was reported, so that by 1910 the membership of the congregations was close to seventeen thousand. Following World War I, Andreas Udvarnoki, who was trained at Hamburg, was selected as the president of the seminary which was erected with the help of Southern Baptists. Because Hungary lost so much territory in the peace settlement, a good portion of the Hungarian Baptist membership was lost to other nations.

In Bohemia and Moravia the Anabaptist movement early obtained a good footing and rapidly increased; however, the Catholic campaign of extermination broke the work down completely. It was during the nineteenth century that the Anglo-American societies came to minister. Even the German Baptists exercised some influence. The first Baptist pioneer was A. Meereis, a colporteur in the service of the British and Foreign Bible Society. The first baptism took place in 1877, but it was not until 1885 that the first Baptist congregation was organized in the vicinity of Prague. Heinrich Novotny was elected pastor. He and Meereis, in spite of persecution, continued to advance the cause of the Baptists. Other men also labored in Moravia, including converted emigrants from the United States. When World War I broke out in 1914, there were several congregations in three major districts in Bohemia, Moravia, and Slovakia.

In the new republic of Czechoslovakia which was formed after World War I, enveloping the three countries just mentioned, the Baptist work was free to continue. Novotny died in 1912, and his son Josef continued with the work. Josef had studied at various universities and seminaries, including Hamburg and schools in England. Prague became the center of the Baptist work; a new church was erected and a theological seminary was founded in 1921 under the leadership of Dr. H. Prochazka. A few years before, the churches had organized into a union which included approximately four thousand members. This work has been supported by the Northern Baptists in the United States, as well as English Baptists. Just as in other eastern European countries, this work has experienced a number of unfavorable circumstances. Accurate reports about present conditions are not available.

Romania gained new territories after World War I. Having a progressive ministry, the Baptists grew here and in a few years became the fourth largest continental Baptist body. A well-established work came into being in Bucharest in 1878, as a pastor was chosen as a director of a Bible depot. This action took place under the initiative of E. Millard. A seminary for preachers was also established in Romania after the war, largely through the generous support of the Southern Baptists.

In Bulgaria, German colonists from Russia were the Baptist pioneers. The colporteurs from the British and Foreign Bible Society were also instrumental in working for the cause in Bulgaria. In 1880 the first two Baptist churches were established, and in 1894 work was begun in the capital city of Sophia. An American preacher lived here, and American money provided for the erection of a chapel. In Bulgaria, as in the other countries in southeastern Europe, a veil is now drawn over the present state of affairs.

During the nineteenth century the Baptists in Yugoslavia made little progress. After World War I activity increased in this country, especially after the return from Russia of prisoners of war who had been baptized and emigrants returning from America who had been converted to the Baptist position. A denominational organization was formed in 1925, and now there are several churches with about 3,500 members. During the German occupation up until 1945, missionary activity was hindered considerably. In this as in other countries, Southern Baptists have given significant aid.

In the Roman Catholic countries the free church movement has always met strong resistance, and therefore the gains have been meager. Robert Haldane influenced the forming of Baptist-minded groups in France, and Swiss and American missionaries baptized people during the 1820's and 1830's. As usual, there followed imprisonment and fines for the pioneers. However, it was not until after the establishment of the French Republic and the inauguration of religious freedom in 1871 that any appreciable gain was made. Churches were organized in a number of the leading cities such as Paris, Lyon, and Marseilles, and at the close of the century there were forty-five churches with about two thousand members in an organized work. Later theological and personal opposition arose to hinder the progress of the work. During World War I a large number of the churches as well as the organizations were destroyed in northern France. The last war and Nazi occupation also seriously crippled the work. The Belgians and French-speaking Swiss have worked together with the French Baptists. The French Baptists are divided into three groups. The original denomination has only about a thousand members. American assistance has greatly aided the work.

During the 1860's some English preachers started Baptist work in Italy, but only after 1870 when Italy became united did the work begin to progress. The Southern Baptists have for many decades aided the work here. At the turn of the century, congregations had been established in such cities as Rome,

Bologna, Naples, Venice, Milan, and Turin. A theological seminary was started in Rome in 1901, but it was discontinued in 1932. After World War I the Southern Baptists assumed responsibility for assisting the Italian churches. A new seminary was opened in 1949 in Turin, while in Rome a school for young women and a children's home have expanded Baptist work. The entire denomination numbers a membership of about five thousand.

The colporteurs prepared the soil for the Baptist ideas in Spain as they did in Italy. From England and America came support, and it was through the ministry of an American preacher that the first Spanish people were won to the Baptist position. In 1870 converts were baptized, and the first Baptist church in the country was organized in Madrid. From the beginning of the 1880's Baptists from Sweden were engaged in the ministry in Spain; such names should be mentioned as Erik Lund, Juan Uhr, C. A. Haglund, and Nils Bengtsson. Since World War I the Southern Baptists have supported the work in Spain. During the Franco regime the Baptists, together with other Protestant groups, have suffered severe hardships. About twenty-four congregations with approximately 1,600 members make up the entire fellowship of Baptists in this ultra-Catholic country.

In Portugal there are twenty Baptist churches with about 1,200 members, but these churches have divided into two groups. Baptist efforts began there during the 1880's, and for a number of years they were supported by the Baptists from Brazil, who sent missionaries and supported the native pastors and their mission stations. Since World War II, a Baptist group from America, the Conservative Baptists (fundamentalists), has entered Portugal and won over some churches to their cause.

This treatise has given considerable attention to the spread of the Baptists on the European continent because the Baptists are the oldest and the largest free church movement in Europe. We now turn to the other energetic, evangelistic denomination of the Anglo-American world, the Methodists. As the Baptists made Germany their chief headquarters, so also the Methodists spread out through the Continent with this country as a base. Initial work of the Methodist mission has already been treated. After the 1860's there was gradual development but no great progress among the Methodists. Only in Sweden did the Methodists experience dramatic expansion, especially during the decades of the 1870's and 1880's.

The two branches of German Methodism, the Wesleyan in the south and the episcopal in the north, both had established their work by the end of the 1860's. This was also true in other German-speaking territories, especially in northern Switzerland. This period which extends to the present has been marked by a steady development within German-speaking territories. By 1870 the Wesleyans had established a foothold in Vienna, and shortly thereafter in München, Augsburg, Nürnberg, and a number of places in Bohemia. In the meantime, it became very difficult for the Methodists to work in Catholic-controlled territories, and the Wesleyans were unable to make the same numerical gain here as did the episcopal group in northern Germany.

John C. Barratt (d. 1892) led this mission, which increased its scope of activity. He was supported by the Wesleyans of Great Britain. When in 1872 a new law for dissenters was issued in Württemberg, the Wesleyans decided to constitute their own free church. It was not until 1875, however, that the first German pastors were ordained by English Methodist pastors. It was at this time that the Methodist chapels began to increase in number. Stuttgart and the suburb of Cannstatt formed a strategic center, for in this area a number of Englishmen resided who were engaged in various industries. There was a small English church here, and in Cannstatt a small seminary was established in 1875.

In the middle of the 1870's the Methodists in Germany felt the influence of the Moody and Sankey revivals in Great Britain. The well-known holiness preacher, R. Pearsall Smith, came to Stuttgart at this time and conducted revival meetings which caused some unrest among the leading men of the Wesleyans but stimulated the activities of the mission. The Methodist work expanded at this time to Silesia and Westphalia. Several new church buildings were erected, support for this project coming from England. In 1879 a beautiful church was built in Stuttgart, and the seminary in near-by Cannstatt, staffed by English teachers, had several students. During this period of progress an active conflict between state-church clergy and the Methodists was taking place. The Methodists were severely attacked, and though religious freedom was formally sanctioned, there were many opportunities to make infringements upon this free church. The same situation existed in northern Germany, where the episcopal group encountered clergy of the state who claimed a religious monopoly.

When the Wesleyan mission celebrated its fiftieth jubilee in 1882, a memorial church was dedicated at Winnenden. The English Methodists contributed generous amounts to this building as well as other chapels and church building projects. This memorial celebration was indicative of a new upsurge within the entire Methodist movement. In Bavaria the Methodists received legal status as an independent church denomination, but it was not until 1890 that the first chapel could be dedicated. This took place in Nürnberg. In other Catholic territories, such as Vienna, persecution was so severe that the membership increased slowly. It became more and more clear to the Wesleyans ministering in the southern districts that the union with the Methodists of the north was profitable. After Barratt's death in 1892, a series of negotiations led to an agreement which involved receiving large economic contributions from England for the many churches and other buildings in the mission of German Wesleyanism. In 1897 both sides reached an agreement, and since that year German Methodism has pursued the episcopal polity. This church was united with the mother church in the United States, and American bishops presided at its conferences.

While only 2,500 Wesleyans joined the Methodist Episcopal church in Germany at this unification, a large number of churches, preaching places, and lay assistants placed themselves under its control.

After Jacoby's passing from the leadership of the mission in 1868, district superintendents had been installed. At the conferences the bishops from the United States were present. The work proceeded normally in spite of various difficulties which hindered progress. In Saxony the Methodists were long denied the freedom to carry on their work openly, and even in other provinces the churches in the free movement were very much confined. However, revivals brought many people into touch with the congregations, and the work could not be suppressed. During the middle of the 1870's, the Sankey songs won great approval. Many of the gospel songs were translated into German, and other songs were added and disseminated in special collections which were greeted with great enthusiasm in the various free churches as well as within the fellowship groups in the state churches. The influence of Pearsall Smith's holiness teachings also increased among the northern Methodists.

Because of the revivals among the Methodists, new chapels were built both within the German and the Swiss branches. In Frankfurt on the Main the Methodists more and more came to centralize activities, especially when a mission school (seminary) was moved there in 1869. Support from the United States was significant. Through it all, it was the faithful Methodist minister's daily work which bore fruit in conversions, erection of new church buildings, and establishing of new young people's associations. Among American, English, and German Methodists there was the conviction that Germany needed a strong, free evangelical ministry. This was the real cause behind the sacrifices of money and personal talents.

In 1886 the Methodist Episcopal church divided into a German and Swiss conference. At this time there were about fourteen thousand members and 22,500 Sunday school children in these free church congregations. After this period each conference developed independently. The German group naturally had both the larger field and the greater resources. From 1893 the German conference was divided into northern and southern conferences because of an expanding ministry.

In 1895 a central council was established for the European conferences, which had significance for Methodism in other countries. Many churches were erected, the ministry of the deaconesses was enlarged, and other social work was increased, including the cause of temperance. By means of the union between the Wesleyans and the episcopalians in 1897, new possibilities opened up, and this fact was used to the best advantage. J. H. Vincent, the American bishop, presided at the Jubilee Conference of 1900 at Bremen, for he had received the commission from the General Conference in the United States to stay four years in Europe, residing in Zürich. At this time the reported membership of the Methodist churches in Germany and Switzerland was twenty-six thousand, and the work was well established in this German portion of Europe. Now the Methodists began to convene European congresses, and there were approximately sixty thousand Methodists on the European continent. After the four-year mission of Vincent, William Burt came to Zürich, where he remained for eight years as bishop.

A significant action was taken when the General Conference in the United States in 1912 appointed John L. Nuelsen as bishop over the European churches. Nuelsen was an American citizen, but he was born in Zürich, a son of a Methodist pioneer there. He had received his training in Switzerland, Germany, and America, and he was able to use the German language, something which his predecessor bishops were unable to do. Nuelsen stayed in Europe from 1912 to 1940, and during a critical period he distinguished himself as a church leader of this great territory. Nuelsen was an outstanding theologian, and he was respected as such in educated circles. In 1922 the theological faculty of Berlin University granted him an honorary doctorate.

The organizational structure of European Methodism was enlarged at the General Conference in the United States in 1920, when pastor Anton Bast of Copenhagen was named bishop for the Scandinavian church territory. He was followed in 1928 by Bishop Raymond J. Wade, an American, who made his headquarters in Stockholm, serving until 1940. In 1946 the Northern European Central Conference appointed pastor Theodor Arvidson as bishop over the northern churches. In 1936 the annual conference in Germany organized its own central conference, and the first German Methodist bishop was Otto

Melle (d. 1947). He had been president of the seminary at Frankfurt on the Main. Melle's successor in 1946 was another president of the seminary, Ernst Sommer (d. 1952). The southern Methodists had assumed a definite responsibility for work in eastern Europe, and in 1922 they established a number of annual conferences under the leadership of special bishops. The General Conference in the United States (northern states) in 1920 had established a bishopric which had southern European countries and North Africa under its care, but it ceased in 1932. After the union of the Methodist churches in the United States in 1939, a reorganization took place. Since 1944 Bishop Paul N. Garber has had the responsibility of the Methodists in southern Europe and North Africa.

After World War I Methodists made new gains with aid from the United States. The new German constitution now extended religious freedom. Consequently, it was possible to plan the work better. The various phases of the work, such as literature, school work, and ministry of the deaconesses, were revived. During the 1930's the free churches again suffered hardships because of coercive Nazi policy. During World War II all of the churches suffered severe losses, especially in the destruction of church buildings. Generous support came from the United States, however, for rebuilding the destroyed churches. In 1939 there were forty-five thousand Methodists in Germany, and by 1949 this number had increased to sixty-two thousand.

As previously mentioned, the Swiss Methodists were closely allied with the German. In 1886 the Swiss Methodists organized their own conference with about 5,300 members. Like the Baptists, Swiss Methodists did not have their own literature at the beginning of their work but were dependent on the German publication house in Bremen to assist them. After the independent conference was established, a Swiss publishing enterprise was begun. The same action took place with regard to the deaconess and hospital ministries. In social and community moral matters the Swiss Methodists have made valuable contributions. With the assistance from the United States, several new buildings were erected, while at the same time interest in the distress in other countries during and after the two world wars was expressed in actions of benevolence. At the present time there are twelve thousand Methodists in Switzerland, and their churches are now self-supporting.

Methodists in France, like the Baptists, do not have an encouraging history. The Wesleyans' early ministry during the nineteenth century made insignificant progress. During the 1850's the French organized their own conference with about a thousand members. A church was dedicated in Paris in 1862, and in connection with it a school and a publishing house were erected. After World War I about sixteen hundred members belonged to this French Wesleyan church organization.

When the Methodist Episcopal Church assumed the work in France, it discovered that progress on the field was difficult. The Americans did not step in until after the separation of church and state in 1905. Bishop Burt, who was stationed at Zürich, visited France in 1907 and gathered together small groups and organized congregations in Lyon, Grenoble, Avignon, and Marseilles. After 1918 Americans made significant contributions, especially in behalf of the children and young people; but the great depression in the United States following 1929 curtailed this program of assistance. The organized annual conference ceased to operate, and the churches disbanded to join other churches, primarily the Reformed bodies.

Similar difficulties faced the newly established Methodist work in Belgium when the depression came, but the outcome was not the same as in France. In connection with the aid that was received after World War I, a mission was established in 1922. In Brussels a headquarters building was erected, a school and a children's home were put into operation, and aid was given which made it possible to maintain a Protestant hospital. Early in the 1930's when the crisis came, the American missionaries were recalled, a number of enterprises were closed, and some of the property had to be sold. However, American assistance once again came to the aid when Belgium was liberated from Nazi occupation, new churches were built, and the congregations increased. At the present time there are about five thousand adherents in this Catholic country, and their contributions in various directions are influential.

Italy has been a place of great interest for the Methodists. Even during the 1860's there were some Methodist people in this country, under the leadership of some Wesleyan missionaries. The center for their work was Milan. One of these men was Henry Piggot, who labored for forty years in behalf of Italian Methodism. After 1870 it was even possible to conduct some work in Rome, and consequently Piggot went there. As usual the progress in the Catholic countries was meager. At the close of World War I there were two thousand members.

When Rome was opened to Protestant missions, the Methodist Episcopal church in the United States initiated a work there in 1871. A church was dedicated in Rome in 1875, and in 1886 William Burt came to assume the leadership with a powerful hand until he became bishop in Zürich in 1904. Shortly after World War I the mission was again in operation. A school, a children's home, and a headquarters building were built in Rome, along with a publishing house. During the Mussolini period and the war the Methodist work suffered injury, but in later years it has revived. The entire membership of the Methodists in Italy is approximately four thousand.

Spain, like other Latin countries, has been an unfruitful field for free church ideas, and the Methodists have gained little significant results from their labor there. Early in the nineteenth century the Wesleyans started a mission. It was associated with the Bible distribution of the British and Foreign Bible Society. Revolutions and political unrest have hindered the work, and the Catholic opposition has resulted in severe oppression. After 1870 there was relative freedom and some progress, but soon new difficulties arose which reduced the membership to an insignificant number.

A preacher and a teacher, Francisco Albricias, on his own accord established a school and free church in Alicante at the close of the nineteenth century. He joined his mission and his school with the Methodist Episcopal church in 1919, and Bishop Nuelsen reorganized the mission in 1920. This school had at this time nine hundred pupils. During the Franco regime the Methodists have experienced difficult times. The school was closed and the leaders were compelled to leave the country. This, of course, was part of a general oppression against all free movements in Spain.

Through Methodist relief work there was a spiritual revival in eastern Europe after World War I, leading to the organization of churches in many areas. This was the case in Poland, and when the Polish emigrants pleaded for a Methodist mission in the homeland, a mission was established in 1922. Here, too, importance was given to the establishment of schools and social work. A school for teaching English had eleven hundred pupils just before the last war, and of this number 95 per cent were members of the Roman Catholic Church. The depression also affected the work in Poland. Missionaries were recalled to the United States, half of the Polish preachers had to be dismissed and the schools discontinued. Later the work was revived, but then the German Nazis invaded in 1939. The conditions after the war are uncertain, but no doubt Methodism is still alive in Poland.

In Czechoslovakia, Methodism is a new movement. It was organized in 1922. Two Czechs who had become converted and were Methodist pastors in the United States returned to their native country. Great revivals followed the ministry of these men, and as early as 1926 there were ten thousand adherents in the country. German occupation during the war hindered the work to a great extent and destroyed much of what had already been gained. After 1945 the four thousand remaining Methodists united in a new ministry in young people's work, social missions, and education.

The Methodists came into the Russian territories in 1890's by means of an emigrant who returned from the United States and began to conduct Methodist classes. The first Methodist church was organized in Wirballen in 1909. Methodist influence also came from Finland to St. Petersburg. Of this work, mention shall be made later. The Revolution of 1917 and the establishment of communism were crushing blows to the newly established and weak Methodism in the country. In 1923 a reformed Russian Orthodox group sought to make connections with the American Methodists for help in organization. This unique effort did not prove successful. What remains of Russian Methodism is unknown.

A small group of Methodists had long existed in southeast Europe. The American Board started a Congregational ministry in southern Bulgaria by 1857, and it invited the Methodist Episcopal church to work in the northern portion of the country. Thus a twofold Protestant mission was initiated, yet the work went forward slowly. In 1892 the Methodists organized their work as a "mission conference." The work of the congregations proceeded gradually with but little success, yet influence increased. Above everything else, the educational work was of greatest significance. A school for girls was established in 1882, and this was the best Methodist work in the country between the two world wars. Oppressive persecution has hindered the work of the congregations. Both communism and Nazism have taken their toll, especially during the 1930's and 1940's. When the Nazi regime was crushed in 1944 there were approximately three thousand Methodists in the country.

In old Austria-Hungary the Methodists had a good missionary in Christian Dieterle, who was sent from Germany in 1870 to prepare the way for his church in this Catholic empire. He ministered in Vienna for a number of years, but he was severely oppressed, and consequently he was unable to conduct many services. Only a few joined the Methodist cause in the following decades. In 1900 Otto Melle came to Hungary, and he was able to establish churches among the German-speaking population as well as the Hungarian. From 1905 Budapest became the center of this work. Melle was selected to be the superintendent of this Methodist mission in Austria-Hungary in 1911. During World War I and the decay of the Austro-Hungarian empire, further difficulties troubled the churches. The few Methodists were divided into three countries, namely Austria, Hungary, and Yugoslavia. Because of the wars and all of the related problems, Methodism has had few opportunities for making advancement. At the close of the 1940's only about fifteen hundred Methodists remained in Austria, a thousand in Hungary, and a similar number in Yugoslavia. In the latter two countries the Methodist schools, hospitals, and other property have been confiscated by the authorities. In Austria Catholics have been the primary opponents to the progress of the free churches.

Congregational churches did not grow on the Continent as a result of emigration or other aid from the United States. In this respect their historical development is different from that of the Baptists and Methodists. As has been pointed out, the influence of the British free churches played an important role in Swiss-French Congregationalism and the German free church movement. Among the German churches the spirit of independence and activity increased during this period. The leading church in Wuppertal (Elberfeld-Barmen-Ronsdorf) became very influential. Communion groups, which developed into congregations, were established in several places. A union of these free churches took place in 1874 when a conference was held and the Union of Free Evangelical Churches and Lord's Supper Fellowships was organized. Several important propositions were laid down, one of which was that the individual churches should maintain their own autonomy. At the annual conferences only matters that dealt with common edification and missions were to be handled.

At first this union proceeded very carefully, and only at the beginning of the present century did the work become more purposeful and active. It was not until after World War I that a seminary was established, which now has a four-year curriculum. Young people's work was carried on, and publication and literature distribution were parts of the organizational work. Similar to the other German free church denominations, the Congregationalists maintained a deaconess ministry. The most remarkable enterprise of this nature is the hospital in Hamburg. Because of their common work it became necessary to draw up a closer knit organization. Thus in 1922 the change, involving the name of the union was effected, and the Union of the Free Evangelical Churches in Germany came into being. A brief confession and a model constitution exist for the churches within the union.

As with other Congregational groups, the Germans were careful to guard the independence of each local congregation. In the matter of baptism there existed great freedom so that both infant baptism and the baptism of believers were practiced, and at the Lord's Supper they have practiced open communion. Personal confession of faith is a prerequisite for church membership, and like the other free churches they have strict church discipline. The membership has never been large. In all of Germany there are at present about twenty thousand members.

The Swiss Congregationalists, as has been pointed out, made good progress during the first part of the nineteenth century, both in the French- and the German-speaking sections of the country. In some of the cantons the movement diminished, while in others it continued to develop throughout the latter part of the nineteenth century. A free church was erected in Neuchâtel during the 1870's, and the leading personality was the well-known exegete, Frédéric Godet (d. 1900). In northeastern Switzerland there arose a highly respected preacher, Otto Stockmeier, who arranged for a remarkable revival center at a castle placed at his disposal. In other territories humble laborers paved the way for the revival of the free church mission. Thus the foundation was laid for the greatest of the Swiss free church groups, centered in Winterthur and neighboring districts. The congregations for a long time were only loosely connected. It was in 1910 that the churches united in the Union of Free Evangelical Churches in Switzerland. The membership is about three thousand.

The French free church movement prior to 1870 had been influenced from various directions. This awakening had associations with the continuing movement among the French-speaking Swiss. These relationships continued, but growth was slow nevertheless. A new impulse came from England. Following the unfortunate Franco-German War, an English pastor zealously entered the work in Paris, especially trying to reach the non-Christian laborers. This man was R. W. McAll (d. 1893). His missionary work began in France in 1872. It made encouraging progress. McAll started several preaching stations, and he obtained economic aid not only from his British friends in the faith but also from Americans. This movement primarily attempted to win the working classes, and it developed into a significant enterprise.

In 1885 the British Congregationalists sent a delegation to the French free church synod, and consequently new contributions were made to the work on the Continent. The Union of the Evangelical Free Churches in France had, after the separation of state and church in 1905, other Reformed free churches at its side, but the union differs from these in that its churches demand a personal confession of faith as a condition for church membership. The association has only about a thousand members.

In Holland the idea of the free church has existed in various forms; not only were the Mennonites the pioneers of this concept, but the so-called Remonstrants had also championed this thesis. These churches have continued to exist until the present day in the congregationalistic polity. They make up a denomination of more than twenty thousand. The modern free church movement resulted from the work of a pastor, de Liefde, who visited England, where he became acquainted with the congregational church concept. De Liefde became a zealous pioneer for congregations made up of regenerate believers, and he won many followers. In the matter of baptism, he like many of the other Congregationalists took a twofold point of view. Revival influences from the Continent also made an impression, so that several churches were established. In 1880 these Dutch churches united in the same way as in Germany, Switzerland, and France. In the forty churches there are close to seven thousand members. A theological seminary was established at Apeldoorn in 1926.

In Catholic Belgium a free church movement grew up after World War I. The work began through the efforts of an American evangelist who distributed Bibles to Belgian soldiers. Since this time the work has received aid from many sources. In a short time the movement became a typical revival denomination. A Bible school for French-speaking evangelists was founded in 1919, and three years later a similar school was started for the Flemish. In several of the country's leading cities the denomination has sizable church buildings. Its influence in this Catholic country is not small, especially through the means of energetic Bible, book, and newspaper publications.

As it has been pointed out previously, the Anglo-American Congregationalism did not evidence the same zeal to establish missions in the European countries as did the Baptists and the Methodists. This was due to the fact that the latter groups won so many followers among the emigrants. However, eventually even the English Congregationalists and the Congregationalists in the United States, the American Board, began to support work on the European continent. This was true in Czechoslovakia, where in 1872 some Americans came to Prague to work for the cause of evangelicalism. The Scotch Bible Society also began a typical colporteur ministry here. Persecution faced these representatives and their ministry, and it was not until 1880 that a Congregationalist church was established. Heinrich Novotny was one of the leaders, but soon he became a Baptist, separating from this movement and becoming a pioneer for the Baptists. Others came in the place of Novotny—a Reformed pastor, Franz Urbânek, and Alois Adolf, until 1927 undoubtedly the foremost preacher and leader. The movement won followers not only in Bohemia but also in Moravia and Slovakia. A congregation was even established in Vienna. An American named Clark was the faithful leader of the movement for many years. He worked in relationship with the Scotch Bible Society, which supported colporteurs who preached and spread the revival.

After the close of World War I, a great liberal epoch dawned under the first president, Masaryk, and it was at this time that full religious freedom was proclaimed. Assistance from the Americans continued for some time, but in 1931 the American Board discontinued its support, and it was a difficult struggle for the movement to collect money on its own. The membership of the denomination is about eight thousand, centered in the territories of the old Brethren congregations. It was proper, therefore, for this denomination at its annual meeting in 1919 to take the title "Bohemian United Brethren." This title signified a sense of continuity with the opposition movement of the fifteenth century.

Quite early American and British missionaries had been active in southeast Europe, but little progress had been made. The American Board established a foothold in Greece as early as the 1820's, and at the same time the English missionaries became active in this country. This missionary activity began when Greece achieved its independence from Turkey. In Bulgaria the American Board started work as early as 1858, but progress has hardly been worth mentioning. During the latest decades, the abnormal political conditions have hindered the work. The college operated by the mission has been closed, and the leading pastors have either been put in prison or shut off in one way or another from their ministry.

The Congregational movement has never made any significant progress in the Latin countries, even though friends from England and the United States attempted to work for the cause in Spain, Portugal, and Italy. During recent decades the impact of war and political unrest has caused all Christian work supported by foreign denominations to meet with opposition in these countries.

Only in one Catholic country, Poland, has there been a Congregationalist movement of some significance. During World War I there were revivals. Evangelists who arose from among the common people were successful, and free churches were established by "gospel Christians." These friends received aid from outside of the country, primarily from Germany, for the revival arose in the German-speaking territories of Poland. Before World War II this evangelical group reported about two thousand members in Poland with thirty-eight congregations. The present situation in this country is uncertain, as it is in eastern Europe in general.

The free church movement in the north appeared first in the Baptist form, beginning in Denmark in 1839, then in Sweden in 1848, and in Norway in 1860, as described above. The Baptists were the pioneers in the struggle for religious freedom. This was an epoch-making achievement. During the period following the 1860's, the Baptists advanced consistently here and in Finland and the Baltic countries.

The oldest of these movements was in Denmark. It soon was organized, ready to assume new responsibilities. To be sure, the possibilities of the work were not large, but due to the close connection with the German and American brethren the Baptists of Denmark received substantial economic assistance. A number of young men obtained ministerial education in the United States. At the turn of the century the membership had risen to about four thousand, and at the present time this number has doubled. A "folk high school" was established in 1899, and in connection with this school a seminary class for training of pastors came into being. In 1928, with the help of the Northern Baptists, an institution was established at Töuöse. It consists of a folk high school, a middle school, and a theological seminary.

Social work has also been taken up, such as a children's home and child care. Special mention should be given to the new Köbner Church in Copenhagen which owns the Köbner House, where young people's work has developed. The Danish Baptist denomination has its own publications, and it reveals great interest and support for foreign missions. Special organizations for young people and women are in operation.

In Sweden the Baptists were the only free church organization of any significance before 1870. At that time the Congregational movement swept over the country when P. Waldenström became a popular religious leader. At the same time, the Methodists made great headway and were numerous by the beginning of the 1890's. In the meantime, the Baptists continued with their development. The Baptists maintained close relationship with their friends in the faith in the United States, but as the congregations increased in numbers they became more and more independent. It was especially during the 1880's that the membership gains were large. Large numbers of young men joined with the Baptists and received their education at Bethel Seminary, Stockholm. Colporteurs became pastors. At the fifty-year jubilee in 1898 the membership was approximately forty thousand. The denomination early organized into a number of regional mission societies, and since 1861 district associations have been formed. There are now twenty societies with 530 churches which make up the Baptist denomination. In its legal form this group has been known since 1889 as "Sällskapet Svenska Baptistmissionen."

The churches are completely autonomous, and all of the members, even the minors, have equal rights to take part in voting and making decisions in the congregation. In the annual conference, which consists of delegates of the congregations, a board is elected, which has charge of the foreign and home mission programs. There are several special organizations, such as the young people's union, the women's fellowship, the choral union, and several others. The denomination has its own newspaper, publishing house, and printing establishment, as well as schools and social institutions. Both in matters of doctrine and in practical missionary work there have been individual expressions which have resulted in schisms.

About 1860 the doctrine of sinless perfection came to be accepted in some of the congregations. At the beginning of the 1870's a new separation took place which led to the development of the Free Baptist denomination. The things that divided were partly doctrinal and partly practical, such as organization and the position of educated pastors. The holiness movements from America and England increased in influence, especially when pastor John Ongman (d. 1931), after several years' ministry as a Baptist pastor in the United States, came to Örebro to begin an active work, beginning in the early part of the 1890's. Broady, who was the president of Bethel Seminary, set the tone for leadership by evangelical and anticlerical concepts, making an imprint on the corps of preachers. Anders Wiberg had died by this time, and a line of young leaders in the congregations and in the denomination followed in his stead. Ongman's mission set up its own organization in the Örebro Mission Society, which more and more became an independent denomination. This mission received a special impetus when the Pentecostal movement broke forth after 1905. Ongman was soon wholly engaged in this movement, and in hundreds of the Baptist congregations the evangelists under

Ongman's influence labored. This situation led to a cleavage within the Baptist denomination, although during the time of Ongman it never led to an open division.

Within the Baptist denomination a new and radical center of the Pentecostal movement developed in Stockholm in some of the oldest churches as well as in the Seventh Baptist Church, established in 1910, now the Philadelphia Church. Young Lewi Pethrus came to the Philadelphia Church to serve as pastor in 1911, and soon there was a division with the leading men in the denomination. The question of the Lord's Supper played a certain role as well as baptism of the Spirit, but the decision which determined the split was the insistent opinion of Pethrus that no organization in the Christian ministry could exist alongside the independent, local congregation. The Pentecostal movement under the leadership of the Philadelphia Church grew into an independent free church denomination with an extreme form of congregationalism as its basic principle. The movement was held together through its news organ, the *Evangelii Härold,* through a closely knit corps of preachers, a Bible school, and other co-operative enterprises.

The death of pastor Ongman in 1931 produced a period of uncertainty. Various circumstances led to a real division, and many churches left the Baptist denomination during the 1930's. This move was not really necessary, as many have since freely admitted. Ongman's movement continues on its own way. It has its own mission school, paper, and publishing establishment, foreign mission program, and as the Örebro Mission Society it continues as a denomination according to the definition of the new law of religious freedom. The number of members in its churches is believed to be over twenty thousand, while the Baptist denomination has approximately thirty-five thousand, to which must be added several thousand in the young people's organization. The Pentecostal churches number their membership around ninety thousand.

Another Baptist fellowship is the Holiness Association, which arose during the 1880's out of a spiritual movement in the province of Närke. This movement proclaims the need of genuine conversion and living of a holy life. Much good has resulted from this work, both in home and foreign missions. It has the least possible organization and encourages the ministry of laymen in various ways. Numerically this group has never been very strong, with about four thousand church members at the present time.

The Baptists of Norway, after the organization of the first two churches in 1860, vigorously championed for the free church concept, but the denomination has never grown to a large group. During the first decades the work among the Norwegians was stimulated by the Swedes, and later the exchange of preachers has been extensive. Aid from Americans continued. The early preachers, Rymker and Hübert, were allied with the Seamen's Friend Society, and even in the later years the American Baptists have supported the work. For a generation, pastor J. A. Ohrn of Oslo was the denominational leader. His son, Arnold Ohrn, is at the present time the general secretary of the Baptist World Alliance.

The first annual conference of the Norwegian Baptists was held in 1877, and the next year a preachers' association was organized, which contributed to the shaping of a genuine solidarity among the pastors. Even though the literature work began as early as the 1880's, it was only since 1900 that this movement received strong leadership, which allowed it subsequently to develop in strength. The Baptists of Norway also have special organizations for women and young people. In their social work they have had a special interest in reaching the fishermen and sailors. Together with the Swedish and the Danish Baptists, the Norwegian Baptists have maintained Seaman's Home in America, located in San Francisco.

The entire Baptist population in Norway is about 7,500, which is about the same number as in Denmark, but the churches are spread over a much wider territory. The country is divided into five districts. Similar to the other countries in the north, the Baptist denominational growth has been hindered by the uprising of another Baptistic organization, the Pentecostal movement. In Norway this group has no less than twenty thousand members.

During the 1850's, Baptists in Sweden began to move eastward. In the Swedish-speaking areas of Finland a small Baptist church was established in 1856. This church was on the Åland Islands, and after a few years this movement took hold in the mainland, becoming established with a center in Vasa. At the present time, the Swedish-speaking group has its headquarters in Vasa with a good congregation, a small theological school, a publishing and newspaper ministry. The membership numbers about two thousand. A young people's organization has existed since 1907, and special courses are conducted every year for the training of young people's leaders and Sunday school teachers. The missionary work has been assisted by the Baptists from Sweden, England, and the United States, especially during the recent years.

Since 1922, when the law providing religious freedom was passed, the Baptists, like other free movements, have obtained a better-defined position as a free church denomination. The Baptists joined with other free denominations and started a "folk high school" in 1945 in the vicinity of Vasa which has come to have great significance.

Finnish-speaking Baptists have their own group which numbers only about a thousand members. Since 1949 they have maintained a small theological school in Vasa, and a monthly periodical has been published, but the outreach of the work is modest. Great difficulties faced this denomination during the wars and in the civil strife in connection with the Russian revolution. There is also a strong Pentecostal movement in Finland which in its manner has hindered the Baptist progress.

In the Baltic states Baptists were able to gain a foothold at the close of the nineteenth century. This was especially true of Estonia and Latvia. After World War I, when these two countries became free states, a good Baptist work began. Ministers were trained at theological seminaries, and the young people's work made good headway. The number of followers was, considering the modest extent of these countries, very good. In 1939 in Estonia the Baptist membership was about 7,500, and in Latvia it was close to twelve thousand. During the last war there was great destruction throughout the countries. It is uncertain how the churches fare at present.

After the 1860's the Danish Methodists continued smoothly. In 1887 a theological school was founded in Copenhagen, and later a "folk high school" was started for the training of young people, as well as for Christian leaders in the churches. The Methodist church in Denmark was officially recognized in 1886, and since then its pastors have had such legal rights as performing marriages. This denomination is organized in districts with superintendents, and in 1911 Danish Methodists were able to have their own annual conference. In 1924 this conference joined with other conferences in the north to make up the North European Central Conference. In 1952 there were 4,600 Methodists in Denmark, but the influence of this church is much greater than this number would indicate. The Methodist church has created attention in Denmark by its interest in social problems. In this respect, Pastor Anton Bast of Copenhagen was a remarkable pioneer when he set in motion in 1910 the organization of a children's and young people's home, old people's home, and a mission that provided free food and lodging for the needy. Even the Americans were impressed with this work, and it is believed that due to Bast's contribution in these areas the General Conference in the United States in 1920 elected him to be the first Methodist bishop of the north. Bast was replaced in 1928 by Bishop Wade. However, the Central Mission has continued its ministry which has brought much blessing.

During the Nazi occupation the Danish Methodists suffered severely, but the rebuilding of the work has been through the aid of the Americans. In all of the northern countries there has been a growing interest in foreign missions during these last years, which is also true in Denmark.

After the 1860's Methodism made rapid headway in Norway, so that after a few years churches were established in most of the cities in the nation. This rapid growth led to the development of an annual conference in 1876, when the work had come to a certain maturity. Most of the early preachers were Norwegian emigrants who returned to their native land.

In 1888 a theological school was established in Oslo. As in other Scandinavian countries, the citizens were not allowed to hold certain offices unless they belonged to the state church. For example, they were not allowed to teach religion in the schools. The free church people therefore cannot be elementary school teachers. This situation has been for all of the free churches a repressive condition. Other hindering regulations also stood in the way, but the work could not be thwarted. In both Denmark and Norway aggressive leaders within the Lutheran Church, both preachers and laymen, have carried on a campaign against all "sects." This so-called "home missions" has made a strong impact upon the people.

The Methodists in Norway have given much attention to the social mission, especially the ministry of the deaconesses. In Oslo and Bergen deaconess' homes were erected, and as late as 1939 a modern hospital was built at Skien. Besides these institutions, the work conducted in children's homes and other philanthropic causes have made a remarkable contribution to the work of the mission. There has also been interest for foreign missions in Norway which has been expressed in various ways. In 1952 the membership total for the Methodists was given as 11,400.

The Swedish Methodists, beginning in 1868, made rapid progress under the leadership of a succession of good leaders and preachers. Difficult opposition, in some instances, led to drastic procedures. During the last decades much consolidation has taken place among the Methodists. The statistics for 1952 reveal that the membership was approximately 11,700. With passage of a new dissenter law in 1873, the possibilities to leave the state church became greater, and the existing Methodist churches were recognized as lawful free churches. In 1876 an annual conference was constituted, and the Methodist church emerged as a legal body. Two years prior, Methodists had started a theological school, which for forty years was in Uppsala, but since 1924 has been associated with the Scandinavian Theological Seminary in Göteborg. This seminary unites the schools which had been established formerly in Denmark and Norway.

The Swedish Methodists have shown a great interest in social missionary activities. The establishment and maintenance of children's homes have been an important part of their mission program, and the Central Mission has obtained branch stations in several cities, primarily in Stockholm, Göteborg, and Malmö. The ministry of the deaconesses has developed in a surprising manner; a hospital was built in 1915 in Göteborg, and the Bethany Foundation hospital and nursing school in Stockholm was established in 1932. The Methodists also have a good publication house, their own paper, and a well-organized work divided into three districts, which gives Methodism a stable position. The Methodist publishing house has introduced one of the best-known men of world missions, Stanley Jones, to the people of Sweden by publishing a number of his books. No less than ten of his volumes have been translated into the Swedish language. Methodism in Sweden has also evidenced great interest in foreign missions.

Methodism entered Finland as converts from Bethel Ship in New York returned to their native country and proclaimed the gospel of conversion among the Swedish-speaking people. This took place at the close of the 1860's. Several preachers came from Sweden, and by 1885 the progress was so significant that a Finnish-Swedish Methodist church was organized as a special district within the annual conference of Sweden. Two years later the work reached out to the Finnish-speaking population, and in 1892 a Methodist mission in St. Petersburg was absorbed. In 1911 Finnish Methodists became independent, separating from the Russian mission and the Swedish annual conference, and organized their own conference. By 1923, because of the language difficulties, the Swedish- and Finnish-speaking groups separated.

The Finnish Methodists had to endure hardships, both from the church and the worldly powers. The foremost leader in the Swedish-speaking church during forty years (1904–1943) was pastor Karl Hurtig of Helsingfors, who had many difficulties to overcome. Earlier the situation had been worse. Difficult times heavily plagued Finland during the two world wars. However, the Methodists had great influence with their social missions. The membership is rather small, about 1,700 in the Finnish-speaking church and 1,400 in the Swedish-speaking church. Finnish Methodism has its headquarters in Tammerfors (Tampere). A small theological school for Finnish-speaking students was established in 1897.

The Methodists have also gained a position within the Baltic states. This work began to emerge already in 1904 during the Russian period, and when Estonia, Latvia, and Lithuania became free nations after World War I, the work faced great opportunities. The Methodists in the three countries organized into an annual conference in 1929, and it came under the jurisdiction of the bishop in Stockholm. There were about three thousand Methodists in the Baltic states in 1939. What remains of the work at the present time is uncertain.

In conclusion, a few words should be written concerning Congregationalism in the north, and here Sweden comes to the foreground. The Congregational form of the free church made an unusual progress in Sweden through P. Waldenström (d. 1917), who stood behind the establishment of the Swedish Mission Covenant. This type of Congregationalism has a history which goes back to the sixteenth century in England. In Sweden this church form has had quite a long antecedent history, but it was not until the 1860's and the 1870's that it developed into a powerful free church organization. The old mission societies became the base of operations for this organization of congregations. The celebration of the Lord's Supper in several of the areas among the mission fellowships became the starting point for the movement. Even though Waldenström's doctrine on propitiation played an important role for the colporteurs and their proclaiming free grace and God's unchangeable love, it was in reality the Lord's Supper question which precipitated the covenant church idea.

Already there were prototypes. For several years the Baptists and the Methodists had advocated a clear free church concept, and it was natural that many of the separatists regarding the Lord's Supper in the mission fellowship were inspired by these earlier free church groups. The men of the Evangelical National Foundation attempted to keep their colporteurs and associations in the old fellowship with the state church, and for a while Rosenius' warnings delayed separation. What took place at the minister's meetings in Stockholm in 1876, 1877, and 1878 indicates how impossible it was to remain united in the program of the state church. Several of the mission fellowships went over to the practice of a separate Lord's Supper celebration. It was then that the idea developed that a union of mission supporters should be formed which would also include Baptists and Methodists. Opposition of the Baptists in the matter of baptism and of the Methodists in regard to the question of holiness prevented such a union. Thus Congregationalism became the third major free church in Sweden.

When the Swedish Mission Covenant began to function in 1878 under the leadership of the former curate E. J. Ekman (d. 1915), a new chapter was initiated for the Swedish free church movement. To be sure, the idea of the church was not always so dominant; for a long time the older mission society order continued in many areas. The development until the present has confirmed the fact that it was the idea of the free church that during the 1870's became more and more prominent, even though it was not clear at that time. Waldenström did not want to build a denomination, but his church concept was not clear. He often stated that the Swedish Mission Covenant was a missionary fellowship, not a denomination. From the other point of view, he saw that the state church was not a true church of God, and his opposition to it sharpened in time. When Waldenström as a clergyman in the state church stated that it was justifiable to celebrate the Lord's Supper privately, he had come to the position of Ekman. This took place in 1882; Ekman had done the same in 1879.

E. J. Ekman remained as the leader of the Covenant for twenty-five years and was president of the school for preachers in Kristinehamm. Great numbers joined the congregations and societies, and the Covenant grew rapidly. The chief task was to advance home missions with revival preaching and the building of churches, to which all who professed to have "life by faith in God's Son" were welcome. No dogmatic questions were prominent; not even the teaching of Waldenström regarding propitiation played any role in this regard. It was the foreign mission program that encouraged and gathered the people, and in this respect the Covenant church has made an unusual contribution.

When Ekman left his Covenant post in 1904, Waldenström succeeded him. Before this time, Waldenström had been the spiritual prophet and the dominant theologian without having to busy himself with the problems of organization and administration. In his early ministry he exercised great influence through the newspaper *Pietisten*. After Rosenius' death in 1868, Waldenström had taken over the publishing of this paper, continuing this ministry until his death in 1917. Waldenström also wrote regularly in other papers and periodicals, and his religio-political influence became increasingly important because of his membership in Parliament and as a delegate to church assemblies.

The Swedish Mission Covenant grew rapidly, and soon it became the largest free church denomination in the country, a place of prominence which it still maintains, with about 102,000 members besides several thousand in young people's organizations. These free congregations are represented in annual conferences, and an elected mission board administers the widespread home and foreign mission program. Several special organizations exist which intimately work in collaboration with the Covenant, namely the Young People's Union, the School Association, Women's Work, and Study Union. The Covenant is divided into districts, each with a superintendent. Ever since the beginning in the 1880's, it has had its own paper; a comprehensive publication establishment with printing equipment has developed throughout the years. The theological seminary of the Covenant has since 1908 had a building suitable to its purpose in Lidingö. Several other schools are either owned or supported by the Covenant.

Local churches in the Covenant maintain their independence like those in the Baptist denomination, but the Covenant leaves the individual free in baptism and the Lord's Supper. The Covenant received a Lutheran imprint through Waldenström and Ekman, which was never true of the Baptists or the Methodists. This clarifies the reason why the Covenant won such large numbers of people in the Swedish revival movement, especially those who were trained in the Lutheran catechism and tradition. The Covenant has labored for a free church fellowship, and it took the leadership when in 1918 a co-operative committee composed of representatives from the free church denominations was established. Eight free church denominations belong to this committee, most of which have been mentioned. In this committee there is also the mission society called the Swedish Alliance Mission, which in its structure is similar to the Swedish Mission Covenant. Its sphere of work is more locally circumscribed to Småland and neighboring provinces. The membership is about twenty thousand.

The new law providing religious freedom, of 1951, has given the pastors of the free church denominations the right to perform marriage ceremonies, and it also made it easier for a person to withdraw from the Lutheran church.

In no other country in the north has Congregationalism increased to the same extent as in Sweden. Work started in Norway in the nineteenth century but was very weak. The Lammers movement during the 1850's played an important role, and in this period various mission societies were established, similar to those in Sweden. The influence of Rosenius and Waldenström had its effect on the free church movement of Norway. When the well-known Swedish-American evangelist, Fredrik Franson, visited Norway during the 1880's, new groups of people were won to this cause. The Norway Mission Covenant was established in 1884 on the same congregational basis as the Swedish Covenant. There was even the division into districts. The free congregations were served mainly by laymen or pastors who had never received special or formal training. In 1913 a project for the training of pastors was initiated. Ten years earlier a newspaper for the Covenant had been established, and at the same time a foreign missions program had been adopted by the group. A special ministry was carried on for the fishermen in northern Norway and among the sailors.

The headquarters of the Covenant is in Oslo, where the

publishing house is located. The progress of this free church movement has not been significantly great, especially if one compares it with the Swedish development. The entire membership numbers over eight thousand.

This movement has had little progress in Denmark. As in Norway, the revival outreach developed within the state church organizations when the Congregational movement began in Denmark in the 1880's. This took place with the arrival of a Danish-American, who in the summer of 1882 began to conduct revival services in Copenhagen. A division among the Lutherans resulted, and one of the groups continued independently. Swedish ministers also came, as well as Franson, who conducted revival meetings in the fall of 1884. The result was a great and much disputed movement, which led to Franson's temporary imprisonment and a subsequent expulsion. Instead of hindering the movement, this advanced the cause. The free congregation in Copenhagen grew rapidly. Women also took part as preachers, a situation that became very common even in other northern countries. When several of these congregations had been established, the thought arose of uniting them in a missionary enterprise. Consequently, the Danish Mission Covenant was established in 1888. Among the early leaders for this mission was a layman by the name of Jensen-Maar (d. 1932), who became the editor of the paper and president of the mission.

The Danish Covenant soon had internal problems, some of a personal nature, some because of different teachings. This group was from the very beginning one-sidedly committed to revival. During later years young people's work has been organized, as well as social work which has had a wide outreach. The Covenant's membership was approximately 2,500 in 1948.

The Congregational movement in Finland was naturally influenced by Sweden. The pietistic awakening early gained a strong footing in Finland, and the new evangelical movement under the leadership of F. G. Hedberg won wide acceptance. The movement, however, remained within the state church; to develop a free church program was not intended, but it resulted at the close of the nineteenth century. Two laymen

357

of noble stock became spiritual leaders and preachers. One of these, Constantine Boije, was installed as a missionary in Helsingfors by the Swedish Mission Covenant in 1879. He invited the English evangelist Lord Radstock, and this brought about a great revival, especially in the upper classes of society. The movement spread to several other sections and cities.

The other, Edward Bjorkenheim, was a landowner and public official, but he became a zealous preacher and won many to the revival movement. Other preachers came from Sweden and England, and during the last two decades of the century the free church movement grew. The first congregation to be established among the Finnish-speaking people arose in 1885. In Finland there also developed mission societies which desired to remain within the state church but which had a difficult problem over the celebration of communion. The free churches were strengthened by the private groups which practiced the celebration of the Lord's Supper. Generally, these groups did not separate from the state church. The position was not clear and certain; consequently, many people were attracted to denominations which had a clear free church position. In 1889, at a conference, the mission attempted to develop a stronger union, and it is this action which developed partly into the Free Mission Covenant (Swedish-speaking) and partly into the Finnish Free Church (Finnish-speaking). This division first took place at the beginning of the 1920's, when Finland had won its political independence. The Finnish Free Church established its own theological school.

The work within these organizations has operated similarly to that in other countries. After the law granting religious freedom in 1922, it was natural that the free church position would be secured; however, both of the organizations have never had a large membership: the Free Mission Covenant has approximately twelve hundred and the Finnish Free Church has about 6,700.

This Congregationalist movement extended even to the Baltic countries. A few Swedish evangelists labored in Estonia during the middle of the 1880's. In 1905 there was a great awakening which was especially characterized by an emphasis on holiness and Christian union. This prepared the way for a new free church group. After the country won its freedom following World War I, a great active awakening and development ensued. The leader for the movement was K. L. Marley. When Marley traveled in Sweden, he won great support among the Swedish Mission Covenant churches for the erection of a central church in Tallin (Reval). This building, with seating capacity for a thousand, was dedicated in 1930. Several other mission houses were built, twenty congregations organized, and the work was very promising when World War II and the accompanying difficulties struck an annihilating blow. The membership statistics in 1936 for the Estonian churches was about fourteen hundred.

Colonies and Mission Fields.—England's great colonial expansion during the eighteenth and nineteenth centuries advanced the spread of English free church ideals over the world. The free movement spread to the English-speaking colonies and dominions. Side by side with the erection of Anglican churches, the free churches were built. This was true in Canada, Australia, South Africa, and the South Sea Islands.

Before the European mass emigration to the United States took place, and partly contemporaneous with it, a British migration to the colonies and territories developed. As the great migration to the United States led to an active building of the free churches, when European immigrants organized and developed national denominations, the migration to the new territories within the British Empire also advanced the establishment of the free churches. This is a many-sided history, and here it is only possible to suggest the subject matter.

Canada provides an interesting illustration. In addition to a strong French Catholic migration, the leading free church denominations—Congregational, Baptist, and Methodist—developed a free church movement of great importance. During the 1920's, when arrangements were taking place to bring about a united church, the membership of the Methodists was about four hundred thousand, while the Congregationalists numbered about twelve thousand. After a long period of negotiations, the United Church of Canada was established in 1925, made up of Methodists, Congregationalists, and Presbyterians. In 1945 it was reported that this union church had a membership of close to 750,000. The Baptists have grown to about 150,000. Besides these free churches there are a number of other groups, including Mennonites, which number about a hundred thousand.

In Australia the various free churches generally followed the pattern in the homeland, and the statistics of the largest denominations of this type, according to a recent report, are as follows: Methodists, 871,000; Presbyterians, 743,000; Baptists, 113,500; and Congregationalists, 63,200. This number for the Methodists is much higher than that of the denomination's own report and probably includes families as so-called adherents.

In South Africa the free church movement can be numbered among the white people, but there are large missionary districts among the Negroes without full statistical information. Consequently, this study turns to a wider area, the mission among the non-Christian Negro people. This should invite a survey with the assistance of Kenneth S. Latourette's volumes of the *Expansion of Christianity* in the foreign countries of the world. Here the problem only shall be pointed out.

One fact is certain: the great outreach was through the men and women of the revival who became the pioneers for the modern missionary movement. The English-speaking free churches took the lead during the great nineteenth-century advance. When the British and American free church movements were described, the various pioneer mission societies were also mentioned. Baptists, Congregationalists, and Methodists supported the first pioneer mission stations in India, Burma, Assam, China, south and central Africa, Madagascar, and the South Sea Islands. It was the free church principle that was everywhere proclaimed and practiced. That situation prevails to this very hour.

The great revival groups mobilized large numbers of people for the cause of foreign missions, and to a great extent the people from the free associations went out to the mission fields or supported the work by their gifts. On the mission fields the primitive Christian free church principle was followed: people heard the word, received it, made confession, and joined the church. The local *ecclēsia* again was established in a heathen culture. It gathered around the church building, the school, and the hospital. This is the modern free churches' most remarkable historical enterprise.

At this point a closer examination would reveal a surprising fact. The young mission churches have made such great progress in many places that some congregations have surpassed the homeland congregations in magnitude. This indicates that the Christian free churches during the last century have made a remarkably aggressive invasion around the world. For example, the largest congregation in the Swedish Mission Covenant's mission in Congo has approximately 9,250 members, while the largest congregation in Sweden has only about fifteen hundred members. The same situation is true for the Baptists in Congo, where the largest church has over two thousand members, while the largest Baptist church in Sweden has about eight hundred.

A hundred-and-fifty-year mission history from Carey to Schweitzer and Stanley Jones is full of accounts and descriptions concerning the planting of Christian free churches in other parts of the world. A premonition of the results is gained when one observes that the Methodist fellowship in South Africa includes about 230,000 members and in India nearly two hundred thousand. Baptist churches in India, including Burma and Assam, have nearly four hundred thousand members, and in the Belgian Congo about two hundred thousand. Evangelical ministry in South America, as earlier in the West Indies, has made great advances. The work is old in the West Indies, but the greatest progress of the free churches in South America has taken place in the last few decades. This revival is especially evident in Brazil, where the Baptists have a denomination numbering more than a hundred thousand and the Pentecostals number 120,000 members. Many believe that the Roman Catholic Church, which has reigned there during the last century, is now beginning to break apart and is in some respects being replaced by evangelical churches.

It is natural that the missionary enterprises of the national churches have also had great success on the mission fields. Thus gradually they have laid the stage for another type of church, for these minority churches are free churches in their relationship to the community and state in which they live and minister. Here it should only be pointed out that the free church idea has had a greater outreach than is usually recognized.

Naturally the old weakness in the free church setup has revealed itself also on the mission fields. Division and separation into new denominations and groups have led to serious difficulties. This problem has been clearly presented by Bengt Sundkler's observant work, *Bantu Prophets in South Africa* (1948). On the other hand, it can be pointed out that there have also been union efforts among the various missions. This has taken place in Japan and more lately in India, where the Church of South India since 1947 has been a union of Anglicans, Presbyterians, Methodists, and Congregationalists.

While the free congregations and the free churches in the mission countries develop and progress in various ways, there takes place a secularizing process in the changing world of the white race which surprises visiting Christians from the younger churches. Europeans have accepted the idea that the average person in the West does not believe in God to any visible degree, nor does he have any need to go to church, nor does he have a Christian conduct, nor does he care whether or not his name is written on the church books. Gradually it must be clear to every serious observer that in practice, even in the European state churches, there is a certain acceptance of the free church idea. The claim that all of the people in the nation belong to the church is an evident fiction. There is a real boundary line between the church and the world in the old so-called Christian countries, not only in the heathen mission territories.

This book makes it clear that the free churches have played a much greater role in Christian history than church history handbooks generally indicate. This fact is especially true in the modern period, from the Reformation to the present. None of the exponents and martyrs who during the sixteenth century

362

advocated the misunderstood and condemned ideas of the separated church—the *Sonderkirche* or the gathered church—could ever have anticipated such a harvest from the seed they sowed.

Appendix to the Third Edition

When Congregationalism on the European Continent was mentioned, the new free church in Greece should have been mentioned. The originator of this group seems to be Dr. Const. Metallinos, former financial director of the government. At the present time there are twenty-nine small congregations with a membership of approximately eleven hundred. The organization of the denomination took place in 1946. A Bible institute was established in 1947.

The Pentecostal movement has not been given much attention. This group is so young that it has played a small role in free church development. It has not added anything new to the concept of the church. The characteristic of the Pentecostal movement, at least in Sweden, is that it pushes the congregational idea of the independence of the church to the extreme, at least in theory. It is clear, therefore, that in some respects it has strengthened the free church stream of separation during the last forty years. Moreover, the movement is in constant flux. In some countries this church group has had a good success; in others it has made very little progress. In the United States there are several groups, but all together they make up a comparatively small body alongside the large denominations. Pentecostal groups are enjoying rapid growth in many parts of the world.

Bibliography

ENCYCLOPEDIAS AND GENERAL WORKS

Dictionnaire de spiritualité, ascétique et mystique. Paris, I, 1937, II, 1953.

Encyclopaedia of Religion and Ethics. Edinburgh and New York, 1908–1926.

Kirkeleksikon for Norden. Aarhus and Kobenhavn, 1900–1929.

Lexikon für Theologie und Kirche. Freiburg im Breisgau, 1930–1938.

Mennonitisches Lexikon. Frankfurt a. M. and Weierhof, Pfalz, 1913–1951.

Realencyklopädie für protestantische Theologie und Kirche. Leipzig, 1896–1913.

Religion in Geschichte und Gegenwart. Tübingen, 1927–1932.

ARNOLD, GOTTFRIED. *Unpartheyische Kirchen- und Ketzerhistorie.* Leipzig, I–IV, 1699–1700.

GRUBB, KENNETH G. (ed.), *World Christian Handbook.* London, 1949.

HOLMQUIST, HJALMAR, AND NORREGAARD, JENS. *Kirkehistorie.* Kobenhavn, I, 1946, II, 1949, III, 1940.

———. *Kristendommens historie i romantikens, liberalismens og realismens tidsalder.* Kobenhavn, I–II, 1939.

LATOURETTE, KENNETH S. *A History of the Expansion of Christianity.* New York, I–VII, 1937–1945.

———. *A History of Christianity.* New York, 1953.

MOLLAND, EINAR. *Konfesjonskunnskap.* Oslo, 1953.

MÜLLER, KARL. *Kirchengeschichte.* Tübingen, I, 1938, II:1, 1911, II:2, 1919.

NEIIENDAM, MICHAEL. *Frikirker og Sekter.* Kobenhavn, 1939.

NIGG, WALTER. *Das Buch der Ketzer.* Zürich, 1949.

———. *Det eviga riket.* Stockholm, 1948.

ROUSE, RUTH, AND NEILL, STEPHEN CHARLES (eds.). *A History of the Ecumenical Movement 1517–1948.* London, 1954.

STEPHEN, W. R. W., AND HUNT, WILLIAM (eds.). *A History of the English Church.* London, I–VIII:2, 1912 ff.

THIMME, LUDWIG. *Kirche, Sekte und Gemeinschaftsbewegung vom Standpunkt einer christlichen Soziologie aus.* Schwerin in Meckl., 1925.

TROELTSCH, ERNST. *Die Soziallehren der christlichen Kirchen und Gruppen.* Tübingen, 1923.

———. "Protestantisches Christentum und Kirche in der Neuzeit" in *Die Kultur der Gegenwart.* Berlin and Leipzig, 1909.

WELTER, G. *Histoire des sectes chrétiennes.* Paris, 1950.

WISBORG, SVEN. *Statskyrka och frikyrka.* Motala, 1945.

BIBLIOGRAPHY

SELECTED WORKS

Chapters I–II

BARDENHEWER, OTTO. *Geschichte der altkirchlichen Literatur.* Freiburg im Breisgau, I, 1913, II, 1914, III, 1912.

BAUER, WALTER. *Rechtgläubigkeit und Ketzerei im ältesten Christentum.* Tübingen, 1934.

BENZ, ERNST. *Ecclesia spiritualis.* Stuttgart, 1934.

Bibliothekder Kirchenväter. Kempten and München, 1913–1931.

CAMPENHAUSEN, HANS. *Kirchliches Amt und geistliche Vollmacht in den ersten drei Jahrhunderten.* Tübingen, 1953.

———. *Die Idee des Martyriums in der alten Kirche.* Göttingen, 1936.

CAUZONS, TH. DE. *Les Albigeois et l'inquisition.* Paris, 1908.

COULTON, G. G. *Inquisition and Liberty.* London, 1938.

HARNACK, ADOLF V. *Entstehung und Entwickelung der Kirchenverfassung und des Kirchenrechts in den zwei ersten Jahrhunderten.* Leipzig, 1910.

———. *Die Mission und Ausbreitung des Christentums in den ersten drei Jahrhunderten.* Leipzig, 1924.

———. *Lehrbuch der Dogmengeschichte,* I. Tübingen, 1909.

HENNECKE, EDGAR (ed.). *Neutestamentliche Apokryphen.* Tübingen, 1924.

KNOPF, RUDOLF. *Das nachapostolische Zeitalter.* Tübingen, 1905.

LECHLER, G. V. *Johannes Hus.* Göteborg, 1915.

LEQUENNE, FERN. *Le drame cathare ou l'hérésie nécessaire.* Paris, 1954.

LIETZMANN, HANS. *Geschichte der alten Kirche.* Berlin and Leipzig, I, 1932, II, 1936, III, 1938, IV, 1944.

———. *Från fornkyrkan.* Uppsala, 1935.

LINDBLOM, JOH. *Ekklesia.* Uppsala, 1943.

LINTON, OLOF. *Das Problem der Urkirche in der neueren Forschung.* Uppsala, 1932.

LUCHAIRE, ACHILLE. *Innocent III: La croisade des Albigeois.* Paris 1911.

LÜTZOW, COUNT. *The Life and Time of Master John Hus.* London and New York, 1909.

NELLI, RENÉ, AND BRU, CHARLES P. *Spiritualité de l'hérésie: Le Catharisme.* Paris, 1953.

PUECH, H. CH. *Le Manichéisme, son fondateur et sa doctrine.* Paris, 1949.

SCHNEIDER, JOH. *Die Gemeinde nach dem Neuen Testament.* Kassel, 1939.

SODEN, HANS VON (ed.). *Urkunden zur Entstehungsgeschichte des Donatismus.* Bonn, 1913.

SÖDERBERG, HANS. *La religion des Cathares.* Uppsala, 1949.

WEIZSÄCKER, CARL. *Das apostolische Zeitalter der christlichen Kirche.* Tübingen and Leipzig, 1902.

WESTIN, GUNNAR. *I urkristen tid.* Stockholm, 1944.

————. *I efterapostolisk tid.* Stockholm, 1946.

————. *John Wyclif och hans reformidéer.* Uppsala, 1935–1936.

WORKMAN, HERBERT B., *John Wyclif.* Oxford, I–II, 1926.

Chapter III

Primary Sources

Aktensammlung zur Geschichte der Baseler Reformation in den Jahren 1519–1534. Basel I, 1921, II, 1933.

Beiträge zur Geschichte rheinischer Mennoniten. Krefeld, 1939.

BOSSERT, G. (ed.). *Herzogtum Württemberg.* ("Quellen zur Geschichte der Täufer.") 1930.

EGLI, EMIL (ed.). *Actensammlung zur Geschichte der Zürcher Reformation in den Jahren 1519–1533.* Zürich, I–II, 1879.

FRANZ, GÜNTHER (ed.). *Wiedertäuferakten 1527–1626.* ("Urkundliche Quellen zur hessischen Reformationsgeschichte.") 1951.

KREBS, MANFRED (ed.). *Baden-Pfalz.* ("Quellen zur Geschichte der Täufer.") 1951.

LOSERTH, J. (ed.). *Pilgram Marbecks Antwort auf Kaspar Schwenckfelds Beurteilung des Buches der Bundesbezeugung von 1542.* ("Quellen und Forschungen zur Geschichte der oberdeutschen Taufgesinnten im 16. Jahrhundert.") 1929.

MÜLLER, LYDIA (ed.). *Glaubenszeugnisse oberdeutscher Taufgesinnter.* ("Quellen zur Geschichte der Täufer.") 1938.

MURALT, LEONHARD VON, AND SCHMID, WALTER (eds.). *Zürich.* ("Quellen zur Geschichte der Täufer in der Schweiz.") 1952.

NEFF, CHR. (ed.). *Gedenkschrift zum 400-jährigen Jubiläum der Mennoniten oder Taufgesinnten 1525–1925.* Karlsruhe, 1925.

SCHORNBAUM, KARL (ed.). *Bayern.* ("Quellen zur Geschichte der Täufer.") 1951.

————. *Markgraftum Brandenburg.* ("Quellen zur Geschichte der Täufer.") 1934.

STECK, R., and TOBLER, G. (eds.). *Aktensammlung zur Geschichte der Berner Reformation 1521–1532.* Bern, I–II, 1923.

WOLKAN, RUDOLF (ed.). *Geschicht-Buch der Hutterischen Brüder.* Macleod, Alberta, 1923.

ZIEGLSCHMID, A. J. F. (ed.). *Die älteste Chronik der Hutterischen Brüder.* Ithaca, N. Y., 1943.

BIBLIOGRAPHY

Secondary Sources

BAINTON, ROLAND H. *David Joris, Wiedertäufer und Kämpfer für Toleranz im 16. Jahrhundert.* Leipzig, 1937.

BARGE, HERMAN. *Andreas Bodenstein von Karlstadt.* Leipzig, 1905.

BAUR, AUGUST. *Zwinglis Theologie.* Halle, I–II, 1885, 1888.

BAX, E. BELFORT. *The Rise and Fall of the Anabaptists.* London, 1903.

BECK, JOSEF. *Die Geschichts-Bücher der Wiedertäufer in Oesterreich-Ungarn—von 1526 bis 1785.* Wien, 1883.

———. *Georg Blaurock und die Anfänge des Anabaptismus.* Berlin, VII, 1908.

BECKER, EDUARD. *Wiedertäufer in Oberhessen.* ("Archiv für Hessische Geschichte und Altertumskunde.") Darmstadt, 1914.

BENDER, HAROLD S. *Conrad Grebel, Founder of the Swiss Brethren.* Goshen, Ind., 1950.

———. *Mennonite Origins in Europe.* ("Mennonites and Their Heritage.") Akron, Pa., 1945.

———. *Menno Simons' Life and Writings.* Scottdale, Pa., 1944.

BERGFRIED, ULRICH. *Verantwortung als theologisches Problem im Täufertum des 16. Jahrhunderts.* Wuppertal, 1938.

BERGMANN, CORNELIUS. *Die Täuferbewegung im Kanton Zürich bis 1660.* Leipzig, 1916.

BIRKENMAYER, C. A., and BAUMHAUER, A. *Geschichte der Stadt Waldshut.* Waldshut, 1927.

BLANKE, FRITZ. "Zollikon, 1525," *Theologische Zeitschrift.* Basel, 1952.

BOEHMER, H., AND KIRN, P. (eds.). *Thomas Müntzers Briefwechsel.* Leipzig, 1931.

BRAGHT, THIELEMANN. *The Bloody Theater or Martyrs Mirror.* Scottdale, Pa., 1951.

BRANDT, O. *Thomas Müntzer, Sein Leben und seine Schriften.* Jena, 1933.

BURCKHARDT, PAUL. *Die Basler Täufer.* Basel, 1898.

BÄCHTOLD, C. A. *Die Schaffhauser Wiedertäufer in der Reformationszeit.* Schaffhausen, 1900.

CANTIMORI, DELIO. *Italienische Haeretiker der Spätrenaissance.* Basel, 1949.

CORRELL, ERNST H. *Das schweizerische Täufermennonitentum.* Tübingen, 1925.

EGLI, EMIL. *Schweizerische Reformations-Geschichte.* Zürich, I (1519–1525), 1910.

———. *Die Züricher Wiedertäufer zur Reformationszeit.* Zürich, 1878.

———. *Die St. Galler Täufer.* Zürich, 1887.

GEISER, SAMUEL. *Die Taufgesinnten Gemeinden.* Karlsruhe, 1931.

HEGE, CHRISTIAN. *Die Täufer in der Kurpfalz.* Frankfurt a. M., 1908.

HEYER, FRITZ. *Der Kirchenbegriff der Schwärmer.* Leipzig, 1939.

HOLL, KARL. *Luther und die Schwärmer.* Tübingen, 1923.

HORSCH, JOHN. *The Hutterian Brethren 1528–1931.* Goshen, Ind., 1931.

HRUBY, FR. "Die Wiedertäufer in Mähren," *Archiv für Reformationsgeschichte.* 1933, 1934, 1935.

HULSHOF, ABRAHAM. *Geschiedenis van de Doopsgezinden te Straatsburg van 1525 tot 1557.* Amsterdam, 1905.

JENNY, BEATRICE. *Das Schleitheimer Täuferbekenntnis 1527.* (Reprinted from *Schaffhauser Beiträge zur vaterländischen Geschichte.*) Thayngen, 1951.

KOLB, FRANZ. *Die Wiedertäufer in Wipptal.* Innsbruck, 1951.

KRAHN, CORNELIUS. *Menno Simons.* Karlsruhe, 1936.

KUEHLER, W. J. *Geschiedenis der Nederlandsche Doopsgezinden in de zestiende Eeuw.* Haarlem, 1932.

KÖHLER, WALTER. "Das Täufertum in der neueren kirchen-historischen Forschung." *Archiv für Reformationsgeschichte.* 1940, 1941, 1943, 1948.

LITTELL, FRANKLIN HAMLIN. *The Anabaptist View of the Church.* Chicago, 1952.

LOHMANN, ANNEMARIE. *Zur geistigen Entwicklung Thomas Müntzers.* Leipzig and Berlin, 1931.

LOSERTH, JOHANN. *Doctor Balthasar Hubmaier und die Anfänge der Wiedertaufe in Mähren.* Brünn, 1893.

———. *Die Stadt Waldshut und die vorderösterreichische Regierung in den Jahren 1523–1526.* Wien, 1891.

LÜDEMANN, H. *Reformation und Täufertum in ihrem Verhältnis zum christlichen Prinzip.* Bern, 1896.

MAU, WILHELM. *Balthasar Hubmaier.* Berlin and Leipzig, 1912.

MURALT, LEONHARD VON. *Glaube und Lehren der Schweizerischen Wiedertäufer in der Reformationzeit.* Zürich, 1938.

MÜLLER, ERNST. *Geschichte der Bernischen Wiedertäufer.* Frauenfeld, 1895.

MÜLLER, K. *Kirche, Gemeinde und Obrigkeit nach Luther.* Tübingen, 1910.

MÜLLER, LYDIA. *Der Kommunismus der mährischen Wiedertäufer.* Leipzig, 1927.

NESTLER, HERMAN. *Die Wiedertäuferbewegung in Regensburg.* Regensburg, 1926.

NEUSER, WILHELM. *Hans Hut—Leben und Wirken.* Berlin, 1913.

PAULUS, NIKOLAUS. *Protestantismus und Toleranz im 16. Jahrhundert.* Freiburg im Breisgau, 1911.

PAYNE, ERNEST A. *The Anabaptists of the 16th Century and Their Influence in the Modern World.* London, 1949.

SACHSSE, CARL. *Balthasar Hubmaier als Theologe.* Berlin, 1914.

SCHULTZ, S. G. *Caspar Schwenckfeld von Ossig.* Norristown, Pa., 1947.

SMIRIN, M. M. *Die Volksreformation des Thomas Müntzer und der grosse Bauernkrieg.* Berlin, 1952.

SMITHSON, R. J. *The Anabaptists.* London, 1935.

STOLZE, WILHELM. *Bauernkrieg und Reformation.* Leipzig, 1926.

STAEHELIN, ERNST. *Briefe und Akten zum Leben Oekolampads.* Leipzig, I, 1927, II, 1934.

STAEHELIN, RUDOLF. *Huldreich Zwingli.* Basel, I, 1895, II, 1897.

WAPPLER, PAUL. *Die Täuferbewegung in Thüringen von 1526–1584.* Jena, 1913.

WIPF, JAKOB. *Reformationsgeschichte der Stadt und Landschaft Schaffhausen.* Zürich, 1929.

WISWEDEL, W. *Bilder und Führergestalten aus dem Täufertum.* Kassel, I, 1928, II, 1930, III, 1952.

WOLKAN, RUDOLF. *Die Hutterer.* Wien, 1918.

———. *Die Lieder der Wiedertäufer.* Berlin, 1908.

WOOD, NORMAN. *A Study of the Influence of Religious Uniformity on English Education in the 16th Century.* London, 1931.

TEUFEL, E. "Täufertum und Quakertum im Lichte der neueren Forschung," *Theologische Rundschau.* 1941, 1942, 1943, 1948.

ZWINGLI, HULDREICH. *Briefe* (1512–1530). Zürich, 1918–1920.

·———. *Sämtliche Werke.* ("Corpus Reformatorum.") Berlin and Leipzig, I–X, 1905 ff.

Chapters IV–V

ADDISON, WILLIAM G. *Religious Equality in Modern England 1714–1914.* London, 1944.

ARVIDSON, THEODOR. *Biskopens Budskap till Metodistkyrkans Centralkonferens i Helsingfors den 25–29 mars 1953.*

BETT, HENRY. *The Spirit of Methodism.* London, 1937.

Biskoparnas Budskap till den Europeiska Metodistkonferensen i Köpenhamn den 2–6 augusti 1939. Stockholm, 1939. (English edition, Zürich, 1939).

BJÖRLING, AUGUSTA. *John Bunyan.* Stockholm, 1928.

BRAITHWAITE, WILLIAM C. *The Beginnings of Quakerism.* London, 1923.

BRASH, W. BARDSLEY. *Methodism.* London, 1928.

BROWN, JOHN. *John Bunyan (1628–1688). His Life, Times and Work.* London, 1928.

BURRAGE, CH. *The English Dissenters.* Cambridge, I–II, 1912.

BUTTERWORTH, HEZEKIAH. *Roger Williams och västerns indianer.* Stockholm, 1922.

BYRT, G. W. *John Clifford.* London, 1947.

CARLILE, J. C. *C. H. Spurgeon.* Stockholm, 1935.

CHURCH, L. F. *The Early Methodist People.* London, 1948.

——. *More About the Early Methodist People.* London, 1949.

CLARK, HENRY W. *History of English Nonconformity from Wiclif to the Close of the Nineteenth Century.* London, I, 1911, II, 1913.

COLE, G. D. H. *A Short History of the British Working Class Movement 1789–1927.* London, I–II, 1927.

DALE, A. W. *The Life of R. W. Dale of Birmingham.* London, 1902.

DAVIES, HORTON. *The English Free Churches.* London and New York, 1952.

DIFFENDORFER, RALPH E. *The World Service of the Methodist Episcopal Church.* Chicago, 1924.

EDWARDS, MALDWYN. *Methodism and England.* London, 1944.

EDWARDS, W. *Four Centuries of Nonconformist Disabilities 1509–1912.* London, 1912.

FIRTH, C. H. *Oliver Cromwell and the Rule of the Puritan in England.* London, 1929.

FLYNN, JOHN STEPHEN. *The Influence of Puritanism.* London, 1920.

FOGELKLOU, EMILIA. *William Penn.* Stockholm, 1935.

FRANKS, J. D. (ed.). *European Baptists Today.* Rüschlikon-Zürich, 1952.

FRIEDMANN, ROBERT. *Mennonite Piety Through the Centuries.* Goshen, Ind., 1949.

FULLERTON, W. Y. *C. H. Spurgeon.* London, 1920.

GARBER, PAUL NEFF. *The Methodists of Continental Europe.* New York, 1949.

GOW, HENRY. *The Unitarians.* London, 1928.

HALÉVY, ELIE. *Histoire du Peuple Anglais aux XIXe siècle.* Paris, I, 1930, II, 1927.

HALLER, W. *The Rise of Puritanism.* New York, 1938.

HIGHET, JOHN. *The Churches in Scotland To-day.* Glasgow, 1950.

HOBHOUSE, STEPHEN. *William Law and Eighteenth Century Quakerism.* London, 1927.

HOLMQUIST, HJALMAR. *Ur kristendomens historia mellan världskrigen 1814–1914.* Uppsala, 1918.

——. *Engelsk högkyrka, lågkyrka, frikyrka i deras historiska tillkomst 1559–1689.* Stockholm, 1916.

HORNE, C. SILVESTER. *A Popular History of the Free Churches.* London, 1926.

HORSCH, JOHN. *Mennonites in Europe*. Scottdale, Pa., 1950.

HORTON, DOUGLAS. *Congregationalism*. London, 1952.

HÄNDIGES, E. *Beiträge zur Geschichte der Mennonitengemeinde Elbing-Ellerwald* ("Beiträge zur Geschichte der Mennoniten.") Weierhof, Pfalz, 1938.

———. *Die Lehre der Mennoniten* . . . Kaiserslautern, Pfalz, 1921.

HOENEN, RICHARD. *Die Freien evangelischen Gemeinden in Deutschland.* Tübingen, 1930.

JONES, RUFUS M. *Kväkarnas tro och livsåskådning.* Stockholm, 1943.

———. *The Church's Debt to Heretics.* New York–London, 1925.

———. *Spiritual Reformers in the Sixteenth and Seventeenth Centuries.* London, 1914.

———. *The Faith and Practice of the Quakers.* London, 1930.

JORDAN, W. K. *The Development of Religious Toleration in England.* London, I–IV, 1932–1940.

JÄDER, KARL. *En världsväckare.* Motala, 1937.

———. *En stridernas man.* Stockholm, 1927.

———. *E. Stanley Jones* (Stockholm), 1954.

KEIJER, AUGUSTINUS. *Kristen församlingsbildning.* Stockholm, 1936.

KNIGHT, RACHEL. *The Founder of Quakerism.* London, 1922.

LEHMANN, JOSEPH. *Geschichte der deutschen Baptisten.* Kassel, I, 1912, II, 1900.

LIER, ALF. *Metodismen i Norge i dag.* Oslo, 1950.

LINDERHOLM, EM. *Pingströrelsen—dess förutsättningar och uppkomst.* Stockholm, 1924.

LINGE, KARL. *Fredrik Franson.* Örebro, 1951.

LUCKEY, HANS. *Johann Gerhard Oncken und die Anfänge des deutschen Baptismus.* Kassel, 1934.

LYON, T. *The Theory of Religious Liberty in England 1603–39.* Cambridge, 1937.

MCLACHLAN, H. *English Education Under the Test Acts.* Manchester, 1931.

MANNING, B. L. *The Protestant Dissenting Deputies.* London, 1952.

MATHEWS, BASIL. *John R. Mott—en världsmedborgare.* Uppsala, 1934.

MATHIESON, WILLIAM L. *England in Transition 1789–1832.* London, 1920.

MELLE, F. H. OTTO. *Das Walten Gottes im deutschen Methodismus.* Bremen, 1925.

MOFFAT, JAMES. *The Presbyterian Churches.* London, 1928.

MURRAY, ROBERT H. *Studies in the English Social and Political Thinkers of the Nineteenth Century.* Cambridge, I–II, 1929.

NUELSEN, JOHN E. *Kurzgefasste Geschichte des Methodismus von seinen Anfängen zur Gegenwart.* Bremen, 1929.

NYVALL, DAVID, AND OLSSON, KARL A. *The Evangelical Covenant Church.* Chicago, 1954.

OLSON, ADOLF. *A Centenary History as Related to the Baptist General Conference of America.* Chicago, 1952.

PARKER, IRENE. *Dissenting Academies in England.* Cambridge, 1914.

PAUL, HERBERT. *A History of Modern England.* London, I–V, 1904–1906.

PAYNE, ERNEST A. *The Free Church Tradition in the Life of England.* London, 1944.

———. *The Fellowship of Believers.* London, 1952.

PEEL, ALBERT. *These Hundred Years.* London, 1931.

———. *The Congregational Two Hundred 1530–1948.* London, 1948.

PEEL, ALBERT, AND HORTON, DOUGLAS. *International Congregationalism.* London, 1949.

PEEL, ALBERT, AND CARLSON, LELAND H. (eds.). *The Writings of Robert Harrison and Robert Browne.* London, 1953.

PETRI, LAURA. *John Wesley.* Stockholm, 1928.

RITSCHL, ALBRECHT. *Geschichte des Pietismus.* Bonn, 1880.

ROBINSON, CYRIL E. *A History of England.* London, 1924.

ROBINSON, H. WHEELER. *The Life and Faith of the Baptists.* London, 1927.

RUSHBROOKE, J. H. *The Baptist Movement in the Continent of Europe.* London, 1923.

RUSSEL, E. *The History of Quakerism.* New York, 1942.

RÖNNEGÅRD, SAM. *Lars Paul Esbjörn och Augustana-synodens uppkomst.* Stockholm, 1949.

SELBIE, W. B. *Congregationalism.* London, 1927.

———. *Nonconformity—its Origin and Progress.* London, n. d.

SELECMANN, CHARLES CLAUDE. *The Methodist Primer.* Nashville, Tenn., 1953.

SILLÉN, ELIN. *William Carey. Den moderna världsmissionens fader.* Stockholm, 1934.

SKEATS, HERBERT S., AND MIALL, CHARLES S. *History of the Free Churches of England 1688–1891.* London, 1891.

SMITH, FRANK. *A History of English Elementary Education 1760–1902.* London, 1931.

SMITH, C. HENRY. *Mennonites in America.* ("Mennonites and Their Heritage.") Akron, Pa., 1942.

———. *The Story of the Mennonites.* (Revised by Cornelius Krahn.) Newton, Kan., 1950.

STEPHENSON, GEORGE M. *The Religious Aspects of Swedish Immigration.* Minneapolis, 1932.

SUNDKLER, BENGT. *Bantu Prophets in South Africa.* London, 1948.

————. *Church of South India.* London, 1945.

SUNDSTRÖM, ERLAND. *Trossamfund i det svenska samhället.* Stockholm, 1952.

SYKES, NORMAN. *Church and State in England in the Eighteenth Century.* Cambridge, 1934.

THÖRNBERG, E. H. *Sverige i Amerika—Amerika i Sverige.* Stockholm, 1938.

TORBET, ROBERT G. *A History of the Baptists.* Philadelphia, 1950.

TOWNSEND, W. J., *A New History of Methodism.* London, I–II, 1909.

TREVELYAN, G. M. *England under the Stuarts.* London, 1924.

————. *British History in the Nineteenth Century.* London, 1922.

UNDERWOOD, A. C. *A History of the English Baptists.* London, 1947.

WAKEMAN, H. O. *The Church and the Puritans 1570–1660.* London, 1912.

WARNER, WELLMAN J. *The Wesleyan Movement in the Industrial Revolution.* London, 1930.

WENGER, JOHN C. *Glimpses of Mennonite History and Doctrine.* Scottdale, Pa., 1949.

WESTIN, GUNNAR, NORDSTRÖM, N. J., JULÉN, JONATHAN, AND ANDERSON, AXEL. *De frikyrkliga samfunden i Sverige.* Mariestad, 1934.

WESTIN, GUNNAR. *Kampen om religionsfriheten.* Stockholm, 1942.

————. (ed.). *Missionssällskap, Svenska kyrkans frivilliaa arbete, Frikyrkosamfund.* Stockholm, 1937.

————. *Protestantismens historia i Amerikas Förenta stater.* Stockholm, 1931.

————. *Trossamfund i Sverige.* Tierp, 1951.

WHITING, C. E. *Studies in English Puritanism from the Restoration to the Revolution, 1660–1688.* London, 1931.

WHITLEY, W. T. *A History of British Baptists.* London, 1923.

YODER, EDWARD. *Our Mennonite Heritage.* ("Mennonites and Their Heritage") Akron, Pa. 1945.

Index

375

INDEX